Genesis and Christian

Edited by

Nathan MacDonald

Mark W. Elliott &

Grant Macaskill

WILLIAM B. EERDMANS PUBLISHING COMPANY

GRAND RAPIDS, MICHIGAN / CAMBRIDGE, U.K.

Published 2012 by
Wm. B. Eerdmans Publishing Co.
2140 Oak Industrial Drive N.E., Grand Rapids, Michigan 49505 /
P.O. Box 163, Cambridge CB3 9PU U.K.

Printed in the United States of America

18 17 16 15 14 13 12   7 6 5 4 3 2 1

Library of Congress Cataloging-in-Publication Data

Genesis and Christian theology / edited by Nathan MacDonald,
    Mark W. Elliott & Grant Macaskill.
        p.   cm.
    Proceedings of a conference held July 14-18, 2009 at St. Andrews.
    ISBN 978-0-8028-6725-4 (pbk.: alk. paper)
    1. Bible. O.T. Genesis — Theology — Congresses.
    I. MacDonald, Nathan, 1975-   II. Elliott, M. W. (Mark W.)
    III. Macaskill, Grant.

    BS1235.52.G465   2012
    222′.1106 — dc23

                                        2011039628

www.eerdmans.com

Contents

Abbreviations   ix

Introduction   xiii

GENESIS AND SALVATION HISTORY

Manifest Diversity: The Presence of God in Genesis   3
  William P. Brown

Beginning with the Ending   26
  R. R. Reno

The *Akedah* in Canonical and Artistic Perspective   43
  Gary A. Anderson

Joseph in the Likeness of Adam: Narrative Echoes of the Fall   62
  Timothy J. Stone

"Before Abraham Was, I Am": The Book of Genesis
and the Genesis of Christology   74
  Knut Backhaus

Contents

Genesis 2–3: A Case of Inner-Biblical Interpretation   85
   Christoph Levin

GENESIS AND DIVINE-HUMAN RELATIONS

Gregory of Nyssa on Language, Naming God's Creatures,
and the Desire of the Discursive Animal   103
   Eric Daryl Meyer

Image, Identity, and Embodiment: Augustine's
Interpretation of the Human Person in Genesis 1–2   117
   Matthew Drever

Poetry and Theology in Milton's *Paradise Lost*   129
   Trevor Hart

Sex or Violence? Thinking Again with Genesis
about Fall and Original Sin   140
   Walter J. Houston

GENESIS AND THE NATURAL WORLD

Interpreting the Story of Creation: A Case Study
in the Dialogue between Theology and Science   155
   David Fergusson

Humans, Animals, and the Environment in Genesis 1–3   175
   Richard Bauckham

Reading Genesis in Borneo: Work, Guardianship,
and Companion Animals in Genesis 2   190
   Michael S. Northcott

Covenantal Ecology: The Inseparability of Covenant
and Creation in the Book of Genesis   204
   Brandon Frick

"And Without Thorn the Rose"? Augustine's Interpretations
of Genesis 3:18 and the Intellectual Tradition   216
   Karla Pollmann

Toward a Creational Perspective on Poverty: Genesis 1:26-28,
Image of God, and Its Missiological Implications   228
   Pascal Daniel Bazzell

GENESIS AND THE PEOPLE OF GOD

Did God Choose the Patriarchs? Reading for Election
in the Book of Genesis   245
   Nathan MacDonald

Rebekah's Twins: Augustine on Election in Genesis   267
   Ellen T. Charry

Abraham and Aeneas: Genesis as Israel's Foundation Story   287
   R. Walter L. Moberly

Genesis and Human Society: The Learning and Teaching
People of God   306
   Mark W. Elliott

Food, Famine and the Nations: A Canonical
Approach to Genesis   323
   Stephen B. Chapman

Index of Names   334

Index of Scriptures   338

Abbreviations

AARDS	American Academy of Religion Dissertation Series
AB	Anchor Bible
AJS	*American Journal of Sociology*
ANET	*Ancient Near Eastern Texts Relating to the Old Testament.* Ed. J. B. Pritchard. 3rd ed. Princeton: Princeton University Press, 1969.
AOTC	Apollos Old Testament Commentary Series
ATANT	Abhandlungen zur Theologie des Alten und Neuen Testaments
ATD	Das Alte Testament Deutsch
AugStud	*Augustinian Studies*
BBR	*Bulletin for Biblical Research*
BEvT	Beiträge zur evangelischen Theologie
BKAT	Biblischer Kommentar, Altes Testament
BN	*Biblische Notizen*
BYU Studies	*Brigham Young University Studies*
BZAW	Beihefte zur Zeitschrift für die alttestamentliche Wissenschaft
CBQ	*Catholic Biblical Quarterly*
CC	Continental Commentaries
CCCM	Corpus Christianorum: Continuatio mediaevalis
CCSL	Corpus christianorum series latina
CD	Karl Barth, *Church Dogmatics.* Ed. G. W. Bromiley and T. F. Torrance. Trans. G. W. Bromiley et al. 4 vols. in 14. Edinburgh: T&T Clark, 1936-1969.
COS	*The Context of Scripture.* Ed. W. W. Hallo. 3 vols. Leiden: Brill, 1997-2002.

Abbreviations

CSCO	Corpus scriptorum christianorum orientalium. Edited by I. B. Chabot et al. Paris, 1903-
CTJ	*Calvin Theological Journal*
DDD	*Dictionary of Deities and Demons in the Bible.* Ed. Karel van der Toorn, Bob Becking, and Pieter W. van der Horst. 2nd ed. Grand Rapids: Eerdmans, 1999.
DRev	*Downside Review*
ESV	English Standard Version
FRLANT	Forschungen zur Religion und Literatur des Alten und Neuen Testaments
HeyJ	*Heythrop Journal*
HSM	Harvard Semitic Monographs
HTR	*Harvard Theological Review*
ICC	International Critical Commentary
Int	*Interpretation*
ITC	International Theological Commentary
JB	Jerusalem Bible
JBL	*Journal of Biblical Literature*
JECS	*Journal of Early Christian Studies*
JPS	Jewish Publication Society
JPSTC	JPS Torah Commentary Series
JSJSup	Journal for the Study of Judaism: Supplement Series
JSNTSup	Journal for the Study of the New Testament: Supplement Series
JSOT	*Journal for the Study of the Old Testament*
JSOTSup	Journal for the Study of the Old Testament: Supplement Series
JTS	*Journal of Theological Studies*
JTSA	*Journal of Theology for Southern Africa*
KD	*Kerygma und Dogma*
LCC	Library of Christian Classics
LCL	Loeb Classical Library
LXX	Septuagint
LW	Luther's Works. Ed. Jaroslav Pelikan et al. Trans. George V. Schick et al. 55 vols. St. Louis: Concordia; Philadelphia: Muhlenberg, 1955-1976.
MT	Masoretic text
NAB	New American Bible
NEchtB	Neue Echter Bibel
NIB	*The New Interpreter's Bible.* Ed. Leander E. Keck. 13 vols. Nashville: Abingdon, 1994-2004.
NICNT	New International Commentary on the New Testament
NICOT	New International Commentary on the Old Testament
NIV	New International Version
NovTSup	Novum Testamentum Supplements

NPNF	*Nicene and Post-Nicene Fathers*
NRSV	New Revised Standard Version
OBT	Overtures to Biblical Theology
OTL	Old Testament Library
OtSt	*Oudtestamentische Studiën*
PG	Patrologia graeca
PL	Patrologia latina
RB	*Revue biblique*
RBL	*Review of Biblical Literature*
REAug	*Revue des Études Augustiniennes*
REB	Revised English Bible
SBL	Society of Biblical Literature
SC	Sources chrétiennes
SemeiaSt	Semeia Studies
SVTQ	*St. Vladimir's Theological Quarterly*
TB	Theologische Bücherei
TD	*Theology Digest*
TDOT	*Theological Dictionary of the Old Testament*. Ed. G. J. Botterweck et al. Trans. J. T. Willis et al. 15 vols. Grand Rapids: Eerdmans, 1974-2006.
ThTo	*Theology Today*
TLOT	*Theological Lexicon of the Old Testament*. Ed. Ernst Jenni and Claus Westermann. Trans. Mark E. Biddle. 3 vols. Peabody, Mass.: Hendrickson, 1997.
TRE	*Theologische Realenzyklopädie*. Ed. Gerhard Krause and Gerhard Müller. 36 vols. Berlin: de Gruyter, 1977-2004.
TS	*Theological Studies*
TUAT	*Texte aus der Umwelt des Alten Testaments*
TynBul	*Tyndale Bulletin*
VT	*Vetus Testamentum*
VTSup	Supplements to Vetus Testamentum
WA	Martin Luther, *Werke, Kritische Gesamtausgabe* (Weimarer Ausgabe)
WBC	Word Biblical Commentary
WMANT	Wissenschaftliche Monographien zum Alten und Neuen Testament
WTJ	*Westminster Theological Journal*
WUNT	Wissenschaftliche Untersuchungen zum Neuen Testament
WW	*Word and World*
ZAC	*Zeitschrift für Antikes Christentum*
ZÄS	*Zeitschrift für ägyptische Sprache und Altertumskunde*
ZAW	*Zeitschrift für die alttestamentliche Wissenschaft*
ZBK	Zürcher Bibelkommentare
ZTK	*Zeitschrift für Theologie und Kirche*

Introduction

In the memory of a conference such as that which ran July 14-18, 2009, in St. Andrews, the oddest things stand out: we began the conference with a concert in St. Salvator's chapel, a place with dual identity as a foundation of both church and academy, and rounded it off there with Grant Macaskill preaching. We are inclined to remember conversations over dinner, more relaxed chats in pubs, coffee between sessions, the odd noticeable disagreement, academic jokes, journeys to airports, anything but the papers. Hence all the more reason to make conference papers available, many of which have been rewritten in the light of wisdom received by means of those oddest things. All this in the hope they might serve up the distilled essence of the undertaking. Someone — a spouse, a child, a colleague — might have asked those returning, "What was the result?" In terms of good conscience, one could do worse than point to this book.

When one mentions "Scripture and Theology" (and this was the third in the series, after "John" in 2003 and "Hebrews" in 2006) it would seem that the biblical scholars have an advantage: the agenda is set by a book of the Bible, after all. However, one could argue just as well that the invariable component of all three conferences so far, whether on John, Hebrews, or Genesis, is "Christian theology." The "Christian" epithet is important here, employed in part as a disclaimer against false expectations of some universal theology and in part to recognize and affirm a particular significance of these books within Christian theology. To employ this epithet is to acknowledge that until we have considered the role of these books in relation to Christian theology, the critical task is incomplete and we have not properly understood the object of our study. It is mistaken, then, to perceive biblical scholars to have an advantage over theologians in this task.

But to regard these conferences simplistically as points where two related disciplines speak to one another is naïve. Anyone who has attended the major disciplinary conferences such as AAR and SBL is well aware of the diversity that exists within each discipline. Not every biblical scholar is a redaction critic; not every theologian is a systematician. Methods and approaches can complement or conflict, likewise theologies and readings of history. It is noticeable just how much time the Christian theologians spend sorting out the tradition of interpretation of texts and themes — sometimes positively to affirm it, to show developments, sometimes negatively to criticize its malformations and mutations — often in disagreement with one another. These conferences, then, host encounters between internally diverse fields. Fault lines inevitably emerge and a range of nonnegotiable touchstones come to the surface: the inerrancy of Scripture, the inerrancy of the critical method, Christ-focus, Jewish-rootedness, liberationist imperative, enlightened and sanctified common sense.

If, in his introduction to the volume in this series on Hebrews,[1] Nathan MacDonald drew attention to the growing distance between biblical scholars and systematic theologians, by the time of the approach of the *Genesis* conference in July 2009 this seemed to have the irrevocability and inexorability of continental drift. In the planning of the conference there was an attempt to pair the two disciplines: Brown with Reno, Bauckham with Northcott, and so on. It was not quite the charged atmosphere of a Ryder Cup Singles Match — St. Andrews is too sedate (or douce, as we Scots would say) for such incivility. Yet when, eighteen months later as I write, it comes to digesting the contributions from the point of the Q&A onward, the neat lines between exegesis and doctrine, keynote paper and short paper, seem less to matter. There is and was a lot of fluidity and crosscurrents between papers and genres. However, if one is to try to identify distinct discourses during and after the conference presentations and up to and beyond this moment of publication and reading, then I would discern *four* threads, sometimes tied together but of recognizably different colors: Genesis as setting the stage for salvation history, the God-human connection, the natural world and our place in it, and the delineation of the people of God.

---

1. R. J. Bauckham, D. R. Driver, T. A. Hart, and N. MacDonald, *The Epistle to the Hebrews and Christian Theology* (Grand Rapids: Eerdmans, 2009).

Genesis as Setting the Stage for Salvation History

Bill Brown argues that, in comparison with other places in the Hebrew Bible, theophanies in Genesis are "extraordinarily ordinary," small-scale manifestations of God's presence. God manifests himself as a conversationalist, one who, even on his way to judge, is friendly, or who in the case of Hagar allows her "to be seen." Or again, in the case of Jacob the faces of God and Esau are presented in parallel. God's presence can even be "sneaky," and he makes out of Jacob's pillow a descending and ascending staircase. "In the Priestly strand, word takes precedence over presence." God's presence is largely verbal in P, while the emphasis of the Yahwist is on God's *grounded* presence as one who asks questions. Brown is reminded of an observation made by a Benedictine priest (Sebastian Moore): "God behaves in the psalms in ways he is not allowed to behave in systematic theology." It is being implied here that perhaps systematic theology should be prepared to change its rules of engagement and embrace metaphor. Yet modern systematic theologians would argue that this has indeed been the case. For that subdiscipline is more prepared than before to be flexible with its categories concerning the divine being.

Rusty Reno fights shy of an overly or overtly Christological reading of the early chapters of Genesis. He notices how these chapters are full of false starts and dead ends. From Genesis 3–11 "the primal histories of Genesis go in unproductive circles" and hence subvert the expectation of ancient Near Eastern cosmogonies. And the zooming in to a domestic story of Abraham and his household is further proof of a lack of interest in universal history on the part of the author(s). "In one moment, with a single stab, God thrusts the sharp needle of redemption into the rolled-up fabric of time." Creation is for the sake of Torah, or better, covenant, just as the Priestly writer sets up his account of beginnings. Likewise, the only hope for universal redemption is identification with the particular passion, death, and resurrection of Jesus, and a concurrent "saturation with divine presence." The covenant and its history are more real than the details of the text and these form the basis for interpretation. "Most biblical scholars are rigorously trained to view the laws of history, the principles of cultural development, and the dynamics of tradition and textual transmission as the glue holding together the remarkable diversity and recondite literal particularity of the Bible, not Christ as the eternal Word (or the Torah as the eternal Word)." He does not hold out much hope for most biblical scholars becoming convinced of this.

Gary Anderson considers the famous Sepphoris mosaic and its representation of Aaron from Leviticus 8–9, particularly the offering of the daily sacrifice, and the *Akedah*. The mosaic's theme seems to be "the Lord has made himself visible." "The theophany that happened to Abraham in a singular fashion will be possible for all Israelites at the 'mount of the LORD'" (or Jerusalem, the reader is allowed to understand), on the north or hidden side of the Lord. The emphasis in Jewish interpretation was on Isaac more than on Abraham, with Isaac's (not Israel's) obedience meriting reward in a way unthinkable in Genesis 12. The seventh zodiacal month of Libra marvelously fits with the business of penance and release of debts in the seventh month of the Jewish calendar. "Even the Bible allows for the notion that later generations could draw on the merits of the patriarchs." Such is at the heart of Ephraim and Anselm's soteriology.

Timothy Stone reads Joseph as an antitype of Adam, who did not sin in Adam's likeness. Adam's transgression echoes through Genesis in the lives of Noah, Abraham, and Jacob, until in the Joseph story Adam's folly is overcome by Joseph's wisdom. In Potiphar's house Joseph's situation is analogous to Adam's — everything is put in his charge except Potiphar's wife/food, yet when tempted with this "forbidden fruit," Joseph does not listen to the voice of the woman (Gen. 39:10; cf. 3:17). He not only avoids Adam's transgression, but also succeeds where Adam and others in Genesis failed. He rules over the land, is a blessing to the whole world, and under his care Israel is fruitful and multiplies. If Adam is a type of the one to come, Joseph is more so. Finally, Christ's reversal of Eden in Luke–Acts is analogous to Joseph's.

As a series of conferences that moves between Testaments it was felt important that there be at least some deliberate mention of the New Testament's appropriation of the themes of Genesis — a task entrusted to Knut Backhaus. He explains how the relationship of the New Testament to "its Bible" is not straightforward, but is mediated by already established traditions of interpretation. On the one hand the *relecture* of Genesis is creative; on the other hand Genesis is so much the foundation that the New Testament takes for granted that it belongs to it, even if the assimilation seems to happen through swallowing it up. Genesis is clearly behind the Johannine prologue, and Genesis 28 behind John 1:51; Jacob is present in John 4 and Abraham in John 8. The figure of Melchizedek from Genesis 14 (with help from Ps. 110:4) stamps Hebrews 7, and Hebrews 11 has eight patriarchal characters. In Paul, Christ is the heavenly, eschatological Adam who is just as important as the faithful Abraham. In conclusion there is "a certain consciousness of being 'at home' in this book, of 'dwelling' between its lines." When considering the Creator in Genesis we cannot escape the fact that he is the God who has defined himself in Christ.

Christoph Levin, on inspecting the textual joints, concludes that there was once a creation narrative without a fall. "When no plant of the field was yet in the earth, . . . then . . . God formed man" (Gen. 2:5-7). The more primitive J narrative invites readers to think of desert sand as what existed when God put Adam on earth as a farmer. By naming animals and getting hands dirty the human being participates in creation. The fall narrative is sewn into an earthy account of the garden. The serpent looks like the intrusion of another strand, but that theme is tempered, and the dialogue shows that the woman was fully responsible for her actions, even as she tries to filter what God has said; the serpent carries this spinning of God's message further. Unlike Paul, for the author of Genesis "Being-toward-death belongs together not with sin but with creation." Levin finds dust to have been the fate of humans all along, and what is threatened ("on the day you eat . . . you shall die") is meeting that eventuality sooner. The point is that the tree of life has not been partaken. Genesis 3 reinforces the mortality that it takes Christ to overcome.

Genesis and the God-Human Connection

Eric Meyer reports Gregory of Nyssa's belief that God the Trinity does not require language for communication *intra se*. Language is only required when enfleshment makes the communication of intelligence necessary. Language also serves to lick the material flesh into shape. Yet, unlike Eunomius, Gregory is not certain about the fittingness of words to things: language can neither pinpoint God and reality nor be the means of our transformation in communion. God is to be known beyond our minds and doctrines. Gregory is an ecumenist's delight. Meyer argues that this emphasis on desire ends up undermining the distinction between animal and human in Gregory's thought. The points of greatest continuity with animal life are also the sites where divine grace breaks in and draws the human creature forward in its transformation. "Discourse is not to eradicate passionate desire altogether, but to oversee and enforce a refusal of any closure of the gap within subjectivity (named by the *imago Dei*) that should properly propel the human to seek and contemplate God." Passion is only bad where it forecloses on transcendent desire, and theology's task is to remind us of that. "The continuity between human and animal and the limits of discourse entail that humanity's spiritual service to creation in God's image is not a 'pulling up' from above, in which human beings raise animals to a higher plane of existence;

instead, it is a reconciliatory 'getting down into,' in which a deeper, ecosystemic integration (guided by wisdom) guards the multivalence of desire as an approach to God." So Gregory was not a proto-environmentalist, but was interested in the requirements of human fulfillment.

Matthew Drever thinks that Augustine can be defended as far as his ideas about human creation are concerned. What matters is that "intellectual and material things come into existence in distinct manners," with the intellectual creature formed directly by God, each time a human person is made, and becoming self-knowing and aware of its origin from God. The language of "according to kind" *(secundum genus)* is not used of humans since only one, Adam, was created. Yet, unlike angels, humans know all they know — God included — through their bodies. Body and soul are created according to likeness. So "humans begin with a knowledge of the created order and progress to a knowledge of God, while angels begin with a knowledge of God before coming to a knowledge of the created order." "The image of God is not some 'thing,' part, or faculty imprinted onto an already existing soul; rather it characterizes how the soul forms its most basic identity out of its existence." Humans are not autonomous agents but exist in relation — to God and the world.

According to Trevor Hart, John Milton believed that in scriptural poetry delight came first, and benefit second (echoing Augustine's *delectare et prodesse*), yet that was only in order of effect — the true priority was the reverse. Considering temptation narratives helps the reader to think how s/he would have done better, or could do now. We are hooked as we read on, and start to learn. The orthodox, Augustinian Milton of C. S. Lewis can be used against the heterodox one of Empson, for whom the devil had all the best lines. The great poem, however, leads the reader into temptation only to shock us back to our senses, or as Hart puts it, Stanley Fish's Milton is "a supralapsarian deity who *leads his readers into temptation* precisely in order to deliver them from evil." What one *may* say on Satan's part is that there was a frailty that might account for Adam and Eve's fall, and perhaps they have bought into that idea by their own will. Milton was working well under the influence of Grotius and Arminianism, but in no way Socinian (for Milton they were noble, not "naïve foundlings").

Walter Houston argues that the traditional (Augustinian) doctrine of the fall and original sin has several unsatisfactory features, not least from an exegetical point of view that it is not clear that the account in Genesis 3 intends to describe the origin of sin. He suggests that this account should be read in the context of the P framework of Genesis 1–11. In the P narratives of the creation and the flood, we find a contrast between the goodness of God's original creation (Gen. 1:31) and the "violence" (חמס) of "all flesh" (i.e., all human and animal life) as now experienced (6:11-12). This is encapsulated in the differing charges given to humanity in 1:28 and in 9:1-7. In the original charge they are to rule the creatures by their natural authority; after the flood they must repress violence by force and fear. P, in itself, does not explain the irruption of violence, but Genesis 3 may be read in this context as relating the human decision to reject the divine mandate of justice and peace. The whole narrative must be understood as equally mythical with Genesis 3. But to formulate the doctrine of sin on the basis of Genesis 1–9 as a whole would have the advantage of giving the doctrine an unforced cosmic reach, rooting it in the central biblical value of justice, and assisting in theological reflection on the urgent issue of our responsibility toward the natural world. An appendix discusses possible ways of understanding the text diachronically.

Genesis and the Natural World (and Our Place in It)

David Fergusson homes in on the theological sense of the Christian doctrine of "creation out of nothing," as it was developed by the church fathers in general and Augustine in particular. The dependence of the cosmos on the Trinitarian Creator gives it a certain stamp. The creation theme is happily not as subservient to history as it was two generations ago in the hands of Old Testament scholars like Gerhard von Rad. Although applying "infinity" to the created cosmos does not make sense, nevertheless one cannot enlist the Big Bang in service of *creatio ex nihilo*. And it could be that our anthropically shaped universe is just one of many others in a multiverse setup. Down on the biological ground, the companion Christian doctrine of divine providence has been challenged by Darwinian science, and this is arguably more the neuralgic point than any "doctrine" of the six days of creation. If the Old Princetonian Hodge could not fit natural selection into God's plans, then his successor B. B. Warfield could. It seems better in recent theology to live and let live, or better still see divine spirit as there in the cracks. However, that "God becomes reactive and in important respects dependent upon what has been made" with these developments is one problem. That the God of Jesus is hardly the God who says "Amen" to all that helps the fittest to survive is another. Yet it is surely a bonus that theology is less anthropocentric today than it was a century ago.

Richard Bauckham believes that Genesis 1–2 has often been read as though it was the whole extent of what the Bible has to say about creation. In any case the creation account proceeds according to a spatial, not temporal or progressive, schema. It is not that humans are the summit of a gradually ascending scale. Rather, the seventh day (of rest) is the true culmination. Creation has its existence for reasons that do and that do not altogether relate to humanity. Humans are told to take possession of the land and work it, nothing more. Since 1:28 echoes 1:22 it cannot mean that humans are to compete with animals. They are to rule them, domestic and wild alike, as they would rule other humans — and that means rule justly. Genesis 9:9-10 assumes that animals too are partners in the covenant, not just parts of "the environment." Humans meanwhile are literally *anima*-ls and somehow closely related to the soil. The Renaissance interpretation of the image of God is now being seen for the error it was.

According to Michael Northcott, animals are presented in Genesis 2 as companions to humans, not as objects of domination. Since the Victorian age, embodied in the hunter-scientist A. R. Wallace, and with the more recent clearance of the habitat for the sake of oil palm production, all this has been forgotten. If space is scarce for human and orangutan alike, then the answer is not that they should compete for it, but rather learn to coexist in it. To achieve this is to work against the common reception of Genesis 1–3 as supporting human dominion over a fallen world. Countering voices of a more generous interpretation are to be heard in the Eastern and monastic tradition, which affirm that Adam was called in paradise to be a good farmer, and he was called to this *before* the fall, not as some sort of remedy for it. Manual work was a true means to true holiness. When monasteries became too rich to have to work manually, their point was lost. The reader needs to be transformed by the text. Some Syriac fathers imagined the paradise of coexistence in Adam's naming the animals, even while for the Western fathers the power of naming spoke of the elevation of reason.

Brandon Frick notes that Northcott had also raised concern about the use of the "stewardship" metaphor for elevating humans as though they can control everything for monetary profit. Better, thinks Frick, is that of covenant, for in the first use of this term in Genesis 6 and 9 animals are included as covenant partners. The ark symbolizes the need to coexist. The Noachic covenant covers all creation from head to toe. "The scope of the Abrahamic covenant more fully expresses the cosmic dimensions briefly noted in the Noachic." This might seem counterintuitive, but the blessing for the creation includes land, that is, the whole creation. Barth used the word *Begleiter* for animals (the translation "companion" is better than "attendant"). God might subsequently find animal sacrifice pleasing, but even then such life is sacred, and they are no less parties to the covenant.

Singling out a verse, Karla Pollmann follows the progress of Augustine from allegorizing the "weeds and thistles" of Genesis 3:18 to a more literal interpretation that he will defend with apologetic strength. The tradition rarely followed this departure. Although Avitus does like the idea that wild beasts used their savagery to the detriment of others only after the fall, Bede prefers to give readers the earlier Augustine of the *De Genesi contra Manichaeos*. For Eriugena the "thorns" are mental ones, and the serpent became poisonous after the fall (contrary to Augustine in the later literal commentary). Although the literal commentary did reappear with Lombard, it was hardly known to Luther, and Calvin had a moralizing sort of interpretation. The tradition liked certain things such as the *rationes seminales* idea from the commentary, but did not care to listen to Augustine on all the details.

Perhaps a less obvious reading of Genesis 1:26-28 is provided by Pascal Bazzell, who addresses the theme of poverty. The important point is not to view the poor as having that image effaced. The same verses also show a reflexive capacity in God, and hence an image in God, but this is the very thing that can be skewed, not least in the poor believing in repressive ideology. Networks of relationships are in need of reconciliation and structures need correction, and that is part of the church's missiological task.

The Delineation of the People of God

Nathan MacDonald proposes that "election" in all its separating out and parting of ways is certainly a theme in Genesis, though not quite *the* theme, just as Israel is "the people" but not the *only* people. The Abraham story supplies the dominant note in the chord, and the patriarchal narratives as a whole are clear that blessing abounds within this life unto many nations, even while the distinction between Israel and the rest is strictly maintained. Election *is* for service, but it is service to the Lord God. Deuteronomy might well spoil this party, but there is something inclusive about the atmosphere, as Israel attempts to play "humanity" as chosen by God as "early" as Genesis 1:26. With thanks to Kaminsky's tripartite classification (elect, non-elect, anti-elect) one may discern that only the anti-elect (possibly a smaller group) are doomed, and *they* hardly appear in Genesis. On the other hand, the elect are Torah-obedient rather than purely grateful sinners.

Ellen Charry notes a point that is not as obvious as one might think: Augustine read the Genesis narratives through Paul. How could Romans 9–11, a charter of hope, become also a foundation of a somber doctrine? For Charry the fault lies with Paul himself, who saw Jews as represented by Esau; what Augustine did was to make Jacob and Esau stand for individuals. Humility and fear became the Augustinian legacy, although Thomas Aquinas for one did not believe in it — whether it is a defect of the will or of ignorance, it is still a defect. Is Augustine's view of election pastorally harmful or at best unrealistic? Whether we agree or not, it is a point to ponder; does the Esau-type haunt Western civilization? It is important that Christian theologians think through their psychology of religion.

Walter Moberly provides a comparison of Genesis and a "pagan" foundation story from a civilization's prehistory. Abraham may be compared with Aeneas. Each time it is the hand of Providence that guides their respective journeys. The Israel of these narratives is a peaceable nation, called to peace and to defend itself, much like Aeneas and the Romans, or at least the way the Romans liked to think of themselves and their great ancestor. These narratives announce that something way off in the future was already being prepared for. Just like the location of Rome, Jerusalem too has a visit from the patriarch before it truly exists; and Sodom is comparable to Carthage. The *Aeneid* is less reserved about making explicit the connections across history. It would be simplistic to represent Genesis as anti-Constantinian. Abraham's family are far from perfect, but Balaam's vision "of a people 'not reckoning itself among the nations' indicates a noncompetitive nature for the people of Abraham" and suggests being "self-dispossessingly obedient" and the capacity for blessing in the church today.

Mark Elliott outlines the contours that run between the concepts of community and society and thinks there is a communal extroverted quality to the chosen people in Genesis. In Christian interpretation, the coming of Jesus makes Israel forever and for all. What struck Luther about the patriarchal narratives was humanity in extended families. The City of God is a moral society of forgiveness, and in this Augustine was shaped by his reading of the Genesis narratives. There are both a positive presentation and a realism about what can be expected of sinful people. Luther sees the family as the place where God's people learn thankfulness and joy, and as outward-going, rather than introspectively bourgeois, as in the modern interpretations of the patriarchs (Mann, Wénin).

Stephen Chapman, inspired by Brevard Childs's identification of the *toledot* lists as a structuring principle in Genesis, one that subordinates J to P, sees Genesis 12 and 26 as important, with "famine" as a theme that links to the last section of Genesis. Meanwhile, what Joseph does to provide for all in Genesis 45 is in fulfillment of the divine promise to Abram. Joseph also undoes Adam's bad work, with food as a sign of the blessing's material aspect. God blesses the Egyptians for Joseph's sake. Blessing then becomes contagious and gets reciprocated. With the help of J. Gerald Janzen's commentary on Genesis, Chapman notes how ambivalent the characterization of Joseph becomes as the story goes on. The essay concludes with an application to the church as imparting material bread along with the spiritual as part of its eucharistic discipline.

Introductions by means of summaries are meant to whet the appetite and in no way steal the thunder. I shall end with an admission that, if doctrinal theologians and exegetes were brought together, then it happened in the heads and conversations of participants — in the bar, in the taxi, even now. However, there are signs that although these conversations have a long way to go before we learn to speak the other's language comfortably and pick up its nuances and idioms, there is a realization that both the church and the academy deserve better than artificial though convenient dichotomization of ancient Scripture and Christian theology.

MARK W. ELLIOTT
St. Andrews

Genesis and Salvation History

Manifest Diversity:
The Presence of God in Genesis

William P. Brown

What constitutes a bona fide account of God's presence in Scripture? Clearly something more than a *Wortbericht,* a report of divine discourse. A theophany account must refer in some fashion to God's actual appearance.[1] Related to the literary issue is a theological matter: *Where* is God located in such accounts?[2] Does God remain outside the created order, occasionally breaking in to bless or to disrupt? Or, to take the other extreme, does God's presence fill or permeate the world (see, e.g., Ps. 72:19; Isa. 6:3; cf. 11:9)? Biblical tradition gives no single answer. In addition, what about the consequences of God's manifest presence? There are, on the one hand, the god-awful theophanies that trigger cosmic tremors. On the other hand, three "men" come to visit Abraham one hot afternoon and eat with him, God being among them. The variety of ways God appears in the Hebrew Scriptures is nothing short of staggering.

---

1. An illustrative example outside Genesis is found in 1 Kgs. 19, in Elijah's encounter with God at Horeb. Verse 9 states, "The word of YHWH came to [Elijah], saying, 'What are you doing here, Elijah?'" This is distinguished from what happens next, when God "passes by" Elijah on the mountain (vv. 11-13). Yet the account concludes with the same "word" from God and the identical response from Elijah! Here one can separate out a "word-report" (vv. 9-10) from, one could say, a "presence-report" (vv. 11-14 [+ 15-18]). For further discussion on the latter, see below.

2. This issue is insightfully addressed by Andreas Schuele in his 2007 inaugural address at Union-PSCE in Richmond, Virginia, "In the Vicinity of God: The Idea of Divine Nearness in the Hebrew Bible," available at http://www.union-psce.edu/faculty_staff/fulltime/schuele1/index.php.

The book of Genesis offers its own select array of divine-human encounters. But to establish a basis of comparison, I want to leap briefly beyond Genesis to note a few of the more dramatic examples of divine presence in the Hebrew Bible. The most prominent is God's appearance on Mount Sinai. Though Exodus 19 is a convoluted text from a literary standpoint, it shares a consistency of tone and theme: holy fear and fascination.[3] There is nothing casual or mundane about Israel's encounter with God on the mountain; the account is filled with images of terror and transcendence. This mountaintop theophany requires stringent preparations: the people are consecrated and boundaries are established. God's holy presence tolerates no contact with the impure. Sex is prohibited (v. 15), and touching the mountain is proscribed (vv. 12-13). On the third day, cloud and smoke envelop the mountain accompanied by thunder, earthquake, and shofar blasts. Deuteronomy recalls the mountain as "ablaze with fire to the heart of heaven, shrouded in darkness, cloud, and gloom" (Deut. 4:11).[4] Only Moses and later Aaron are allowed to ascend to the top, where God has descended "in fire" (Exod. 19:18-20).

On the mountain God's presence is made manifest in both sound and visual fury, but the latter serves the former. The fury sets the stage for God's verbal address to all Israel, the Decalogue (Exod. 20:1-17; Deut. 4:13), and the sound establishes its own commanding presence. According to Deuteronomy, only the voice is perceived, albeit a voice "out of the fire" (Deut. 4:12, 15), a voice that the gathered people can withstand only so long. According to one ancient testimony, not only did the Israelites gather at the foothills of Sinai to hear the thunderous voice of God, they *saw* it! The Old Greek of Exodus 20:18a reads, "And all the people saw the voice," which departs from the plural rendering of the direct object in the MT (הקולת) usually taken to refer to lightning bolts.[5] But regardless of how one reconstructs the Exodus text, God's presence at Sinai/Horeb is described as terrifyingly transcendent, requiring the people to stand at a distance and be purified. Displayed in godawful glory, holiness takes a front seat at Sinai.

Jump ahead to Elijah and his sojourn at Horeb in 1 Kings 19. Elijah's encounter with God has all the elements of another Sinaitic encounter:

3. Exodus 19 exemplifies well Rudolf Otto's famous notion of the holy as *mysterium tremendum* in *The Idea of the Holy: An Inquiry into the Non-Rational Factor in the Idea of the Divine and Its Relation to the Rational,* trans. John W. Harvey, 2nd ed. (New York: Oxford University Press, 1958), esp. pp. 12-40.

4. All biblical translations are my own.

5. The Old Greek likely preserves the older reading. See Azzan Yadin, "*Qôl* as Hypostasis in the Hebrew Bible," *JBL* 122 (2003): 617-23.

earth-shattering wind, earthquake, and fire (vv. 11-12; cf. Exod. 33:22). But, as the text makes clear, God was not present in any of these natural, destructive phenomena. Instead, a hush falls (קול דממה דקה),[6] followed by a voice (1 Kgs. 19:12-13). Elijah must come out of his cave to hear it, covering his face with a mantle (v. 13). God commands the prophet with a new commission (vv. 15-16).

One could also consider Isaiah's encounter with the enthroned God in the temple (Isa. 6:1-4). Here God's presence, accompanied by the thunderous acclamations of the seraphim, is visibly palpable. The prophet sees the temple's inner sanctum burst open with the hem of God's robe filling the nave. This dramatic scene has, according to the singing seraphim, a cosmic parallel: God's glory fills the entire world (v. 3). As for the prophet, God's presence so fills him with dread (v. 5) that he must be ritually cleansed (vv. 6-8). As in the case of Elijah at Horeb, God's voice takes center stage to commission the prophet (vv. 8-13).

Perhaps these three accounts are sufficient for our base of comparison, though one must not overlook Moses' encounter with the burning bush, also at Horeb, "the mountain of God" (Exod. 3:1). Moses is instructed to take off his sandals (v. 5; cf. Josh. 5:15) and receives God's most personal yet elusive name: I AM (אהיה, Exod. 3:14-15; cf. 6:2-3; 33:19). There is also the central account of YHWH passing before Moses on Sinai after the Israelites have broken covenant. Moses requests that he be shown YHWH's glory (33:18-19). In response, Moses is granted a theophany that, again, is indelibly marked by divine discourse (v. 19). Nevertheless, he must be protected; he must not see YHWH's face, lest he die (vv. 20-23). Shielded by God's hand, Moses is permitted to see only YHWH's "back" (v. 23). The renewal of the covenant that immediately follows is accompanied by YHWH descending in a cloud and passing before Moses for yet another solemn proclamation, one that reaches the theological summit of the Pentateuch (34:5-7). And, last but not least, one cannot forget the remarkable covenantal meal shared on Sinai by Moses, Aaron and his sons, seventy "elders," and "the God of Israel" (24:9-11). There they behold God (without dying), and the base upon which God stands is vividly described as a gleaming "plate of lapis lazuli" (v. 10).

---

6. Marvin A. Sweeney translates the ambiguous phrase as "sound of faint silence." The Old Greek reads, "(the) sound of a delicate breeze, and there was the Lord." Targum Jonathan attributes the voice to "those who were praising softly." See the discussion in Sweeney, *1 & 2 Kings*, OTL (Louisville: Westminster John Knox, 2007), pp. 220, 232. The closest parallel to the enigmatic use of דממה is found in Job 4:16. See Schuele, "In the Vicinity of God."

From this brief, incomplete survey, we find that each account depicts in richly dramatic ways God's dread-filled, self-disclosing presence, whether on a mountain or within the temple. Such scenes are filled with marvelous special effects, as any ten-year-old would agree. Not so in Genesis, however. No pyrotechnics are featured, not even a descending cloud. Examples of God's presence in Genesis cannot hold a candle, or smoking fire pot (Gen. 15:17), to Sinai's blazing mountain and Zion's smoke-filled sanctum. When the narrators of Genesis report, for example, that "YHWH appeared," the focus is predominantly on the substance of what God says rather than on the substance of God's presence. As is often noted, "holy" is not part of the theophanic vocabulary of Genesis,[7] to which one could also add the word "glory" (כבוד). Notwithstanding two notable exceptions, there is by and large a distinct matter-of-factness that characterizes the accounts, a certain casualness, and in at least one striking case, a casualness with a vengeance. The Genesis theophanies are extraordinarily ordinary. Genesis 12:7 is representative: "Then YHWH appeared (וירא) to Abram, and said, 'To your seed I will give this land.' So there he built an altar to YHWH, who had appeared to him." One could cite other stripped-down examples of divine manifestation: 17:1; 26:2, 24-25; 35:9-10. In all these cases, the Deity's "appearance" is simply reported, with divine discourse taking center stage. Nothing more happens except in certain cases where the patriarch builds an altar, or plants a tree (21:33), so that God's name can be worshipfully invoked (13:4; cf. 4:26).

The Priestly covenant account in Genesis 17 adds one small detail: Abram falls on his face as God speaks (17:3). This reference, which narratively does nothing more than interrupt God's discourse, does acknowledge in its own small way the weightiness of God's presence. But, as is typical of most accounts in Genesis, the narrator dwells not on the palpable but on the verbal. Why, then, this strange matter-of-factness that pervades most of the theophanies in the ancestral narratives? On the one hand, the Genesis narrators insist that these episodes are more than simply *Wortberichte,* for they are frequently introduced with the near formulaic statement, "YHWH/God appeared to PN."[8] Bona fide theophanies they are. On the other hand, nothing, or nothing much, of the numinous is conveyed. In Genesis it appears that God travels lightly, freed from the heavy baggage of divine "glory," perhaps so as not to steal Sinai's thunder or diffuse, for that matter, the tabernacle's

---

7. R. Walter L. Moberly, *The Old Testament of the Old Testament: Patriarchal Narratives and Mosaic Yahwism,* OBT (Minneapolis: Fortress, 1992), pp. 100-103.

8. For example, Gen. 12:7; 17:1; 18:1; 26:2, 24; 35:9; cf. 35:1; 48:3.

impenetrable cloud (see Exod. 40:34-35). These "ordinary" theophanies can be added to the list of other unorthodox elements (unorthodox, that is, in comparison to Mosaic Yahwism) that characterize the so-called religion of the patriarchs, prompting R. W. L. Moberly to call the ancestral narratives of Genesis the "Old Testament of the Old Testament."[9]

Theophanies in Miniature

Now for the more exceptional examples, five particular accounts in Genesis that render a fuller, or at least more complex, picture of divine presence: Genesis 15:7-21 (YHWH's covenant with Abram); 18:1-15 (Abraham hosts three strangers at Mamre); 16:7-14 (Hagar at Beer-lahai-roi); 28:10-22 (Jacob at Bethel); and perhaps strangest of all, 32:22-32 (Jacob at the Jabbok). Nevertheless, they remain "small-scale manifestations" of God's presence.[10] I present them in order of increasing numinosity.

God among Three Persons

The first, then, is Genesis 18, which begins with the typically terse theophanic introduction, "YHWH appeared."[11] Divine manifestation occurs "by the oaks of Mamre" (v. 1; see vv. 4, 8), a site where the patriarch had earlier built an altar after receiving the divine promise of land (13:14-18). This time, however, contrary to most other episodes in Genesis, the narrator divulges what Abraham actually saw. Dramatically introduced by the interjectory particle הנה — perhaps best translated as *voilà!* — Abraham sees "three men standing near him" (18:2). So begins the fabled tale of Abraham's hospitality and the announcement of Sarah's giving birth. The first word that comes out of Abraham's mouth has been the subject of much discussion: אדנָי in MT (*kyrie* in the Old Greek; *Domine* in the Vulgate), the formal address to God, which would be unique in Genesis.[12] Most scholars, however, repoint the

---

9. Moberly, *Old Testament of the Old Testament*, esp. pp. 79-104.

10. I borrow this language from Benjamin D. Sommer's description of the מלאך in *The Bodies of God and the World of Ancient Israel* (Cambridge: Cambridge University Press, 2009), p. 40.

11. Claus Westermann regards v. 1a as a theological "chapter heading," comparable to 22:1a (*Genesis 12–36*, trans. John J. Scullion, CC [Minneapolis: Fortress, 1995], p. 277).

12. אדנָי in Gen. 19:18 is in pausal form.

word as אֲדֹנָי, "my lord," indicating that Abraham does not recognize God in the group.[13] E. A. Speiser, followed by others, sees Abraham identifying one among the three as the leader and speaking specifically to him in v. 3 and then to the others out of courtesy in v. 4.[14] The Samaritan Pentateuch, however, maintains a plural reading throughout the verse, including Abraham's initial word of address. The MT, by contrast, alternates between singular and plural forms throughout the chapter: singular in vv. 1, 3, 10-15, 17-21, 22b-33; plural in vv. 2, 4-9, 16, 22a. Similar shifts occur in the subsequent chapter on Lot and the two מלאכים or divine messengers (19:2, 17-18). Is Abraham entertaining God unawares (cf. Heb. 13:2)?

More telling is the other side of the unfolding dialogue. The strangers speak as one until v. 10. Together they accept Abraham's invitation (v. 5), together they eat (v. 8), and, perhaps strangest of all, they speak in consort when inquiring of Sarah's whereabouts (v. 9).[15] Only one, however, promises to return "when Sarah bears a son" (v. 10). The transition from the many to the one does not call attention to itself with the blaring of trumpets; it is marked simply by a shift in verbal inflection: from ויאמרו ("they said") to ויאמר ("he said" [vv. 9-10]). But divine identity is not fully unveiled until v. 13: "YHWH said to Abraham, 'Why did Sarah laugh . . . ?'" The inquiry is followed by a rhetorical question: "Is anything too difficult for YHWH?" (v. 14). Thereafter a new episode unfolds in which the "men" set out for Sodom (vv. 16, 22), while YHWH remains with Abraham to deliberate over the city's fate (vv. 16-33).[16]

The narrator of this strange tale proves to be a master of subtlety, if not ambiguity. It is unclear whether Abraham recognizes YHWH among the strangers. That the "men" speak and eat together suggests that YHWH is indistinguishable from the other אנשים until v. 10. Divinity emerges from the discourse. Verse 10 thus lifts the veil, and the speaker's identity is fully confirmed in v. 13. The narrative gradually builds to an unveiling of divine iden-

---

13. See, e.g., E. A. Speiser, *Genesis,* AB (Garden City, N.Y.: Doubleday, 1964), pp. 128-29; Victor P. Hamilton, *The Book of Genesis, Chapters 18–50,* NICOT (Grand Rapids: Eerdmans, 1995), p. 3 n. 2. Cf. Westermann, *Genesis 12–36,* p. 278.

14. Speiser, *Genesis,* pp. 128-29, 131.

15. Esther J. Hamori helpfully cites a parallel example of discursive alternation between singular and plural in 1 Kgs. 18:17-18 (*"When Gods Were Men": The Embodied God in Biblical and Near Eastern Literature,* BZAW 384 [Berlin: de Gruyter, 2008], pp. 5-6).

16. For a recent, nuanced treatment of Gen. 18:16-33, see Nathan MacDonald, "Listening to Abraham — Listening to Yhwh: Divine Justice and Mercy in Genesis 18:16-33," *CBQ* 66 (2004): 25-43.

tity from "three men" to "one" to YHWH. No shock of recognition, however, is registered on the part of Abraham. Sarah's role, however, is another matter: upon realizing the stranger's divine status, she registers fear. The transition from laughter to fear parallels YHWH's self-disclosure (vv. 10-14). But as for Abraham's reaction, the narrative is silent. God's presence remains casual throughout, beginning with a degree of concealment. YHWH's appearance to Abraham is consistently less than a full appearance. Here we find a very humanlike Deity pondering which course of action to take with Abraham concerning the "outcry" against Sodom and Gomorrah (vv. 17-33).

The two remaining "men" are referred to as divine messengers (מלאכים) in the following chapter (19:1) and later as משחתים ("destroyers," v. 13). Yet they again find themselves eating an evening meal at Lot's house in Sodom (v. 3) and are later referred to as "men" (vv. 8, 10, 12; see the tight interchange in vv. 15-16). Lot addresses them as "my lords" (אדנָי, v. 2; cf. v. 18 in pausal form). However divine these "men" are, they cannot pass up an invitation and a good meal before exercising their superhuman powers.

Seeing Is Believing: The Deity at the Well

The theophany recounted in Genesis 16:7-14 is, likewise, casually ambiguous, for it is declared only in retrospect and begins with a figure other than the Deity. Hagar's flight from Sarah's harsh treatment takes her into the wilderness, where she is "found" by the מלאך יהוה beside a desert spring (v. 7). Nothing, however, is said of the messenger's *appearance;* only his words are recounted, four times no less. Each verse of the messenger's discourse is introduced with ויאמר ("and he said," vv. 8-11), culminating with the promise of a son, whose name, Ishmael, is itself testimony to God's *hearing* (vv. 11-12), as dramatically attested in the Elohist's counterpart to the Yahwist's account (21:17).

In 16:13-14, however, the focus shifts abruptly to God's *seeing*. In response to the child's naming by God, Hagar provides her own set of names. She first names the God whom she has encountered through the medium of the מלאך as אל ראי, "God of seeing/sight." She then names the location of her encounter: "The Well of the Living One Who Sees Me" (באר לחי ראי). The emphasis falls upon the Deity's power of sight, as evidenced in God's response to Hagar's plight. Lamentably, the clause between these two naming reports is textually uncertain. Literally it reads: "for she said, 'Have I really seen here after the one who has seen me?'" (הגם הלם ראיתי אחרי ראי,

v. 13b). This seemingly obscure clause has prompted a widely accepted reconstruction, proposed first by Julius Wellhausen, which renders the clause to read, "Have I really seen God and lived?" (הגם אלהים ראיתי ואחי).[17] The difference is considerable. Is Hagar awestruck over having seen God and survived (cf. Exod. 33:20), or is she marveling over the fact that she could still see after having been seen by God? I propose that Hagar's question is simply elliptical: "Have I really seen (God) here after (his) seeing me?" Apart from this curious clause, the subject of seeing is God, in parallel with the God who hears. Given the ambiguity of Hagar's question, the narrative straddles the line between theophany and mere divine discourse. It is as if Hagar were asking, "Was this really a theophany?" Indeed, with the emphasis placed on the God who finds and sees Hagar, this concealed theophany is more an "anthrophany," more the case of Hagar appearing in God's sight than the reverse! In any case, the narrative progresses from the messenger to the Deity, from the מלאך to YHWH and El, another case of the Deity's manifestation in miniature.

The Wrestling Match: God's Obscure Presence at Peniel

A far stranger account of a retrospective theophany in Genesis is found in the story of Jacob at Jabbok (32:22-32 [MT 23-33]).[18] God's presence this time takes place under the cover of darkness. The narrative is a redaction of two non-Priestly sources, whose combined effect renders a story filled with irony, ambiguity, and paradox.[19] Despite the narrative's succinct style, Gerhard von Rad notes its "spaciousness in content."[20] More pointedly, Stephen Geller acknowledges the text's "pregnant ambiguity," which "allows intimations of all possible answers" to the question of the wrestler's identity.[21]

Jacob's encounter with God at the Jabbok begins with an איש ("man") in the night (v. 25). But the story and its background begin much earlier. The Jabbok episode is nested within the larger narrative of Jacob's homeward-bound journey and his impending encounter with Esau. The scene opens

17. See the discussion in Speiser, *Genesis*, pp. 118-19.
18. Henceforth I will cite only MT versification.
19. For a compelling treatment of ambiguity in this narrative, see Stephen A. Geller, *Sacred Enigmas: Literary Religion in the Hebrew Bible* (London: Routledge, 1996), pp. 9-29.
20. Gerhard von Rad, *Genesis*, trans. John H. Marks, 2nd ed., OTL (Philadelphia: Westminster, 1972), p. 319.
21. Geller, *Enigmas*, p. 23.

with a poignant parting between Jacob and Laban (32:1). Jacob is set on his way only to be suddenly met by "the messengers of God" (מלאכי אלהים), to which he exclaims, "This is God's camp/company" (מחנה אלהים זה). But apparently Jacob sees double, for he calls the place מחנים ("Two Camps/ Companies"; v. 3). Does the name indicate Jacob's camp and God's camp or suggest that God has two camps? The text does not clarify the matter. The dual name does, however, anticipate an element in the scene that follows (vv. 3-13a), which begins with Jacob sending his own messengers (מלאכים) to Esau (v. 4). They return with news that Esau is coming to meet him along with a veritable army. Panicked, Jacob strategically divides his own retinue "into two companies" (לשני מחנות, v. 8).[22]

Human and divine realms become tightly intertwined as Jacob makes repeated reference to Esau as "my lord" (אדני) in the narrative, eight times no less, and to himself as his brother's "servant" (four times). Is it coincidental that Jacob also refers to himself as YHWH's "servant" in his prayer (v. 11)? For the first time in the Jacob cycle, this heel-grabbing supplanter expresses humility, declaring himself "the least (worthy) of all the acts of benevolence and of faithfulness" YHWH has shown him. Jacob pleads that he be delivered (הצילני נא, v. 11). Jacob's prayer to God, effusive in its expressions of reverence and humility, anticipates his encounter with Esau. Is Jacob practicing for his impending encounter with Esau?

The "Elohist" version offers Jacob an alternative plan (vv. 13b-21): instead of shrewdly dividing his company into two, Jacob plans to present Esau with a lavish gift in hopes that his brother will be appeased and that he will "see his face" and "be accepted" by him (v. 21). The language of appeasement employs a verb (כפר) that in other contexts designates atonement and indicates forgiveness.[23] Moreover, Jacob's gift to Esau, his מנחה, elsewhere refers to tribute and political submission to an overlord, human (Judg. 3:15-18) or divine (Gen. 4:3). It can even be used to appease the Deity's anger.[24] Jacob's approach to Esau thus resembles a supplicant's approach to an angry god. Indeed, Esau is introduced to Jacob in the same manner as the three divine strangers are introduced to Abraham in 18:2. In both scenes the patriarch

22. The "camp" (מחנה) motif also sets up a wordplay with the repeated word מנחה ("gift") in vv. 13, 18, 20-21 (MT 14, 19, 21-22).

23. For atonement see, e.g., Exod. 32:30; Lev. 4:20; 23:28; Deut. 32:43; Ezek. 45:15. For forgiveness see, e.g., Pss. 65:4; 78:38; 79:9.

24. See 1 Sam. 26:19; Jacob Milgrom, *Leviticus 1–16*, AB (New York: Doubleday, 1991), pp. 195-98.

"lifted his eyes, and saw, and *voilà!*" (וישׂא . . . עיניו וירא והנה, 33:1) — Esau appears! So does his entourage.

The impending crisis that Esau poses in the narrative constitutes the backdrop of Jacob's encounter with the mysterious nocturnal wrestler.[25] At the outset, he is a "man" of inferior strength, but he cheats. Upon seeing that he is "unable to prevail," he dislocates Jacob's thigh[26] with a sucker punch (v. 26), a blow that also packs great national import (v. 33).[27] But victory is snatched from the jaws of defeat, for Jacob refuses to release his opponent until he receives a blessing. That predawn blessing marks the turning point in the Jacob cycle. Jacob's name change is nothing short of a game changer. He is now deemed the eponymous ancestor of all Israel for having "striven with (שׂרית עם) God and with men and prevailed (ותוכל)" (v. 29).[28] And on which side of the divine-human spectrum does the wrestler's identity fall? Both![29] His countenance, to be sure, remains shrouded in darkness.[30] But the wrestler's refusal to surrender his name reveals, paradoxically, his divine status (v. 30; see Judg. 13:18),[31] for immediately thereafter Jacob pronounces the name of the site (v. 31). In Jacob's own words, according to the Yahwist: "I have seen God face to face (פנים אל פנים), and yet my life has thus been delivered (ותנצל נפשׁי)." Jacob's prayer has been answered: he has been delivered (see v. 12). Yet Esau, his fraternal foe, has not yet arrived on the scene! With the sun rising, Jacob leaves with a new name and a limp. Blessed

25. Drawing from Gunkel, Westermann argues that Jacob's opponent is a demon, but does so only by deleting vv. 26b, 28-29, 31b, 33, effectively taking God out of the story (*Genesis 12–36*, pp. 514, 516, 519, 520-21). He even suggests that the naming of the site in v. 31a has suppressed an older naming account of the Jabbok (p. 519). But even if the growth of the text can be delineated in this way, the question of divine presence is by no means evaded but simply shifted to the interpretation of the text in its later form. It is disingenuous of Westermann to state categorically: "all the profound theological consequences drawn from Jacob's supposed encounter with God . . . have no basis in the text" (p. 519). Such "consequences" have a basis in the biblical text, just not in Westermann's eviscerated text.

26. Specifically his hip socket.

27. As attested in the etiology (v. 33). See Geller, *Enigmas*, p. 19.

28. This folk etymology (see also Hos. 12:4) is only phonetically related to the name Israel, whose original meaning is probably "El rules." See the discussion in Hamilton, *Genesis 18–50*, p. 334.

29. Perhaps the poetic parallel between "with God" and "with men" in v. 29 suggests a tight coordination, even interchangeability, between Deity and human, apropos to the shifting identity of the wrestler in the text.

30. An ironic connection is found in Gen. 29:21-25, in which Leah's identity on Jacob's wedding night is discovered only "when morning came" (v. 25).

31. Geller, *Enigmas*, p. 16.

though he is, successful though he is in prevailing over "God and men," Jacob is now in no position to either fight or flee as Esau and his formidable host advance.

Jacob approaches Esau bowing to the ground seven times — deference fit for a god (33:3). But Esau charges Jacob, as if to attack: he "clinches" Jacob, "falling on his neck" (v. 4). Indeed, what turns out to be a fraternal embrace of reconciliation is described by the phonetically similar verb to "wrestle" in the previous scene: the Piel of חבק.[32] A wordplay is born.[33] At this point in the plot, there is little difference between the nocturnal wrestler and Jacob's kin, until the two brothers are said to kiss and weep. Next comes the clincher: Jacob implores Esau, "Take my gift (מנחתי), for truly I have seen your face as one sees the face of God, and you have accepted me" (v. 10). In Jacob's eyes the face of God and the face of Esau have much in common. Esau's face reflects the face of God, who, Jacob states, "has dealt graciously with" him (חנני, v. 11). Esau, in turn, has "favorably received" Jacob (ותרצני, v. 10b). In Jacob's testimony Esau and God are cast as parallel agents. Both have spared Jacob's life.

As for the wrestler's identity, Hosea's unsympathetic portrayal of the Jabbok/Jacob story explicitly holds a divine messenger (מלאך) in parallel with God (אלהים) (12:4). But the Genesis narrative refuses to be so overt; the links are too thick and numerous to separate out categorically the God of heaven from Esau of Seir, divinity from humanity (cf. Deut. 33:2). Ronald Hendel calls these connections ironic.[34] I call them iconic. While approving Jacob's name for the site, Peni-el ("the face of God"), the narrator teases the reader's imagination with Peni-esau ("the face of Esau").[35] The ambiguity runs deep. The identities of the actors are not clarified except at the end of verses (vv. 26, 28). Geller calls them examples of "annoying ambiguity."[36] But there is nothing annoying about the human-divine interchange that pervades the narrative. No supernatural wonder is performed to signal un-

---

32. See, e.g., Prov. 5:20; Song 2:6; 8:3; Gen. 29:13; 48:10; Prov. 4:8.

33. The narrator could have easily used the more common verb for wrestling, פתל (see Gen. 30:8). Geller calls the wordplay "the most striking example of verbal linkage" in the narrative (*Enigmas*, p. 13).

34. Ronald S. Hendel, *Epic of the Patriarch: The Jacob Cycle and the Narrative Traditions of Canaan and Israel*, HSM 42 (Atlanta: Scholars Press, 1987), p. 130.

35. Nahum Sarna goes so far as to suggest that the mysterious figure is "Esau's alter ego," specifically "the celestial patron of Esau," as found in midrash (*Genesis*, JPSTC [Philadelphia: JPS, 1989], p. 404).

36. Geller, *Enigmas*, p. 15.

equivocal divine status. That itself is a "surprise."[37] Perhaps the greatest ambiguity is that Jacob's victory seems to mark him as semidivine, as Geller
argues, in a league with Gilgamesh.[38] But Geller fails to note that this "pregnant ambiguity" also signals the story's greatest irony. By prevailing over the
nocturnal assailant, Jacob is wounded. His prevailing has led to his being in-
jured and thus deprived of strength. Jacob is now damaged goods and, in
turn, humbled to the point of giving up his blessing, his ברכה, the one he
had stolen from Esau (33:11; see 27:35).

As it stands, the narrative is set up in such a way as to effect an unexpected reversal. By day, Jacob discerns the face of God in the benevolent face
of Esau. But at night, the angry face of Esau is reflected in the hidden face of
God. Esau's wrath, no doubt nurtured as Jacob sojourned, is played out in a
deity's wrestling with a trickster. But wrestling at night, so the larger narrative claims, paves the way for reconciliation by day. Wrestling matches do
have their conciliatory consequences. Just ask Gilgamesh.[39] But Jacob's wrestling is more complex, given the larger narrative. Just as Esau's birthright and
blessing were stolen by Jacob, Esau is now deprived of his anger. Nevertheless, something of that anger manifests itself in the dead of night, whosoever
it is: Esau's, Laban's, Isaac's, God's.[40] In any case, the results are transformative. No longer harboring hostility, Esau shows himself noble and gracious.
Unlike Cain, Esau seems to have prevailed over his own anger as much as Jacob has over his opponent (cf. Gen. 4:5-7).

The story of Jacob at the Jabbok and its surprising aftermath suggests
that God's grace is demonstrated in Esau's grace, and that God's "weakness"
is related to Jacob's humility. As the night visitor yields a blessing to Jacob, so
Jacob gives up his blessing to Esau. Jacob, the underdog, accepts his new status as Israel's eponymous hero but as "the least of all." He is a "trickster in
transition."[41] But God, too, engages in trickery: assaulting Jacob at night, en-

37. Ibid.
38. Ibid., p. 22.
39. Tablet II of the epic. See the typological comparison between the Old Babylonian
Epic of Gilgamesh and the Jacob/Esau narrative in Genesis in Hendel, *Epic of the Patriarch*,
pp. 117-21.
40. Perhaps even Jacob's. See J. Gerald Janzen, *Abraham and All the Families of the
Earth: Genesis 12–50*, ITC (Grand Rapids: Eerdmans, 1993), p. 131. One can also read the story
as an account of Jacob's wrestling with his *own* demons (personal communication from
Alan Cooper).
41. Susan Niditch, *Underdogs and Tricksters: A Prelude to Biblical Folklore* (San Francisco: Harper & Row, 1987), p. 117.

gaging him *mano y mano* or פנים אל פנים, yet "losing" and thereby preserving Jacob's life, but not without a parting injury and a new name, a blessing and a bane. No interjectory הִנֵּה introduces this deity in the night. "Elusive" does not fully capture God's presence in this most enigmatic of ancestral stories. "Sneaky" comes closer.

From Pillow to Pillar: God's Grounded Presence in Bethel

No altar is built at Peniel. Its episode is too threatening and enigmatic to be claimed a cultic site. Only the name persists, and even that with variant spelling.[42] Not so with Bethel, the counterpart, or better counterpoint, to Peniel. To be sure, Genesis 28:10-22 bears unmistakable parallels to Genesis 32–33. Both stories bracket Jacob's conflict with Esau. Like Hagar in flight from Sarah, it is in his flight from Esau that Jacob encounters God at Bethel, and it is in his return to Esau that he meets God at Peniel. Both theophanies occur at Jacob's most vulnerable moments on his journey; they are entirely unexpected.[43] They also occur at night, and awareness of God's presence is gained only after the fact. Nevertheless, there are enough differences to suspect that one serves as the foil for the other. The Bethel theophany is more spatially grounded. The word for "place" (מָקוֹם), repeated six times in the passage, brackets Jacob's angelic vision (vv. 11, 16-17, 19). As an urban site, this "place" was known by another name, Luz (v. 19). No such parallels are found in the Jabbok's deep gorge.[44]

The account of Jacob at Bethel is a complex literary melding of sources and supplements,[45] and it contains all the elements of a full-blown theophany. It begins at night. With a stone as his pillow, Jacob dreams and sees three things, each introduced by the interjectory הִנֵּה: (1) a stairway (סֻלָּם)[46]

---

42. Geographically, the Jabbok River was an area of territorial contention (see Deut. 2:37; 3:16; Judg. 11:13, 22).

43. Verse 11, with the verbal construction פגע ב, indicates the "randomness with which Jacob chose this place to pass the night" (Hamilton, *Genesis 18–50*, p. 238).

44. Although reference is made to a tower in Penuel in Judg. 8:4-9.

45. Rolf Rendtorff, for example, identifies five discrete stages of development in "Jakob in Bethel: Beobachtungen zum Aufbau und zur Quellenfrage in Gen. 28,10-22," *ZAW* 94 (1982): 511-23.

46. The word is a hapax legomenon perhaps related to the verb סלל, "heap up," although it may also be connected with Akkadian *simmilltu*, "stairway," by way of metathesis. See Hamilton, *Genesis 18–50*, p. 239.

set up on earth and reaching heavenward (v. 12a); (2) God's messengers or angels ascending and descending on it (v. 12b); and (3) YHWH standing next to Jacob (נצב עליו),[47] promising protection, offspring, and land (vv. 13-15).[48] Divine presence manifests itself in two ways: by word and by space. God's word ensures that the God of Jacob's ancestors is the patriarch's *personal* God, one who intends to care for him and guide him, to be responsible for him in times of distress.[49] In this awe-filled place (v. 17), a word comes to Jacob ensuring him that this resident God is committed to his well-being and to that of his descendants.

Jacob's nocturnal vision reveals a seemingly nondescript place as no less than the convergence of heaven and earth. The narrative unfolds as an oracular incubation scene, in which a revelatory dream is induced through certain actions, including sleeping at a sacred site. No ritual purifications, however, are performed to induce the vision. Jacob does not even take off his sandals. He does, however, take a stone as a pillow, but does so not knowing what will transpire (v. 16). At most, Bethel is a site of unintended, unmediated incubation. But what a site it is! Bethel reveals itself as the theological counterpoint to Babel, itself patterned after the Mesopotamian *Etemenanki,* the "House of the Foundation of Heaven and Earth," Marduk's towering ziggurat. But Jacob's stairway is not for human ascent. Filled with divine "messengers" going and returning, "ascending and descending," Bethel is God's axis of communication. Modest as it may seem, this "House of God" and "Gate of Heaven" that Jacob stumbles upon matches the "Gate of the Gods" (Akkadian *Bâb-ili*).

Jacob responds with fear, declaring what has been unexpectedly revealed to him (v. 17). Jacob then takes his stone pillow, sets it up as a מצבה, and pours oil on its "head" (v. 18), a practice condemned in later biblical tradition.[50] Such actions indicate the place-bound nature of this theophany. At Bethel, God becomes "incarnate in the betyl."[51] As the vision reveals the numinosity of Jacob's lodging site, so Jacob makes sacred his stony pillow.

---

47. Or "above it." The former rendering, however, is more likely, given what Jacob says in v. 16.

48. A fourth הִנֵּה introduces v. 15, YHWH's announcement of protection.

49. Drawing primarily from the psalms and their ancient Near Eastern counterparts, Thorkild Jacobsen so describes the "rise of personal religion" in Mesopotamia in *The Treasures of Darkness: A History of Mesopotamian Religion* (New Haven: Yale University Press, 1976), pp. 147-64.

50. See, e.g., Exod. 23:24; 34:13; Deut. 7:5; 12:3; 16:22.

51. Sommer, *Bodies of God,* p. 50.

Indeed, the pillar itself resembles the heavenly stairway. The top (or "head" [רֹאשׁ]) of each structure is deliberately referenced: the top of the stairway, which reaches heaven (v. 12; cf. 11:4), and the top of the pillar, which receives consecrating oil (28:18).[52] Though the language of holiness (קָדֹשׁ) is lacking, as is typical of the ancestral narratives in Genesis, the matter of holiness is certainly assumed in this narrative.[53] Of all the theophanies in Genesis, this one comes closest to the kind of "sanctuary-centered relationship between YHWH and Israel" that is more fully developed in Exodus and beyond.[54] The pillar that once served as a pillow takes on transcendent proportions: it is the heavenly stairway in miniature!

The episode concludes with Jacob's vow, one that parallels YHWH's promise in vv. 13-15. But Jacob is interested more in the immediate concerns of food and clothing than in offspring and being the medium of blessing for all the families of the earth. If YHWH follows through as promised, taking care of Jacob's physical needs, and becomes his own personal deity (v. 21), then Jacob will respond with a tithe.[55] Thorkild Jacobsen aptly underscores the paradoxical character of personal religion in Mesopotamia by noting "its conspicuous humility curiously based on an almost limitless presumption of self-importance, its drawing the greatest cosmic powers into the little personal world of the individual, and its approach to the highest, most awesome, and the terrifying in such an easy and familiar manner."[56] Jacob's "religion" at Bethel fits well such a profile. God's manifestation is all about him, his care and feeding, his little world. To borrow a line from the Sumerian poem "Man and His God" (so-called): "a man without a god would not have anything to eat."[57] Without YHWH, Jacob does not even have a prayer.

The Bethel account is not complete in chapter 28, for it jumps ahead to the end of the cycle with Jacob instructed by God to return to Bethel. He is commanded to build an altar, which prompts Jacob to purge his own house-

---

52. Compare the Priestly parallel in 35:14, which makes no mention of the pillar's head in the act of consecration.

53. Cf. Moberly, *Old Testament of the Old Testament*, pp. 100-102.

54. Ibid., p. 104.

55. There is the question as to where the protasis ends and the apodosis begins in Jacob's vow (vv. 20-22). Most translations take v. 21b as the division. However, there is stronger evidence that the apodosis begins in v. 22. Note the change in verbal consecution from *wĕqāṭal* forms through v. 21 to conjunctive *waws* + nouns followed by the imperfect in v. 22. See also Hamilton, *Genesis 18–50*, p. 248.

56. Jacobsen, *Treasures of Darkness*, p. 161.

57. Jacob Klein, "Man and His God" (1.179), *COS* 1:573-75, here p. 573.

hold of foreign gods (35:1-4). The Priestly version of God's revelation at Bethel concludes the account (vv. 9-15). It lacks the vision of angels and mysterious encounters. In their place is the Deity's speech to Jacob, reiterating the promise of land and offspring, even nations (vv. 11-13). And it is at Bethel, according to P, that Jacob's name is changed to Israel (v. 10). In Priestly hands, Bethel overshadows Peniel. Jacob commemorates the divinely delivered promise with a "pillar of stone" drenched with oil *and* a drink offering (v. 14). The final verse is telling: "So Jacob called the place where God had spoken with him Bethel" (v. 15), similar to Hosea 12:4b. It does not say "where God had *appeared* to him." In the Priestly strand, word takes precedence over presence (cf. v. 1 from E).

Deep Sleep: Abraham's Vision

One final theophany worth noting, albeit briefly, is another vision, one that provides a solemn background to YHWH's covenant with Abram in Genesis 15:7-21. YHWH promises the land to Abram, and does so accompanied by a supreme act of self-obligation in the form of a self-imprecation. God binds God's self through a bloody covenantal ceremony that entails cutting (בתר) various animals in two. Then, in the darkest of dreams, Abram receives a vision, introduced once again by the interjectory הִנֵּה: "a smoking fire pot (תנור עשׁן) and a flaming torch (לפיד אשׁ) passing between these pieces" (v. 17), followed by a report of YHWH "cutting" (כרת) a covenant with Abraham (v. 18).[58]

Mysterious though these images are, particularly in the dead of night, they, like Jacob's pillar, represent in miniature something of God's numinous presence, which later in the pentateuchal narrative is manifest in both smoke and fire in leading the community out of Egypt (e.g., Exod. 13:21-22) and in signifying God's presence at Sinai/Horeb (e.g., Exod. 19:18; cf. Deut. 4:11-12).[59]

58. The ritual and legal backgrounds to this dark episode are rich. In addition to Jer. 34:18, there are numerous extrabiblical parallels and background texts. See Theodore J. Lewis, "Covenant and Blood Rituals: Understanding Exodus 24:3-8 in Its Ancient Near Eastern Context," in Seymour Gitin, J. Edward Wright, and J. P. Dessel, eds., *Confronting the Past: Archaeological and Historical Essays on Ancient Israel in Honor of William G. Dever* (Winona Lake, Ind.: Eisenbrauns, 2006), pp. 341-50, here p. 344.

59. One could call it a "humble manifestation," as Sommer does in describing the burning bush theophany vis-à-vis the Sinai account in Exod. 19 (Sommer, *Bodies of God*, p. 41).

The Genesis narrative, moreover, features them as inseparably wedded, as part of the same symbolic package, and appropriately so.[60] As these symbols of divine presence pass through the dismembered pieces, YHWH becomes bound to the dire consequences of a violated covenant, a covenant sealed as a self-curse. The enigmatic scene offers solemn confirmation of the promise that Abram's descendants will receive the land before him (vv. 18-20).

A Manifest Diversity

These theophanic accounts in Genesis seem to share little. Yet with respect to the matter of divine presence, there are overlapping characteristics. Each account is surprising in its own way. With regard to the Deity's appearances at Mamre and Peniel, we find a surprising immanence at work: God appears as a human, eats like a human, wrestles like a human.[61] Recognizing the human form as divine, moreover, may not be immediate. But are these accounts simply cases of a patriarch's inability to "ascertain the divinity of a supernatural visitor"?[62] Clearly that is so for Jacob at the Jabbok, perhaps also for Abraham at Mamre. But even if we grant that such accounts are about mistaken identity or, better, mistaken divinity, that is only half the story. The other half is the God who appears as a human being, an אִישׁ among אנשים, in contrast to the God who appears in full transcendent glory elsewhere.

At Bethel, things are different. Nevertheless, it too packs a surprise. As at the Jabbok, Jacob is caught unawares. The object of surprising discernment on the part of the patriarch includes not just the matter of divine identity — the God who is standing beside Jacob — but also divine space. This account is the closest a theophany in Genesis comes to portraying the holiness of God. Divine presence is felt in terms of a surprising revelation of location. And Jacob's reaction is one of fear (28:17) — the only time in the ancestral stories when a patriarch is described as being afraid in God's presence.[63]

The other revelatory encounter occurs in Genesis 15. In an unnamed location and in a passage dominated by divine discourse, God appears in a

---

60. The verb עבר in v. 17 is singular with a dual subject.
61. Hamori classifies both narratives as "*'îš* theophanies," concrete examples of "anthropomorphic realism" (*When Gods Were Men*, pp. 96, 101-2, 126).
62. So Hamilton, *Genesis 18–50*, p. 330, who cites both Gen. 18–19 and 32. Hamilton finds comparable episodes in Judg. 6 and 13.
63. Cf. Gen. 3:10; 18:15. On the other hand, three times God addresses someone with the command not to be afraid: 15:1; 21:17; 26:24.

bloody covenantal ceremony to assure Abram of God's commitment regarding the land. This revelation is full of dread and darkness (אימה חשכה גדלה, v. 12b). The extreme length to which God goes to confirm the promise is the surprise: God *physically* takes on the covenantal curse, sealed, as it were, in God's blood! This account, moreover, is the only place in all of Genesis that refers explicitly to Egyptian bondage and settlement of the land (vv. 13-16; cf. vv. 18-21). The theophanic imagery of smoke and fire (v. 17) may very well anticipate the exodus. Like Jacob's pillar, the flaming torch and smoking pot represent in miniature God's numinous, guiding presence for the larger community.

What could these diverse theophanies in Genesis possibly have in common? All are by and large miniature manifestations of divine presence or divine space to certain individuals. All revolve around divine discourse. Even the exceptional encounter at the Jabbok involves a climactic name change. All other accounts of God's appearance reflect God's "personal endearment and commitment" to the individual.[64] And God's endearment most often revolves around the promise of land. Even the altars erected throughout Canaan, beginning with Abram's altar at Shechem, under the oak of Moreh (12:7), and concluding with the altar at Bethel (35:7), constitute both Israel's foothold in the land and God's commitment to a people. These sites are, to be sure, not beachheads for a military blitzkrieg. (That is reserved for Joshua.) The patriarchs, by contrast, exhibit no aggression toward possessing the land. They are simply promised it. Nevertheless, these cultic sites represent tangible claims to the land as Israel's ancestors sojourn peaceably upon it.

The manifest diversity, including geographical diversity, of God's presence reflects proleptically Israel's manifest destiny in the land. And not just altars: also trees and pillars dot the landscape. They are all the cultic counterparts to Abraham's burial plot at the cave of Machpelah, so meticulously and humorously detailed in P (23:1-20).[65] The only other time in Genesis that land is purchased is when Jacob buys a plot next to the city of Shechem, where, yes, he erects an altar, calling it El-Elohe-Israel, "El, the God of Israel" (33:18-20). Jacob's penultimate altar makes clear that God, land, and people are bound together. In the narrative cycles of Israel's ancestors, *Orts-*

64. Simon J. De Vries, *The Achievements of Biblical Religion* (Lanham, Md.: University Press of America, 1983), p. 69.

65. See the analysis in Joseph Blenkinsopp, "Abraham as Paradigm in the Priestly History in Genesis," *JBL* 128 (2009): 225-41, here 239-40.

gebundenheit is bound up with *Volksgebundenheit*. As God binds God's self to individuals and to the land in surprising ways, God in Genesis is found to be personally and profoundly incarnational. Only later, when the people are fully constituted, does God exhibit a full manifestation, whether on a mountain, in the tabernacle, or in the temple.

That these theophanies are preserved at all, in all their variety, reflects an ecumenical broadening of orthodox Yahwism, as it is defined by the Priestly and Deuteronomic sources, whose perspectives and prescriptions differ significantly from these ancestral traditions. That they are included at all suggests a larger narrative concern to recount not only the history of a people sojourning and seeking a land to call their own but the story of God personally claiming a people as God's own — a story in progress.

Creation and Divine Presence

While devoid of clear parallels with Mosaic Yahwism as expounded in Exodus through Deuteronomy, the "miniature" manifestations of divinity that populate the ancestral history do find some grounding in the opposite direction, specifically in the creation narratives of Genesis. While the Priestly story of creation (Gen. 1:1–2:4a) lacks an account of divine manifestation, it does set the framework and context for it. As often noted, creation in Genesis 1 is cast in the image of a temple. It unfolds according to the tripartite structure of a typical Northwest Semitic temple.[66] And typical of such temples was their accommodation of divine images. God's "image" also takes its rightful place in God's cosmic temple. Indeed, the Hebrew term for "image" (צלם) is elsewhere used for idols, such as the cult statues of false gods.[67] But this is not the case here. Genesis 1 recasts the language of divine image by relating the *imago Dei* to human beings, who alone bear an iconic relation to the divine, a uniquely theophanic presence in creation.[68] But there is also the

66. See, e.g., S. Dean McBride Jr., "Divine Protocol: Genesis 1:1–2:3 as Prologue to the Pentateuch," in William P. Brown and S. Dean McBride Jr., eds., *God Who Creates: Essays in Honor of W. Sibley Towner* (Grand Rapids: Eerdmans, 2000), pp. 3-41, here pp. 11-15; William P. Brown, *The Seven Pillars of Creation: The Bible, Science, and the Ecology of Wonder* (New York: Oxford University Press, 2010), pp. 37-41.

67. E.g., Num. 33:52; 2 Kgs. 11:18; 2 Chr. 23:17; Ezek. 7:20; Amos 5:26. For more detailed discussion of the semantic range of this term, see J. Richard Middleton, *The Liberating Image: The Imago Dei in Genesis 1* (Grand Rapids: Brazos, 2005), pp. 45-46.

68. McBride, "Divine Protocol," pp. 15-18.

converse: the image in which humankind is created naturally reflects back on the Creator. That is, something about the human form or substance bears an essential resemblance to God. If human beings are "theomorphic" by design, God, in turn, must in some sense be anthropomorphic in relation. The relational link between God and humanity manifested in the various theophanies of the ancestral narratives finds cosmic precedence in the Priestly account of creation, specifically in the *imago Dei.*

If the entire cosmos is constructed as a temple in time, where then is God? Genesis 1 leaves unsaid anything about God's entrance into or presence *in* creation. In holiness, God remains wholly apart from creation. Moreover, no spatial center, no conduit between heaven and earth, is identified in P's cosmogony.[69] There is nothing equivalent to Esagila or Zion or Bethel in Genesis 1. Yet, paradoxically, there is a possible point of entry, an adumbration of God's presence in creation: the final day, Sabbath, foreshadows God's indwelling, a formal entrance into creation that is postponed until a community is formed. In Exodus 25–40 a people liberated from Egypt embarked on a construction project that would mirror the course of creation itself, the tabernacle. As the climax to the book of Exodus, God's holy presence or "glory" fills the tabernacle in the form of a "cloud," one so dense that even Moses could not enter, denser than the cloud at Sinai (Exod. 40:34-35). This event inaugurates God's full and formal entrance.[70] Between creation and tabernacle, God's "presence" from the Priestly perspective is primarily verbal. Palpable, overwhelming, glorious presence is entirely lacking.

But such lack is also God's gain: God remains free to appear and to speak wherever, whenever, and however God wills.[71] Like Abraham living as a "stranger and an alien" seeking a burial place for his beloved in the land (Gen. 23:4), God too is a stranger to creation seeking to be a tabernacling presence, and ultimately does so with a people as they continue to sojourn in and beyond the land. Genesis 1 and Exodus 39–40 serve as the "bookends of a single narrative," one that documents the desire of a transcendent God to

69. See Schuele, "In the Vicinity of God."

70. For the numerous parallels between Gen. 1:1–2:4a and the account of the tabernacle's construction in Exod. 25–40, see Joseph Blenkinsopp, "The Structure of P," *CBQ* 38 (1976): 275-92; Eric Elnes, "Creation and Tabernacle: The Priestly Writer's Environmentalism," *Horizons in Biblical Theology* 16 (1994): 144-55; Jon D. Levenson, *Creation and the Persistence of Evil: The Jewish Drama of Divine Omnipotence* (San Francisco: Harper & Row, 1985), pp. 78-99.

71. Cf. Hamori, *When Gods Were Men,* p. 64.

become immanent in creation.[72] The prologue to John's Gospel extends the narrative arc by claiming the incarnation, the "Word made flesh," as God's full entrance into the world created "in the beginning" (John 1:1, 14). God in Christ recalls the scaled-down, personal theophanies of ancestral religion but, in so doing, places the personal nature of God's presence on a new and paradoxical level. Jesus, friend and savior, is God for the nations, indeed for all creation. In Christ the cosmic God becomes the personal God in the flesh. According to John's Gospel, Christ himself is the staircase to heaven (John 1:51; cf. Gen. 28:12).

The Ground of Being: Genesis 2:4b–3:24

In the Yahwistic account of creation, an alternative perspective is given. God exchanges the royal decree for a garden spade. The God from on high becomes the God on the ground, a down-and-dirty Deity. While the Priestly account teeters on the edge of cosmic abstraction, the Yahwist story revels in the drama of dirt. As both gardener and potter, God works naturally and intimately with creation. As "the divine farmer,"[73] God is found grubbing about in the soil, planting trees and fingering clay. And highlighting God's organic work with the earth, the Yahwist depicts the garden, literally the "garden of plenty," the centerpiece of creation.

There God casually strolls, enjoying the company of the garden's denizens. The God of the Yahwist is no outsider waiting for the right time to gloriously enter creation. No, it is in YHWH's nature to enter nature and enjoy creation's good company. But on one occasion, instead of greeting God, the human creatures hide from God's presence (3:8). For the first time, God's presence inspires fear. God demands an explanation. The man blames the woman ("whom you gave to be with me"), who blames the serpent (it "misled me"). The blame game, however, stops before coming full circle, at least within the narrative's scope, for God chooses, for whatever reason, not to question the serpent. Had God done so, the serpent could have easily responded with, "I only told the truth," putting God on the defensive,[74] the

---

72. Sommer, *Bodies of God*, pp. 74, 111.

73. Theodore Hiebert, *The Yahwist's Landscape: Nature and Religion in Early Israel* (Oxford: Oxford University Press, 1996), p. 67.

74. See Danna N. Fewell and David M. Gunn, "Shifting the Blame: God in the Garden," in Timothy K. Beal and David M. Gunn, eds., *Reading Bibles, Writing Bodies: Identity and the Book* (London: Routledge, 1997), pp. 16-33.

God who created the tree and the crafty serpent in the first place.[75] But by refusing to interrogate the serpent, God reveals a measure of vulnerability, even defensiveness.

Guarded by formidable gatekeepers, the garden is now a secret garden, a barred temple,[76] and the man and the woman must eke out their existence outside it. God strolls inside the garden, in an inner sanctum now cut off from human contact. But the primal couple are not cut off from God's providential presence. Before their expulsion, they are clothed by God (3:21). As seamstress, God equips the couple for a harsher life. Outside the garden God helps Eve in procreation (4:1). God even protects Cain (4:15). The case of Cain is particularly telling. Cain laments his curse: "Today you have driven me away from the soil, and I shall be hidden from your presence [or face]; I shall be a fugitive and a wanderer (נע ונד) on the earth" (4:14). For Cain, productive soil and divine presence share common ground. And so "Cain went away from YHWH's presence" and founded a city (4:16-17). For the Yahwist, God's presence is a grounded presence, tied to the soil's fecundity.[77] If in Genesis 1 God is King of the cosmos, in Genesis 2 God is King of the compost.

Outside the garden, God continues to react to new situations brought on by humanity's exercise and abuse of freedom. God's vulnerability is matched by humanity's freedom, for good and for woe. YHWH appears threatened by the opportunity of the אדם to partake from the tree of life (3:22). At Abraham's initiative, YHWH must negotiate the terms of urban destruction (18:16-33). In grief YHWH comes to accept that the "inclination of the human heart is evil from youth" (8:21). In the Yahwist's ear, divine discourse in Genesis is peppered with searching questions: "Where are you?" (3:9); "Who told you . . . ?" (v. 11); "What is this that you have done?" (v. 13); "Why are you angry?" (4:6); "Where is your brother Abel?" (v. 9); "What have you done?" (v. 10); "Hagar . . . where have you come from and where are you going?" (16:8); "Where is your wife Sarah?" (18:9); "Shall I hide from Abraham what I am about to do?" (18:17); "What troubles you, Hagar?" (21:17); "What is your name?" (32:27). In the Priestly strand, God is never caught asking a question.

75. Note that the man, in his defense, holds God responsible for having created the woman.

76. The walls of the temple, not fortuitously, were engraved with the figures of the cherubim, palm trees, flowers, and lions to re-create the primeval garden (1 Kgs. 6:29-35; cf. Ezek. 41:18-20).

77. See e.g., Gen. 26:12-33, in which Isaac's agricultural prosperity is acknowledged by Abimelech as the result of YHWH being "with" Isaac (v. 28).

Conclusion

Two sides of God are evident in these two creation accounts: the God from on high, executing creation by command, and the God from below, grubbing about in the dirt and wondering what to do next. One could call this combination a polarity of sorts, the polarity of transcendence and immanence. But there is more here than rarified theological concepts. This divine polarity is replete with nuance and dynamic complexity. I am reminded of an observation made by Sebastian Moore, a Benedictine priest: "God behaves in the psalms in ways he is not allowed to behave in systematic theology."[78] One could say the same about God in Genesis. God takes on human form; God eats; God wrestles; God loses; God utters a self-curse. God appears in the darkest of night and under the burning sun.

The manifest diversity of God's presence in Genesis reflects the peculiar versatility of God's character and conduct. Not that this diversity is significantly minimized after Genesis: within a single chapter in Exodus, we find Moses speaking to God "face to face, as one person speaks to another," in the tent of meeting (33:11), and only a few verses later we read of YHWH shielding Moses from the fatal glory of the divine countenance (vv. 20-23). The obscurely personal "God of the fathers" still comes to Moses, patriarch and lawgiver,[79] even when descending as a "pillar of cloud" (33:9; see Num. 12:7-8). More than simply quaint and antiquated stories that merely serve to preface God's full manifestation before a constituted people at Sinai, the ancestral narratives in Genesis model God's freedom to appear and to choose, the freedom to be unilaterally bound to a people and a land, the freedom to choose even the nonchosen, as in the case of Hagar and Ishmael. The variety of ways God appears suggests one way of interpreting the personal yet elusive name that God reveals to Moses: אהיה אשר אהיה, "I will be whatever I will be" (Exod. 3:14). God in Genesis chooses to be king and farmer, nighttime wrestler and daytime guest, heavenly and earthly, friend and foe, vulnerable and magisterial, sneaky and self-disclosive, human and divine. And accompanying God's presence is a voice filled with blessing and full of surprises.

---

78. Quoted in Kathleen Norris, "Why the Psalms Scare Us," *Christianity Today* 40, no. 8 (1996): 18-24, here 20 (or http://www.christianitytoday.com/ct/1996/july15/6t818a.html).

79. In Num. 14:11-12 YHWH offers to "make of [Moses] a nation greater and mightier than [Israel]" (cf. Gen. 12:2-3).

Beginning with the Ending

R. R. Reno

The opening chapters of the book of Genesis invite exegetical adventure. The first chapter outlines the architecture of reality and the second evokes the inner springs of desire that provide the motor for human history. Therein lies the problem for any interpreter. Genesis is seminal, and explaining what the text says easily opens out onto an account of all reality. Not surprisingly, therefore, Bonaventure's *Hexameron* reads like a treatise on metaphysics, anthropology, and systematic theology rather than a commentary in the usual sense of the word. The impulse, moreover, is not limited to traditional figures. In *The Book of J*, for example, Harold Bloom turns the Yahwist tradition into a literary phenomenon that provides an occasion to expostulate on a whole range of philosophical and theological issues. The primeval sources seem to promise an endlessly fertile set of interpretive possibilities.

For biblical critics concerned with textual control over exegesis, the expansive tendency of traditional commentaries, as well as some of the more ambitious, freewheeling modern readings, can raise eyebrows. Genesis 3 provides a good example. There is nothing about the tasty apple and the fateful first bite that suggests the mud-filled trenches of the Somme or the ash-stained winter skies above Auschwitz or the bodies frozen into the cruel Soviet Siberian mud or the shadows of men and women burned into the concrete of Hiroshima — nothing, that is, except the first-ness, the original-ness of the transgression that so quickly bears the fruit of Cain's murder of Abel. Here, then, in just a few short verses, the interpreter finds the whole sad history of humanity painfully relevant, crowding in and demanding exposition.

Modern biblical scholars can protest that the doctrine of original sin is not present in the short account of Eve, the serpent, and the forbidden fruit; and in a strict sense that is certainly true. But readers invariably tumble forward out of the text and into their conceptions of the dark shape of human history. Promising to reveal the origins of reality, Genesis exhales consequence.

We find expansive readings of Genesis throughout the Christian tradition, almost always keyed to the mystery of salvation. The Letter to the Colossians is typical. Paul evokes the division of light and darkness on the first day of creation, and he transfers this original parsing of reality to the ongoing work of redemption in which the Father pries the faithful out of the dominion of darkness and delivers them to their inheritance of light (Col. 1:12-13). Paul is not simply providing a symbolic, poetic use of the images of light and darkness. This passage from Colossians functions as an interpretation of Genesis 1. In Christ, Paul writes, "all things were created in heaven and on earth, visible and invisible, whether thrones or dominions or principalities or authorities — all things were created through him and for him" (1:16).[1] The crucified Christ is "the mystery hidden for ages and generations" (1:26). Therefore, once the truth of Christ is made manifest, all things — especially the source and origin and purpose of all things — become clear.

Were I more thoroughly Barthian, I would call this approach Christological. However, I am not, in large part because I have become increasingly concerned about the tendency of theological conceptualities to become omnipotent.[2] Barth once said of Schleiermacher that he tried to talk about God by talking about man in a loud voice. I worry sometimes that Barth tries to talk about God by pronouncing theological formulations in a loud voice. Moreover, I am impressed by important parallels between traditional Jewish and Christian readings of the early chapters of Genesis, especially Genesis 1, parallels that are obscured rather than clarified by direct appeals to Christology. As a result, in this paper I will not offer a singular Christological reading of Genesis. Instead, I want to provide more exploratory and preliminary observations about the overall role of theological convictions in our interpretations of creation. As I have tried to understand and articulate the project of theological exegesis of the Bible, I have come to see the fittingness of the privileged role that traditional readers give to the mys-

---

1. Biblical translations are from the RSV.

2. See R. R. Reno, "Biblical Theology and Theological Exegesis," in Craig Bartholomew, Mary Healy, Karl Moeller, and Robin Parry, eds., *Out of Egypt: Biblical Theology and Biblical Interpretation* (London: Paternoster, 2004), pp. 385-408.

tery of salvation in their interpretations. It turns out that some of the literary features of Genesis positively invite readers to import theological convictions from later portions of the biblical witness. The grand scenes of the opening chapters suggest that we seek the fullness of the beginning in its end.

The Scandal of Particularity

By the usual modern way of thinking, the genres of cosmogony and primal history help explain why the opening chapters of Genesis invite exegetical invention. The material may suffer from what Hegel termed "picture thinking," but as later biblical scholars have recognized, the mythic idiom serves as a suitable literary mechanism for conveying deep insights and expansive intuitions. Indeed, this mythic quality can seem quite appealing, because it so obviously makes literal questions of historical event and sequence irrelevant, leaving the interpreter free to explore the larger themes rather than trying to reconcile the biblical time line with modern cosmology or scientific study of the origins of human culture. For example, according to Kant, Genesis 3 represents to us the reality of radical evil in story form.[3] In the eyes of modern biblical scholars, other themes come to the fore. In his widely used textbook, *The Old Testament: A Historical and Literary Introduction to the Hebrew Scriptures,* Michael Coogan suggests that the primeval snake should be read as a sexual symbol and the larger episode of the forbidden fruit as a story of sexual awakening.[4]

If we take this approach, then we can introduce academic rigor into our interpretations of the early chapters of Genesis by turning toward comparative mythology. Close comparisons of the early chapters of Genesis with other creation stories in the ancient world such as *Enuma Elish* and the Gilgamesh Epic promise to provide the proper path toward disciplining modern critical exegesis, allowing us to distinguish between alien intrusions of later doctrinal concerns and legitimate speculations about original mythic meaning. Scholars can identify key parallels — the taming of chaos from *Enuma Elish*, for example, or sexual awakening from the Gilgamesh Epic — and thus feel reassured that these themes constitute the original

---

3. Immanuel Kant, *Religion Within the Boundaries of Mere Reason,* trans. Allen Wood and George di Giovani (Cambridge: Cambridge University Press, 1998), pp. 63-65.

4. Michael Coogan, *The Old Testament: A Historical and Literary Introduction to the Hebrew Scriptures* (New York: Oxford University Press, 2006), pp. 16-17.

meaning of the passages. Shared mythic material points to shared mythic meaning, or so the comparative approach assumes.

The larger structure of the book of Genesis, however, seems to encourage a very different judgment. As we read through the opening chapters, we find that the literary forms generally associated with cosmogony and primal history take on a negative, futile, repetitive quality that undermines easy assumptions about the relevance of comparative mythology. Take a look, for example, at the long genealogy flowing from Adam in Genesis 5. God's creation of humanity is retold, but this time the entire episode in the garden and the conflict between Cain and Abel are simply omitted. The birth of Seth is substituted, with a series of long-lived descendants to follow. The significance seems obvious. After the transgression of Adam and Eve cascades toward death in the murder of Abel, and then the depravity of Lamech, the Bible appears to endorse a redemptive strategy of forgetfulness. God seems to adopt a practical and therapeutic view. If things do not work out, then one needs to put the mistakes to the side and start over again. The problem of transgression will be solved by rebooting human history.

Closer examination, however, shows that the new beginning through the genealogy following from Seth comes to yet another bad end. By the time readers get to chapter 6, things have again gone rotten. The network of episodes that constitute the story of Noah, the flood, and its aftermath is very complicated. At one level the material seems to represent a new cosmogony. The original waters of chaos return and destroy the world, allowing God to restrain "the foundations of the deep" (8:2), thus restoring order and solidity to creation, an echo of the third day of creation. Yet it is fascinating that this strategy of worldwide cleansing and re-creation goes bad as well, ending no more successfully than the genealogy that erases the memory of Cain and Abel. After the flood, Noah is mysteriously shamed by his son Ham. The curse of Cain reappears. This time it is given an even more pathetic and painful form because it is pronounced by a father on the progeny of his own son.

The ensuing story of the tower of Babel reinforces our sense that the primal histories of Genesis go in unproductive circles. The episode recapitulates Genesis 3. Just as God in the garden of Eden is anxious about the seemingly limitless, nearly divine human capacity for transgression ("Behold, the man has become like one of us, knowing good and evil; and now, lest he put forth his hand and take also from the tree of life," 3:22), the Lord looks down on what the men are building in their great city and expresses a similar concern: "This is only the beginning of what they will do; and nothing that they will propose to do will now be impossible for them" (11:6). In view of this parallel, the confusion of languages and scattering the peoples function in the same way as the expulsion of Adam and Eve from the garden. Both divine interventions forestall the danger of unlimited human agency. In an important sense, therefore, Genesis 11 simply returns the reader back to the final verses of Genesis 3, giving the intervening material a strangely futile, immobile significance.

In view of this circular motion, the significance of chapters 5–11 within the larger context of the book of Genesis seems strangely self-defeating. The literary forms of cosmogony and primordial history promise insight into the meaning and purpose of creation. Yet the episodes go nowhere as they cycle through the sequences of creation, failure, and re-creation. The three accounts of the creation of humanity and the origins of history — chapters 2–4, 5–6, and 7–11 — recapitulate rather than correct or change the original cycle of creation and fall. The overall effect cannot help but discourage readers who want to use the literary form of myth as a privileged means for gaining knowledge of the life-giving sources of reality.

Indeed, as these chapters exhaust themselves in a series of dead ends, the entire sweep of Genesis 1–11 can be read as a cleverly constructed parody of the genres of creation narrative and primeval history. It is as if the biblical authors (or editors) wished to introduce a critical moment into our usual expectations, planting the seed of the thought in our minds that there is something wrong with the genres of cosmogonies and primeval legends, genres suspiciously popular among the Babylonians and other neighboring cultures. As I consider the weird way in which the basic pattern of creation followed by failure repeats itself in Genesis 1–11, I find myself wondering if the final form of the book of Genesis is trying to guide us away from the usual ancient Near Eastern literary forms of cosmogony and primal history.

If we allow ourselves to think in this way about the first chapters of Genesis, then some interesting historical-critical conclusions suggest themselves. We might find ourselves saying that the borrowings from ancient Near Eastern cosmogonies in Genesis express a subtle polemical agenda. "This popular way of thinking about human origins and destiny," we can read these chapters as saying, "isn't going to get us anywhere." In other words, it may very well have been the case that the ancient Israelites did not only think the surrounding religious culture had the wrong stories of creation. They might have viewed the seemingly popular ancient Near Eastern genre of myth with suspicion. And if this is so, then the use of comparative mythology in our exegesis may do more harm than good in our efforts to uncover the original meaning. We risk missing the point. The historical borrowings do not reflect overlapping views of reality that are to be corrected by an Israelite retelling. Instead, the very expectation of an original, orienting mythic narrative is being called into question.

My historical-critical speculations about the mental outlook of the authors (or editors) of Genesis are probably hyperbolic, and certainly speculative. In any event, while the opening chapters of Genesis may mock borrowed creation myths, they do so only in part. Genesis 1, for example, has a definite magisterial cadence, and the pathos of human failure throughout Genesis 3–11 seems earnest. Nonetheless, the overall thrust of the book of Genesis provides additional support to the suspicion that the editors of the material making up the final form of Genesis never intended readers to treat creation and primeval history seriously on their own terms. The twelfth chapter of Genesis throws the circular immobility of the well-known episodes in the early chapters into sharp relief. As Gerhard von Rad observes, "The transition from primeval history to sacred history occurs very abruptly and surprisingly. . . . All at once and precipitously the universal field of vision narrows. . . . Previously the narrative concerned humanity as a whole, man's creation and essential character, woman, sin, suffering, humanity, nation, all of them universal themes. In [Abraham's call], as though after a break, the particularism of election begins."[5] From chapter 12 onward, Genesis is concerned with one household, one tiny and otherwise invisible portion of humanity. The shift cannot but seem a shocking reduction in the focus of the text. Like a large building suddenly sagging and giving way, the global and world-historical perspectives of the opening chapters of Genesis collapse into a narrowly local and tribal frame of reference.

The feeling of collapse finds reinforcement in the narrative thrust of Abraham's story. God does not call Abraham and then tell him to affirm his creaturely condition. God does not instruct Abraham in a "sacramental worldview." He does not encourage him to develop an "incarnational ethic." On the contrary, instead of affirming creation, God cuts to the bone of the natural order of things and rends the fabric of history: "Go from your country and your kindred and your father's house to the land that I will show you" (12:1). The consequence is hardly an affirmation of human history that tumbles forward in the genealogies of the earlier chapters. Instead, we find a divine invasion, an offensive campaign against the doleful trajectory of his-

5. Von Rad, *Genesis,* trans. John H. Marks, rev. ed., OTL (Philadelphia: Westminster, 1972), p. 154.

tory that plucks a family out of the cascade of generations. As the career of Abraham unfolds, the body is not affirmed; on the contrary, human flesh is given over to the knife of circumcision, and in the person of Isaac it is bound on the altar of sacrifice.

The forward-looking, future-oriented promises of Genesis 12 reinforce the conclusion that God is not interested in "history" in a generic sense, as if the six days of creation were meant to march forward with regal significance. God does not use Abraham in order to give a serene benediction to our condition as creatures; he does not provide a plenary affirmation of human historical existence. On the contrary, the promises to Abraham contract all hope for the future of humanity into the thin thread of the particular history of a single clan. To be sure, the end point is universal. God promises, "In you all the families of the earth shall be blessed" (12:3; see Acts 3:25 and Gal. 3:8). But the blessing, however universal in scope, turns on Abraham and the fate of his descendants. In this contraction we find the first expression of the scandal of particularity in the Bible. God loads Abraham and his progeny with responsibility for the future of human history, indeed, with responsibility for the future of creation as a whole. In one moment, with a single stab, God thrusts the sharp needle of redemption into the rolled-up fabric of time.

Our natural religious instincts are gnostic. We prize the timeless, the disembodied, the universal, because we sense the fragility of the particular, as well as its unreliable arbitrariness. The ensuing story of Abraham and his descendants offers no metaphysical reassurances, accentuating instead the terrible, narrow character of the divine invasion. The main source of drama of chapters 12–22 comes from the threats that infertility, paternal blindness, family conflicts, brotherly enmity, and foreign domination pose to the impossibly fragile line of inheritance, culminating in the mysterious divine threat in the commandment to Abraham to offer his son as a sacrifice on Mount Moriah, a commandment that dramatizes the blind, inscrutable meaning of God's investment in the particular. Our natural and gnostic spiritual intuitions seem vindicated: no sensible religious person would invest all hope in something so vulnerable as Abraham and his clan's survival — or in a God so reckless.

And the Bible does not stop with Abraham! On top of unlikely survival of his progeny, God adds the requirement of obedience to his commandments, which he foresees will be violated again and again by his chosen people. This divine prophecy sets up the Christological scandal of particularity, the incarnation of the eternal Son, whose death secures obedience and whose resurrection ensures survival, thus bringing the recklessness of Abraham's election to a crescendo by drawing God himself into the disintegrating realm of particularity, the perilous reality of finitude that teeters at every moment on the edges of nothingness.

Overall, therefore, the trajectory of the Bible is clear. The narratives move toward an intensification of the divine investment in the particularity of Abraham. At each turn biblical history seems to come to a dead end — disobedient people, faithless kings, captivity and exile, all of which are summed up in the Pauline reading of Genesis 3 as the source of human bondage to sin and death. In each instance, the way forward involves a further, deeper divine involvement in the particularity of covenant, never a step back to the universal perspective suggested by the first chapters of Genesis. This ever-deeper involvement magnifies the scandal of particularity and explodes the religious significance of myth. As the Bible as a whole testifies, the inner secrets of reality and the true trajectory of history are found in Genesis 12 — "the particularism of election" — not in Genesis 1 and the universal perspective, not in Genesis 2–11 and the stylized visions of the origins of humanity.

Judaism and Christianity are extraordinarily text-sensitive traditions, and therefore both make the scandal of particularity central to their exegesis and doctrine. Yes, history plays an intrinsic role in human fulfillment. And, yes, the created world remains germane. Yet Abraham is called for something different from the good things of creation, something further, something greater, something more. For Jews, the *more* is the Torah, the invasion of divine law into every nook and cranny of everyday life, and thus into the subtle fabric of soul. For Christians, the *more* is Christ crucified and risen, with whom, as Paul teaches, we die in baptism, and with whom we rise to new life, becoming instruments of his righteousness (Rom. 6:4-13). The differences are profound, but the logic of these soteriological affirmations remains strikingly similar. Both Jews and Christians treat Genesis 12 and the ensuing history of the covenant as a more fundamental revelation of God's purpose for creation than Genesis 1–11, because only in Abraham do we begin to see the way into the *more*. "You who pursue deliverance," we read in the Servant Songs that function for Christian interpreters as one of the primary textual hinges between Sinai and Golgotha, "you who seek the LORD, look to the rock from which you were hewn, and the quarry from which you were digged. Look to Abraham your father and to Sarah who bore you" (Isa. 51:1-2). God created humanity on the sixth day, but our future is not found in our finite, created condition — and therefore it is not to be discovered in the language of myth. Our future is revealed in the still deeper sources of reality, in the divine project of intimacy, the project begun in Abraham.

It is not the case, however, that Jewish and Christian readers set aside the universal language of the opening chapters of Genesis. Traditional readers recognized the way in which the scandal of particularity that presses beyond creation also raises a problem that scholastic Catholic theology formulates in terms of nature and grace. How can grace perfect and complete our humanity without somehow ignoring or destroying our created nature? "God saw everything that he had made, and behold, it was very good" (Gen. 1:31). Given this affirmation, shouldn't the remedy for sin and transgression be found in a restoration of our created humanity rather than the strange intensification, concentration, and change initiated in Abraham? In other words, shouldn't we look to universal truths about our common humanity as the proper basis for the spiritual life, not the oddly particular and endlessly divisive teaching unique to our religious tradition? Isn't the way forward to be found in natural reason rather than revealed truth, in something like the open expanses of the gnostic dream of transcendence rather than the narrow and constrained way of faith? And if this is so, then isn't the particularity of the call of Abraham a distraction, because it leads away from the universality of creation? Aren't the genres of myth and primeval history therefore fitting sources of spiritual insight?

Both Judaism and Christianity take these questions seriously, and this seriousness has led to salvation-historical approaches to the opening chapters of Genesis. Both traditions recognize the way in which the primordial material in Genesis collapses into the particularity of Abraham, setting in motion the ever-deeper loyalty of God to his people. Thus, although Judaism sees Moses and Sinai as the fulfillment of the divine investment in Abraham, while Christianity sees Jesus and Golgotha, both traditions have sought to give exegetical form to the theological judgment that grace perfects rather than destroys nature. Their goal is formally identical: to show how the collapse of perspective from the cosmic ambiance of Genesis 1 into the impossibly focused atmosphere of Genesis 12 reflects a coherent, overall divine plan rather than a sudden swerve or radical departure. The scandal of particularity fulfills creation rather than annulling its universal scope. Showing how this is so involves the bold interpretive approaches to Genesis 1 that read the call of Abraham back into the beginning. Or to change the direction of the metaphor, both Jews and Christians employ exegetical strategies that pull the creation myth forward, incorporating it into covenant history rather than allowing it to stand alone as the orienting template for our vision of reality.

Creation for the Sake of Covenant

At the outset of his commentary on Genesis, the great medieval commentator Rashi reiterates the ancient rabbinic opinion that the Pentateuch should have begun with Exodus 12:2 rather than Genesis 1:1. The assertion seems fanciful at first, but on closer examination the claim is not an objection to Scripture but rather an interpretation. Exodus 12:2 contains the first commandment that God gives directly to the people of Israel, and by a certain reading the verse represents the beginning of the covenant fully adumbrated on Mount Sinai. Thus the ancient rabbinic opinion that stipulates that the Bible *should* have begun with Exodus 12:2 is meant to convey a theological judgment: God creates for the sake of his commandments, for the sake of the Torah. Something in the future — the Passover sacrifice, the covenant, the commandments, and so forth — is deeper and more fundamental than the structure and solidity of the created order.

As modern intellectuals and idea merchants, we often find ourselves satisfied with theoretical statements. Yes, we might say, God creates for the sake of covenant. One ancient gloss of Genesis 1:1 stipulates, "God looked into the Torah . . . and created the world."[6] Karl Barth says essentially the same thing: covenant is the inner basis of creation. But more than theological formulation is at work in Rashi's use of the odd rabbinic claim about where the Bible ought to have begun. It turns out that the first commandment to Israel echoes the key, fraught word from Genesis 1:1 — "beginning." Exodus 12:2 reads: "This month shall be for you the beginning of months; it shall be the first month of the year for you." Exodus 12 as a whole goes on to command the preparations for the Passover. Given this context, the commandment seems very odd, because the Jewish calendar does not, in fact, begin with Nissan, the month of the Passover. Thus Exodus 12:2 is not just a handy verse to use in order to convey a theological judgment about the relation of creation and covenant. It is a troublesome verse, one that seems falsified by a Jewish tradition that claims to prize the authority of the Bible.

The solution rests in specifying the proper sense of "beginning," and this approach gives an intensely verbal form to the larger rabbinic project of subsuming creation into covenant. In a substantive rather than temporal or sequential sense, the Passover serves as the beginning for Israel's lunar calendar. God is saying, in effect, "The months and the lunar calendar exist for the sake of marking the time of the Passover." More bluntly, God is saying to the

---

6. *Genesis Rabbah* 1.1.

35

Israelites as they prepare to depart from Egypt: "I made time and history for the sake of *this* moment, for the sake of *this* sacrifice." Or, to summarize a traditional Jewish midrash, God looked into his Torah and saw that an entire world of space and time would be necessary for the performance of the Passover sacrifice, and so he set about to ensure that it would be so.

I lack the clear and precise theoretical language necessary to describe the rich hermeneutical interplay at work in what at first glance seems like the strange and whimsical rabbinic view that the Bible should have begun with Exodus 12:2. Indeed, there may be no hermeneutical generalizations capable of capturing the nuance and genius of traditional exegesis, which is in any event more fundamental than theoretical observations about its logic. At one level, the motives are obviously theological. Rabbinic readers felt the pressure of particularity that I have suggested is present in Genesis 12, a pressure made all the more intense by Sinai. The particularized focus of salvation history needs to be reconciled with the grand cosmogony of Genesis 1. But the localized need to account for the seemingly unfilled commandment in Exodus 12:2 also plays a role. What fascinates me is the way in which the two exegetical problems operate on very different levels — one broadly conceptual and the other narrowly literal — and yet they interact and are solved with the same insight. The "beginning" needs to be understood substantively, that is, in view of the end for which it comes to be.

In view of the fact that the New Testament ascribes universal redemptive significance to the concrete particularity of the passion, death, and resurrection of Jesus, we should not be surprised that John 1:1-3 interprets Genesis 1:1 in precisely the same way. The prologue of the Gospel of John asserts that all things were made through the Word and without him nothing was made. With this formulation, the implicit theology of creation in the Gospel of John follows the ancient rabbinic pattern. Reality exists for the sake of the fulfillment of the covenant, which the writer of the Gospel affirms as existing eternally as the divine Word, now incarnate in the person of Jesus Christ. The seemingly stable and fixed architecture of creation is not, therefore, simply a given, unchanging fact. It is mobilized from the outset as the medium for the unfolding divine plan. Creation is not just creation; it is creation for the sake of consummation.

History is full of ironies, not the least the history of modern biblical study. I have been struck by the fact that modern historical-critical readings of Genesis 1 reinforce rather than undermine the logic of traditional Jewish and Christian readings of creation. The distinction between the P source and J source is fundamental to modern interpretations of Genesis. This approach encourages us to situate our exegesis in the larger body of Priestly writings. As modern historians, therefore, the first and most important thing to say about Genesis 1 is that it stems from a Priestly tradition that wishes to place temple and sacrifice at the center of our perceptions of the deepest logic and purpose of reality. Put somewhat differently, the modern historian says that the Bible does not so much begin with Genesis 1:1 as with the Priestly tradition that gives shape to the final form of the first chapter as a whole. We assume that the Priestly tradition does more than borrow from other creation myths; this tradition reshapes the borrowed material for the sake of an already existing and highly particularized religious vision.

With this common historical-critical approach, modern scholars thus place covenant "before" creation, and in so doing provide arguments that cut against any tendency to read the creation story in a naïve, mythological fashion, putting readers much where Rashi and John's Gospel left us. To be sure, there are important differences. The traditional rabbinic opinion holds that God creates for the sake of the Torah, while the traditional Christian view presumes that the eternal Word was with God in the beginning. In contrast, modern scholars direct our attention toward sociological rather than theological truths. Certain religious ideologies and political loyalties characteristic of the Priestly tradition shape the final form of the biblical text, or so we are told. Nonetheless, the logic of interpretation is the same. For everybody, it seems, Genesis presents the days of creation in terms of a substantive goal or purpose: God's saving plan for traditional readers, Priestly ideology for modern historical scholars.

In view of this striking consensus, I find myself facing an invincible temptation to digress. These days biblical scholars favor translations of Genesis 1:1 as: "In the beginning when God created" or "When God began to create." Among the reasons adduced for these thin, temporally focused formulations are the links between Genesis 1 and other ancient Near Eastern cosmogonies that picture a divine power acting upon and ordering a preexisting chaos. The impulse to treat comparative mythology as a "scientific basis" for biblical scholarship remains very strong. This impulse, however, cuts against the grain of the biblical text, which is oriented toward the particularity of the covenant, as modern historians know but often forget. Again, I reiterate the consensus: Genesis 1:2 hovers over the waters and the face of the deep, so to speak. *Everyone* seems to be using the covenant as the interpretive key to Genesis 1. It does not matter that Rashi will say that God creates for the sake of the Torah over and against the author of John's Gospel, who implies that God creates for the sake of the incarnation of his Word — and that both are contradicted by the modern biblical scholar, who says that the writer or writers of the creation account formulated the seven-day sequence in order to reinforce a Jerusalem-oriented temple theology. All agree that creation emerges out of a prior plan or purpose, traditional readers putting the plan in the mind of God, and modern historians putting the plan in the tradition that animates the P source. Perhaps I am simply dull, but it seems obvious to me that this striking consensus speaks against the interpretive authority of comparative mythology, as well as against the contemporary preference for a thin, temporally focused reading of Genesis 1:1. After all, everyone seems to agree that Genesis has a "beginning" out of which everything emerges.

As we move from the first verse of Genesis to the second, we can see another closely related instance of covenant history absorbing the genre of creation myth. It is easy to see that the first verses of Genesis do not entail the doctrine of creation out of nothing. On the contrary, the second verse positively suggests the preexistence of an unformed matter that God subsequently organizes and shapes: "The earth was without form and void, and the darkness was upon the face of the deep, and the Spirit of God was moving over the face of the waters." Here again comparative mythology presses against the traditional approach. When read in conjunction with *Enuma Elish*, a much more richly elaborated creation myth, Genesis 1:2 strongly suggests a preexisting chaos that is tamed and ordered by divine power.

Traditional readers sensed the problem. Augustine, for example, recognized that the plain sense was against him. Nonetheless, in his comments on this verse he insisted that "we are bound to believe that God is the author and founder of all things," and he found a way to explain away the passage, which seems to speak so clearly against the doctrine of creation out of nothing.[7] It is important to see that Augustine was not championing doctrine for the sake of doctrine. Creation out of nothing turns out to be an integral part of the traditional Jewish and Christian theological vision that affirms the scandal of particularity. The Bible itself offers a nice way to frame the problem that creation out of nothing solves. On the one hand, we read, "Behold, heaven and the highest heaven cannot contain thee" (1 Kgs. 8:27). The metaphysical affirmation of God's transcendence is straightforward. God is wholly other and cannot be framed within the finite world. On the other hand, God is a character within the biblical story. He calls Abraham and speaks to him. Here we find the scandal of particularity in metaphysical

---

7. *Unfinished Literal Commentary of Genesis* 4, found in *The Works of Saint Augustine*, vol. 1/13: *On Genesis*, trans. Edmund Hill (Hyde Park, N.Y.: New City Press, 2002), p. 123.

form: God is strangely loyal to a discrete and unique dimension of the created order. He has a people he calls his own, and calls them intimately rather than at a distance. This intimacy seems to contradict God's transcendence.

These days most of us tend to opt for transcendence at the expense of particularity. The bumper sticker declaration that asserts, "My God is too big for any one religion," reflects the conviction that one must be loyal to 1 Kings 8:27 to the exclusion of Genesis 12. One must affirm the universal Deity over against the LORD who has a particular name and elects a particular people. Needless to say, the apparently inevitable and contrastive choice between universality and particularity is all the more dramatic in classical Christology, which should be understood as an intensified version of the election of Abraham in Genesis 12. Divine transcendence seems utterly inconsistent with incarnation.

Creation out of nothing plays an important role in resolving this problem, because it formulates God's transcendence in terms of uniqueness rather than difference or supremacy. Prior to creation, there is no eternal "stuff" present with God. As a result of this ontological parsimony, what makes God divine is nothing other than his identity ("I am who I am"), and this self-defined identity, as opposed to divine identity defined in relation to other eternal "stuff," allows God to be intimate with and present to finite reality. God leaves nothing behind. He neither betrays nor contradicts his divinity by drawing near. As a consequence, one can affirm both 1 Kings 8:27 and Genesis 12. God is wholly other than the world — as creation out of nothing makes clear — and as such, God has no contrastive or zero-sum relation to the world. This allows the interpreter committed to the transcendence of God to give a robust account of the call of Abraham and the ensuing covenant. God does more than use Abraham to signify or symbolize a larger, more mobile religious truth. He allies himself to Abraham; God marries his holiness and power to Abraham. Put somewhat differently, God saturates the cultural and historical particularity of Abraham and his descendants with his presence. The ontological parsimony of the doctrine of creation out of nothing provides the crucial metaphysical background for the view of God's transcendence — one common to both Jewish and Christian traditions — that allows for an interpretation of election as an act of divine love.[8] It is for this reason that traditional Jewish and Christian readers

8. For a more extended account of the exegetical significance of the doctrine of creation out of nothing, see R. R. Reno, *Genesis*, Brazos Theological Commentary on the Bible (Grand Rapids: Brazos Press, 2010), pp. 39-46.

have imposed the doctrine onto their reading of Genesis 1:2, and just such an imposition shows once again the larger pattern of traditional exegesis. The creation myth is not read on its own terms; instead, it ends up subordinated to the more fundamental exigencies of providing a cogent interpretation of covenant history.

The Metaphysical Impasse

I could go on with more examples: the light of the first day of creation, humanity made in the image and likeness of God, Adam cleaving to Eve and becoming one flesh, and the serpent in the garden. These and other passages are traditionally interpreted in the same forward-looking way as Genesis 1:1 and 1:2. The implicit reading of Genesis 2 that we find in Ephesians 5 — a primeval nuptial union between man and woman that foreshadows the union of Christ with the church — is just one example among countless others. In each instance, the mythic character of the opening chapters of Genesis is absorbed into the salvation-historical drama that begins in chapter 12. We can see the same absorptive move at work in traditional interpretations of the wisdom literature, another portion of the Bible that seems to convey a broad, universal perspective that transcends covenant particularity. To take only one instance: traditional readings of the Song of Songs set aside its literal sense as broadly human love poetry, reading the poem as an allegory of God's love affair with those whom he has chosen.[9] By my reckoning, this absorption of a seemingly universal moment of Scripture into the particularity of the covenant constitutes one of the basic strategies of theological reading. It is the exegetical form of the scandal of particularity, a transformation of material seemingly universal in meaning into a coded form of covenant history. And this approach should not surprise us. Genesis tumbles so quickly from the mythic genre and cosmological frame of reference into the narrow particularity of Abraham and his progeny that a sensitive reader feels quite acutely the invitation to think of the broad sweep of creation and the universal scope of human experience in terms of covenant history.

Indeed, even if my suggestions about the early chapters of Genesis and

---

9. "Anyone who explains this book, in accordance with the literal meaning of the words, as referring to sensual love, defiles its sanctity and denies the Oral Torah," Joseph B. Soloveitchik, *And from There You Shall Seek*, trans. Naomi Goldblum (Jersey City, N.J.: Ktav, 2008), pp. 152-53.

their relation to chapter 12 are unconvincing, we should recognize that the tendency of theological reading to solve exegetical puzzles by recourse to covenant history is the outcome of deep assumptions about the true source of reality and history. As interpreters, we invariably seek to expound texts by identifying their power to disclose or refer to something real, something true. This is why modern historical scholars pay so much attention to the editorial processes, tradition history, and *Sitz im Leben*. Historians are confident that these phenomena, however dimly suggested by ancient texts, are at least real. Surely they are right on that score. History and culture have a solidity and depth that saturate texts. Needless to say, however, if one believes in the God of Abraham, Jacob, and Isaac, then no matter how one handles particular episodes in salvation history, no matter what aspects of the modern historical-critical method one employs to analyze discrete portions of the text, one invariably regards the covenant as even more fundamental. Indeed, for faithful readers, the covenant emerges as supremely real, because it is infused with the permanence and trustworthiness of the divine promise. Therefore, we should not be surprised that faithful Jews and Christians turn to the particularity of the covenant as a solid basis — a real and reliable and true basis — for thinking through difficult passages and, as in the passages I have considered, pinning down the meaning of the open-ended and suggestive initial chapters of Genesis.

This appeal to covenant should not trouble us. Faith in the reality of the covenant does not rule out an affirmation of and interest in the historical dynamics that contribute to the production, dissemination, and transmission of texts. It is possible for the Torah (or Christ) to fulfill creation and history by perfecting rather than destroying its natural reality. Indeed, it was to endorse just such a possibility that interpretations of Genesis 1 in terms of the seemingly alien, future-oriented notions of covenant were formulated. Obviously, if Christ is the eternal Word incarnate, and if God created all things in and for his Word (or if God created for the sake of the Torah), then the surpassing interpretive power that traditional exegesis gives to covenant particularity should allow for the usual sorts of historical-critical questions modern scholars ask about the biblical text. If the end is in the beginning, then creation can be creation and at the same time lean toward the calling of Abraham. The P writer can disclose a cosmological imagination formed by temple theology — and point toward covenant fulfillment in Christ.

If I am right about the way in which theological interpretation is open to historical-critical questions, then I am naturally led to explain the presumption against theological reading among modern critics as arising largely from a metaphysical stance, a horizon of assumptions about what is the fundamental truth about reality, rather than a unique sensitivity to or regard for the integrity of the biblical text. Historical scholars object to covenant-oriented interpretations of creation because they have very definite ideas about what is solid, permanent, and real, which is why most of their talk about respecting the integrity of the text actually reduces to metaphysics. Most biblical scholars are rigorously trained to view the laws of history, the principles of cultural development, and the dynamics of tradition and textual transmission as the glue holding together the remarkable diversity and recondite literal particularity of the Bible, not Christ as the eternal Word (or the Torah as the eternal Word). By this view, a view held tacitly and unconsciously even by modern biblical scholars who would like their scholarship to serve the community of faith, covenant particularity cannot be seen as saturated with the divine reality that is the source of all truth; or if it is, then this divine reality ends up treated as subordinate to the more powerful "laws of history." In view of these metaphysical assumptions, the use of Christ (or the Torah) as a deep explanation for biblical texts such as Genesis 1:1 or 1:2 cannot but seem a whimsical abuse of Scripture.

I do not see any way beyond this impasse. I have suggested that the odd circular character of the opening chapters of Genesis invites readers to put aside naïve readings that take the creation stories as sufficient on their own terms, and I have drawn attention to the radical shift toward covenant particularity in Genesis 12. The text itself would seem to encourage a reading of the universal beginning of the Bible in terms of its salvation-historical end. But these arguments rarely persuade. We read under the guidance of our conceptions of what is most deeply real, most fundamentally true, and these conceptions do a great deal to shape our interpretive practices. Therefore, we should see the usual modern complaints about the way in which traditional exegesis abuses or ignores the biblical texts for what they are: large-scale disagreements about what is real rather than exegetical arguments per se.

The *Akedah* in Canonical and Artistic Perspective

Gary A. Anderson

In this essay I would like to consider the story of the binding of Isaac, known as the *Akedah* in Jewish tradition, as it is represented in a mosaic from the city of Sepphoris.[1] As the excavators of this site have determined, the mosaic dates from the fifth century and covered almost the entire floor of a very important synagogue within this city. My interest is in how the exegesis of Genesis 22 has informed the way in which the floor can be read. I make no pretensions of offering a complete interpretation of the contents of the mosaic — like any work of art its purpose and function were multiform and many different readings are possible. But before jumping directly into exegetical matters, let us pause for a moment and consider the mosaic as a whole.

The Mosaic at Sepphoris

A quick perusal of the floor will demonstrate that the mosaic is divisible into seven horizontal registers that reflect three subjects (see fig. 1 on p. 44). Registers two through four have to do with the inauguration of cultic life in the

---

1. See the publication of the results of the excavations: Zeev Weiss, *The Sepphoris Synagogue: Deciphering an Ancient Message through Its Archaeological and Socio-Historical Contexts* (Jerusalem: Israel Exploration Society, 2005). My discussion of the mosaic is heavily indebted to this extraordinary exposition.

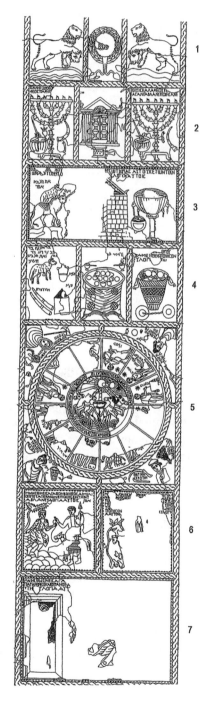

Figure 1. Fifth-century mosaic from the floor of the Sepphoris Synagogue.

Courtesy of Prof. Zeev Weiss, The Sepphoris Expedition, The Hebrew University of Jerusalem.

Drawing by Pnina Arad.

44

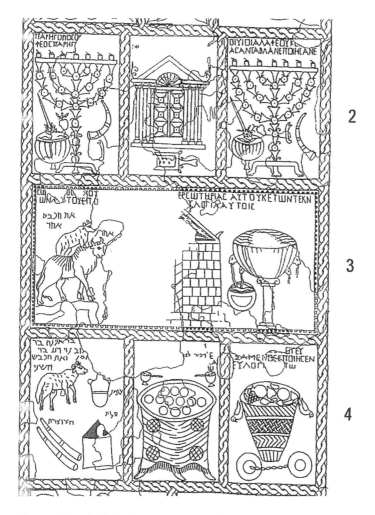

Figure 2. Detail of the floor mosaic, panels 2-4.

tabernacle that is described in Exodus 25–40 and Leviticus 8-9 (see fig. 2 above). The largest register in the middle (#5) depicts the zodiac. At the center of this register are twelve individual representations of the months of the year that, in turn, surround a figure of the sun driving a chariot. In the four corners of the register we find representations of the seasons. The bottom two panels (#6 and #7) depict the story of the annunciation of Isaac's birth and his ordeal at Mount Moriah.

Let us begin with a consideration of the third and fourth registers (fig.

2). In this long horizontal panel, we see Aaron assuming his role as priest at the altar. (The scene should be read from right to left.) We begin with the washbasin where Aaron would have cleansed himself before approaching the altar. In the middle we find Aaron beside the altar ready to offer the sacrifice. Most of his figure has been destroyed, but there is sufficient evidence of the hem of his vestment and the bells that would have been attached to that hem to make this identification. To the left of the altar there is a bull. No doubt the reference here is to the bull that Aaron must bring to inaugurate the tabernacle that Moses has brought to completion. The book of Exodus commands that Aaron "shall bring the bull before the tent of meeting. Aaron and his sons shall lay their hands upon the head of the bull, and [Aaron] shall kill the bull before the LORD, at the door of the tent of meeting" (Exod. 29:10-11).[2] According to the book of Exodus, this rite is to last for seven days in order to complete the consecration process. Once the rites of this seven-day service of ordination are completed — as depicted in scrupulous detail in Leviticus 8 — Aaron and his sons are finally ready to assume responsibility for the public liturgy. In Leviticus 9, the rites of the eighth day, once Aaron fulfills the commands that Moses gives him, God's glory makes a dramatic appearance and consumes the sacrifices upon the altar: "Fire came out from the LORD and consumed the burnt offering and the fat on the altar; and when all the people saw it, they shouted and fell on their faces" (Lev. 9:24). This is clearly the very heart of the Sinaitic revelation. God had told Moses that the sole reason for bringing Israel out of Egypt was "to dwell among them" and thus become their God (Exod. 29:42b-46). The moment had now arrived — God had taken up residence among his people.

But let us not move along too quickly. The inauguration of Aaron to the priesthood is not the only thing going on in this panel. Next to the bull seen in the third register is a lamb, and if we look down into the fourth register on the left we see a second lamb. To our good fortune, the artisan has taken care to label these two animals — אֶת הַכֶּבֶשׂ אֶחָד, "the first lamb," and הַשֵּׁנִי אֵת הַכֶּבֶשׂ, "the second lamb." By so doing, we know that these two lambs refer to the *tamid* or daily sacrifice (see Exod. 29:38-42a and Num. 28:3-8).

According to what Moses reveals at the close of the ordination service (Exod. 29:38-46), the entire purpose for the establishment of the tabernacle is to provide a place in which God can dwell and be served. Through God's gracious act of revealing to Moses the design of his hearth and home, he has

---

2. Biblical translations are from the NRSV. All translation of rabbinic texts are my own.

granted Israel the right to serve his table in the morning and evening. The text in question reads:

> Now this is what you shall offer on the altar: two lambs a year old regularly each day. One lamb you shall offer in the morning, and the other lamb you shall offer in the evening; and with the first lamb one-tenth of a measure of choice flour mixed with one-fourth of a hin of beaten oil, and one-fourth of a hin of wine for a drink offering. And the other lamb you shall offer in the evening, and shall offer with it a grain offering and its drink offering, as in the morning, for a pleasing odor, an offering by fire to the LORD. It shall be a regular burnt offering throughout your generations at the entrance of the tent of meeting before the LORD. (Exod. 29:38-42a)

If we return to the mosaic (fig. 2) we will see that alongside the consecration of Aaron and the onset of the daily *tamid* sacrifice, a number of other important moments in Israel's liturgical life are also represented. In the second register, we see two lampstands that flank the façade of the doors of the temple. The lampstands were among the most sacred objects to be found within the shrine and were constructed of solid gold (Exod. 25:31-40). Beside the lampstands is a set of tongs that would be used to trim the wicks as well as items that are related to two of the three pilgrimage festivals: the four species that are specific to the Feast of Booths (palm branch, myrtle, willow, and ethrog) and the shofar that is part of the rites of the New Year Festival. In front of the façade of the temple is an incense shovel, which would have been used to service the incense altar (Exod. 30:1-10) that stood before a curtain that was directly in front of the ark of the covenant (Exod. 25:10-22). In the fourth register (fig. 2), just below the scene of Aaron's ordination, we find the table of presence (Exod. 25:23-30) and the basket of firstfruits that were to be brought to the altar year by year (Deut. 26:1-11).

At the bottom of the mosaic (the sixth register in fig. 1) we see a depiction of the binding of Isaac. At the left are the two servants that Abraham leaves behind and on the right is the sacrifice itself. Below these two scenes in the bottom register is a depiction of the arrival of the angelic visitors in Genesis 18 who announce that Sarah, who is postmenopausal, is about to conceive and bear a son. Now the question becomes how the cultic artifacts that we have seen in these upper registers relate to the sacrifice of Isaac below.

Gary A. Anderson

The *Akedah* as Etiology

Biblical scholars have long noted the etiological sense of Genesis 22.[3] The story of the theophany that Abraham experiences on this mountain is not simply a one-time event but marks the founding of a site for worship. This seems to be clear from the wordplay that takes place in 22:14. Having just been commanded to stay his hand and spare Isaac, Abraham lifts up his eyes and discovers a ram caught in the thicket. After he has offered this animal in place of Isaac, the narrative informs us that Abraham "called the name of that place 'the LORD will see/the LORD has made himself visible' [both translations are possible on the basis of the consonantal text]. And so it is said even now, 'At the mount of the LORD, he has made himself visible.'"

The implications of the last phrase would seem to be clear: the theophany that happened to Abraham in a singular fashion will be possible for all Israelites at the "mount of the LORD." In this respect the narrative is similar to the story of Jacob's dream in which he saw angels going up and down a ladder whose head reached the heavens. That story concluded when Jacob rose the following morning, set up a stone as a pillar, and poured oil over it. He named the site Bethel, a location that would become a prominent place of worship in the northern kingdom (see 1 Kgs. 12:25-33). Genesis 22 is a bit unusual, however, in that it leaves the specific geographical location unstated, preferring to identify the cult site with the generic title, "mount of the LORD." But this may not be surprising given that the city of Jerusalem is never mentioned explicitly in any pentateuchal text even though it would become the worship site of the highest prestige in the subsequent history of Israel. Though Jerusalem is not mentioned explicitly in Genesis 22, there is a tacit reference at the very beginning of the story when Abraham is instructed by God to take Isaac and offer him as a sacrifice in the "land of Moriah." Though this location remains uninterpreted in the book of Genesis, according to 2 Chronicles 3:1 Mount Moriah is the spot on which Solomon began to build the temple within the city of Jerusalem.

By the early Second Temple period, we can confidently say that readers of the book of Genesis presumed that the sacrifice of Isaac took place precisely at the location where Israel would later offer their sacrifices. The sacral nature of the location is made evident in the mosaic by the fact that Abra-

---

3. See Jon D. Levenson, *The Death and Resurrection of the Beloved Son: The Transformation of Child Sacrifice in Judaism and Christianity* (New Haven: Yale University Press, 1993), especially the chapter titled, "The Aqedah as Etiology," pp. 111-24.

ham and Isaac have removed their shoes prior to approaching the altar. As one can learn from Exodus 28, the chapter that describes the vestments of Aaron and his sons, there is no mention of any sort of covering for the feet. No doubt this is because the wearing of sandals on sacred ground was thought to be an affront to the demands of holiness. When God called Moses from the burning bush he addressed him in an emphatic fashion: "Moses! Moses!" To which Moses replied, "Here I am." Thereupon God declared: "Come no closer. Remove the sandals from your feet, for the place on which you are standing is holy ground." Similarly when God called out, "Abraham! Abraham!" Abraham responded, "Here I am." God did not need to say anything about the removal of shoes in this instance — our early interpreter presumed — because Abraham and Isaac had already removed them prior to approaching the altar.

The artist who designed the mosaic at Sepphoris had a good precedent for linking the sacrifice of Isaac in Genesis 22 to the sacrifices that were regularly offered at the tabernacle and temple. Although this linkage has a biblical foundation, the Bible does not develop in any meaningful way what we are to make of it. This question, however, was of great importance to early biblical interpreters, and to the results of their inquiries we now turn.

The *Akedah* and Sacrifice

The first text that I would like to look at is an imaginative midrash on Leviticus 1:11.[4] In this chapter of Leviticus we learn how to sacrifice the burnt offering. This is relevant for our concerns because the *tamid* or daily sacrifice that was of such interest in register three of the mosaic was a burnt offering. And the specific instructions that govern the way in which that sacrifice was to be offered are detailed in the opening chapter of Leviticus.

According to this text there are rules specific to how one should sacrifice a bull (vv. 3-9), a sheep or goat (vv. 10-13), and a bird (vv. 14-17). It just so happens that the sheep or goat, unlike the bull, is to be slaughtered "on the *north* side of the altar." The texts in question read:

The bull   shall be slaughtered   before the Lord. (v. 5)
[The sheep] shall be slaughtered *on the north side of the altar* before the Lord. (v. 11)

4. *Leviticus Rabbah* 2.11.

The additional geographical reference in v. 11 is an odd detail to be sure (were the other animals sacrificed on a different side?), but one that most modern readers pass by without much attention. But for the rabbinic reader, that the offering of the lamb was treated uniquely could not be accidental. It must reveal some deeper truth. What is it about the lamb that distinguishes it from the other animals?

In order to understand how the rabbis will solve this puzzle, we need to know two other basic facts. First, every morning and evening in Jerusalem a lamb was offered as a burnt offering in the temple (Exod. 29:38-42 and Num. 29:3-8). The second fact we must attend to is that it was at the future site of the temple that God had commanded the offering of Isaac. According to rabbinic readers, the sacrifice of Isaac was a foundational offering that paved the way for the ongoing liturgy in the temple.

The midrashic interpretation opens by citing the biblical verse, "It shall be slaughtered on the north side (צפנה) of the altar, before the Lord" (Lev. 1:11). The exposition of the verse reads, "When our father Abraham bound Isaac his son, the Holy One (blessed be He!) established the institution of the two lambs, one in the morning and one in the evening (Exod. 29:38-42). Why so much? Because when Israel would sacrifice the daily offering on the altar and recite this verse ("on the צפנה side of the altar"), the Holy One (blessed be He!) would remember the binding of Isaac."

I left צפנה untranslated because it is the key to understanding this text. The Hebrew text was originally written without vowels, and so the rabbinic reader always felt free to explore other ways of vocalizing a word. The consonants צפנה are commonly rendered צָפֹנָה and translated "north side" as a consultation of any modern translation of the Bible will confirm. But the rabbis eschewed the obvious sense of this word in order to link this text to the story of Isaac. They accomplished this by playfully misreading the word as צְפֻנָה, a feminine passive participle meaning "hidden." The word "hidden" would then refer to the story of the binding of Isaac (known in Hebrew as the *aqedah* ["binding"], commonly spelled *akedah*, a feminine noun that would match our feminine passive participle). On this reading we could paraphrase the end of the midrash as follows: "Why sacrifice a lamb every morning and evening? Because when Israel would sacrifice those lambs on the altar and at the same time recite this verse — 'hidden (צְפֻנָה before the Lord' — the Holy One (blessed be He!) would remember the *akedah* of Isaac." In other words, in the rabbinic mind, Israel's daily sacrificial service was nothing other than a way of memorializing the heroic self-offering of the patriarch Isaac. Every time Israel made their sacrifice on earth, God contemplated Isaac's merits that were stored in heaven.

Perhaps even more surprising, especially to Christian readers who are forever tempted to think of Judaism in narrow, parochial terms, is that this verse from Leviticus is imagined to have universal consequences. The text ends with a dramatic intervention on the part of God himself, "I call heaven and earth to witness against me: Whenever anyone — Gentile or Jew, man or woman, male or female slave, reads this verse ('on the north side before the Lord'), the Holy One (blessed be He!) remembers the binding of Isaac, as it is written: 'on the north side in the presence of the Lord'" (*Leviticus Rabbah* 2.11).

The *Akedah* and Eschatology

The second text I would like to consider explores the relationship of the *Akedah* and the temple in relationship to eschatology. This may at first appear surprising because nothing that I have said so far about the contents of this mosaic has been explicitly eschatological. Yet one must bear in mind that the upper registers that document the story of the founding of the sacrificial liturgy were not solely of antiquarian interest in rabbinic eyes. At the end of days, Israel would be redeemed from servitude to the foreign nations, return to the land of Israel, and rebuild the temple in a fashion befitting the prophecies granted the great prophets of old. Isaiah 60 is an outstanding example of what this new temple would look like. Its ongoing utility in Second Temple Judaism is evident in the famous prayer of thanksgiving that Tobit gives voice to at the end of the book that bears his name (Tob. 13). Zeev Weiss makes the additional observation that in rabbinic thought the redemption of Israel is often linked to merits of the patriarchs.[5] This is quite evident in the first benediction of the Amidah, a prayer recited in the synagogue three times a day,

> Blessed are you, O Lord our God, God of our fathers, God of Abraham, Isaac, and Jacob; great, mighty, and revered God, God Most High, who does good deeds, created all things, and who remembers the good deeds of the patriarchs, and who will graciously bring a redeemer to their children's children for the sake of his name. . . . Blessed are you, O Lord, shield of Abraham.

5. Weiss, *Sepphoris Synagogue*, pp. 240-42.

In the following midrash from the Palestinian Talmud (*Ta'anit* 2.4; 65d) we can see a specific linkage made between the merits that accrued to the sacrifice of Isaac and the redemption of Israel at the end of time.

A. And was not Isaac redeemed on Mount Moriah? Since Isaac was redeemed, it was as if all Israel was redeemed. . . .

B. "And Abraham said, 'God will see. . . .'" [This means] You will be reminded for their sake of the binding of Isaac their father, and will be filled with compassion for them.

C. What is written afterward? "And Abraham lifted up his eyes and looked *after,* and behold, there was a ram *caught in the thicket* (נאחז בסבך). . . ." What is the meaning of *"after"*? R. Judah b. R. Simon said: *After all generations* your children are going to be *caught* (ליאחז) by their sins and *entrapped* (להסתבך) in troubles. But in the end they will be redeemed by the horns of this ram.

This section begins (unit A) by noting that God "redeemed" Isaac by allowing Abraham to sacrifice a ram in his stead. Because Isaac is the progenitor of the entire nation, the redemption of his person quite literally was the redemption of all of Israel. In B the midrashist is struck by the answer Abraham has given to Isaac's question, "Where is the lamb for the burnt offering?" (v. 7). Abraham's response when translated word-for-word reads: "God will see it." The midrash understands this to mean that in the future God will continue to contemplate the extraordinary sacrifice that was required of Abraham and Isaac and the many merits they secured by complying with this command. The specifically eschatological element, however, is drawn from another peculiar phrase found later in the story after Abraham is told to stay his hand. The Hebrew text could be read as follows: "And Abraham lifted up his eyes and saw a ram *afterward* (אחר) *caught in the thicket* (נאחז בסבך)." The usage of the word אַחַר meaning "afterward" is quite strange, and most modern translations emend to אֶחָד (". . . saw *a* ram caught in the thicket"). But the rabbis utilized this odd word to infer that Abraham looked beyond this present moment ("afterward") and saw the implications of Isaac's redemption for the people Israel. The midrash continues:

> What is the meaning of *"after"*? R. Judah b. R. Simon said: *After all generations* your children are going to be *caught* (ליאחז) by their sins and *entrapped* (להסתבך) in troubles. But in the end they will be redeemed by the horns of this ram.

Just as the ram was caught (נאחז) in the thicket (בסבך), so would Is-rael be "caught" by their sins and ensnared (להסתבך) in their troubles. In the end both Isaac and Israel would be redeemed by the horns of a ram. Yet this interpretation of R. Judah does not specify how the horns of a ram might be directly relevant to the salvation of Israel. That point is made clear by R. Hunah in the following midrash.

> R. Hunah in the name of R. Hinenah bar Isaac said: "For that entire day Abraham saw that the ram would get caught in one tree and free itself and then get caught in a bush and free itself and then get caught in a thicket and free itself." The Holy One (blessed be He!) said to him: "Abraham, this is how your children in the future will be *caught* by their sins and *entrapped* by the kingdoms, from Babylonia to Media, from Media to Greece, from Greece to Edom [= Rome]." Abraham responded: "Lord of the ages! Is that how it will be forever?" God responded: "In the end they will be redeemed by the horn of this ram." [As Scripture says:] "The Lord God will sound the *ram's horn* (שופר) and march forth in the whirlwinds of the south" (Zech. 9:14).

The *Akedah* and Atonement

The third and final theme that I would like to address concerns the Jewish New Year (Rosh Hashanah). New Year's Day falls on the first of Tishri, just ten days before Yom Kippur (the tenth of Tishri). During those ten interven-ing days numerous prayers of contrition and repentance are uttered. Ac-cording to Jewish tradition, God inscribes in the heavenly books the fate of each and every person on New Year's Day. Those verdicts will be finalized on the Day of Atonement but are subject to revision during the intervening days.

It cannot be accidental, given this highly charged spiritual atmosphere in which one's future hangs in the balance, that during the second day of the New Year's liturgical rites, the Torah portion is none other than Genesis 22. The reading of the *Akedah* is intended to remind God of the merits that ac-crued to Abraham and Isaac as a result of this awesome sacrifice. The Baby-lonian Talmud asks: "Why do we blow the horn of a ram [on New Year's Day]?" And the answer is straightforward: "so that [God] may *remember* for your benefit the binding of Isaac, son of Abraham, and account it to you as if you had bound yourselves before me" (*Rosh Hashanah* 16a). During the

Figure 3. Detail of the floor mosaic, panel 5.

prayers of remembrance *(zikronot)* that are said during the additional prayer service of New Year's Day, one is to repeat at the conclusion of one set of petitions the refrain: "and remember the binding of Isaac this day in mercy unto his seed."

The importance of these liturgical rites is deeply embedded in each of the three sections of the mosaic. We have already noted the presence of the shofar in panel two (fig. 2). It is worth recalling that the talmudic text I just cited accords more significance to Isaac than to Abraham. God is asked to remember Isaac's deed rather than that of Abraham. This accords nicely with the rabbinic idea that Isaac, because he was thirty-three years old during the ordeal, must have freely consented to be bound by his father. But equally important is the request that God "accounts it to us" as though we had been bound and not Isaac. The idea that stands behind this prayer is *zekut 'abot,* the "merits of the fathers." The supplicants acknowledge that they do not merit redemption but ask God to consider what was accomplished by Isaac, and allow the grace of that founding moment to be shared by them.

Though it might not seem obvious at first, if we look carefully at the zodiac we will see that it is also relevant to this theme (see register five in fig. 1). In rabbinic thought, as in most of Second Temple Judaism and a good swath of early Christianity, the predominant metaphor for sin was that of a debt that one owes to God.[6] (Consider, for example, the metaphoric language of the Our Father: "forgive us our *debts* . . ."). Because sin was conceived of in this mercantile manner, one way to picture God's behavior toward the sinner was to imagine God as a shopkeeper with a set of scales putting debits on one side and credits on the other in order to determine whether one merited absolution or punishment. By a happy accident of providence the month of Tishri, in which the Day of Atonement falls, is marked by the zodiac sign of Libra, or in Hebrew מאזניים, "scales" (see fig. 3). Therefore all three panels come together during the "days of awe": the shofar, the scales of Libra, and the binding of Isaac. The linkage of the zodiac with the midrash is nicely made in an early piece of liturgical poetry written by Yannai the Paytan for the eve of Rosh Hashanah.[7] In the middle of his acrostic poem we read,

> *(Tet)* The heavenly array of the seventh month — its constellation is a pair of scales/For [at that time] the LORD will weigh both debits and merits upon a set of scales.
> *(Yod)* With his own hand God will remove [some] debits; as the *shofar* sounds we shall shout for joy/God shall push the pan of merits down [and declare] my innocence.

One additional image is worth mentioning, even though it is considerably later than the mosaics from Sepphoris. It is found in a *mahzor,* or liturgical book, from the Rhine valley in South Germany (14th century). This particular image (fig. 4) is taken from the top third of a page that contains a liturgi-

---

6. I give a succinct account of this problem in "From Israel's Burden to Israel's Debt: Towards a Theology of Sin in Biblical and Early Second Temple Sources," in Esther G. Chazon, Devorah Dimant, and Ruth A. Clements, eds., *Reworking the Bible: Apocryphal and Related Texts at Qumran* (Leiden: Brill, 2005), pp. 1-30.

7. I was directed to this *piyyut* by Steven Fine in his book *Art and Judaism in the Greco-Roman World: Toward a New Jewish Archaeology* (Cambridge: Cambridge University Press, 2005), p. 188. I have modified his translation in consultation with the original.

Figure 4. Image of the scales of justice, a detail from a fourteenth-century German manuscript of a Jewish prayer book for the high holidays.
Courtesy of The Bodleian Libraries, University of Oxford, MS. Reggio 1, fol. 207v.

cal prayer *(piyyut)* that would have been spoken at the *musaf* ("supplementary") service on New Year's Day. The Hebrew word *melek* ("king") sits at the center while on the left side, just beyond the Hebrew letter *kaph,* we see a hand reaching down from heaven that holds a set of scales. The pan on the right (presumably holding the sins of Israel) is higher than the one on the left (holding Israel's merits) and thus indicates Israel's innocence. But a demonic figure has both arms wrapped around the higher pan, evidently trying to pull it down so that Israel will be condemned. (On this particular role of Satan, see my discussion a few paragraphs below.) This illumination indicates how deeply embedded the metaphor of scales was in Jewish thought. It was not a passing fashion. In some sources the month of Tishri was interpreted to mean "forgiveness of a sin [debt]." Hence the midrash asks: "Why is the month called Tishri? [Because we implore God to] release [*tishri*] and forgive our debts" (*Pesikta Rabbati* 40.7).

For many modern persons, the image of God as a shopkeeper who carefully tends to his account books in heaven is not appealing. Indeed, I think it is fair to say that it has been the source of a considerable degree of anti-Semitic rhetoric. Perhaps the most famous is the character of Shylock, the Jewish moneylender in Shakespeare's *Merchant of Venice,* a person so bound and determined to collect his pound of flesh that he dismisses mercy altogether. Nothing trumps the necessity of collecting what one is owed.

The first thing to be said in defense of the *piyyut* is that the imagery it employs is deeply biblical. It is the common inheritance of both Judaism and Christianity.[8] Although the construal of sins as debts appears for the first time in Second Isaiah and the Holiness Code (Lev. 17–26), the best place to illustrate their appearance is in the prophet Daniel's speech to King Nebuchadnezzar. In order to forestall a terrible punishment that awaits this pagan king, Daniel urges him to give alms (צדקה) and show mercy toward the poor in order to redeem (פרק) himself from sin (Dan. 4:27 [MT 24]).[9] The mention of redemption brings to mind Leviticus 25, the laws that govern the manner in which a debt slave can be redeemed. Nebuchadnezzar is also imagined as a debt slave whose sins — conceived of as debts — have put him in his dire state.

Why then does Daniel urge so strongly the giving of alms? The logic of this piece of advice is to be derived from the contemporary books of Tobit and Ben Sira.[10] They show us that giving alms to the poor is the most efficient means of funding a heavenly treasury. If we take this notion of storing currency in heaven and set it side by side with the predicament that our king is in — having debts that he has no other means of repaying — then the logic of Daniel's advice is quite clear: fund a treasury in heaven that can repay your debts. The logic of Leviticus 25 (repay your debts in order to be redeemed from slavery) has been moved to a heavenly sphere.

But even if I have established that this rabbinic image has deep biblical roots, this does not eliminate the problem of the debt metaphor itself. Have we not turned God into a heartless debt collector? Or to put the matter in terms bequeathed to us from the Reformation: do we not achieve our salvation by virtue of human works? On the face of it, Daniel's advice to King Nebuchadnezzar seems to put the burden of forgiveness solely in the hands of humankind: by showing mercy to the poor you purchase your own salvation. It should not surprise us to learn that the advice Daniel has provided became one of the most contested verses in all of Scripture in the wake of the Reformation.

---

8. The development of this motif is the subject of my book *Sin: A History* (New Haven: Yale University Press, 2009).

9. Not all would translate פרק as "redeem." A justification of that translation can be found in Anderson, *Sin: A History,* pp. 137-44.

10. See Tob. 4:9 and Sir. 29:11. Both texts assert that the giving of alms to the poor will result in the donor funding a "treasury in heaven."

In order to get at these thorny theological problems, let us consider a text from *Pesikta Rabbati,* a collection of homilies on the major festivals of the Jewish liturgical year. The homily in question, Homily 45, is dedicated to the Day of Atonement.

> "An instruction of David. Happy is the one whose wrongdoing is carried away, whose sin is covered over" (Ps. 32:1). This is what David means: you have carried away the sins of your people, all their sins you have covered up.
>
> [What this means is depicted in the following story:] Once, on the Day of Atonement, Satan came to accuse Israel. He detailed her sins and said, "Lord of the Universe, as there are adulterers among the nations of the world, so there are in Israel. As there are thieves among the nations of the world, so there are in Israel." The Holy One (blessed be he!) itemized the merits of Israel. Then what did he do? He took a scale and balanced the sins against the merits. They were weighed together and the scales were equally balanced. Then Satan went to load on further sin and to make that scale sink lower.
>
> What did the Holy One (blessed be he!) do? While Satan was looking for sins, the Holy One (blessed be he!) took the sins from the scale and hid them under his purple royal robe. When Satan returned, he found no sin, as it is written, "The sin of Israel was searched for, but it is no longer" (Jer. 50:20). When Satan saw this he spoke before the Holy One (blessed be he!), "Lord of the World, 'you have borne away the wrongdoing of your people and covered over all their sin'" (Ps. 85:3). When David saw this, he said, "Happy is the one whose wrongdoing is borne away, whose sin is covered over" (Ps. 32:1).

It is important to note that Satan is not the personification of evil we might expect. He is rather a cipher for the principle of justice. His claim is that Israel does not deserve forgiveness; their debits outweigh their credits. God, however, will not allow strict accountancy procedures to govern his heart. Even if Satan is correct, he cannot win. God amends the situation by "bearing away" the sin of Israel. In this case, God does not remove a weight from someone's shoulders, as the biblical expression would require, but rather some bonds from one set of scales.[11] With those bonds removed, the merits of Israel prevail; God can "justly" forgive his people.

11. It is true that the image of a set of scales does conjure the notion of weight — for it is the weight placed on the pan that will determine what the price of a certain set of goods

But one element in this midrash remains unaccounted for. The forgiveness of Israel is not normally attributed to an act of God pure and simple — there is almost always an important role for human agency. In particular, the merits of the patriarchs quite frequently play a crucial role. As Walter Moberly has pointed out, one of the most important elements of the *Akedah* is the second angelic address wherein the angel reveals that Abraham's obedience (or Isaac's in rabbinic thought) was so stupendous that the divine promise to Israel would now be grounded in that act.[12] Whereas Genesis 12 had grounded the promise to Abraham in God's inscrutable will and (save for the midrash) had accorded no role whatsoever to human deeds, Genesis 22 provides a very different picture: "By myself I have sworn, says the LORD: *Because you have done this,* and have not withheld your son, your only son, I will indeed bless you, and I will make your offspring as numerous as the stars of the heaven and as the sand that is on the seashore" (22:15-17). Only against the background of the reformulation of the original promise can we make sense of Israel's urging that God *remember* the merits of Isaac when they find themselves in dire straits. It was upon Isaac's merits, not Israel's, that the redemption of the nation would depend.

It is worth giving some attention to one of the most important intercessory prayers in the Hebrew Bible. After Israel builds the golden calf, God calls Moses aside and informs him of his intentions to destroy the nation he has brought out of Egypt and to create a new nation from the loins of Moses. Moses resists the suggestion with his entire being and urges God: "Remember Abraham, Isaac, and Israel, your servants, how you swore to them by your own self, saying to them, 'I will multiply your descendants like the stars of heaven and all this land that I have promised I will give to your descendants, and they shall inherit it forever'" (Exod. 32:13). The midrash understands the words of Moses to be a plea that God remember the merits of the

---

will be. But here it should be noted that the idea of weight has been fully subsumed into a commercial context. What is being weighed are not the sins of the individual but the bonds that those sins have created. It should be recalled that sin has a certain "thing-ness." In the First Temple period the "thing" that is created at the point of sin is a weight that is loaded upon one's shoulders. That weight could be so heavy that one would have to load it upon carts in order to transport it. In the Second Temple period the picture is wholly transformed: a bond is drawn up that must be repaid. In this particular midrash it is the bonds that are put on the pan of a set of scales; this is very different from the picture we see in First Temple texts.

12. R. Walter L. Moberly, "The Earliest Commentary on the Akedah," *VT* 38 (1988): 302-23.

patriarchs.[13] Most modern commentators resist this suggestion and argue that the text is not calling human acts of obedience to God's attention but rather the Deity's own solemn oath, which was repeated several times in the book of Genesis. In terms of the specific intention of the author of this prayer, this seems right. But in light of the larger canonical narrative, it is very difficult to read Exodus 32 in isolation from Genesis 22. If the most solemn and sacral act of the entire book of Genesis concludes with the notice that the divine promise is now reworded so that it is a reward for a specific act of human obedience, why would not this very reformulation carry over to the words of Moses' intercessory prayer? The midrash, when read in light of Israel's full canonical witness, must be given due respect. Even the Bible allows for the notion that later generations could draw on the merits of the patriarchs.

The idea that virtuous deeds generated merit was hardly unique to Judaism. Early Christian thinkers came to similar conclusions. The fourth-century Syrian theologian Ephrem once wrote:

> Blessed is he who endured, withstood, and triumphed; his head is
> held high with its crown.
> He is like a creditor who demands his fee with a bold voice.
> He is not like me, too weak to fast, too weary for the vigil,
> the first to succumb. My enemy is skillful.
> When he overcomes me, he lets me rise only to throw me down
> once more.
> O Sea of Mercies, give me a handful of mercy,
> so I can wipe out the note of my debt.[14]

The hero of this text is Christ, who is like a heavenly banker who holds the notes of indebtedness that mortals have "signed" when they sinned. Ephrem, who understands himself as too weak to secure the means of repayment, appeals to the vast treasury in heaven that Christ had accumulated on the cross. He prays that a portion of this wealth may be transferred to his account in order to cover the debt that he owes.

Ephrem's formulation of the problem calls to mind Anselm's classic

13. *Exodus Rabbah*, ad loc.
14. *Hymns on Fasting* 1.13. The translation is my own. For the edition consult Edmund Beck, ed., *Des heiligen Ephraem des Syrers: Hymnen de Ieiunio*, CSCO 246-47 (Louvain: Peeters, 1964).

essay, *Cur deus homo (Why God Became Man).* At one point in his argument, while pondering the infinite merits that Christ's sacrifice had accrued, he turned to his dialogue partner and asked: "What, indeed, can be conceived of more merciful than that God the Father should say to a sinner condemned to eternal torments and lacking any means of redeeming himself, 'Take my only begotten son and give him on your behalf'?"[15] We could easily translate that back into the language of Jewish theology that inspired our synagogue floor: "What, indeed, can be conceived of more merciful than that the God of Israel should say to his people, 'Take Abraham's only-begotten son and give him on your behalf'?" Much has been made in the last few years about how slow was the process that led to the eventual separation of Judaism from Christianity.[16] Perhaps this example shows why that might have been the case.

Over the course of this essay I have made a number of points. Let me pick out just four that are worthy of special attention. First, I have shown that the link of the *Akedah* to temple sacrifice that is well attested in the midrash goes back to the last redactional stage in the composition of the Bible. Second, the result of this linkage was to extend the benefits of the *Akedah* to all subsequent individuals who invoked its memory. The sounding of the shofar during the liturgy of New Year's Day served to recall its foundational significance. One hoped that God would recall it during the ten days of penitence in order to rule in favor of his people for the coming year. But one also hoped that the merits of Isaac would prod God to redeem Israel at the eschaton. And for those moments of ordinary time that stood apart from the High Holidays and the eschaton, one could benefit from the merits of the binding of Isaac by studying the laws for temple sacrifice. Third, I have emphasized that the merits of Isaac proved to be a very important motif for the way in which rabbinic Judaism understands the fundamental mechanics of the forgiveness of sin. In a world that viewed sins as debts, the merits of the *Akedah* often proved to be the best hope one had before the judgment seat of God. And last but not least, to the degree that we have grasped the soteriological function of the *Akedah* in rabbinic Judaism we have cast new light on the way in which Christians have understood the saving work of the cross. Anselm and the rabbis are not as far apart as one might have guessed.

---

15. *Cur deus homo* 2.20, from *Anselm of Canterbury: The Major Works,* ed. Brian Davies and G. R. Evans (New York: Oxford University Press, 1998).

16. For an example of this sort of scholarship, see Daniel Boyarin, *Border Lines: The Partition of Judaeo-Christianity* (Philadelphia: University of Pennsylvania Press, 2004).

Joseph in the Likeness of Adam: Narrative Echoes of the Fall

Timothy J. Stone

According to Gerhard von Rad, "The Joseph story is in every respect distinct from the patriarchal narratives which it follows."[1] Many others agree, though Claus Westermann observes: "The result of the uniqueness and independence of the Joseph story over against the preceding patriarchal stories is that too often not enough attention has been paid to their continuity and what they have in common."[2] Yet even he does not entertain the possibility of continuity between the Joseph story and the entire book of Genesis.[3] In my view, the Joseph story is the culmination and the conclusion of Genesis[4] rather than an intrusion to the book or merely a necessary historical bridge to the opening chapters of Exodus. This paper explores one particular thread of continuity running through the entire narrative, even across the book's

1. Gerhard von Rad, "The Joseph Narrative and Ancient Wisdom," in *The Problem of the Hexateuch and Other Essays*, trans. E. W. Trueman Dicken (New York: McGraw-Hill, 1966), p. 292; cf. p. 299.

2. Claus Westermann, *Genesis 37–50*, trans. John J. Scullion, CC (Minneapolis: Augsburg, 1986), p. 27.

3. Brevard Childs, *Introduction to the Old Testament as Scripture* (Philadelphia: Fortress, 1979), p. 156, notes that this question is seldom raised.

4. Bruce Dahlberg, "The Unity of Genesis," in Kenneth R. R. Gros Louis and James S. Ackerman, eds., *Literary Interpretations of Biblical Narrative*, vol. 2 (Nashville: Abingdon, 1982), p. 128, takes a similar position, though he focuses on the thematic and textual *inclusio* formed by Gen. 1–11 and 37–50, which I admit is stronger than the connections between Gen. 12–36 and the Joseph story. The development of the themes in Gen. 1–11 in Gen. 12–36, however, plays an essential role in framing Joseph's story.

different sources and varied literary forms.[5] I begin by tracing the repeating story of the fall[6] as it moves along before taking a surprising turn in Joseph's story. Then I briefly sketch some ways in which Joseph surpasses those before him. I conclude by looking at the relationship between Joseph and Jesus.

Adam

The blessings of creation are significantly diminished by the fall. Eve eats the forbidden fruit, gives it to Adam, who is with her, and he eats. Adam listens to his wife's voice and disobeys the command of God. There is division on every level: between humans, animals, the land, and God. Instead of multiplying seed, the pain of procreation is multiplied; instead of ruling over the animals, the man will rule over the woman; instead of cultivating the ground and receiving food as a gift of God, man toils over the cursed ground with its thorns and thistles. Humanity's exile from Eden banishes them from the tree of life; they die and return to dust. Exiled from Eden, Eve gives birth to Cain and Abel, yet Cain rises up and kills his brother Abel. Abel's blood cries out from the ground against Cain, who is then cursed from the ground. The fall's division increases until Cain's violence fills the earth in Noah's days (Gen. 6:11, 13; cf. 1:26).

Noah

Lamech hopes that Noah will ameliorate God's curse on the ground (5:28-29). After the judgment of de-creation and death caused by the flood, Noah emerges from the ark with the animals into a new creation as a man of the ground, a new Adam, appearing to lessen the impact of the curse on the ground by planting a vineyard. Yet, like Adam before, Noah and his three sons have a fall narrative.[7] Noah partakes of the vine, becomes drunk, and uncovers himself inside his tent.[8] Ham, seeing the nakedness

---

5. This observation is not intended as a denial of different sources in Genesis.

6. I would prefer not to use the term "fall," but since it is the one in common usage, I will use it throughout the paper.

7. These parallels are often listed, e.g., Bruce Waltke with Cathi J. Fredricks, *Genesis* (Grand Rapids: Zondervan, 2001), pp. 127-28.

8. Interpreters of Genesis divide over Noah's culpability. Waltke and Fredricks, *Genesis*, p. 148, suggest that Noah's behavior is condemned in the narrative, while Nahum Sarna, *Genesis*, JPSTC (Philadelphia: JPS, 1989), p. 65, attaches no blame to Noah for the incident.

of his father,[9] shares his discovery with his brothers, as Eve shared the fruit with Adam. Like God covering Adam and Eve, the brothers cover the nakedness of their father. Awaking from his wine, Noah knew, as Adam and Eve knew their nakedness, what Ham had done. This results in a divided family and a curse on Ham. The re-creation of Noah's day does not escape the fall. Though there is a degree of flexibility, through the use of key words,[10] images, and motifs, Noah's fall echoes Eden's.[11]

Abraham

From all the families of the earth Abraham is called out to be blessed and to be a blessing to the nations. Abraham's call is a response to the fall and its consequences. Through him, God's original creational blessings will flow.[12] Yet for all his faith and mighty acts, Abraham does not escape the repeating fall story. In Eden God puts Adam into a deep sleep (תרדמה, 2:21), then brings him Eve. Abraham falls into a deep sleep (ותרדמה, 15:12),[13] then receives a covenant that his descendants will possess the land of Canaan. Yet, after ten years in Canaan, Abraham has no son. Sarah says that the Lord has prevented her bearing, so she takes over, advising Abraham to go into Hagar, her maid. Like Adam before, Abraham listens to his wife's voice (וישמע אברם לקול שרי, 16:2)[14] and goes into Hagar, following the conventional practice. Like Eve with the Edenic fruit, Sarah takes (ותקח, 16:3) and gives (ותתן, 16:3) Hagar to her husband with unexpected and disappointing results. Abraham, like Adam, is a passive character in Sarah's unfolding scheme.[15] This mini-rerun of the fall again brings division into the family culminating in Hagar and her son's (tem-

---

9. There may be some sordid details lurking in this truncated story; see Sarna, *Genesis*, pp. 63-66.

10. Some of the key words are: ערוה, ראה, אדמה, and ידע.

11. Noah's connection to the fall story is widely recognized, e.g., Joseph Blenkinsopp, *The Pentateuch: An Introduction to the First Five Books of the Bible* (New York: Doubleday, 1992), p. 58.

12. For more on this see Terence E. Fretheim, "The Book of Genesis," *NIB* 1:422-26.

13. These two texts are the only places in Genesis where this word is found. In the OT it occurs only five more times (1 Sam. 26:12; Isa. 29:10; Job 4:13; 33:15; Prov. 19:15).

14. This exact construction occurs in Genesis only here and in 3:17.

15. By themselves these two verbs are extremely common, but in these exact forms, when taken together in this order, they occur in close proximity just four times in the OT: Gen. 3:6; 16:3; 30:9; and 2 Chr. 22:11. They also occur together in Gen. 27:15-17; in this instance, explored below, they are slightly more separated.

porary) exile.[16] Echoes from Eden frame Sarah and Abraham's failed attempt to bring to fulfillment God's promise of a son.

Jacob

The promise of blessing is passed on from Abraham, to Isaac, and then to Jacob. Though somewhat diffused, a scene in his story may echo the fall narrative.[17] Rebekah, overhearing Isaac's plan to bless Esau, decides to deceive her husband into blessing her favorite, Jacob, instead. Echoing Eve, she commands Jacob to listen to her voice twice; as Eve took the desirable fruit, so Rebekah takes (ותקח, 27:15) the most desirable (החמדת, 27:15)[18] clothes of Esau, puts them on Jacob, then gives (ותתן, 27:17) to Jacob the savory food with which to deceive his father. In the garden the serpent is cursed for his deception of Eve; Rebekah is willing to be cursed for her deception of Isaac. Not unlike Adam, Jacob is passive in the entire affair.[19] Again, this results in family division, and Jacob goes into an exile of sorts with his cousin Laban in Haran.

16. Werner Berg, "Der Sündenfall Abrahams und Saras nach Gen 16:1-6," *BN* 19 (1982): 7-14; Gordon Wenham, *Genesis 16–50*, WBC (Dallas: Word Books, 1994), pp. 6-13; and John Sailhamer, *The Pentateuch as Narrative* (Grand Rapids: Zondervan, 1995), p. 153, all support the position presented here and add a few arguments of their own. This confirms Gerhard von Rad, *Genesis*, trans. J. H. Marks, rev. ed., OTL (Philadelphia: Westminster, 1972), p. 196, who sees the episode as an example of a "fainthearted faith that cannot leave things with God and believes it necessary to help things along."

17. To listen to someone's voice (שמע לקול) is a common idiom in Hebrew, but when a woman is the subject of the verb it occurs only seven times in Genesis: 3:17; 16:2; 21:12; 27:8, 13, 43; and 30:6. Not all these instances are negative: in 21:12 God tells Abraham to listen to the voice of Sarah; in 30:6 Rachel says that God has listened to her voice; and in 27:43 Jacob's life is probably spared because he listens to the voice of Rebekah. It is not therefore refusing to listen to a woman's voice per se that Genesis is driving at; rather, individuals in Genesis are confronted with something similar to the wisdom decision in Prov. 1–9 between listening to the voice of Dame Folly or that of Dame Wisdom. There is a time when it is wise and there is a time when it is foolish to listen to the voice of the woman in Genesis. While this could be construed as misogynistic, in my view this would misunderstand and artificially isolate this motif from the narrative logic of Genesis.

18. Apart from the use of נחמד in 2:9 and 3:6 as a Niphal participle, its appearance as a superlative noun החמדת in 27:15 is the only other occurrence of the root in Genesis.

19. Wenham, *Genesis 16–50*, pp. 207-8, explains in detail the way the narrative artfully highlights the passive, maybe even reluctant, role of Jacob.

Joseph

The fall story echoes through Genesis, taking on new and surprising tones in the Joseph story. Though Joseph is a slave in Potiphar's house in Egypt, the Lord is with him and causes everything in his hand to prosper.[20] Seeing this, Potiphar favors him, trusting all his affairs — except his food, which is probably a euphemism for his wife — to Joseph.[21] Within the narrative the only thing withheld from Joseph is Potiphar's "food"; later Joseph explains everything has been placed in his hand except his master's wife. The convergence of a single exception from Joseph's domain makes Potiphar's wife the forbidden food. Here Joseph is in an analogous situation to Adam in Eden. In God's "house," Adam rules over everything — yet the tree of the knowledge of good and evil is forbidden. Though Adam and Joseph each rules over the entire house, their authority is not absolute, since one thing remains outside their domain.

For Potiphar's wife, functioning like Eve in this incident, Joseph — beautiful in form and appearance — is her forbidden fruit. Joseph's beauty tempts Potiphar's wife to look on Joseph in the same way as Eve covetously viewed the Edenic fruit, which was a delight to the eyes.[22] Daily, Potiphar's wife attempts to seduce Joseph, saying: "lie with me." With great moral restraint Joseph continually refuses her; acquiescing would constitute not only a betrayal of his master's trust but also a great sin against God. Undeterred by his moral fiber, she continues her advances — Joseph responds by *not* listening (ולא שמע, 39:10) to her, thus distinguishing himself from those before who, like Adam, fell precisely because they listened to the woman's voice. During the temptation, Adam and Eve are not separate, as Milton would have it; rather, Adam is described as being "with her" (עמה). By contrast, Joseph rejects Potiphar's wife's pursuit to the point of refusing to be "with her" (עמה).[23]

---

20. For ancient interpreters this episode was the central story of Joseph's life; see James Kugel, *Traditions of the Bible* (Cambridge: Harvard University Press, 1999), p. 442.

21. This interpretation is well attested in the tradition. See Michael Maher, *Targum Pseudo-Jonathan: Genesis* (Collegeville, Minn.: Liturgical Press, 1966), p. 130, and the rabbinic sources cited there in n. 7. Cf. Sarna, *Genesis*, p. 272.

22. Susan Brayford, *Genesis*, Septuagint Commentary Series (Boston: Brill, 2007), p. 403, observes how the LXX-G portrays Joseph as very beautiful but also as very ripe (ὡραῖος) in appearance. She concludes, "Joseph's appearance alludes to the 'ripe' (ὡραῖος) fruit in the primeval Garden (3:6)."

23. This preposition with a feminine singular suffix occurs only three times in Genesis: 3:6; 30:16; and 39:10.

One day when the house is empty,[24] however, she catches his garment and says, "lie with me"; he flees, leaving his garment in her hand. Adam broke God's command, but Joseph keeps his commandments, refusing to commit adultery (Exod. 20:14). Adam and Eve went from naked to clothed in the fall story; Joseph, in reverse, goes from clothed to naked. Adam and Eve's nakedness indicates their guilt; their nakedness is covered by God's provision of clothes. By contrast, Joseph's garment is used as material "evidence" in Potiphar's wife's accusations, which result in Joseph's imprisonment, mirroring the earlier deceptive use of Joseph's garment by his brothers. This adds an ironic twist to the story, since the reader knows the loss of Joseph's garment reveals his innocence because it makes clear the rapid nature of his flight from temptation. As he says, Joseph has done nothing to deserve being twice put into a pit (Gen. 40:15; cf. 37:20-28).[25] Reversing the significance of nakedness and clothing in the Eden story, Joseph's story flips the motif on its head — his nakedness indicates his innocence. Like Adam, Joseph is tempted, loses his position, and is judged; unlike Adam, Joseph does not yield to the temptation and is innocent of wrong. Joseph is *like* Adam and the others in fall stories in Genesis, yet he overcomes their folly.

Joseph not only succeeds where those before him failed, he surpasses in other areas as well. Noah's flood and Joseph's famine, threatening all the land, are analogous disasters. Both Noah and Joseph are warned by God of the coming disaster, gather food in preparation (6:21; 41:48-49), and are responsible for preserving the life of humans and animals on the land (6:19-20; 47:4, 17).[26] The ark delivers Noah's family from the flood's judgment, while Joseph's wise planning saves not only his family but also the whole earth from the devastating results of the famine (41:54-57).

Also, for the first time the family, torn apart at the story's beginning, is reconciled by the end. The conflict and division begun in the garden continue to characterize family relationships from Cain and Abel, to Ishmael and Isaac, and to Jacob and Esau. Joseph's story repeats many themes of the Cain and Abel episode, but as an intricate reversal of this brotherly tale and its tragic

---

24. It may be important that Adam and Eve were alone in the garden as Joseph is here with Potiphar's wife. Both God and Potiphar are not present during the temptation.

25. In my view Joseph's "bratty" behavior is often exaggerated, yet he certainly could have been wiser in his dealings with his brothers. His faults, even if they are significant, are not in proportion to the brothers' evil actions against him.

26. There are no linguistic similarities between the two episodes, but the situations are similar enough as to invite comparison.

outcome.[27] Joseph is nearly killed by his brothers; as with Abel there is a reckoning for his blood,[28] yet Joseph is not dead but alive in Egypt. Instead of taking revenge, Joseph patiently and wisely leads his brothers to repentance for their actions against him (well, at least Judah), uniting the family in Egypt.[29] When his brothers fear for their lives, he reassures them that God had other plans for their evil actions than they intended and it has turned out for the preservation of life. Finally, Joseph promises to care for his brothers and their children. Thus Joseph breaks Genesis's repeating story of family conflict.

The patriarchs were to be instrumental in spreading the blessings of creation to the nations, yet such hopes remain in the future for them; their lives are characterized instead by conflict with the nations. Lot receives compassion because of Abraham, and Laban is blessed due to Jacob's presence, but both of these individuals are part of Terah's family. Nevertheless, Jacob's situation in Laban's house is comparable to Joseph's situation in Potiphar's. Exiled from Canaan because of his brother's hatred, Jacob manages Laban's flocks, much like Joseph. As the Lord is with Jacob wherever he goes (28:15), so the Lord is with Joseph (39:2) causing all that either does to prosper (30:43; 39:2, 23). Laban and Potiphar are the only two characters in Genesis who realize that God has blessed (ברך) them on account of the one from Abraham's family serving in their house. Yet when Jacob leaves Laban he takes the blessings with him (31:1). In contrast, nothing reveals that Joseph's blessing on Potiphar is removed when he is cast into jail. Moreover, the episode in Potiphar's *house* foreshadows the greater blessing Joseph will be to the world (41:53-57) in Pharaoh's *house* (39:4; 41:40).[30] For the first time in Genesis, one of Abraham's seed is a blessing to the families of the earth!

In this manner Joseph restores, to a small degree, the blessings that Adam and Eve diminished in the garden. He provides food and preserves life on earth. Joseph is a picture of what Adam might have been, had he not succumbed to temptation. As such, Joseph is the most significant antitype of

---

27. For a more detailed explanation see Jon Levenson, *The Death and Resurrection of the Beloved Son* (New Haven: Yale University Press, 1993), pp. 143-68.

28. Reuben's words in Gen. 42:22 echo 9:5. Also, "blood" is a consistent word of choice in Gen. 1–11 and Gen. 37–50, but is not found in the patriarchal narratives.

29. Robert Alter, *The Art of Biblical Narrative* (New York: Basic Books, 1981), pp. 174-75, explains the adept way Joseph leads his brothers to repentance.

30. In both instances the Hebrew for "over the house" (Gen. 39:4: על ביתו; 41:40: על ביתי) is similar and limited to these two descriptions of Joseph's position. Also, the term "house" is a strange way to refer to Pharaoh's kingdom and unique to this instance, inviting a comparison between Joseph's rule in the two houses.

Adam in Genesis. Adam was to rule over the land, mirroring and extending God's own rule. Adam was to subdue the land and rule over the animals, but the serpent ruled over Adam. Though Abraham at times appears kingly (e.g., Gen. 14), none of the main characters in Genesis rule like this over the land, despite the expectation that kings will come from Abraham's seed (17:6; 35:11). This expectation is heightened in Genesis 36, which lists the kings of Edom who reigned "before any king reigned over the Israelites" (Gen. 36:31 NRSV).

The stage thus set, it is unsurprising that Joseph is presented in the next chapter as one who will reign over the sons of Israel. In every situation, Joseph is the ideal ruler. He rules over Potiphar's house, in jail, and finally over all Egypt, which due to the famine included all the land (41:57). Slavery and even imprisonment do not thwart Joseph's successful rule. In both situations everything is immediately placed under his control. Genesis is clear that Joseph succeeds not from innate ability but because the Lord is with him. Even Pharaoh recognizes that Joseph has a divine spirit and sets him over his entire kingdom. In each situation, Joseph exercises his rule under the authority of another: first Potiphar, then the chief jailer, and finally Pharaoh. He never usurps their authority; in the case of Potiphar he is especially conscientious not to violate his master's trust or transgress his command. Perhaps this indicates that Adam and Eve's disobedience to God's command involved mishandling their position as rulers *under* authority (cf. Ezek. 28). Significantly, by contrast, Joseph emphasizes to Potiphar's wife that his actions would constitute sin against God. Confronted with the cupbearer's and baker's dreams, Joseph prefaces his explanation by stating plainly that interpretations belong to God. Before Pharaoh, Joseph takes no credit for his ability to interpret dreams, repeatedly referring to God as the one who has revealed what is about to take place and who will quickly bring it about (Gen. 41:16, 25, 28, 32). Joseph is an ideal ruler.[31]

After Jacob's death, Joseph's brothers fear for their lives because of the

---

31. How can *Joseph* be the ideal ruler when it is from *Judah's* line that the scepter will not depart? In view of the messianic afterlife of Jacob's blessing on Judah, I suggest that Joseph is a type of the ruler to come from the line of Judah. As part of Judah's blessing in the latter days (Gen. 49:8c), Jacob says that the sons of Israel will bow down to Judah (ישתחוו לך בני אביך). This is similar to Jacob's words in response to Joseph's dreams: "Shall we indeed come, I and your mother and your brothers, and bow to the ground before you?" (37:10b) (הבוא נבוא אני ואמך ואחיך להשתחות). The image invoked by Joseph's dreams sets the stage for Joseph's rule, playing a central role in its culmination. Transferring this image to Judah's blessing may suggest that in the latter days a ruler will arise from Judah who will look like Joseph.

evil they did to Joseph. Again, Joseph clarifies that he is not in God's place, instead saying: "you intended evil against me, but God intended good in order to keep this day many people alive."[32] Joseph realizes that his brothers' evil, and, by extension, the evil done to him in Potiphar's house, brought about life for the world. The evil of Joseph's own fall story was necessary to preserve life on earth. As the culminating antitype to Adam in Genesis, Joseph's words form a theological interpretation of Adam's fall. The echoes of Eden in this passage reverberate back through Genesis explaining humanity's role and God's reason for the fall. Adam and Eve intended it for evil, but God intended it for good. In sum, Joseph resists temptation, living under the authority of God by ruling *for* him — not *instead* of him.[33] In a striking connection to the creation story, under Joseph, the blessing given to Adam finally begins: Israel is fruitful and multiplies (47:27).

Joseph and Jesus

Ancient readers and even some contemporary readers of Genesis have made much of Joseph as a type of Christ. Jon Levenson and Gary Anderson are two recent scholarly examples.[34] This typological framework can be strengthened by viewing Joseph as an antitype to Adam who does not succumb to the temptation of the fall and rules under the authority of God.[35] The relationship between Old Testament and New Testament is not one of type to antitype, but already in the Old Testament Joseph prepares the way, as an antitype to Adam, for the greater antitype, Jesus. In the Gospels, Jesus, while tempted like Adam (and Israel) passes the test (Matt. 4:1-11; Mark 1:12-

32. My translation throughout unless otherwise indicated.

33. Joseph is not guilty of the ruler of Tyre's pride (cf. Ezek. 28).

34. Levenson, *Death and Resurrection*, pp. 143-69, although he does not share the ontological attachment that Christians typically give to such readings; Gary Anderson, "Joseph and the Passion of Our Lord," in Ellen Davies and Richard Hays, eds., *The Art of Reading Scripture* (Grand Rapids: Eerdmans, 2003), pp. 198-215.

35. Adam-Christ typology is well established; see Leonhard Goppelt, *Typos: The Typological Interpretation of the Old Testament in the New*, trans. Donald H. Madvig (Grand Rapids: Eerdmans, 1982), pp. 129-36. Kristian Heal, "Joseph as a Type of Christ in the Syriac Literature," *BYU Studies* 41 (2002): 37, records how Narsai elaborated on the seduction of Potiphar's wife to include the murder of her husband and the promise to install Joseph as king and lord of the house if he will only sleep with her. This forms a direct comparison with the temptation of Jesus in Matt. 4 and Luke 4. More importantly, after praising Joseph for his resistance to temptation, Narsai says, "The Chief of the Air hid a snare for you by the agency of Eve."

13; Luke 4:1-13) and rules as one under the authority of God the Father. In this manner, Jesus undoes the folly of Adam; then, through his death and resurrection, he puts the creational project back on track, albeit significantly refigured (Matt. 28:16-20; John 20:21-23).

Like the other Gospels, Luke stresses Jesus' fulfillment of *all* Scripture.[36] In Luke–Acts Jesus is the Messiah, the son of David, and in the tradition of the prophets of old like Elijah and Elisha, he is the prophet greater than Moses.[37] Where is Adam in all of this? With Luke's focus on God's plan to bring salvation to all, first Jew and then Gentile, and a genealogy for Jesus extending back to Adam, a more pronounced Adam-Christ typology in Luke might be expected. After all, the genealogy climaxed by Adam as the son of God directly precedes Jesus' temptation in Luke 4. Though Luke 4:1-13 may contain general echoes of the serpent's temptation of Eve and Adam, the main thrust of the passage foregrounds a comparison between Israel wandering in the wilderness for forty years and Jesus in the wilderness for forty days being tempted by the devil. Jesus, in his obedience to the Scriptures, succeeds where Israel, constantly disobeying God in the wilderness, failed. In Luke 4 Jesus symbolically embodies Israel's story, but also overturns it. Luke certainly presents Jesus' story in Luke–Acts as a "continuation of biblical history,"[38] but at the same time as its reversal. Luke views Jesus' relationship to Adam as one of reversal as well, but for a story portraying Jesus in comparison to Adam, one must wait until the climactic moment in Luke's Gospel when Jesus reveals himself to the disciples after his resurrection.

In Luke 24 the risen Christ makes clear that everything written about him in the Scriptures must be fulfilled. The chapter, however, is relatively empty of allusions to the Old Testament, making any that remain stand out. After explaining the Scriptures to the two travelers coming from Jerusalem, Jesus stays with them, taking part in a meal. With allusions to Genesis 3:6-7, this first meal after the resurrection reverses the first meal of Adam and Eve in Eden. During it Jesus *takes*, blesses, breaks, and *gives* the bread to his disciples and then their *eyes are opened* and they *know* him (Luke 24:29-32).[39] Af-

---

36. I am grateful to Christopher Hays, who gave me several suggestions on this portion of the essay.

37. Beverly Roberts Gaventa, "Learning and Relearning the Identity of Jesus from Luke–Acts," in Beverly Roberts Gaventa and Richard B. Hays, eds., *Seeking the Identity of Jesus: A Pilgrimage* (Grand Rapids: Eerdmans, 2008), pp. 157-59.

38. Joseph Fitzmyer, *The Gospel According to Luke I–IX*, AB (Garden City, N.Y.: Doubleday, 1981), p. 92.

39. The echoes of Gen. 3:6-7 in the passage are unmistakable. Compare the Old Greek

ter taking the forbidden fruit, Adam and Eve knew their nakedness — indicating that they had acquired knowledge of good and evil. Contrastingly, the disciples' eyes are opened (διηνοίχθησαν) to the identity of the risen Jesus the moment he breaks the bread. This new knowledge is grounded in a scriptural understanding of Christ since Jesus had opened (διήνοιγεν) the scriptures (24:32) prior to the meal and in his next appearance he opens (διήνοιξεν) their minds to understand the same scriptures (24:45).[40] In the garden it was the word of God that Adam and Eve disobeyed; here Jesus reveals that his death and resurrection fulfill the Scriptures. Jesus' undoing of the fall narrative in Luke finds analogy in the Joseph narrative. Joseph's reversal of the fall anticipates Jesus' greater and final reversal of the folly of Adam. This reversal realigns God's creational plan for the world so that "repentance and forgiveness of sins should be proclaimed in his name to all nations, beginning from Jerusalem" (Luke 24:47 ESV).

This plan unfolds in Acts through the work of Jesus' Spirit; this should not be characterized as a period of "Jesus' absence but of his presence in a new and more powerful way."[41] Through the power of the Holy Spirit, Jesus' witnesses preach and heal "in his name."[42] This unfolds according to Luke's constant attention to the theological implications of geography. In Luke, Jesus' work is oriented in relationship to approach and entry into Jerusalem; in Acts, as is well known, the book carefully tracks Jesus' followers, empowered by the Holy Spirit, as they witness "in Jerusalem, and in all Judea, and Samaria and to the ends of the earth" (Acts 1:8b ESV). Luke sums up the spread of the Christian mission at key points in his narrative, speaking of it as being fruitful (ηὔξανεν) and multiplying (ἐπληθύνετο). In Acts 6:7 the "word of God was *fruitful* and *multiplied* the number of disciples greatly in Jerusalem"; in Acts 9:31 the church in all Judea, Galilee, and Samaria *multiplied;* in

---

of Gen. 3:6-7: καὶ <u>λαβοῦσα</u> τοῦ καρποῦ αὐτοῦ ἔφαγεν καὶ <u>ἔδωκεν</u> καὶ τῷ ἀνδρὶ αὐτῆς μετ' αὐτῆς καὶ ἔφαγον. Καὶ <u>διηνοίχθησαν</u> οἱ ὀφθαλμοὶ τῶν δύο καὶ <u>ἔγνωσαν</u> ὅτι γυμνοὶ ἦσαν, and Luke 24:30-31: μετ' αὐτῶν <u>λαβὼν</u> τὸν ἄρτον εὐλόγησεν καὶ κλάσας <u>ἐπέδιδου</u> αὐτοῖς. Αὐτῶν δὲ <u>διηνοίχθησαν</u> οἱ ὀπθαλμοὶ καὶ <u>ἐπέγνωσαν</u> αὐτόν. The combination of διανοίγω, ὀφθαλμός, and γινώσκω occurs only in these two passages in the Old and New Testament combined. N. T. Wright makes this same connection in *The Resurrection of the Son of God* (Minneapolis: Fortress, 2003), p. 652. The words "take," "bless," "break," and "give" also form an inner-textual echo of the feeding of the five thousand (Luke 9:16). On this see Joel B. Green, *The Gospel of Luke*, NICNT (Grand Rapids: Eerdmans, 1997), p. 849.

40. Green, *Luke*, p. 850.

41. Luke Timothy Johnson, *The Writings of the New Testament: An Interpretation* (London: SCM, 1986), p. 223; Gaventa, "Learning," pp. 161-63.

42. Johnson, *Writings*, p. 222.

Acts 12:24 "the word of God was *fruitful and multiplied,*" in the midst of persecution and the spread of the gospel to the Gentiles; in Acts 19:20, while Paul is in Ephesus, the "word of the Lord continued to be *fruitful* and prevailed mightily."[43] Throughout Acts the spread of God's word is virtually synonymous with the increase of the disciples.[44] This language describing the spread of the Christian mission occurs consistently in Acts, but is limited to Acts in the New Testament. Why does Luke use this language? Luke is aware that during Joseph's time in Egypt Israel was fruitful and multiplied (Acts 7:17), which may influence his terminology, but the textual background is probably better located in Adam's commission in Genesis 1:28. Adam was blessed or, as some argue, commanded to be fruitful, multiply, and fill the earth; as noted above, the first time this takes place is in Joseph's days. Jesus' first resurrection meal reverses the meal in Eden; as biblical history continues unwinding, the coming of the Spirit in Acts 2 reverses the story of Babel;[45] from this point on, the gospel spreads from Jerusalem to fill the earth. This reversal of Israel's history is not without significant setbacks, where the church repeats Israel's folly, not least Acts 5, which can be read as a typological repeat of the fall story and/or Achan's debacle in the book of Joshua.[46]

Adam-Christ typology appears to influence Luke's account of the work of Jesus in Luke–Acts. While Adam is surely but one thread in Luke's typological cord — alongside Moses, Elijah, Israel, and others — he is a significant thread. Whether Joseph's reversal of Adam's folly shapes Luke's typological account is unclear. Nevertheless, regardless of influence, Joseph's reversal of the fall prepares the way for Jesus' final reversal that puts back on track God's creational purpose to fill the earth with his image. As an interpretation of the fall, Joseph's words at the end of Genesis in the fuller scriptural context take on added significance. Adam intended it for evil, but God intended it for good, that through the death and resurrection of Christ, the last Adam, he might redeem fallen humanity, filling the earth with his disciples.

---

43. On the spread of the gospel see also Acts 2:47 and 16:5.

44. Johnson, *Writings,* p. 214.

45. Although this reading has its detractors, it is well attested in modern commentaries and ancient sources.

46. Daniel Marguerat, *The First Christian Historian,* trans. Ken McKiney, Gregory Laughery, and Richard Bauckham (Cambridge: Cambridge University Press, 2002), pp. 155-78.

"Before Abraham Was, I Am":
The Book of Genesis and the Genesis of Christology

Knut Backhaus

> *No retrospect will take us to the true beginning; and whether our prologue be in heaven or on earth, it is but a fraction of that all-presupposing fact with which our story sets out.*
>
> George Eliot, *Daniel Deronda*

Survey

At first sight the book of Genesis is quoted comparatively rarely in the New Testament literature. Further examination shows that it plays a crucial role in the development of Christology, in that it presents to the early Christians the primordial base of being, salvation history, and hope. For as long as these core themes were not integrated, Christology would not have reached its target, so that the Christian *relecture* of the Bible would remain nothing but some embarrassing sort of "reading other people's mail."[1]

---

1. The phrase is borrowed from Paul Van Buren, "On Reading Someone Else's Mail: The Church and Israel's Scriptures," in Erhard Blum, Christian Macholz, and Ekkehard W. Stegemann, eds., *Die Hebräische Bibel und ihre zweifache Nachgeschichte: Festschrift Rolf Rendtorff* (Neukirchen-Vluyn: Neukirchener Verlag, 1990), pp. 595-606.

I am much indebted to my Munich colleague Professor Alexander J. M. Wedderburn for checking my English.

The overall number of thirty-one direct quotations from the Greek Genesis in the New Testament seems indeed amazingly small, at least when seen against Psalms or Isaiah, which constitute what may be called the biblical horizon of the New Testament literature.[2] In contrast, it may come as no surprise that the Abraham cycle is the focus of New Testament writers, that Genesis 2:24 and 15:6 are the most often cited passages,[3] and that Romans 4 and 9,[4] Galatians 3 and 4,[5] and the book of Hebrews[6] show the most frequent use of Genesis. The significance of a biblical book is, of course, broader than quotations will reveal. We may be sure that wherever the great leitmotifs of creation, fall, promise, and destination are brought up or one of the heroes and patriarchs of old is dealt with, Genesis is, in one way or another, involved. However, the nature of such involvement is hard to trace.[7] We must always take into consideration that — even in the case of direct quotations — there is no purely literary relationship between the New Testament and "its Bible" but a complex interaction of biblical intertexts, their

---

2. Synoptic Gospels: 3 quotations; John: 1; Acts: 4; Romans: 7; 1 Corinthians: 2; Galatians: 4; Ephesians: 1; Hebrews: 7; James: 1; Revelation: 1. Sometimes a quotation refers to an intertext that is multiply represented in Genesis or it may be composed of several Genesis passages. Moreover, the boundaries between citations and other forms of references (e.g., "allusions") are not always clear-cut.

3. Gen. 2:24 = Matt. 19:5/Mark 10:7; 1 Cor. 6:16; Eph. 5:31; Gen. 15:6 = Rom. 4:3, 23; Gal. 3:6; Jas. 2:23.

4. Rom. 4:3 = Gen. 15:6; Rom. 4:17 = Gen. 17:5; Rom. 4:18 = Gen. 15:5; Rom. 4:23 = Gen. 15:6; Rom. 9:7 = Gen. 21:12; Rom. 9:9 = Gen. 18:10, 14; Rom. 9:12 = Gen. 25:23.

5. Gal. 3:6 = Gen. 15:6; Gal. 3:8 = Gen. 12:3; 18:18; Gal. 3:16 = Gen. 13:15; 17:8; 24:7; Gal. 4:30 = Gen. 21:10.

6. Heb. 4:4 = Gen. 2:2; Heb. 6:14 = Gen. 22:17; Heb. 7:1-2 = Gen. 14:17-20; Heb. 7:4 = Gen. 14:20; Heb. 11:18 = Gen. 21:12; Heb. 11:21 = Gen. 47:31; Heb. 13:5 = Gen. 28:15.

7. A more general approach that focuses on Gen. 1–4 with the canonical motifs of creation, fall, curse, and promise is taken by Paul S. Minear, *Christians and the New Creation: Genesis Motifs in the New Testament* (Louisville: Westminster John Knox, 1994); see also Peter C. Bouteneff, *Beginnings: Ancient Christian Readings of the Biblical Creation Narratives* (Grand Rapids: Baker Academic, 2008), pp. 33-54. On OT actors on the NT stage see Markus Öhler, ed., *Alttestamentliche Gestalten im Neuen Testament: Beiträge zur biblischen Theologie* (Darmstadt: WBG, 1999): the genealogies (Robert Oberforcher, pp. 5-26); Adam (Michael Ernst, pp. 27-39); Cain and Abel, Enoch and Noah (Wolfram Uebele, pp. 40-53); Abraham (Josef Pichler, pp. 54-74); Isaac, Jacob, Esau, Joseph (Hermut Löhr, pp. 75-96); Sarah and Hagar, Rebekah, Rachel (Marianne Grohmann, pp. 97-116). A subject that deserves closer investigation is the possible background of the *Akedah* (Gen. 22:1-19) in Mark 1:9-11 (and parallels), Rom. 8:31-32, and Heb. 11:17-19; for a general overview in the context of the canonical approach, see Brevard S. Childs, *Biblical Theology of the Old and New Testaments: Theological Reflection on the Christian Bible* (Minneapolis: Fortress, 1993), pp. 325-36.

conventional early Jewish modes of understanding and application, and the specific horizon of the New Testament writer. Thus, on the one hand, where a particular subject that Genesis deals with is at stake, there may be perhaps merely a vague cultural remembrance of its locus classicus in the Tanakh. On the other hand, some subjects are not mentioned in Genesis at all but are associated with it in later strata of tradition, such as Satan, who would merge with the serpent of Eden in his early Jewish career.

In general, the New Testament writers show a vivid interest in rooting the Christ event deeply within Israel's immemorial history reaching back to the archaic beginnings in the first book of the Bible. The genealogies in Luke and Matthew trace Jesus back to his Genesis roots, and Paul does not hesitate to turn the offspring of God's blessing to Abraham into a Christological singular (cf. Gal. 3:16). Frequently, Genesis serves to give a certain biblical undertone to a line of thought in order to make it more plausible. The *relecture* of the New Testament writers proves overall to be no less creative than that of their Jewish contemporaries, and it is far from uniform. The most striking example, of course, is Genesis 15:6, where we see Abraham enacting righteousness by "justice of faith" for Paul (Rom. 4:3, 22-23; Gal. 3:6) and "justice by works" for James (Jas. 2:23) (my trans.). Doubtless the really interesting case is where Genesis has inspired an entire theological discourse. In my view, this is the case with the Christological model of preexistence with regard to which Genesis has exerted its influence on the three major theologians of the New Testament: Paul, John, and the author of Hebrews.

In a devotional manner, we may say that John has christened Abraham, Hebrews has christened Melchizedek, and Paul has christened Adam. In a less devotional manner, we may say that they have swallowed them. Then we cannot but ask (with Stanisław Lec): "Is the cannibal entitled to speak in the name of those he has eaten?" The answer, "Yes, if the cannibal is a Christian," may seem a bit unrealistic. The canonical approach tends instead to speak of a dialogue between the Old and New Testaments. With respect to cannibals, however, it is not without danger to speak of dialogue when we mean digestion. So let us take a closer look into the hermeneutical jungle. We start with John.

A Heavenly Ladder: Genesis in the Fourth Gospel

In the Septuagint, the book of Genesis starts with the phrase Ἐν ἀρχῇ ("in the beginning"). It seems hard to imagine that it is just by chance that the

Fourth Gospel begins in the same bold way. Rather this very beginning is intended to signalize by connotation: *Introite, nam et hic Biblia sunt* ("Enter, for here too is the Bible")![8] The noun ἀρχή, however, does not denote the same thing in both cases. In Genesis it refers to the cosmological beginning of the created world, while in John it denotes the ontological origin of all being. In a scriptural mode Genesis, so to speak, demarcates the primeval beginnings of being and the theological scope beyond which creational beginnings end and eternal origins remain. Therefore, on a deeper level the connotation runs: "Behold, something greater than any creation, any 'genesis,' is here!"

We note that the reference to the first book of the Bible, as the very first impression the Gospel gives, will determine the whole horizon of the readers' understanding. It opens the Johannine prologue, which initiates the reader mystagogically into the eternal provenance of the Word, λόγος, dealing with his participation in creation, his self-revelation, and his redemptive work. In the *inclusio* of the prologue as well as in the *inclusio* of the whole narrative corpus, Christ is called "God" (John 1:1, 18; 20:28). It is made clear from the beginning what this predication means: divine provenance, "God from God as light from light" (cf. Philo, *Somn.* 1.229-30, 239-41, on Gen. 31:13).[9] So, as in Job or, following that scheme, Goethe's *Faust*, the prelude provides the reader with a margin of knowledge. In contrast to the actors in

---

8. On the quasi-canonical self-enactment of the Fourth Gospel, cf. Thomas Söding, "Die Schrift als Medium des Glaubens: Zur hermeneutischen Bedeutung von John 20,30f," in Knut Backhaus and Franz Georg Untergaßmair, eds., *Schrift und Tradition: Festschrift Josef Ernst* (Paderborn: Schöningh, 1996), pp. 343-71. For an evaluation of the motif of preexistence in John, see Jürgen Habermann, "Präexistenzchristologische Aussagen im Johannesevangelium: Annotationes zu einer angeblich 'verwegenen Synthese,'" in Rudolf Laufen, ed., *Gottes ewiger Sohn: Die Präexistenz Christi* (Paderborn: Schöningh, 1997), pp. 115-41. For a detailed assessment of the Christologoumenon in NT literature, see Jürgen Habermann, *Präexistenzaussagen im Neuen Testament*, Europäische Hochschulschriften XXIII/362 (Frankfurt am Main: Peter Lang, 1990). The possible background of John 1:1-18 in early Jewish creation traditions is explored by Masanobu Endo, *Creation and Christology: A Study on the Johannine Prologue in the Light of Early Jewish Creation Accounts*, WUNT II/149 (Tübingen: Mohr Siebeck, 2002).

9. For further discussion see William S. Kurz, "Intertextual Permutations of the Genesis Word in the Johannine Prologue," in Craig A. Evans and James A. Sanders, eds., *Early Christian Interpretation of the Scriptures of Israel: Investigations and Proposals*, JSNTSup 148 (Sheffield: Sheffield Academic Press, 1997), pp. 179-90, esp. 181-82; John Painter, "Rereading Genesis in the Prologue of John?" in David Edward Aune, Torrey Seland, and Jarl Henning Ulrichsen, eds., *Neotestamentica et Philonica: Festschrift Peder Borgen* (Leiden: Brill, 2003), pp. 179-201.

the narrated world, he or she will know who the main character really is. In the prologue, thus, Genesis forms the archaic base from which the reader may throw a glance at the perpetual light before all times. It is John the Baptist who testifies to this true light: "He who comes after me ranks ahead of me because he was before me" (John 1:15; cf. 1:6-8).[10]

No later than in the home stretch of the same chapter do we come across the first and only direct quotation from Genesis in John. Nathanael is identified as a true Israelite searching for the Messiah in Moses and the prophets. He is overwhelmed by what Jesus intrinsically knows about him, and he seems to realize that he now perceives "the Son of God, . . . the King of Israel," as he in turn was perceived by him (cf. Ps. 139:1-7). But Jesus indicates — not only to his various disciples present with him, but also to his later disciples reading this passage — that something greater than knowledge lies ahead: "you will see heaven opened and the angels of God ascending and descending upon the Son of Man" (John 1:51).

It is impossible to overlook the reference to Jacob's dream of the heavenly ladder at Bethel here (cf. Gen. 28:12).[11] Nevertheless, it is now "the Son of Man" who turns out to be the "house of God" and the "gate of heaven" (28:17), and this all the more so since the next chapter will reveal what the temple really means: "Destroy this temple, and in three days I will raise it up" (John 2:19). Christ is the place where God dwells and where humans may encounter him. To know about that means to know about Christ's provenance. The patriarch's archaic God-experience literally becomes flesh with Christ.

Jacob contributes another significant setting: it is his well at the foot of Mount Gerizim where Jesus guides the Samaritan woman "to worship in spirit and truth" (John 4:24). Their exchange is the most intense dialogue offered by the Fourth Gospel, and Jesus again reveals some mystifying personal knowledge. "Are you greater than our ancestor Jacob?" the woman asks, somewhat surprisingly (John 4:12). The reader already knows the implicit answer: "Behold, a greater than Jacob is here." Worship in spirit and truth includes the personal interrelation between the worshiper and Christ in the eternal realm. Once again, Genesis draws the archaic scenery that makes it the more relevant to ask after Christ's origin. It is this "Where is this man from?" that so often bewilders the actants in John (e.g., 7:25-29). We, on

10. All biblical quotations are from the NRSV unless otherwise noted.

11. On the most vivid reception of this story in ancient Judaism, see James L. Kugel, *The Ladder of Jacob: Ancient Interpretations of the Biblical Story of Jacob and His Children* (Princeton: Princeton University Press, 2006), pp. 9-35.

the other hand, are not bewildered to learn that this question is again settled on the forum of the book of Genesis. Jesus' provenance is an issue of life and death discussed between the Revealer and the "Jews," who represent the godless κόσμος in John. It is at this juncture that the Johannine Jesus rebukes those who flatter themselves by claiming to be descendants of Abraham for being descendants of the devil instead: "You are from your father the devil, and you choose to do your father's desires. He was a murderer from the beginning and does not stand in the truth, because there is no truth in him. When he lies, he speaks according to his own nature, for he is a liar and the father of lies" (8:44).

This is probably the harshest anti-Jewish statement of the New Testament and obviously alludes to the scene of seduction in Eden (Gen. 3; cf. Wis. 2:24).[12] But once more Genesis echoes not so much past beginnings as present origins. That is, the origins of darkness and death are contrasted with the Revealer himself, who originates from light and life (cf. John 1:1-18). The question asked by the "Jews," meanwhile, sounds familiar: "Abraham died, and so did the prophets; yet you say, 'Whoever keeps my word will never taste death.' Are you greater than our father Abraham, who died?" (8:52-53). Jesus' answer is both indirect and unambiguous: "'Your ancestor Abraham rejoiced that he would see my day; he saw it and was glad.' Then the Jews said to him, 'You are not yet fifty years old, and have you seen Abraham?' Jesus said to them, 'Very truly, I tell you, before Abraham was, I am'" (8:56-58).

In a sense, Genesis serves to illustrate that Jesus is older than fifty years of age, as the notoriously "cosmic" misunderstanding takes it to mean. In light of the prologue, the readers know that Jesus is immemorially old, because he ever has been. He will not taste death forever, for he is incarnation of life. His combatants, representing all those who are born blind in the deepest sense (cf. John 9:39-41), will never come to see the "light from light." They do know, however, that after this self-disclosure the stakes could not be higher: "So they picked up stones to throw at him, but Jesus hid himself and went out of the temple" (8:59) — in order to be, as the reader knows, the temple in person.

In sum, the book of Genesis and Abraham serve here to open the perspective for the eternal origins of Christ.

---

12. See Rudolf Schnackenburg, *The Gospel according to St. John,* trans. Kevin Smyth et al., 3 vols. (New York: Crossroad, 1968-1982), 2:213-15; George R. Beasley Murray, *John,* WBC (Waco, Tex.: Word, 1987), p. 135.

Priesthood and Faith: Genesis in Hebrews

Here I can offer only a few brief remarks. First, more than any other New Testament book, Hebrews is characterized by the Christological motif of preexistence, which begins right from the scriptural catena in the first chapter.[13] However, it is not until the central part of Hebrews that Genesis plays its Christological role. In chapter 7 the story of Melchizedek (Gen. 14:17-20) is retold in a somewhat inventive reading: *Quod non est in Tora, non est in mundo* ("what is not in the Torah does not exist"), and since Genesis does not happen to mention father, mother, ancestors, the beginning or the end of his life, Melchizedek proves to be without any earthly provenance or limitation and thus "resembles the Son of God, remaining a priest forever" (cf. Heb. 7:1-3). What is more, he even blesses the patriarch; and Abraham for his part gives tithes to Melchizedek, thereby prefiguring the Levitical priesthood in its inferiority to the eternal priest "according to the order of Melchizedek." So Genesis 14, combined with Psalm 110:4 ("You are a priest forever according to the order of Melchizedek"), the only other Old Testament verse hinting at this enigmatic priest-king, helps the author of Hebrews to take the Levitical priesthood off its hinges. Without fostering any interest in Melchizedek as such, he eventually has a biblical prototype or, to say it more accurately, a vertical archetype that allows him to establish the high priesthood of Christ, which in fact has preceded the whole priesthood of Mount Sinai because Melchizedek's order is nothing but the order of eternity.

Second, the famous and powerful "tract on faith" in Hebrews 11 shows us a long procession of the Old Testament "pilgrim fathers and mothers," beginning with Abel and ending with more recent Jewish martyrs. It is the book of Genesis that enriches this chapter with the most, and the most impressive, images of the old heroes' hope and desire: Abel, Enoch, Noah, Abraham, Sarah, Isaac, Jacob, and Joseph — most of them dying, all of them believing, each of them a true wanderer through earthly deserts looking out for a better country, that is, a heavenly one: "Therefore God is not ashamed to be called their God; indeed, he has prepared a city for them" (11:16). Gratefully, we may note that this "Ode to Faith" is that part of the New Testament in which Genesis has its classical entry on the stage of Christianity. It is,

---

13. For analysis and interpretation see Knut Backhaus, "'Licht vom Licht': Die Präexistenz Christi im Hebräerbrief," in Laufen, ed., *Gottes ewiger Sohn*, pp. 95-114: Otfried Hofius, "Biblische Theologie im Lichte des Hebräerbriefes," in Sigfred Pedersen, ed., *New Directions in Biblical Theology: Papers of the Aarhus Conference, 16-19 September 1992*, NovTSup 76 (Leiden: Brill, 1994), pp. 108-25.

moreover, doubtless the most "intertestamentary" chapter of the whole Bible. Nevertheless, the heroes of Genesis are not perfected without us, as we — so may we add — are not perfected without them. It is Christ, "the pioneer and perfecter of faith," who is to be seen through "so great a cloud of witnesses" from all times. As a human being, he is one of the believers in the chain of faith, but as the eternal Son, "the same yesterday and today and forever" (13:8), he belongs to "the realization of what is hoped for and evidence of things not seen" (11:1 NAB).[14] From the point of view taken by Hebrews, Christ is not only a member of what Augustine calls the *ecclesia ab Abel* ("church from Abel"), but also, surprisingly enough, a main character in the book of Genesis.

A Human Ground: Genesis in the Pauline Letters

Paul's image of Christ centers on the cross and resurrection, not on the provenance of the Lord. It is the *pro*-existence of Christ rather than his *pre*-existence that preoccupies the apostle. But to consistently bear out his soteriology Paul needs the premise of the Savior's heavenly origin (cf. Rom. 8:3-4; 2 Cor. 8:9; Gal. 4:4-5).[15] Far from being a meteorite from lonely skies, Pauline Christology shares the horizon of understanding with Hellenistic Christianity, as it has developed before, beside, and after Paul. How important the preexistence motif was for the early Christological approach — especially within the scheme of descent, incarnation, and ascension — is illustrated in the poetic mode rather than in the narrower field of speculation, though we should add at once that New Testament poetry is the text type that has generated part and parcel of the church's Christology in the age that was to come. Both the Philippians hymn (Phil. 2:6-11) quoted by Paul and

---

14. The concept of faith in Hebrews is, to be sure, a theocentric one, but since God has created the world through the Son and defined himself once and for all in the Christ event (cf. 1:1-4), Christology is but the other side of the theocentric coin.

15. The passages cited are brief and not beyond dispute. For a comprehensive reappraisal see Thomas Söding, "Gottes Sohn von Anfang an: Zur Präexistenzchristologie bei Paulus und den Deuteropaulinen," in Laufen, ed., *Gottes ewiger Sohn*, pp. 57-93. A different (in my view, less plausible) interpretation dispensing with the motif of personal preexistence is argued for by James D. G. Dunn, *Christology in the Making: A New Testament Inquiry into the Origins of the Doctrine of the Incarnation*, 2nd ed. (London: SCM, 1989), esp. pp. 113-28; idem, *The Theology of Paul the Apostle* (Grand Rapids: Eerdmans, 1998), pp. 266-93.

the Colossians hymn (Col. 1:15-20) are the most distinct examples of this Christological trajectory. At least Colossians is perhaps inspired by Genesis (cf. 1 Cor. 8:6) and certainly pushes forward to the theological ground held by Genesis in order to plant the Christological flag there: "He is the image [cf. Gen. 1:26] of the invisible God, the firstborn of all creation; for in him all things in heaven and on earth were created, things visible and invisible" (Col. 1:15-16). Some have even argued (though, to my mind, not convincingly) that there is a sort of Adam-Christ speculation in the background of the Philippians hymn.

At any rate, it is sure that Paul, while utilizing the Abraham tradition as far as his theology of justification is concerned, presupposes some sort of "ecumenical" Adam tradition in matters of Christology (1 Cor. 15:20-28, 42-49; Rom. 5:12-21; cf. also the covert paradisiacal scene in Mark 1:12-13). The function of Genesis in this respect is to broaden the scope beyond any ethnic, social, and religious boundary by transcending to the forefather of all humankind, thereby dodging even the gap between the Jews and the pagans.[16] The goal Paul pursues with the Adam-Christ typology is, to be sure, an eschatological one. Nevertheless, the first man, who *was* of dust from the earth, mirrors the second man, who *is* from heaven: "Just as we have borne the image of the man of dust, we will also bear the image of the man of heaven" (1 Cor. 15:49). To appreciate the heavenly Son and his work of salvation, Christians then are expected to read the first book of their Bible. Genesis provides soteriology and eschatology with both their anthropological base and a sort of preconceptualization of Christ. To understand redemption we must understand creation, and to understand creation we must read Genesis.

Conclusions

First, in a general way (which is hard to control in particular), the book of Genesis serves to provide New Testament literature with *knowledge of provenance,* an immemorial history, biblical ancestry, a specific cultural background, and the great leitmotifs of creation, fall, promise, and destination.

---

16. For closer analysis see Deborah F. Sawyer, "The New Adam in the Typology of St Paul," in Paul Morris and Deborah Sawyer, eds., *A Walk in the Garden: Biblical, Iconographical and Literary Images of Eden,* JSOTSup 136 (Sheffield: Sheffield Academic Press, 1992), pp. 105-16.

Second, the New Testament writers make infrequent but vivid use of the book of Genesis. We cannot identify a specific (overall) method of interpretation (e.g., "typology" or *Heilsgeschichte*), but rather see a certain consciousness of being "at home" in this book, of "dwelling" between its lines. From the early Christian point of view, this book does not treat past beginnings but ever-present origins seen in the light of the Christ event. Genesis is not an interesting book for learned discussion. It is a mirror of early Christian self-experience. Christ is in the center of this experience. Thus he is in the center of Genesis. It is this pivotal experience that allows a *creative relecture*. Christ, so to speak, occupies the hermeneutic center of the cognitive universe. In this manner he becomes an invisible but decisive "third man" between the book of Genesis and its early Christian readers.

Third, we are not to confuse such a Christologically inventive reading with hermeneutical arbitrariness. What we have observed is a hermeneutic triad of *rooting, comparing, and relating:* (a) The New Testament writers anchor their own belief system on the biblical foundation (the rhetorical figure of ancient lineage). (b) They use Genesis as a broad framework to demonstrate that "behold, a greater than Abraham, Jacob, Abel, creation is here," thereby stepping down to the realm beyond all beginnings (the rhetorical figure of *synkrisis*). (c) Above all, they read Genesis to establish coherence with the greater drama God scheduled ἐν ἀρχῇ (the rhetorical figure of theocentric consistency): It is the Creator Genesis deals with who has defined himself in Christ, and it is not possible to understand the redemptive work of Christ in any other relationship.

Fourth, we have focused our attention on the Christological motif of preexistence, in regard to which the three major theologians of the New Testament — Paul, John, and the author of Hebrews — show remarkable interest in Genesis as a platform to develop what we may call fundamental Christology.

In John, Genesis invokes the foretimes and forms the biblical edge that the reader needs to surpass the foretimes and to look into the bottomless deep of eternity, only to retrieve Christ there. The first book of the Bible is the authority that demonstrates that Jesus is above all religious boundaries and historical developments.

In Hebrews, Genesis — or, rather, what Genesis does not tell: its indeterminate sections or gaps — presents the archetype of a priesthood above time as well as the believers of old who bear testimony to the heavenly land of promise, thereby paving the way to Jesus as both the pioneer of faith and the personal bridge to that land.

In Paul (apart from the Abraham tradition, which inspires his message of justification), Abel forms the model of undivided humankind, which is fulfilled, restored, and redeemed in Christ.

In short, in Paul Genesis provides the human and worldwide ground for Christ, in Hebrews it provides a heavenly perspective on his work of salvation, and in John it provides the eternal origins of his being.

Thus, fifth, our opening metaphor turns out to be a bit unsatisfactory: there is certainly no "dialogue" between the New Testament and Genesis, but there is more than a process of cannibalic digestion. Rather, the New Testament writers pull apart the letters to enter the jungle behind, only to find Christ there. They share this primordial ground with other biblical inhabitants. This has been the cause of many hermeneutical fights in the past, but this is also the best *precondition for a dialogue* — not of books, but of literary neighbors reading a book "about that all-presupposing fact" with which our story sets out.

Genesis 2–3:
A Case of Inner-Biblical Interpretation

Christoph Levin

The biblical story about paradise and the fall was already subject to interpretation in biblical times. As everywhere in the Bible, the present text shows many traces of textual growth or, we might say, signs of a *Wirkungsgeschichte* that is part of the biblical tradition itself. "Sacra scriptura sui ipsius interpres" — "Holy Scripture is self-interpreting," and this is true even in terms of literary history. If we can talk about the biblical text's final shape at all — which may be doubted in view of the divergences within the textual tradition — then this shape is for the most part unintentional; it has rather grown out of many later ideas based on and added to an already existing text. The idea that the present text is the outcome of a deliberate redactional shaping is not only unnecessary; it is certainly wrong. Canonicity is not primarily the end result of the Bible's history; from the very beginning it provided the necessary condition for the development of the biblical text. In the light of literary history, what Erich Zenger calls "the final shape as theological concept"[1] is an error that brings theological hermeneutics to a dead end. Abraham Kuenen in 1886 rightly stated: "The redaction of the Hexateuch, then, assumes the form of a continuous diaskeuē or diorthōsis, and the redactor becomes a collective body headed by the scribe who united the two

---

1. Erich Zenger, Heinz-Josef Fabry, and Georg Braulik, *Einleitung in das Alte Testament,* 2nd ed. (Stuttgart: Kohlhammer, 1996), p. 34.

Thanks to Margaret Kohl for translating this essay into English.

Christoph Levin

works . . . into a single whole, but also including the whole series of his more or less independent followers."[2] In St. Andrews it is appropriate to remember the late Professor William McKane and his famous concept of the "rolling corpus," a concept shared to some degree by Professor Robert P. Carroll of Glasgow University (who died much too early).[3] This is true not only of the book of Jeremiah, on which both these scholars worked; it applies to the whole of biblical literature.

The following observations about the story of paradise and the fall cannot cover the whole development of today's text. They are confined to four topics: (1) the earliest discernible form of the narrative, and its relationship to the mythologies of the ancient Near East; (2) the fundamental anthropological viewpoints; (3) the nature of sin; (4) the question about the origin of mortality and the possibility of eternal life.

The Earliest Form of the Narrative

The text shows the existence of different literary strata. For this assertion it may be sufficient to draw attention to the most important clue. The man's reaction after God has hurled his curse at him is quite incomprehensible: "By the sweat of your face you shall eat bread until you return to the ground, for out of it you were taken; you are dust, and to dust you shall return. And the man named his wife Eve, because she was the mother of all who live" (3:19-20). Julius Wellhausen pinpointed the paradox: "After 3:19 we should expect to find the man distressed and cast down, waiting to see what else God is going to do with him . . . instead he takes the opportunity to name his wife Eve, for which there was really no occasion at this point."[4]

Wellhausen got over the unevenness by excluding the verse as a later addition. J. G. Herder had already considered that it might be an interpolation.[5] But the suggestion only avoids the problem; it does not solve it. No ed-

2. Abraham Kuenen, *An Historico-Critical Inquiry into the Origin and Composition of the Hexateuch,* trans. Ph. H. Wicksteed (London: Macmillan, 1886), p. 315.

3. William McKane, *A Critical and Exegetical Commentary on Jeremiah,* 2 vols., ICC (Edinburgh: T&T Clark, 1986-1996), 1:l-lxxxiii; Robert P. Carroll, *Jeremiah: A Commentary,* OTL (Philadelphia: Westminster, 1986), p. 46.

4. Julius Wellhausen, *Die Composition des Hexateuchs,* 4th ed. (Berlin: de Gruyter, 1963), p. 10.

5. Johann Gottfried Herder, "Über die ersten Urkunden des Menschlichen Geschlechts. Einige Anmerkungen" (1764-69), in R. Smend, ed., *Schriften zum Alten Testament,* Werke 5;

itor would have been so blind as to create the sequence of scenes as it stands. Moreover, the naming of the woman is indispensable. Her name, Eve, is presupposed in what follows (4:1). Since the difficulty cannot be overlooked, the only solution is the converse: the naming of the woman is not later than the surrounding passage — it is earlier.

This conclusion is supported by a second observation. The sequence of the woman's creation and her naming follows the same sequence as that between the creation and the naming of the animals:

> 2:19And . . . God formed . . . every animal of the field and every bird of the air, *and brought them to the man.* . . . 20*And the man gave names to all the birds of the air, and to every animal of the field.* . . . 21Then . . . God caused a deep sleep to fall upon the man, and he slept; then he took one of his ribs and closed up its place with flesh. 22And . . . God made the rib into a woman *and brought her to the man.* . . . 3:20*And the man named his wife Eve,* because she was the mother of all who live.[6]

The possibility of this connection is self-evident. It suggests that we can skip the greater part of chapter 3 without detriment to the sequence of events. This includes the first naming of the woman in 2:23, which competes with 3:20. It has been added later. The conclusion is far-reaching: there was once a creation narrative without a fall.[7]

This differentiation is not without foundation, as is endorsed by the beginning of the narrative. We are first told: "God planted a garden in Eden, in the east; and there he put the man whom he had formed" (2:8). But then the proceeding is repeated, and now the details that are important for the fall are added:

> 2:9And out of the ground Yahweh God made to grow every tree that is pleasant to the sight and good for food, . . . and the tree of the knowledge

---

Bibliothek deutscher Klassiker 93 (Frankfurt am Main: Deutscher Klassiker Verlag, 1993), pp. 9-178, esp. 116.

6. Biblical translations are based on the RSV with some alterations.

7. Werner H. Schmidt, *Die Schöpfungsgeschichte der Priesterschrift*, 3rd ed., WMANT 17 (Neukirchen-Vluyn: Neukirchener Verlag, 1973), pp. 194-229, judges similarly. Admittedly he maintains that the unevennesses "can only derive from the preliterary stage of textual development" (p. 195), and he also fails to see the key significance of 3:20-21; he goes along with received opinion in considering that they have been interpolated (p. 218). An interpolation of this kind can only be a literary one.

of good and evil. . . . 15Yahweh God took the man and put him in the garden of Eden to till it and keep it. 16And Yahweh God commanded the man, saying, "You may freely eat of every tree of the garden; 17but of the tree of the knowledge of good and evil you shall not eat, for in the day that you eat of it you shall die."

The original story that emerges on the basis of such indications ran roughly as follows:

2:5When no plant of the field was yet in the earth, . . . 7then . . . God formed man . . . and breathed into his nostrils the breath of life. . . . 8And . . . God planted a garden in Eden, in the east; and there he put the man whom he had formed. . . . 19And . . . God formed . . . every animal of the field and every bird of the air, and brought them to the man. . . . 20And the man gave names to all the birds of the air, and to every animal of the field. . . . 21Then . . . God caused a deep sleep to fall upon the man, and he slept; then he took one of his ribs and closed up its place with flesh. 22And . . . God made the rib into a woman and brought her to the man. . . . 3:20And the man named his wife Eve, because she was the mother of all who live. 21And . . . God made garments of skins for the man and for his wife, and clothed them. . . . 4:1Now the man knew his wife Eve, and she conceived and bore Cain.

The story begins with the previous status quo, a condition in which the earth certainly existed but nothing else. For the time before creation the inhabitants of Palestine had in their mind's eye the desert of sand, flint, and rocks. On the fringes of the cultivated land the desert merged into the steppe covered with sparse tufts of grass. It was thought that this change from the desert to the steppe had not yet taken place, the steppe being the scantiest form of vegetation that makes the raising of small animals in a modest way possible, and thus human life on its poorest level. The account stands for the absence of any foundation for living at all — for the world before creation.

The description exposes a dilemma that is characteristic of the ancient creation narratives. People were unable to think of nothingness. The imagination was dominated by the world that was present. As a makeshift, the condition before creation was conceived of as the negation of that which is present here and now, as that which is "not yet." In several Egyptian and Mesopotamian texts we find the world before creation described with almost identical "not yet" statements.[8] The most famous of them is the beginning of *Enuma Elish,* the Babylonian epic about the creation of the world (I 1-9):

> When on high the heaven had not been named, firm ground below had not been called by name, naught but primordial Apsu, their begetter, and Mummu-Tiamat, she who bore them all, their waters commingling as a single body; no reed hut had been matted, no marsh land had appeared, when no gods whatever had been brought into being, uncalled by name, their destinies undetermined — then it was that the gods were formed within them.[9]

The Babylonian parallel shows something else in addition: the importance of naming. Creating and naming are virtually one and the same. For a name is a definition, a delineation, and therefore means order in contrast to undefined, uncreated chaos. The ancient world had a distinct feeling for the necessity of a world order. Only the ordered, defined world is the habitat in which being is possible. We find the close connection between creation and naming in the first three works of the first creation narrative too (Gen. 1:5, 8, 10). In the second account, the motif recurs in the creation of the animals and the woman (2:20; 3:20). This time it is the man who confers the names. He participates in the ordering formation of the world. The world of life is certainly God's prevenient gift; but it is also the space of civilization, and as such belongs within the responsibility of the human being.

The man's particular position also emerges from the sequence of the acts of creation. According to *Enuma Elish* (which in this respect is representative of a number of creation myths), after the introductory "not yet" condition, the gods are created first of all. It is only after all kinds of entanglements and conflicts that the gods create human beings, who are intended to serve and nourish them. In Genesis this is different: "When no plant of the field was yet in the earth, then God formed *man.*" Here the man is the first work of creation. He alone is God's counterpart. Whereas in Israel's environment the world is interpreted as the outcome of conflicting forces — that is,

---

8. For Egypt see Hermann Grapow, "Die Welt vor der Schöpfung," *ZÄS* 67 (1931): 34-38. For Sumer Willem H. P. Römer presents two examples in *TUAT* III/3: *Mythen und Epen I* (Gütersloh: Mohn, 1993), pp. 353-56.

9. *ANET,* 61 (trans. E. A. Speiser); cf. *COS* 1:391 (text 1.111; trans. Benjamin R. Foster).

in ancient terms, it proceeds from the struggle of the gods — here everything divine is absorbed by the *one* God, who performs his work as potter and gardener unrivalled.[10]

That the Creator acts like a potter rests on a simple analogy. Images, especially figurines of gods such as could be found in every considerable household, were made of clay.[11] The Gilgamesh Epic tells on its first tablet how the goddess Arura creates Enkidu (I ii 33-35): She thinks out a concept, wets her hands, nips off clay, and forms the figure: "When Aruru heard this, a double of Anu she conceived within her. Aruru washed her hands, pinched off clay and cast it on the steppe. On the steppe she created valiant Enkidu, offspring of . . . , essence of Ninurta."[12]

We do not possess such obvious parallels for every detail of the biblical story. But there is no doubt that the way the Deity cares for the first human being also echoes widespread ideas: the laying out of the garden, the creation of the animals and of a companion similar in kind; the invention of clothing, which completes the creation of the human being.

After this, the primal man mates with the primal woman (Gen. 4:1). With the birth of Cain, a genealogical list begins that reaches as far as Noah, and is adorned with all kinds of basic inventions belonging to the history of civilization, such as the laying out of towns, the raising of cattle, music, forged weapons, and lastly alcohol (4:17-22; 9:20-21). Following Noah's three sons, Shem, Ham, and Japheth, the whole human race is described, according to their peoples, dwelling places, and languages (10:2-18*, 20-25, 31).[13] The mythical primeval era passes swiftly into history.

10. I have described this picture of God as "integrative monotheism." See Christoph Levin, "Das Alte Testament auf dem Weg zu seiner Theologie," *ZTK* 105 (2008): 125-45, esp. 141-42.

11. Illustrations may be found in Othmar Keel and Christoph Uehlinger, *Gods, Goddesses, and Images of God in Ancient Israel*, trans. Thomas H. Trapp (Minneapolis: Fortress, 1998), pp. 325-36, regarding the so-called pillar figurines (§§190-95).

12. *ANET,* 74 (trans. E. A. Speiser).

13. The connection of the anthropogeny with the table of nations is the foundation for the pre-Yahwistic primal history; see Christoph Levin, "Die Redaktion R^JP in der Urgeschichte," in Martin Beck and Ulrike Schorn, eds., *Auf dem Weg zur Endgestalt von Genesis bis II Regum: Festschrift H.-Ch. Schmitt*, BZAW 370 (Berlin: de Gruyter, 2006), pp. 15-34, esp. 17-18. The basic form of the table of nations probably reflects the world of the 7th century.

The Fundamental Anthropological Viewpoints

In the biblical context, this anthropogeny has been interpreted as the beginning of God's history with humanity, and with Israel especially. It continues with the election of the patriarchs and leads on to the liberation of the Israelites from oppression in Egypt, after which Yahweh brings them through the wilderness into the land of Canaan. The interweaving of such essentially disparate material has to be the work of a redaction that we can call "Yahwist" in accordance with the earlier Documentary Hypothesis because of the name for God used, and also according to its literary extent.[14] This redaction has left pronounced traces in the narrative. It is due to this redaction that the Israelite divine name, *Yahweh,* is regularly added to the mention of God (Hebrew *Elohim*). But above all, this redaction has crafted the earliest description of the fall, and in doing so has added to the creation of humanity the counterpoise that is theologically so important.[15]

The fall acquires its contours against the background of a particular anthropology. Fundamental to it are the ties between man and the earth.[16] In Hebrew the roots of the two terms are related: אדם, "man," and אדמה, "ground, earth." Even before creation begins, it is said that the man's task will be "to till the ground" (2:5). That is the purpose for which God has created him. And just as the earth is the purpose of his existence, it is also his origin. The description of the way God makes the man is accompanied by a declaration about the material he uses: "out of the ground" (2:7). In the earlier account the material is tacitly taken to be clay. In the case of the animals too it is subsequently emphasized that they have been formed "out of the ground" (2:19). And of course the plants have the same origin: "Out of the ground Yahweh God made to grow every tree" (2:9).

For the whole term of his life, the man is there to cultivate the earth. This is the commission with which Yahweh sets him in the garden, "to till it and keep it" (2:15).[17] And it is with the same commission that Yahweh expels

---

14. See most recently Christoph Levin, "The Yahwist: The Earliest Editor in the Pentateuch," *JBL* 126 (2007): 209-30.

15. See Christoph Levin, *Der Jahwist,* FRLANT 157 (Göttingen: Vandenhoeck & Ruprecht, 1993), pp. 82-86.

16. This has often been described. See esp. Joachim Begrich, "Die Paradieserzählung," in *Gesammelte Studien zum Alten Testament,* TB 21 (Munich: Chr. Kaiser, 1964), pp. 11-38, esp. pp. 26-27. The key word אדמה runs right through the primeval history of the Yahwist (Gen. 2:5, 7, 9, 19; 3:17, 19, 23; 4:3, 10, 11, 12; 5:29; 6:1, 7; 7:4, 23; 8:8, 13, 21; 9:20) and connects it via 12:3 with the history of the patriarchs.

17. The curious feminine suffixes refer to אדמה.

him from it: "Yahweh God sent him forth from the garden of Eden, to till the ground from which he was taken" (3:23). At the end of his life the man will return to his origin: "Until you return to the ground, for out of it you were taken" (3:19). The details are blended together into an overall statement: according to God's will, the man is by nature a settled farmer.

This lets us realize what it means when, as the punishment for disobedience, the earth is cursed because of him. Certainly lightning does not strike him dead, as one might have expected. But when it strikes the ground beside him,[18] he is touched to the depths of his being: his origin, the commission given him, and his finite goal are all affected. From that time on he lives as if he had been torn away from his roots. So his existence becomes toil and trouble, a drudgery ending only with death.

A second fundamental anthropological element is the close mutual bond between woman and man. This motif is already latent in the earlier account, where the woman is created from the man's rib; now it is emphasized. Other than at the creation of the man, which God goes about without further explanation, here Yahweh makes a resolve: "It is not good that the man should be alone" (2:18). According to this, the purpose of the woman's existence is to be the man's "helpmate" or companion, the cohuman being per se. The unique character of this relationship is effectively staged. Yahweh makes the resolve even before he begins to create the animals. When he brings these to the man, he meets with a setback in the light of what he intends. "The beasts are living witnesses of the failure of His experiments."[19] It is only when he takes the woman from the man, as he has previously taken the man from the earth, that what he has in mind succeeds. The man's cry of rejoicing confirms the success, and again the close bond between the two human beings: "This at last is bone of my bones and flesh of my flesh" (2:23). Man and woman act before God as a unity. Together they commit the sin leading to the fall. And, just as in the man's case, the purpose of the woman's existence is affected by the punishment inflicted on her: as the man's companion, she is also subjected to him (3:16). The man's supremacy counts, not as an order of creation, but as an unnatural curse — a revolutionary assertion for the ancient world.

18. See Walther Zimmerli, *1. Mose 1–11: Die Urgeschichte*, 3rd ed., ZBK 1/1 (Zurich: Theologischer Verlag, 1967), p. 175.

19. Julius Wellhausen, *Prolegomena to the History of Ancient Israel*, trans. J. S. Black and A. Menzies (1885; repr. Atlanta: Scholars Press, 1994), p. 306.

The Nature of Sin

According to the narrative, we are supposed to think of the newly created human pair as being like children, not immediately in possession of their ability to judge; for nothing other is meant by the phrase that they "do not know good and evil" (see Deut. 1:39; Isa. 7:15, 16; also Jonah 4:11). The narrator illustrates this when he lets them lack the sense of shame (2:25), which as we know only develops naturally from about the age of five. After the fall, the two suddenly rediscover themselves as adults who are conscious of their nakedness, and consequently hide when Yahweh approaches, thereby showing him what has happened (3:7-8). With the famous question "Where are you?" they are called to account.

What constitutes the fall? The story does not provide a definition. Its aim is no more than to show generally an initial disobedience and its consequences. For this a commandment was needed. A subject for this commandment was found in something that belonged to the scene in addition to God and the man: the garden, or rather its trees. Since the result of the disobedience is the knowledge of good and evil, the forbidden tree became "the tree of the knowledge of good and evil" (2:9).

In spite of all the rigor of later theological interpretation, the disobedience has the features of a tragic misunderstanding. The woman triggers it. She has hardly been introduced when she sees that what the tree bears is good to eat (3:6) — that is, she perceives what was said about the trees at the beginning: God made them "pleasant to the sight and good for food" (2:9). Unsuspectingly, she reaches out for the fruit; for when God uttered the prohibition she was not yet in existence. But the man's offense is not against the tree; he takes the fruit from the woman. Whether he knows what he is eating is left open. His protestation that the woman gave him the fruit from the tree (3:12) suggests that he did not. And God seemingly accepts the excuse, for when he gives his reason for cursing the man, he points to the woman (3:17). Irrespective of this, the full responsibility is laid on man and woman alike. "Thus there appears externally and fortuitously what has to be recognized as inward and necessary."[20] The Babylonian Talmud (*Sanhedrin* 38b) tried to soften the objectionable passage by maintaining that the narrative sequence does not reproduce the sequence of events: God pronounced the prohibition only after the creation of the woman, indeed — since we are all affected by

---

20. Friedrich Tuch, *Kommentar über die Genesis* (Halle: Buchhandlung des Waisenhauses, 1838), p. 48.

the fall — after the birth of her children. Accordingly, the event of the creation of human beings and the event of the fall took place on a single day. In the seventh hour the woman was created, in the eighth the first human couple were given their offspring, in the ninth the prohibition was promulgated, in the tenth it was infringed, in the eleventh the judgment was pronounced, and in the twelfth man and woman were driven out. Otherwise the punishment would not have been lawful.

It was only later reflection that elucidated the deeper character of the sin, paradoxically because of the attempt to exonerate the human being from direct guilt. The tempter enters the stage:

> 3:1 The serpent was more crafty than any other wild animal that Yahweh God had made. He said to the woman, "Did God say, 'You shall not eat from any tree of the garden'?" 2 The woman said to the serpent, "We eat of the fruit of the trees of the garden; 3 but God said, 'You shall not eat of the fruit of the tree that is in the middle of the garden, nor shall you touch it, lest you die.'" 4 But the serpent said to the woman, "You will not die; 5 for God knows that when you eat of it your eyes will be opened, and you will be like God, knowing good and evil."

It has always been recognized that this scene differs from the rest of the story. The most noticeable feature is that instead of the usual term "Yahweh Elohim," a simple "Elohim" is used four times. Since there is no discernible reason for the change, here another author was probably at work, with "handwriting" of his own. His intention is obvious. By introducing the character of the seducer, he wishes to some extent to exonerate the human beings. When the woman justifies herself: "The serpent tricked me, and I ate" (3:13), this too God accepts. He turns without hesitation to the serpent and curses it, as the author of the transgression.

Of course this subsequent interpretation could not prove successful. Talk about the serpent does not do away with the fact that the initiative to the disobedience comes from the woman — at the decisive moment the serpent has disappeared — nor is the punishment mitigated in the slightest because the serpent is cursed beforehand. Although man and woman have been tempted to the sin, that sin is entirely their own responsibility. This remaining unevenness is one of the features that lends the story its profound truth.

The serpent is described when it is introduced. It is "more subtle" than all the other animals. This characteristic is by no means a negative one. In

Old Testament wisdom, cleverness is accounted a high-ranking attribute, worth striving for. We are not told that the serpent was an evil beast — only that it was a clever one. It proves that this is the case: it can talk. Talking beasts are a fairytale motif. Nevertheless, the woman is not taken aback for a moment. Nor is the reader really surprised. The serpent has a function to fulfill, but does not in itself embody a separate entity. The woman has to have an interlocutor; but on the stage of world history, except for her, only two beings were endowed with reason: God and the man.

There may have been other reasons as well for the choice of the serpent. Because of its closeness to the earth, and because it sheds its skin (which is interpreted as an enigmatic relationship to death and life), and not least because it can be poisonous, it can appear as a being of ambivalent power. That is the basis of its veneration as an earthbound deity, as representative of forces that are annihilating and healing, evil and good.[21] In our passage the mythical background has retreated. We might almost say that the serpent is merely something like the woman's alter ego, for it hardly puts forward anything that in these circumstances the woman might not have said for herself. That is one reason for the casualness that is so surprising a mark of the dialogue between woman and serpent.

This dialogue is the most cleverly contrived scene to be found in the Old Testament.[22] It "has always excited the delight of sensitive readers through its mastery of psychological description. In the few words and actions with which he describes his characters, the narrator makes their inner lives clear."[23] Everything that is about to come is already implicit in the first sentence: "Did God say, You shall not eat from any tree of the garden?" The allegation is absurd. Why should God have issued a prohibition that would have denied the human being the foundation for living? On the contrary, right at the beginning was his generous permission: "You may freely eat of every tree of the garden" (2:16), permission given with only a single stipulation: "Of the tree of the knowledge of good and evil you shall not eat" (2:17). The truly devilish thing about the hypothetical question is that it reverses the proportions between God's goodness and God's prohibition, as if the fact that this single prohibition exists turns the generosity as a whole into its opposite. It is an all-or-nothing attitude, which spoils everything: if God for-

---

21. See Ronald S. Hendel, "Serpent נחשׁ," *DDD* 744-47.

22. See the sensitive description in Gerhard von Rad, *Genesis,* trans. John H. Marks, rev. ed., OTL (Philadelphia: Westminster, 1972), pp. 87-90.

23. Hermann Gunkel, *Genesis,* trans. Mark E. Biddle (Macon, Ga.: Mercer University Press, 1997), p. 16.

Christoph Levin

bids the one, it is just as if he had forbidden everything — simply because a prohibition at all exists that makes clear to the human being that he is not the lord of the world but is the recipient of what God gives him. Basically speaking, the test of obedience requires only one thing: recognition of the difference between God and man. The Babylonian Talmud (*Sanhedrin* 56b) records that R. Judah read the introduction to the speech, ויצו יהוה אלהים על־האדם (usually translated: "And Yahweh God commanded the man"), in such a way that אלהים is the object: "And the Lord commanded *God* to the man [i.e., that the man remember the Godhead]." It is this requirement that the human being fails to meet.

Here the serpent is free of all responsibility. It is allowed to raise a question, hypothetical though it may be. However, it requires an answer from the woman. She takes up the challenge, and falls into the trap laid for her by the serpent and by herself. For the woman does not confront the serpent with the prohibition as it stands. She makes a momentous mistake: instead of talking about what *God* has done and commanded, she talks about the human act: "We eat of the fruit of the trees of the garden." In this assertion two details are missing. First: "all." This allows a stipulation to stand that contradicts God's generosity. Second, and most important: the woman omits to mention that this eating is in accord with God's permission. There is no reference to the fact that when the human beings live from the fruits of the trees they are in relation to God, who gave the trees to them. Under these circumstances it need not surprise us that the "all" is missing — the enjoyment of what is more than necessary, what is more than the mere eking out of existence.

With this reply, which — so forgetful of God — is fixated on human action, the woman has nothing more with which to counter the serpent. She should have recollected God's generosity. But, blinkered as she is, she does not look beyond her own restricted view. The bare answer, "We eat of the fruit of the trees of the garden," is not a rejection of the serpent's insinuation. It is still possible that by eating, man and woman really are setting aside that absurd, total divine prohibition (which neither does nor can exist) — that therefore life is not a gift but a robbery. But in this way for the woman the total prohibition also comes into effect. This is the beginning of the undue dominance of the misunderstood commandment, on which man founders under the actual limitations set for him by God, limitations that, however, he is not prepared to recognize (Rom. 5:13, 20; 7:10-13).

Suppressing God's permission, the woman goes on to talk instead about the prohibition. She even repeats it accurately, and in so doing cor-

96

rects the serpent's rendering. Only she calls "the tree of the knowledge of good and evil" "the tree in the middle of the garden," as if she wants to avoid putting a name to its true meaning. But because the tree is characterized not according to its attributes but according to its place in the garden, the prohibition at once appears to be arbitrary, as if God simply wanted to vex human beings.

The woman changes the prohibition in a second way as well. She expands it: "neither shall you touch it." God had by no means forbidden them to touch the fruit, and had no need to do so, for his prohibition was clear enough. By intensifying the prohibition on her own initiative, the woman shows that she has already allowed herself to be drawn into the undertow of the totality of the prohibition that the serpent has alleged. She makes God much stricter and more precise than he is. Yet at the same time she has already thought about touching the fruit, and thus about violating the prohibition — a possibility that she has now to forbid for herself. And in this way the prohibition suddenly becomes more rigorous than God had meant.

At the end the woman also cites the threat of punishment that went with the prohibition. But she avoids the formula about the death penalty: "you shall die" (2:17), and formulates a negative final, or purpose, clause instead: "lest you die." Whereas the prohibition is intensified to a nonsensical degree, the threat of punishment is softened.

At this point the serpent begins again, and directly contradicts the woman by disputing the threat of punishment. The contradiction of God is now an open one. But at the same time, according to the rest of the story, what the serpent puts forward is nothing other than the truth. It is true that the fall was not immediately followed by death. But preservation from the death penalty, which has to be called an act of God's grace, is made the occasion for disputing the efficacy of the commandment. It is the alteration that constitutes the blasphemy.

The rest too is no less than the truth: "God knows that when you eat of it your eyes will be opened, and you will be like God, knowing good and evil." It is true that after the fruit has been eaten the eyes of man and woman are opened and they arrive at an adult ability to judge — what the Hebrew calls the "knowledge of good and evil": the ability to weigh up and decide on reasonable grounds. It is this attribute that distinguishes the human from the animal, the adult from the immature child, and the wise from the incorrigible fool. It is not in itself in contradiction to God's will. The case is not being put for a religious or romantic hostility to reason. On the contrary, for Old Testament wisdom, the ability to judge rightly is a divine attribute (Job

21:22; 28:23-24; 37:16; Prov. 3:19-20; Qoh. 2:26; etc.). Consequently it is also correct to say that inasmuch as the man can distinguish between good and evil, he is like God. At the end of the story this is stated quite simply by God himself: "Behold, the man has become like one of us, knowing good and evil" (3:22).

The essential point, however, is the way the human being acquires this attribute. The ability to judge is ruined from the outset if it is not received as a gift with which God makes man like himself, but is seen as a claim with which man makes himself like God. The difference seems to be a small one, hardly more than a sophism, and yet it signifies the fundamental distinction between God and man, between the Creator and the created, between the one who gives and the one who receives. If the ability to judge ignores this fundamental distinction, it is compromised to its very roots. It is then no longer innocent but, as the true capacity for judging, is itself called into question.

The Origin of Mortality and the Possibility of Eternal Life

Finally, the serpent's words raise the question: What has the story to say about death? In this connection Christian readers think of Paul: "Sin came into the world through one man, and death came through sin" (Rom. 5:12). "The wages of sin is death" (Rom. 6:23). That interpretation is not covered by the Old Testament text. And this is so not because we should then have to say that the serpent was right in saying "You will not die" (which after all was true only in the short run) but because the story presents human existence from the outset in no other way than as being mortal. Being-toward-death belongs together not with sin but with creation.

The threat "in the day that you eat of it you shall die" (2:17) is easily read in the sense: "You shall become mortal." But such an interpretation is contrary to its intention. The statement "you shall die" or — more correctly — "you shall be put to death" is in Old Testament law a customary formula for the punishment threatened in the case of capital offenses. The way the formula is used in Genesis 26:11 shows that this form of case or casuistic law should be understood as the law of royal promulgation. It was the king who had the power to issue and to enforce punitive sanctions in general. The earliest instances have to do with circumstances in the family, in which the pater familias was the guilty person. When the prohibition against eating from the tree of the knowledge of good and evil is subjected to this sanction, the premise is that the person threatened is mortal. Indeed, the curse is not followed by death but, for both man and woman, by the toil and trouble of life: "Cursed is the ground because of you; in toil you shall eat of it all the days of your life . . . until you return to the ground, for out of it you were taken" (3:17-19*). Death here is named not as punishment but as the end of life. It is only afterward that we find a postscript — too late, in view of the importance that the motif later acquired — that includes transitoriness as well: "for you are dust, and to dust you shall return" (3:19b). It seemed obvious to interpret the human being's forfeiture to death particularly as part of the tribulation, indeed as its profoundest point — although for the Israelite it is not death as such that is the terrible thing; it is the irreversible separation from God that it means: "When you hide your face, your creatures are dismayed; when you take away their breath, they die and return to their dust" (Ps. 104:29). *Dust* is the image of transience (see Ps. 103:14; Job 10:9; 34:15; Qoh. 3:20; 12:7). It is such laments that later gave rise to the idea that it was from dust that man was created.

How little the text starts from the assumption of a lost immortality is shown by the *tree of life*. The description of the trees given in the course of the narrative is confusing. We are told at the beginning that among the trees in the garden, God planted two that were special: "the tree of life in the midst of the garden, and the tree of the knowledge of good and evil" (2:9). But in what follows the tree of life is never mentioned again, neither in God's prohibition nor in the conversation with the serpent. It is only at the end that it provides the reason why man is expelled, "lest he reach out his hand and take also of the tree of life, and eat, and live forever" (3:22). After that, God sets the cherubim and the flaming sword in front of the garden in Eden, "to guard the way to the tree of life" (3:24). The motif is not carried through the narrative consistently.

Its proper place can be found at the end. We become witnesses of a kind of epilogue in heaven. God sums up the consequences of the fall and wishes to avert the perils it has led to: "Behold, the man has become like one of us, knowing good and evil; and now, lest he reach out his hand and take also of the tree of life, and eat, and live forever." In content, this speech casts back to the words of the serpent: "You will be like God." It seems as if this assertion is the source of the theological reflection.

Its purpose is to establish the difference between God and human on a new foundation. The boundary that humans have overstepped is laid down for them with conclusive force.[24] God does this by blocking the way to the

---

24. Gen. 3:22 forms part of an edition that according to Markus Witte, *Vom Leiden zur*

tree of life with mythical beings who act as guards.[25] The "sword flaming and turning" is the weapon of the weather god, a synthesis between lightning and spear. It symbolizes the mighty presence of God. In ancient Near Eastern iconography, *cherubim* are composite beings with human faces who unite the power of the lion or the bull with that of the griffin. Giant cherubim guard the entrance to the king's palace and to the sanctuary. We several times find the tree of life flanked by cherubim.

The motif of the tree of life is widespread in Canaanite-Syrian iconography. The symbol stands for the divine power of order and life. But we can also think of the φάρμακον ἀθανασίας. At the command of Utnapishtim, Gilgamesh fetches from the underworld a prickly herb that confers immortality, but loses it to the serpent when he stops to bathe on the way, since which time the snake has been able to rejuvenate itself by sloughing off its skin. Gilgamesh laments his fate with tears.[26]

We, on the other hand, do well not to take the frustrated snatch at eternal life in a tragic sense. It is no more than logical that the frontier that the human being transgressed but that God restored for his own sake and for the sake of the human being should be felt as a painful end.

But it is rather the limitation of life that now challenges us to accept that limitation from God as our destiny. For it is not the jealous envy of the gods before which we now stand helpless; it is the God who in his death on the cross has himself overstepped the border to us, and by so doing has once again thrown open the gate to paradise. So it can be that the still remaining frontier, in spite of its irrefutable harshness, proves a gracious limitation — for the person who perceives in it not a tragic fate but the almighty and merciful God himself, and who thereby proves that he is indeed able to distinguish between good and evil.

Lehre: Der dritte Redegang (Hiob 21–27) und die Redaktionsgeschichte des Hiobbuches, BZAW 230 (Berlin: de Gruyter, 1994), p. 230, may be named the "humility edition" ("Niedrigkeitsbearbeitung"). Other instances of this edition are Gen. 2:7 (only עָפָר, "dust"), 9bα; 3:16 (only וְהֵרֹנֵךְ, "and your childbearing"), 18a, 19aα, b, 24b (from אַתְּ onward); 6:3aα, b; and 11:6a. See Levin, "Redaktion R^JP," 23; and Markus Witte, *Die biblische Urgeschichte,* BZAW 265 (Berlin: de Gruyter, 1998), pp. 79-99.

25. See Hartmut Gese, "Der bewachte Lebensbaum und die Heroen: zwei mythologische Ergänzungen zur Urgeschichte der Quelle J," in *Vom Sinai zum Zion,* BEvT 64 (Munich: Chr. Kaiser, 1974), pp. 99-112.

26. Gilgamesh XI 263-96; *ANET,* 96.

Genesis and Divine-Human Relations

Gregory of Nyssa on Language, Naming God's Creatures, and the Desire of the Discursive Animal

Eric Daryl Meyer

The controversy between Gregory of Nyssa and Eunomius of Cyzicus over the origin and nature of human language might profitably be mapped across the tension between the two creation narratives in the opening chapters of Genesis. Eunomius, emphasizing the hexameron, finds the world a place of order divinely structured; Gregory, reveling in paradise, theologizes in a more mythopoetic mode. Eunomius places great weight on the text's assertion that God verbally calls the light "day" and the dark "night" — a clear indicator for him of the divine origin of language.[1] In contrast, Gregory invokes the moment in the paradise narrative when God summons all the animals to Adam to see what he would call them. For Gregory, although the faculty to speak and understand is a gift of God, language itself is a creative human enterprise. Eunomius understands Adam to learn grammar and syntax directly from God,[2] but Gregory understands Adam's act of naming to be

---

1. All citations of *Contra Eunomium II* refer to the page number in *Gregory of Nyssa: Contra Eunomium II: An English Version with Supporting Studies*, ed. Lenka Karfíková, Scot Douglass, and Johannes Zachhuber, trans. Stuart George Hall, Vigiliae christianae Supplement 82 (Boston: Brill, 2007); hereafter *CE II;* and to the Greek text in Werner Jaeger, ed., *Contra Eunomium Libri*, vol. 1 of *Gregorii Nysseni Opera* (Leiden: Brill, 1960); hereafter *GNO.* Eunomius's argument from Gen. 1 in his nonextant *Apologia Apologiae* can be found (via Gregory) in *CE II*, p. 199 (*GNO* 1:269-70).

2. According to Gregory, Eunomius "uses perverse exegesis of this passage to make a forced argument that the animal species were not named by Adam" (*CE II*, p. 159 [*GNO* 1:444]); cf. *CE II*, p. 117 (*GNO* 1:263).

genuinely inventive — a creative interaction between the human and the animal that results in the production of meaning before God's attentive ear.

> Our own claim is that he who made all things by wisdom, and who gave living form to this discursive creature (τὸ λογικὸν τοῦτο πλάσμα), merely by bestowing discourse (τὸν λόγον) on the species added the whole capacity to speak articulately (πᾶσαν τὴν δύναμιν τὴν λογικὴν). . . . We claim [that] the thinking power of the mind . . . observes things, and to prevent the information falling into confusion, attaches signals in the form of words (σήμαντρα) as labels to every thing. Such a doctrine was confirmed by great Moses when he said that names were attached to the dumb animals (τοῖς ἀλόγοις τῶν ζῴων) by Adam, writing in these words: [quoting Gen. 2:19-20].[3]

In this essay I take Gregory's emphasis on Genesis 2:19-20 as a starting point for examining the way in which Gregory's account of language structures his theological anthropology, particularly insofar as language is implicated in Gregory's articulation of the differences and similarities between humans, animals, and God. I contend that while Gregory *explicitly* uses language to distance/differentiate the human from the animal and to connect/compare humanity to God, Gregory's careful attention to the limits of language sets up a basic structural parallel between human and animal life focused on the orienting and compelling power of desire. In light of this parallel, both God's image and God's redemption of humanity can be seen as events that stand open to the animal rather than points of differentiation and exclusion.

---

3. *CE II,* pp. 149-50 (*GNO* 1:400-402); translation altered. Throughout the paper I render λόγος, λογικός, etc., by means of the terms "discourse, discursive." This is not an unproblematic translation, but insofar as "discourse" connotes internally coherent patterns of *both* speech and thought, I think that it best approximates the semantic plasticity in Gregory's usage. The reader should not collapse the term too quickly into either speech or thought, as I am relying on a measure of ambiguity to maintain the inner connection that Gregory assumes. In any case, for the purposes of this essay "discourse/discursive" is certainly preferable to both the traditional translation as "reason/rational" and to John Behr's rendering of Gregory's ζῶον λογικὸν as "word-bearing animal," John Behr, "Rational Animal: A Rereading of Gregory of Nyssa's *De hominis opificio,*" *JECS* 2 (1999): 219-47, here 231.

The (Exclusively) Human Nature of Language

One of the more unexpected entailments of Gregory's argument in *Contra Eunomium* is that language is natural to human beings alone. The "proper" possession and use of language marks a difference between human beings and animals; but perhaps counterintuitively Gregory also sees it separating human nature from God. Let us examine more closely how (or where?) language "places" Adam in the cosmos between the animals and God.

On the one (divine) side, language is unnatural to God on account of the formal necessities of *using* language. The use of language presupposes dimensionality in both space and time, because any speech presumes a listener, some interval of space that is spoken across, and the duration of time required to enunciate syllables in succession.[4] Gregory mocks Eunomius for subordinating the Son, not only to the Father, but also to time and space by suggesting that language is proper to God.[5] For the consubstantial persons of the Trinity meaning is shared without inhibition; the "action of the mind" itself is somehow communicative. It is foolish to think that the holy Trinity should have need of language to communicate, because there is no temporal or spatial medium — no separation of οὐσία at all — in which that linguistic communication could take place.[6] While *discursiveness* (that is, being λογικός) is shared by God and human beings, *language* is the necessary means of communicating meaning for intelligent beings separated by space and time:

> No one, I believe, is so stuffed up with choking snivel as to be unaware that the Only-begotten Son, who is in the Father, and perceives the Father in himself, has no need of noun or verb (ὀνόματος ἢ ῥήματος) for the knowledge of the subject, . . . for where the immaterial and intelligent nature is concerned, the action of the mind is a word (λόγος) which has nothing to do with the physical use of organs. . . . As it is, since the thoughts which arise in us are unable to make themselves apparent because our nature is enclosed in its fleshly garment, we are obliged to

---

4. The best extended reflection on spatiotemporality as proper to creatures and not to God in Gregory's thought remains the first chapter of Hans Urs von Balthasar, *Presence and Thought: An Essay on the Religious Philosophy of Gregory of Nyssa*, trans. Mark Sebanc (San Francisco: Ignatius Press, 1995), pp. 27-35, esp. n. 46. See also Johannes Zachhuber, *Human Nature in Gregory of Nyssa: Philosophical Background and Theological Significance* (Boston: Brill, 2000), p. 154.

5. *CE II*, p. 105 (*GNO* 1:212-14).

6. *CE II*, pp. 105-6 (*GNO* 1:212-18).

attach various names to things as signs, and thereby to make the processes of the mind accessible to other people.[7]

Thus Gregory sees language as a necessary corollary of the *enfleshment of intelligence.*

On the other (animal) side, while language is a function of the conditions of bodiliness, it cannot simply be attributed to materiality for Gregory, for not every body uses language. Gregory's favored term for the animals is ἄλογοι ("nondiscursive") — which signifies both irrationality and the inability to communicate intelligibly.[8] Yet the distinction between discursive and nondiscursive animals is not merely intellectual; it is inscribed in the *anatomical* differences between human and animal flesh. In human beings the shape and placement of limbs and organs have been altered to facilitate discourse. Human hands are Gregory's favorite example. Because the human being was made upright she no longer needs forelegs to support half her weight. This means that her hands are free to carry and manipulate objects, to build and to sow according to the patterns set forth in her mind. But the shape of her hands also allows her face and mouth to be put to a different purpose than animals'. Where animals gather and tear their food with their mouths, using powerful lips and tongues and teeth, the human being does all these things (more or less) politely with her hands. In turn the mouth, lips, and throat are freed to become delicate instruments capable of the fine motor movements that speech requires.[9] Thus, while language is a function of intelligence enfleshed, language exerts a counterforce that influences the very shape of flesh itself.

In summary, language arises out of humanity's unique place in the cosmos and has no proper "place" in the cosmos besides the human. This situation is reflected perfectly in Genesis 2. Adam stands among the assembled creatures as one of them in hair, flesh, and bone; and yet, even as he interacts with all the surrounding creatures, Adam's body and mind are the site of an intersection with a different plane altogether.[10] For the sounds that Adam makes are subject to divine interest and divine scrutiny in a manner

7. CE II, p. 147 (GNO 1:390-91).
8. For examples see CE II, pp. 150, 152, 154, 159 (GNO 1:402, 412, 421, 444).
9. Gregory of Nyssa, *De hominis opificio* 10.1-2 (PG 44:152b); translations are drawn from Philip Schaff, ed., *NPNF* 5 (repr. Grand Rapids: Eerdmans, 1954).
10. Alden Mosshammer, "Disclosing but Not Disclosed: Gregory of Nyssa as Deconstructionist," in *Studien zu Gregor von Nyssa und der christlichen Spätantike* (New York: Brill, 1990), p. 105.

unlike the sounds of all the other animals. Because Adam shares derivatively in the discursiveness of God, human language is the enfleshment of meaning in the dimensions of space and time.

The Limits of Discourse: Language and the Eschatological Horizon

Having established that language is *unique* to human beings in Gregory's cosmology, in this section I examine the degree to which language is *essential* to the structure of human life. To answer this question, it will be instructive to examine both Eunomius's and Gregory's accounts of language more closely.

Eunomius sees a strong connection between language — particularly the words by which objects and actions are named — and the essences of language's referents; there is a *fit* between words and things. In Eunomius's understanding, Providence determines semantics. Out of the bounty of divine wisdom God has placed words and things together so that language not only bears knowledge about the state of things, but also supporting arguments that shore up such knowledge as secure and certain. Eunomius's certainty applies not only to descriptions of terrestrial matters, but to theological language about God as well.[11] Through God's providential ordering of the linguistic realm, language is a reliable medium for secure knowledge and correct praise. Gregory caricatures Eunomius's epistemological confidence and rigorism as the ramblings of a rationalistic pedant more concerned with the integrity of his own (private) systematic theology than with a genuine encounter with God. Eunomius falsely regards discourse as a means of ensconcing essences in knowledge, so that, in the hands of the "truly wise," language is a clear map to navigate the world with mastery.[12]

---

11. For Eunomius, if the Son is not *essentially* derivative and subordinate to the Father, then the terms "begotten" and "Son" are equivocal and misleading. The underlying premise for Eunomius's position — the very point at which Gregory disagrees so strongly — is that there is a strong, providential fit between language and reality that makes language a reliable tool for the production and exchange of genuine knowledge about God and the world. See Eunomius of Cyzicus, "Liber Apologeticus," in *Eunomius: The Extant Works,* trans. Richard Vaggione (Oxford: Oxford University Press, 1987), p. 45. See also John A. Demetracopoulos, "Glossogony or Epistemology? Eunomius of Syzicus' and Basil of Caesarea's Stoic Concept of Ἐπίνοια and Its Misrepresentation by Gregory of Nyssa," in *CE II*, pp. 388-90.

12. Gregory argues that by trying to metaphysically interweave names and essences,

In contrast, Gregory's understanding of language is marked by a chaste attention to its limits. He recognizes the limits of language on two fronts: first, the ineradicable slippage between reality, thought, and language that renders language imprecise and misleading; second, the fundamental inadequacy of language for both description and instruction with regard to the transformative communion of human beings with God.

For Gregory, human finitude entails that every interchange between reality, thought, and language also marks a loss. Because Gregory eschews any providential determination of language beyond God's gift of the *ability* and *impetus* to speak, there can be no master signifier beyond sociolinguistic conventions that would metaphysically establish firm connections between words and things. Gregory sees language as a creative endeavor undertaken by the human community in attempts to guide, instruct, entertain, and control one another. Even so, language never communicates perfectly. Some unrecoverable remainder is always lost in moving from perception, to conception (ἐπίνοια), to speech.[13] This loss, however, is not a cause for despair in

---

Eunomius naturalizes language, attributing to it a definitive grip on reality more powerful than any other human capacity for sensation or thought; see *CE II*, p. 94 (*GNO* 1:163-66). From Gregory's epistemologically reserved perspective, this amounts to an arbitrary absolutizing of one narrow linguistic and cultural moment. The strong metaphysical component to Eunomius's notion of language cannot account for the multiplicity, fluidity, and diversity of languages across time and space. See *CE II*, pp. 192-93, 114-16, 122-23, 151 (*GNO* 1:546-47, 246-61, 284-88, 406-9). See also Arabatzis, "Limites du Langage, Limites du Monde dans le Contre Eunome II de Grégoire de Nysse," in *CE II*, pp. 379-80.

13. "What word is not fleeting as soon as it is spoken? . . . If therefore what makes him [Eunomius] characterize the word as a concept is that it does not remain a word but vanishes together with the sound of the voice, he cannot avoid calling every word a concept, since no substance remains to any word once it is uttered" (Gregory of Nyssa, *CE II*, p. 69 [*GNO* 1:44-45]; see also Mosshammer, "Disclosing but Not Disclosed," pp. 102, 104). Demetracopoulos argues that by deploying ἐπίνοια linguistically in addition to its more traditional epistemological application, Gregory introduces a slippage between words and thoughts that (according to Demetracopoulos) causes Gregory to misunderstand and slander Eunomius (as well as overextending Basil's use of the term). Demetracopoulos provides a great service in clarifying Eunomius's position against his many detractors; nevertheless, in the process he crucially mischaracterizes Gregory's disagreement with Eunomius as an *ignoratio elenchi,* when in fact Gregory marks *both* Eunomius's epistemology and his understanding of language as overconfident. Gregory does not restrict his criticism of Eunomius concerning ἐπίνοια to the latter's failure to recognize the validity of *linguistic* inventiveness, but regards Eunomius's confidence in the "fit" between concepts, words, and things to be unfounded. Demetracopoulos mistakes this more comprehensive disagreement for confusion on Gregory's part. See Demetracopoulos, "Glossogony or Epistemology," pp. 393-94.

Gregory's mind; rather, it generally necessitates a multiplication of words and images (all of which remain partially inadequate) to more accurately mark out what is meant, even though that asymptotic process always remains incomplete.[14]

The everyday limitations of language, however, are overshadowed by its theological inadequacies. According to Gregory, our faltering attempts to describe God are instructive, capable of guarding against false conceptions and guiding toward better ones, but are ultimately only preliminary sketches that fail in all but the most rudimentary description of God. Even the language of Scripture does not describe God in the mystery of the divine essence, but points to God's modes of self-presentation and to God's acts.[15] Theological language is a series of illuminating gestures in the direction of the Divine, attempts to find the most fitting concepts and language for God, who exceeds every boundary of thought and speech.[16] The intensity of God's infinity overwhelms every discursive approach, so that all language about God remains a hermeneutic attempt to render sensible that which outstrips sense entirely.

Not only does language fail to convey the deepest knowledge possible of God, it is also impotent in the human spiritual ascent toward God — language can convey only so much knowledge. Thus language's limit marks a transition to another mode of approach to God, rather than the terminus of that approach.[17] The *failures* of discourse carry as much significance for Gregory as do its successes. In spiritual ascent, *discourse* is swept up and subsumed in *desire* as the propulsive force drawing the human being onward into a deeper knowledge of God. God's epistemological elusiveness and the failure of language to comprehend the divine nature become a kind of lure

---

14. "Therefore, when the mind is exercised upon high and invisible subjects, which the senses cannot reach — and I am speaking about the divine and ineffable Nature, on which it is rash to seize on anything hastily with the mind, and still rasher to commit the interpretation of the idea engendered in us to casual words. . . . No suitable appellations being available for these [ideas] which might adequately represent the subject, *we are obliged to reveal the idea of the Deity engendered in us by many and various titles, in whatever way we can*" (*CE II*, p. 189 [*GNO* 1:576-77], emphasis added). See also the very ambitious and perhaps insufficiently nuanced study by Anna Williams, *The Divine Sense: The Intellect in Patristic Theology* (New York: Cambridge University Press, 2007), p. 131.

15. *CE II*, p. 83 (*GNO* 1:105).

16. *CE II*, p. 72 (*GNO* 1:60-61). See also Mosshammer, "Disclosing but Not Disclosed," pp. 108-9.

17. Tina Dolidze, "The Cognitive Function of Epinoia in *CE II* and Its Meaning for Gregory of Nyssa's Theory of Theological Language," in *CE II*, p. 447.

that spurs the human being on to seek another path beyond discourse's limitations.[18] Thus, from Gregory's perspective, by exaggerating the capacity of human discourse to know and communicate about God, Eunomius cuts off the path of desire and makes God an object of knowledge rather than a focal point of human longing. Eunomius's rationalistic theology appears to Gregory not only as a linguistic circumscription of the Divine, but also as a truncation of human nature, a premature collapse of the human into the symbolic realm of discourse, and a failure to recognize that the whole structure of human life stretches out beyond even the lofty reach of reason.

One key piece of evidence in this regard is Gregory's discussions of *human* incomprehensibility as a primary mark of God's image.[19] Every attempt of discourse to come to grips with human consciousness — whether it be to explain it or to guide human life toward full satisfaction — necessarily excludes, divides, and reduces so that whatever comprehension results is only a parody of the human. Human nature eludes every attempt to grasp it because human life is fundamentally structured in God's image around a void of incomprehensibility. Paradoxically, this gap at the heart of human nature is not a deficiency or a problem to be solved, but is integral to humanity's perfection insofar as at the heart of human nature there lies an inexhaustible impulse for ascent, a structuring desire that carries the human being beyond the limits of discourse toward the Divine.[20] The epistemology of discourse gives way to an alternate epistemology of desire, productive of a very different kind of knowledge — the sort that Gregory describes best with the imagery of the blessed darkness of the cloud on Sinai, or the rapture of union in

18. For this reason, the anti-Eunomian writings should be regarded as the hardened edge of a much more expansive body of thought. The restrictions of polemic writing and the precision and narrowness of focus required by the genre necessarily exclude more expansive, metaphorically rich accounts of the subjects under treatment. The polemic is only the hard shell protecting a complex, living and moving body of thought. Sarah Coakley is surely right to insist that Gregory's pastoral and exegetical writings are equally representative (if not more so) of Gregory's theology. See Coakley, "Rethinking Gregory of Nyssa: Introduction," in *Rethinking Gregory of Nyssa*, ed. Sarah Coakley (Malden, Mass.: Blackwell, 2003), pp. 6-8.

19. Incomprehensibility is one of many expressions of the divine image in humanity and is developed at several points in Gregory's writings. See *De hom. op.* 11.3 (PG 44:156a); *CE II*, p. 83 (*GNO* 1:106-8).

20. According to von Balthasar, Gregory's attribution of incomprehensibility to the human soul "is perhaps the first time a Greek thinker considered the incomprehensibility of a thing . . . as a perfection" (*Presence and Thought*, p. 94). See also Lewis Ayres, "Deification and the Dynamics of Nicene Theology: The Contribution of Gregory of Nyssa," *SVTQ* (2005): 375-94, here 393.

the Song of Songs. Language, for all its power to shape human life, remains secondary to desire within the human being's salvific transformation. Thus Adam's ability to name, and the corporate function of human language more generally, must finally be seen as secondary to desire in inhabiting the divine communion that finally envelops human life. Gregory does indeed speak of the human as the discursive animal,[21] yet there remains plenty of evidence within Gregory's writings that any reductive inattention to the *animal* that is discursive will produce an aberrant distortion. God's intensive mystery only grows darker and richer the more the human is enveloped in grace and love, and the growing immediacy with the Divine only fans the insatiable drive to reach further.[22]

The Function of Discourse along the Trajectory of (Animal) Desire

At this point, having articulated the opacity of the thinking human subject to herself as an aspect of the *imago Dei* and the terminus of discourse in desire, we are prepared to return to Adam and the animals with fresh insight. I submit that Gregory's attention to the limitations of language and the centrality of desire to both Gregory's theological anthropology and his account of spiritual ascent mark a fracture where the purity of his distinction between the discursive human and the nondiscursive (ἄλογοι) beasts breaks down and the animal returns to play a theologically positive role, despite Gregory's disavowal. That by which Gregory marks off human difference from the animal, namely discourse, finally turns the human back toward the animal by virtue of its limits. In other words, the *imago Dei* does not exclude the animals Adam names so much as it blesses and leads them forward.

First, Gregory describes a dependence of human life on animal life at three points, of which I will articulate one. In addition to a developmental or evolutionary dependence based on Gregory's notion of vegetable, sensual, and discursive soul, and a physical dependence that directly correlates to dominion, another point of dependence is found where human virtue and vice are built from the "raw material" of animal desire. For Gregory, the passions

21. *De hom. op.* 8.8 (PG 44:148c).
22. Recognizing the function of (animal) desire in the trajectory of spiritual ascent somewhat reduces the tension in Gregory's soteriology (between the cosmic/bodily aspect and the contemplative/psychic aspect) noted by J. Warren Smith, "The Body of Paradise and the Body of the Resurrection: Gender and the Angelic Life in Gregory of Nyssa's *De hominis opificio*," *HTR* 99 (2006): 207-28, here 227.

of the animals are simply "natural" or "fitting," that is, without *moral* weight. Gregory mentions examples like the "greed" that enables herbivores to gather enough grass to sustain themselves, the "lust" that enables rodents and insects to reproduce in such great numbers, or the "fear" that drives animals into flight for self-preservation. All these are present within the human being as well, but discourse sets these movements within an *ethical* plane. The particular enactment of the animal drives present within human life is subject to ethical judgment and indicative of a broader moral and spiritual trajectory. Nevertheless, both virtue and vice draw upon the energy of animal passion and thus, despite Gregory's predominant stress on the latter, both virtue and vice are *materially dependent* on animal passions.[23]

The second point in this synthesis is to note that although Gregory generally invokes the *imago Dei* to shore up human difference relative to animals, its function within his theological anthropology when he is not focused on differentiating human beings actually sets up a precise structural parallel between human and animal life. In Gregory's conception, animals are creatures of necessity whose lives are determined by desires for food, bodily well-being, and procreation.[24] But whereas the lives of animals are subject to necessity, transparently ordered toward self-preservation and reproduction, the lives of humans are opaque, because, although human beings share the activities associated with these animal desires, human life is marked by the freedom and self-reflection of discursiveness.[25] Yet for all the

---

23. Thus, under the proper guidance of a well-trained discursive faculty, animal drives become the strength of virtue. "So, on the contrary, if discourse assumes sway over such emotions, each of them is transmuted to a form of virtue; for anger produces courage, terror caution, fear obedience, hatred aversion from vice, the power of love the desire for what is truly beautiful; high spirit in our character raises our thought above the passions, and keeps it from bondage to what is base" (*De hom. op.* 18.5 [PG 44:193bc]; translation altered). On the other hand, if a subject gives himself over to the plain expression of his animal passions and subordinates discourse to the pursuit of animal drives, he will inevitably (and "unnaturally") become a greedy, lascivious, or cowardly person. "These attributes, then, human nature took to itself from the side of the brutes; for those qualities with which brute life was armed for self-preservation, when transferred to human life, became passions; for the carnivorous animals are preserved by their anger, and those which breed largely by their love of pleasure; cowardice preserves the weak. . . . The rising of anger in us is indeed akin to the impulse of the brutes; but it grows by the alliance of thought: for thence come malignity, envy, deceit, conspiracy, hypocrisy; all these are the result of the evil husbandry of the mind" (*De hom. op.* 18.2-4 [PG 44:192b-93b]).

24. *De hom. op.* 18.2-9 (PG 44:192b-96a).

25. *De hom. op.* 15.2; 18.3 (PG 44:177a, 192cd); see also Smith, "Body of Paradise," p. 210.

difference that discourse inscribes, the fundamental structuring element of both human and animal life is propulsive desire, not discourse, inasmuch as human life is ultimately oriented toward a communion with God that floods the human capacity for understanding or description. The human approach to God depends on a willingness to be fundamentally oriented by a lack or hunger in which discourse is powerless to grasp the object of desire (God), the path of desire's ascent, or even the nature of being a desiring subject.[26] It is no accident in Gregory's mind that Scripture speaks of desire for God with metaphors of hunger, thirst, shelter, warmth, and sexual drive, for it is through and with these desires that the *whole* human person might be oriented toward the transcendent and drawn into spiritual ascent.[27]

All of this affinity with animal life decisively settles the propriety of assertions (such as those made by Harrison, Laird, Burrus, and Hart) that, for Gregory, the points of greatest continuity with animal life are also the sites where divine grace breaks in and draws the human creature forward in its transformation.[28] It becomes abundantly clear in Gregory's *Commentary on the Song of Songs* that the area in which Gregory regards human nature as closest to the animals — the consuming grip of sexual passion — also provides an indispensable metaphorical anchor for human desire for

26. "Since, then, those who know what is good by nature desire participation in it, and since this good has no limit, the participant's desire itself necessarily has no stopping place but stretches out with the limitless" (Gregory of Nyssa, *The Life of Moses,* trans. Abraham Malherbe and Everett Ferguson [Mahwah, N.J.: Paulist Press, 1978], 1.5-7 [PG 44:300d-301a]). See also Rowan Williams, "Macrina's Deathbed Revisited: Gregory of Nyssa on Mind and Passion," in Lionel R. Wickham and Caroline P. Hammond Bammel, eds., *Christian Faith and Greek Philosophy in Late Antiquity: Essays in Tribute to George Christopher Stead* (Leiden: Brill, 1993), p. 242; and von Balthasar, *Presence and Thought,* p. 45.

27. "She calls him who cannot be comprehended by any name, is taught by the guards that she loves him who is unattainable. . . . Because the desire for her beloved is frustrated, her yearning for his beauty cannot be fulfilled. But the veil of despair is removed when the bride learns that the true satisfaction of her desire consists in always progressing in her search and ascent: when her desire is fulfilled, it gives birth to a further desire for the transcendent. Thus the veil of her despair is removed, and the bride will always see more of her beloved's incomprehensible beauty throughout all eternity" (Gregory of Nyssa, *Commentary on the Song of Songs,* trans. Casimir McCambley [Brookline, Mass.: Hellenic College Press, 1987], p. 225 [*GNO* 6:370-71]).

28. Verna Harrison, "Allegory and Asceticism in Gregory of Nyssa," *Semeia* 57 (1992): 113-30; Martin Laird, *Gregory of Nyssa and the Grasp of Faith: Union, Knowledge, and Divine Presence* (New York: Oxford University Press, 2007); Virginia Burrus, *"Begotten, Not Made": Conceiving Manhood in Late Antiquity* (Stanford: Stanford University Press, 2000), p. 81; Mark Hart, "Gregory of Nyssa's Ironic Praise of Celibacy," *HeyJ* (1992): 1-19, here 10.

God.[29] The *rhetorical* freight borne by this metaphor points to a *theological* freight that Gregory conscientiously avoids thematizing: the centrality of "animal" life within the economy of human salvation. Thought and language are incapable of conceiving or naming God in all but the most oblique and indirect terms, yet the incomprehensible gap at the core of human subjectivity generates a straining desire that reaches out toward the even more incomprehensible allure of God and draws the human being onward and upward in a simultaneous rapture and craving that are indiscernible from one another.

In this vein, the ἀπάθεια that Gregory enjoins upon his readers can be seen as the refusal to prematurely seize on any aspect of creation as the site of fulfillment. So long as human beings are overcome with passion, they are deceived into thinking that some object or action present to experience is capable of resolving the discordant interval within their own psyche into a full and complete harmony. Discourse is not to eradicate passionate desire altogether, but to oversee and enforce a refusal of any closure of the gap within subjectivity (named by the *imago Dei*) that should properly propel the human to seek and contemplate God.[30] The height of human wisdom consists in recognizing that even the presence of God does not close or heal this gap in subjectivity, but opens it even wider as the fitting receptacle for the dark immediacy of God's love.[31] In Gregory's ἀπάθεια, discourse functions to di-

29. "What could be more paradoxical than to make nature purify itself of its own passion and teach detachment (ἀπάθεια) in words normally suggesting passion (πάθος)? Solomon does not speak of the necessity of being outside of the flesh's impulses or of mortifying our bodily limbs on earth, or of cleansing our mouths of talk of passion; rather, he disposes the soul to be attentive to purity through words which seem to indicate the complete opposite and he indicates a pure meaning through the use of sensuous language" (*Song* 50; *GNO* 6:29). See also Harrison, "Allegory and Asceticism," 124.

30. In this regard, Rowan Williams's definition of passion as an "impulse or affect divorced from the proper ends of a reasoning being, impulse as leader not as instrument" ("Macrina's Deathbed Revisited," p. 237) is to be vastly preferred to that of Anthony Meredith: "Passion is whatever originates in the elements either of desire or of aggression within us, born of our animal nature and not strictly belonging to our rational nature" ("What Does Gregory of Nyssa Mean by ΠΑΘΟΣ (*Pathos*)?" *DRev* 126, no. 442 [2008]: 57-66, here 64-65). Though he is correct to note Gregory's overwhelmingly negative assessment of passion (πάθος), Meredith certainly cannot sustain the argument that Gregory views "our rational nature" as the primary means for the human approach to God over and against desire and those elements of the human that are continuous with "animal nature." Both definitions, however, miss the point that what is destructive about passion is its *closure to transcendence* through fixation on what can be grasped immanently, whether in understanding or in pleasure.

31. "This truly is the vision of God: never to be satisfied in the desire to see him. But

rect desire toward its transcendent goal by militating against any premature collapse of desire into its "merely" animal expression, or worse, its misdirection in vice. By contrast, Eunomius's disavowal of the animal is thorough and decisive. Given that discourse is the medium of certainty concerning the divine essence (as ἀγένητος) and suffices as an approach to God, Eunomius relegates both desire and the animal to the margins of theological irrelevancy. The animal is merely the object of human dominion; desire only fogs the precision of discourse.

The fracture in Gregory's thought whereby the animal escapes Gregory's disavowal and reenters his theological anthropology with a positive role indicates the fluidity of the human-animal distinction and the possibility of rethinking the role of animals in conceptualizing humanness. Gregory's recognition of discourse's limits might reconcile discourse with the animal through the openness of animal desire to a transcendent trajectory of transformation that exceeds the capacity of any discursive grasp.[32] So, although Adam's language sets him apart from the animals, that separation ultimately creates the space for a deeper synthesis. *The human is not the animal* because of the presence of discourse, but at its limits discourse is subsumed and "animal" desire draws the human further in divine communion. What remains is a negation of the negation: the final function of discourse is not to differentiate the human from the animal but to guard and guide the animal that stretches out toward the glory of God. The continuity between human and animal at the limits of discourse entail that humanity's spiritual service to creation in God's image is not a "pulling up" from above, in which human beings raise animals to a higher plane of existence; instead, it is a reconciliatory "getting down into," in which a deeper, ecosystemic integration (guided by wisdom) guards the multivalence of desire as an approach to God.

---

one must always, by looking at what he can see, rekindle his desire to see more. Thus, no limit would interrupt growth in the ascent to God, since no limit to the Good can be found nor is the increasing of desire for the Good brought to an end because it is satisfied" (Gregory of Nyssa, *Moses* 2.239 [PG 44:404d-5a]).

32. This argument is neither an attempt to argue that Gregory was a proto-environmentalist nor an attempt to exonerate Gregory from contributing to theological patterns that underwrite illegitimate exploitation of creation. It is my hope that careful attention to the strange thought-world of ancient Christian writers can dislodge ecologically destructive "commonsense" notions of being human and open up space for a relocation of the human in the cosmos that remains faithful to the tradition and open to the Spirit's leading in the present.

Eric Daryl Meyer

Adam's naming of the creatures in the garden is a mode of description undertaken before God that labors to understand *in order to guide, protect, and foster desire.* Naming, properly speaking, produces an understanding that is not closed (with pretense to a totality of comprehension, or a grasping of essences), but is an understanding in transit — desirous of divine communion and open to the transformation effected by divine grace. Adam's naming, a speech that is borne on the breath of the incomprehensible God, is a gift of the human to creation whereby its ecosystemic integrity might be guarded, directed, and preserved — provided that discourse does not close itself off from both the animals and from God in a presumption to mastery. Adam's naming is not the establishment of a "grip" on reality, but an opening (through God's image) for the "meaning" of animal life to stretch out toward communion with God.

Image, Identity, and Embodiment: Augustine's Interpretation of the Human Person in Genesis 1–2

Matthew Drever

Introduction

Recent trends in patristic studies have shown renewed interest in how the wider context of developing Nicene theology frames the conceptual, rhetorical, polemical, and exegetical strategies in Latin and Greek Christianity.[1] This has invited scholars in Augustinian studies to reappraise his thought in light of emerging Nicene Trinitarian and Christological issues. In turn, this prompts reassessments of Augustine's anthropology, considering how closely the topics of Trinity, Christ, and human being are intertwined for him.[2] It should also lead to new examinations of his biblical theology, given that some of Augustine's most sustained theological analyses of the human being,

---

1. For example, see Lewis Ayres, *Nicaea and Its Legacy: An Approach to Fourth-Century Trinitarian Theology* (New York: Oxford University Press, 2004); Michael Barnes, "Augustine in Contemporary Trinitarian Theology," *TS* 56 (1995): 237-50.

2. The connection of these issues has received renewed attention in various scholarly circles. For representative samples of this scholarship see Lewis Ayres, "The Discipline of Self-knowledge in Augustine's *De trinitate* Book X," in Lewis Ayres, ed., *The Passionate Intellect: Essays on the Transformation of Classical Traditions, Presented to I. Kidd* (Brunswick, N.J.: Rutgers University Press, 1995), pp. 261-96; Johannes Brachtendorf, *Die Struktur des menschlichen Geistes nach Augustinus: Selbstreflexion und Erkenntnis Gottes in "De Trinitate"* (Hamburg: Felix Meiner, 2000); Norbert Fischer and Dieter Hattrup, eds., *Selbsterkenntnis und Gottsuche. Augustinus: Confessiones 10* (Paderborn: Ferdinand Schöningh, 2007); Rowan Williams, "*Sapientia* and the Trinity: Reflections on the *De Trinitate*," *Augustiniana* 40 (1990): 317-32.

Christ, and God are found in his commentaries on Genesis and Psalms. But if Wilhelm Geerlings's bibliography of contemporary secondary scholarship on Augustine is indicative, there remains a paucity of work in this area.[3] This is particularly true of *De Genesi ad litteram,* Augustine's longest and most mature commentary on Genesis. It is a commentary that offers detailed studies of human nature, which intersect theology, biblical exegesis, and philosophy.[4]

Further examinations in this area are needed, and are particularly apropos in light of the continued influence of Augustine on contemporary theological and philosophical discussions of human nature. Augustine's contribution to this area is evident in the variety of recent scholarship that has drawn on his thought.[5] Augustine's influence, however, is not without its critics. For example, some have contended that his anthropology helps ossify relational polarities of the classical world (e.g., mind/body, matter/spirit, God/world) into oppositional dualisms in the classical world (e.g., mind/body, matter/spirit, man/woman, and God/world). This feeds into a related criticism that Augustine is mired in metaphysics inconsistent with contemporary philosophical methods,[6] and that his thought is contrary to current theoretical

3. Geerlings cites only two recent works on *Genesi ad litteram,* in contrast to the dozens he cites for Augustine's other major texts, in *Augustinus — Leben und Werk: Eine bibliographische Einführung* (Paderborn: Schöningh, 2002), p. 141. This is in line with Hubertus R. Drobner's survey of secondary scholarship on Augustine, "Studying Augustine: An Overview of Recent Research," in Robert Dodaro and George Lawless, eds., *Augustine and His Critics: Essays in Honour of Gerald Bonner* (New York: Routledge, 2000), pp. 18-34.

4. In this essay *Gn. litt.* refers to Augustine's *Literal Commentary on Genesis.* Augustine began writing the commentary between 399 and 404, and it was published in 416. The first nine books were probably revised by 410, and the final three books were finished between 412 and 415. Additional abbreviations of primary texts by Augustine include: *Conf.* (*Confessions*), *Trin. (On the Trinity), Civ. Dei (The City of God), Div. qu. (On Eighty-Three Varied Questions).* Primary text references of Augustine are cited according to book, chapter, and paragraph number. Latin quotations are taken from Migne's *Patrologia latina,* but have been critically compared against the *Corpus Christianorum Series Latina.* English translations of *Literal Commentary on Genesis* are taken from Augustine, *On Genesis,* trans. Edmund Hill (New York: New City Press, 2002).

5. Recent examples of how Augustine has been integrated into such discussions include: Kathryn Tanner, *Christ the Key* (New York: Cambridge University Press, 2010); Jean-Luc Marion, *Au lieu de soi: L'approche de saint Augustin* (Paris: Presses universitaires de France, 2008); James K. A. Smith, *Speech and Theology: Language and the Logic of Incarnation* (New York: Routledge, 2002); John D. Caputo and Michael J. Scanlon, eds., *Augustine and Postmodernism: Confessions and Circumfessions* (Bloomington: Indiana University Press, 2005); Lieven Boeve, Mathijs Lamberigts, and Maarten Wisse, eds., *Augustine and Postmodern Thought: A New Alliance Against Modernity?* (Leuven: Peeters, 2009).

6. For example, see Wittgenstein's famous critique of Augustine's theory of language:

trends and ethical convictions in areas such as gender and ecological studies.[7] As we will see, there is some basis for such criticism, especially with regard to Augustine's views on the nonhuman world. But we should not move too quickly to condemn his anthropology. We will also see that his views have surprising resonances with contemporary portraits of the human person: the Augustinian person is fluid, tenuous, troubled by temporality and problems of freedom, and influenced by language, history, and society.

From Genus to Image of God

Augustine's understanding of the human person is closely tied to the interpretation of the soul's nature and origin that he draws out of his reading of the Genesis creation narrative. This interpretation is itself rooted in his cosmology. Like many of his Christian predecessors, Augustine uses a Platonist theory of the *rationes* (ideas) to develop a formal cosmology out of the creation narrative in Genesis 1.[8] In Augustine's version of the theory the Son holds within his divine nature the *rationes primordiales* (eternal ideas) that govern the creation of all intellectual and material things.[9] From the eternal ideas comes a lower rational ordering principle, called the *rationes seminales* (seminal ideas), that directly governs the existence of material creation.[10] Augustine uses this basic schema to help develop a speculative account of the origin of the human being in Genesis 1. This speculative approach is on display from the opening of *Genesi ad litteram,* where Augustine claims that Genesis 1:1 — "In the beginning God made heaven and earth" — indicates that creation is divided into an intellectual creation ("heaven") and a material cre-

---

Ludwig Wittgenstein, *Philosophical Investigations,* trans. G. E. M. Anscombe (Oxford: Blackwell, 1997), pp. 1-3.

7. For example, see Catherine LaCugna, *God for Us: The Trinity and Christian Life* (San Francisco: Harper & Row, 1973), pp. 81-109; Rosemary Radford Ruether, *Gaia and God: An Ecofeminist Theology of Earth Healing* (San Francisco: HarperCollins, 1992), pp. 134-39, 184-88.

8. For studies of the *rationes seminales* in Augustine's thought see Etienne Gilson, *The Christian Philosophy of Saint Augustine,* trans. L. E. M. Lynch (New York: Octagon Books, 1983), pp. 205-9; Michael J. McKeough, "The Meaning of the *Rationes Seminales* in St. Augustine," diss., Catholic University of America, 1926.

9. *Gn. litt.* 1.10.17-20; 1.18.36; 2.8.16-19; 3.12.18; 4.24.41-25.42; 5.12.28; 6.11.19.

10. *Gn. litt.* 2.8.16-19; 2.15.30; 3.12.18-20; 5.4.9-11; 5.7.20; 6.6.10-11; 6.10.17; 6.14.25; 7.24.35; 9.17.32. Aquinas comments on the multiple levels of divine causation latent in Augustine's theory of the *rationes* in *Summa theologica* Ia.105.5; Ia.115.2. See also Aquinas, *Summa contra Gentiles,* 3.94; 3.69; 3.70.8; 3.67.

ation ("earth").[11] The former includes all forms of created intellect: angels and the human soul.[12] The latter consists of the material universe: the earth, plants, animals, and all other material objects, including the human body.

With this intellect/matter schema before him, Augustine moves further into the opening chapter of Genesis in search of a greater understanding of the origin of intelligence, matter, and the human person. One of his favorite exegetical strategies is to identify an underlying meaning in particular word choices or phrase repetitions. Of interest to him in Genesis 1 is the repetition of a few phrases associated with intellectual and material creation, which he argues provide the hermeneutical key for deciphering different origins. Augustine associates intellectual creation with the creation of light in Genesis 1:3, and notes that its creation is unique within the overall creation narrative because only light comes into existence immediately and fully following the phrase "et dixit Deus: Fiat" (and God said: "Let it be made"). He interprets this to mean that the creation of intellectual beings is an unmediated act: God creates intellectual beings in their actual existence without intermediate steps according to the *rationes primordiales* held in the Son.[13]

By contrast, the creation of material beings (e.g., plants, animals), whose description occupies Genesis 1:6-25, occurs after three phrases: "et dixit Deus: Fiat," "et sic est factum" (and thus it was made), and "fecit Deus" (God made it).[14] Augustine interprets this to mean that the creation of material beings is a three-step process. From the *rationes primordiales* held in the Son, God creates the *rationes seminales,* which themselves hold the principles and power from which flows the actual creation of material things.

Accordingly, intellectual and material things come into existence in distinct manners. God creates material beings indirectly through a universal principle (i.e., *rationes seminales*) external to, and independent of, the individual existence of each being. The intellectual creature, by contrast, is created directly by God in an active relation with God.[15] Its origin is tied to its own intellectual act. The creation of light is the creation of enlightenment — the creation of intelligence — and it is an immediate coming into existence — "et dixit Deus: Fiat."[16]

---

11. In this essay, citations of Genesis are drawn from *Genesi ad litteram.* Augustine uses a pre-Vulgate, Latin version of the Bible.

12. See also *Conf.* 13.2.3.

13. *Gn. litt.* 1.3.7-5.10; 1.9.15-10.20; 1.15.29; 1.17.32; 3.20.30-32.

14. *Gn. litt.* 2.8.16-19; 3.20.30-32.

15. *Gn. litt.* 2.8.16.

16. Augustine's understanding of enlightenment is related to his concept of illumina-

I would underscore that an everyday type of intellectual act is not what is at issue here. It is not the act of an existing creature that thinks about something to come to an understanding of it. Rather, it is an immediate knowing that itself constitutes the existence of the intellectual creature — self-awareness in its most basic sense. This is what it means to be *intellectual* creation. God's creative act results immediately in the creature's own act of knowing, an act of knowing turned toward God. This makes the origin of the intellectual creature intimately tied to its own creation and constituted by its responsiveness to God. In the very act of being, the creature acknowledges (worships) its creator.

Image and Identity

The unique relation forged between God and intellectual creation carries over into Augustine's discussion of the formation of human identity. His judgments here again form around his exegetical strategy of tracing the distinctive application of terms to material creation and human beings. One term Augustine focuses on is *similitudinem* (likeness), and the manner of its occurrence in the description of plants (1:11-12) and the human being (1:26).

Though not in the Vulgate, the phrase *secundum similitudinem* (according to likeness) appears in the account of the creation of plants found in Genesis 1:11-12 of Augustine's Latin version.[17] Augustine notes that it is conjoined to the phrase *secundum genus* (according to genus), a phrase Augustine interprets to indicate the capacity in creatures to reproduce offspring of the same kind.[18] He argues that the conjunction of these phrases means that the likeness that orders the identity of plants is associated with their genus. After Genesis 1:11-12 the phrase *secundum similitudinem* does not recur, though

---

tion, which is a debated topic. For an overview of the issue see C. E. Schuetzinger, *The German Controversy on Saint Augustine's Illumination Theory* (New York: Pageant Press, 1960).

17. *Gn. litt.* 2.12.25. Augustine's Old Latin version of Gen. 1:11-13 is as follows: "Et dixit Deus: Germinet terra herbam pabuli, ferentem semen secundum genus et secundum similitudinem; et lignum fructiferum faciens fructum, cuius semen sit in ipso secundum similitudinem suam super terram. Et factum est sic. Et eiecit terra herbam pabuli, semen habentem secundum suum genus, et secundum similitudinem, et lignum fructiferum faciens fructum, cuius semen eius insit secundum genus super terram. Et vidit Deus quia bonum est. Et facta est vespera, et factum est mane dies tertius."

18. *Gn. litt.* 3.12.18-20. Animals of each *genus* come from a common "seed" *(semen),* which has the power to transmit the identity of the creature through succeeding generations.

secundum genus is repeated following the creation of the animals. Augustine claims that *secundum similitudinem* is implicitly understood in the creation of animals since every animal reproduces offspring of the same likeness.[19]

In Genesis 1:26 the creation of humans is also associated with the term *similitudinem,* but now the term is joined to *ad imaginem* (to the image) rather than *secundum genus.*[20] Augustine wonders why *secundum genus* is not added to the verse, and notes initially that *genus* is unnecessary in the case of humans because only one individual is created (i.e., Adam). In the case of plants and animals multiple kinds are created, and the *genus* of each kind of plant and animal demarcates it from the others.[21] This initial conclusion intimates Augustine's conviction that the human person is singularly unique in creation such that the language of *genus* is not needed to distinguish it from other similar creatures.[22]

No other creature is similar to the human person, because the person finds its likeness in the image of God. For Augustine, this represents an important shift in the creation narrative that points to the special relation between God and the soul.[23] Material creatures bear a general likeness to God on account of their participation in the *rationes seminales.* Humans, however, are created according to the image of God. Image is a special category of likeness, designating a more direct dependency of the creature on that which it images.[24]

The direct nature of this relation between God and the soul leads Augustine to distinguish how the basic identity of humans and other material

19. *Gn. litt.* 3.12.19. "Hoc est ergo secundum genus, ubi et seminum vis et similitudo intelligitur succedentium decedentibus."

20. *Gen. litt.* 3.12.20. Gen. 1:26 reads: "Et dixit Deus: Faciamus hominem ad imaginem et similitudinem nostram."

21. *Gn. litt.* 3.12.20.

22. *Gn. litt.* 3.19.29. I focus here on Augustine's discussion of the creation of Adam. In later books of his *Literal Commentary* (7.28.40-42; 10.3.5) Augustine claims that post-Adamic humanity is created according to the *genus* of Adam. Elsewhere I have argued that the language of *genus* here functions analogously to the way the language of *rationes* functions in the early books of the *Literal Commentary* to describe the creation of Adam and Eve. See my dissertation, "Created in the Image of God: The Formation of the Augustinian Self," University of Chicago, 2008, pp. 75-79.

23. See also *Conf.* 13.22.32.

24. Augustine does not distinguish between image and likeness as clearly or consistently as do some in the Greek tradition. His most explicit delineation of the terms is found in *Div. qu.* 74. See also James J. O'Donnell, ed., *Augustine: Confessions,* vol. 3 (Oxford: Clarendon, 1992), p. 395; R. A. Markus, "'Imago' and 'similitudo' in Augustine," *REAug* 10 (1964): 125-43.

creatures is transmitted. The likeness of plants and animals is found in their *genus* and transmitted through reproduction. Humans reproduce as well, but the distinctive nature of their identity is not transmitted in this manner.[25] The divine image is transmitted to succeeding generations of human souls not through an original seed *(genus)* in a biological act, but rather by the direct, spiritual act of God. The spiritual nature of this act lies in the twofold fact that the image is of God (Spirit), and the image is found in the mind, not the body.[26]

Augustine's conclusion on the source of identity for the soul and material creation builds from his arguments on the origin of the intellectual (heaven) and material (earth) spheres. The identity of material objects derives from, and is ordered to, the likeness of their *genus,* which is held within the *rationes seminales.* This whole system provides a preestablished, universal structure that governs the way all individual things in the material world come into existence. The benefit of this system, from an Augustinian standpoint, is that it gives a clear order and stability to material creation.[27] But the *genus* is external and prior to the particular existence of each material object. The identity of material things is governed by a potential-actual dynamic and oriented toward a universal structure *(genus)* that stands outside it. Accordingly, the identity of material objects is removed both from the direct action of God and from the object's own particular existence.

The situation is different for the soul. The immediate and intimate relation between God and the soul generated by its origin is complemented by a similar situation in its identity. As part of intellectual creation, the soul exists, primordially speaking, in an intellectual act oriented toward God. The intimate relation generated here opens onto the identity of the soul as the image of God. This in turn offers another angle to understand Augustine's skepticism toward having a created principle, such as the *rationes seminales,* mediate in any causal sense between the creation of the individual soul and the direct act of God.[28] In Augustine's terminology, an image (as opposed to

---

25. *Gn. litt.* 3.12.20; 10.3.5.

26. Augustine's version of Gen. 1:26 does not specify which dimension(s) of the human being is the *image of God.* But citing Paul (Eph. 4:23-24; Col. 3:10), Augustine is clear that the image of God is found in the soul or illuminated mind (*Gn. litt.* 3.20.30): "satis ostendens ubi sit homo creatus ad imaginem Dei, quia non corporis lineamentis, sed quadam forma intelligibili mentis illuminatae." See also *Gn. litt.* 7.24.35.

27. *Gn. litt.* 3.12.18-20; 6.14.25. See also Gilson, *Christian Philosophy of Saint Augustine,* pp. 206-7.

28. Augustine entertains theories on how the soul might originate through an inter-

a likeness) requires a more direct relation. God's act of creation is reflected, or imaged, in the creature's existence. This reflection itself structures the intellectual act of the creature, an act that is an acknowledgment of its creator. In its very existence the creature acknowledges God as its creator — the creature worships God.

The Question of Embodiment

Augustine's two-substance account of creation (intellect/matter) leads to a two-source anthropology in which there are distinct spheres for the origin of the soul (intelligence) and the body (matter). The difficulties that arise from a two-source anthropology are not hard to ascertain. For example, how exactly are the two sources brought together in the unity of the human being? Does this two-source approach potentially open the way for the type of oppositional dualism much criticized in contemporary thought? Augustine himself is aware of, and comments on, problems his model raises, and at various points offers some resources to address the tensions.[29]

One such resource is the contrast he draws between humans and angels, a contrast that leads him to directly face the question of the psychosomatic unity of the human being. Puzzling over the repetition of the phrase "evening and morning" in Genesis 1, especially in its occurrences prior to the creation of the heavenly bodies in 1:14, Augustine hypothesizes that it may refer to a movement in the intellect of the angels.[30] In their original creation angels know all creation, including themselves, through the Word rather than through themselves. Augustine speculates that "evening" could describe the movement of angelic intellect from its contemplation of creation in the Word to its contemplation of creation in itself. "Morning" could then describe the return of angelic intellect to the direct contemplation of God. Augustine characterizes this overall movement as less epistemological than doxological. The return of the angels to God is an act in which the angels give to God the praise due the Creator.[31]

Augustine's angelology may appear overly speculative, but the "evening-

---

mediate principle with its own causal efficacy, such as an angelic act. But for the most part he rejects such theories in favor of a direct act of divine creation. *Gn. litt.* 10 is dedicated to this issue, though see also 7.6.9–9.13; 7.22.32–28.42.

29. *Gn. litt.* 6.6.9; 6.9.15; 7.22.32–27.39.
30. *Gn. litt.* 1.10.18; 4.21.38–35.56.
31. *Gn. litt.* 4.21.38–35.56.

morning" creation of angelic intelligence stands as an important contrast to the creation of human beings. The crux of the difference centers on the issue of human embodiment: humans first exist and come to know themselves, their environment, and God through their bodies. Human existence is characterized by psychosomatic unity.[32] This claim resonates widely in Augustine's anthropology: in his rejection of both the preexistence of souls prior to embodiment and their transmigration after death;[33] in his adherence to the bodily resurrection;[34] and in his more general claims that human identity forms through embodiment.[35] And this leads him to conclude that human formation moves in the reverse direction of the angels: humans begin with a knowledge of the created order and progress to a knowledge of God, while angels begin with a knowledge of God before coming to a knowledge of the created order.[36]

This reversal is significant because of the qualifications it requires to Augustine's discussion of the soul's participation in the intellectual creation. The creation and conditioning of angelic identity run parallel: both begin with, and end in, the knowledge of God. In the case of humans, the situation is more complex. The soul is part of intellectual creation and so enjoys a type of immediacy to God. But this immediacy must be interpreted within the historical development of the human being.[37] To harmonize these accounts, we might say that the immediacy of the soul to God is the formal order of its creation, which is always conditioned through its embodied existence. The order of being and knowing is reversed within human knowledge: the soul is created in the image of the immaterial God, but its growth and development begin in material creation and move toward God. This process of identity formation means that we must distinguish but not separate body and soul. The real identity of the person is found in

32. *Gn. litt.* 2.8.16-19; 4.23.40–24.41; 4.32.49-50; 5.4.9-10.

33. *Gn. litt.* 7.9.12–12.18.

34. *Gn. litt.* 6.6.9; 6.9.15; 6.19.30–28.39; 9.3.6; *Civ. Dei* 13.16-23; 22.14-21.

35. Working from a basic Platonist epistemology modified by his own model of the relation between faith and reason, Augustine argues that human understanding progresses through empirical experience — knowledge of the created order — toward the vision of God. For example, see *Gn. litt.* 4.32.49; *Conf.* 7.17.23; *Trin.* 11.1.1.

36. *Gn. litt.* 2.8.16-19; 4.23.40–24.41; 4.32.49-50.

37. It should be noted that Augustine interprets the two creation narratives of Gen. 1–2 as two accounts of creation, the first an atemporal, simultaneous account of how all things were made and the second a temporal account of how things were created in historical sequence. The immediacy of the soul to God is described within the first account, while its historical development is underscored in the second account.

the unity of soul and body, a fact that applies not only to the historical but also to the resurrected human being.[38]

Judgments about the separation between the intellectual and material spheres in Augustine's cosmology, and about potential dualisms inherent in his larger theology (e.g., mind/body, spirit/matter), must consider his specific claims on the psychosomatic unity of the human being and his more general conception of the relation between intellect and matter. The human person exists only in its embodiment. Material reality exists only through created intellectual principles (i.e., the *rationes seminales*). This cautions the reader against deriving an oppositional dualism from Augustine's intellect/matter account of creation and importing it into his anthropology. This has been the trend in some recent feminist and ecological scholarship.[39] The pernicious nature of dualisms in Augustine is sometimes overstated, as for example concerning his claims about the body and sexuality.[40] Augustine certainly distinguishes between intellect and matter, often in strong terms. But they come together in irreducible unity to form the human being. One must be careful to formulate the nature of the relation between intellect and matter to acknowledge the range of claims about the human being Augustine develops in his doctrine of creation.[41]

Conclusion: Augustine in the Context of Contemporary Debates

Allow me to highlight a few implications of Augustine's exegesis of the opening chapters of Genesis that are not his — they are my own — but that I think offer suggestions pertinent to a theological anthropology engaged in

38. This does not mean the physical body perdures. "Body" is a term that can be applied in both a physical context and a spiritual context. For example, see Augustine's discussion of the difference between Adam's "animal" body and the "spiritual" body humans will have at the resurrection (*Gn. litt.* 6.19.30–26.37).

39. See LaCugna, *God for Us;* and Ruether, *Gaia and God.*

40. For balanced critiques on the importance of the body, material reality, and sexuality in Augustine's thought, see Margaret Miles, *Augustine on the Body,* AARDS 31 (Missoula, Mont.: Scholars Press, 1979); John Rist, *Augustine: Ancient Thought Baptized* (New York: Cambridge University Press, 1994), pp. 112-21.

41. Developing a harmonious conception of the intellect/matter relation becomes more imperative when one expands beyond Augustine's doctrine of creation into his Christian claims on the goodness of creation and the incarnation. Carol Harrison's work offers an excellent analysis of these issues: *Beauty and Revelation in the Thought of Saint Augustine* (Oxford: Clarendon, 1992).

contemporary discussions on human identity. In Augustine's reading of Genesis 1–2 we see glimpses of an anthropology sought by scholars trying to develop post-Enlightenment anthropologies that move beyond conceptions of the human person as an autonomous, rational agent.[42] For Augustine, the identity of the soul is forged in its imaging of God. The image of God is not some "thing," part, or faculty imprinted onto an already existing soul; rather it characterizes how the soul forms its most basic identity out of its existence. This identity is internal to the soul and not externally received as in the case of material objects (i.e., via the *rationes seminales*). The soul exists in a type of reflective immediacy in which its primordial identity is given to it from that which the soul is not (i.e., God). This leads to the paradoxical conclusion that the soul is most itself when it is least its own.

This should raise skepticism toward claims that Augustine's concept of the soul grounds the modern (Enlightenment) idea of the self as an autonomous, rational agent.[43] For Augustine, human identity is never forged *autos.* As I am created according to the image of another (God), so I am most myself not when I am myself (i.e., imaging creation) but when I am according to another (i.e., imaging God). This idea of human identity formation, what I am calling its reflective immediacy, has closer affinities with Heideggerian phenomenology and its attempts to understand human nature not in terms of determinate structures grounded in universal categories like being or genus, but rather as a dynamic and malleable entity formed through relations that are always outside one's control.[44] In some respects Augustine is at the juncture of classical (substance) and postclassical metaphysics: he relies on categories of substance (material/spiritual, genus), but his anthropology calls into question the adequacy of such categories for interpreting how the image of God forms human identity.

In Augustine's reading of Genesis 1–2, the image of God is at the core

---

42. See n. 5 for a list of authors.

43. Charles Taylor, *Sources of the Self: The Making of the Modern Identity* (Cambridge: Harvard University Press, 1989), pp. 127-42.

44. These relations are conceived differently in this tradition: Heidegger's being-with, Levinas's face of the other, and Marion's being-given. For Heidegger, and the methodological atheism that frames his phenomenology, the world of the person does not transcend the human world (of *Dasein*). Beginning with Levinas, and continuing with Marion, French phenomenology pushes against these methodological parameters to some extent, opening onto an ethical (Levinas) and erotic (Marion) realm that transcends one's own personal subjectivity (e.g., Levinas's face of the other) and begins *potentially* to hint at a divine realm (e.g., Marion's saturated phenomenon).

of the identity of the human person. But his anthropology does not reduce to a narrowly spiritualized view of the person or conceive the soul (spirit) and body (matter) in oppositional categories.[45] Augustine's anthropology is a careful orchestration of the spiritual and material. It attempts to offer an ever-elusive view of humanity sought after in contemporary circles of a self anchored to time and history but also free and rational. Augustine uses the language of *similitudinem* to describe the creation of both body and soul, but precisely from the distinct ways this language applies to the soul emerges its unique status as that which is according to the image of God.

Of course, questions linger about how this insight into the nature of the soul applies to the historical existence of the human being. If the soul belongs to the intellectual creation and so has its existence in its knowing, and this knowing reflects (on) God (i.e., the image of God), how exactly does this relate to questions of embodiment, sin, and salvation? This opens onto wider questions about Augustine's account of nonhuman, material creation that emerge from the way he juxtaposes it to the soul. Is the material world a stable order dictated by the *rationes seminales,* or is it more like the dynamic, relational nature that characterizes human existence?

Without resolving such problems, Augustine nevertheless argues that it is on the issue of the body and its temporal, historical nature that humans and angels differ. Human identity is formed through embodiment and humans exist only as embodied intelligence. Embodiment is not a punishment for sin or a degradation of human intellectual excellence. Rather, it constitutes the distinctive nature of human existence beyond the purely intellectual existence of the angels, and so contributes to the diffuse variety that characterizes the goodness of God's creation.

---

45. Authors who raise these charges against Augustine include LaCugna, *God for Us;* Ruether, *Gaia and God.* Similar contemporary critiques are found in John Zizioulas, *Being as Communion: Studies in Personhood and the Church* (New York: St. Vladimir's Seminary Press, 1985), pp. 25, 41 n. 35, 88, 95, 100, 104 n. 98; Colin Gunton, *The Promise of Trinitarian Theology* (Edinburgh: T&T Clark, 1997), pp. 42-45.

Poetry and Theology in Milton's *Paradise Lost*

Trevor Hart

To Instruct and to Delight

In his 1925 study *Milton: Man and Thinker,* Denis Saurat urged upon his readers the importance of the attempt to "disentangle from theological rubbish the permanent and human interest of [Milton's] thought."[1] The thought is the familiar modern one that what really matters in poetry, as elsewhere, transcends the accidents of time and place (and particular theological commitment), and may only be had by a painstaking process of stripping these away. In his *Preface to Paradise Lost,* C. S. Lewis responded, in typically forthright and colorful fashion, that this was somewhat like "asking us to study . . . centipedes when free of their irrelevant legs, or Gothic architecture without the pointed arches."[2] Somehow the very point of the matter has been missed, or at least wantonly denied. "Milton's thought," Lewis insisted, "when purged of its theology, does not exist." Much more recently, Theo Hobson has laid an analogous charge at the door of post-Romantic approaches to Milton's poetry as "Literature" that regularly laud him as a great poet, yet assess his worth as such without reference to those ideas that, on another view of the matter, appear to be the very lifeblood of his poetry itself. This, Hobson suggests, is like celebrating Jesus as a "great moral

---

1. Denis Saurat, *Milton: Man and Thinker* (New York: Dial Press, 1925), p. 111.
2. C. S. Lewis, *A Preface to Paradise Lost* (London: Oxford University Press, 1942), p. 65.

teacher"; the judgment is not itself false, but it hardly scratches the surface of what really matters about his teachings.[3]

As a pre-Romantic, Milton himself would not have recognized the point of a tribute to his or anyone else's poetry in terms of its aesthetic and "literary" aspects alone. Of course he understood perfectly well that poetry was gratuitous beyond any utility it might also possess. Indeed, as Frank Kermode notes, "From all that Milton says about the way poetry works, it is clear that he asks of it not that it should *immediately* instruct, but that it should immediately delight."[4] It is also true that "Milton wrote a theological treatise; but *Paradise Lost* is not it."[5] *De Doctrina Christiana*, in effect a work of systematic theology, was composed over several decades and probably completed at the end of the 1650s, just seven years before the publication of *Paradise Lost*.[6] But the aestheticist notion of art produced "for art's sake" was unknown in Milton's day, and the words of poetry mattered for much more than their music alone. In an early anti-prelatical tract Milton himself articulates a vision of the poet as one uniquely gifted by the Spirit to gauge the verities of human life under God and, by showing these forth in ways sufficient to capture the popular imagination, transform the conditions of personal and public life alike.[7] Instruction and delight, he clearly believed, could and should interpenetrate, and in this sense the poet could and must properly be a "theologian" too.

Milton's poetry issues from (and situates itself explicitly within) the intellectual, practical, and affective world of Christian faith in the early-modern period. This was, William Poole observes, a period when the narrative center of gravity of *Paradise Lost* (in Gen. 3) and doctrinal constructs at-

3. Theo Hobson, *Milton's Vision: The Birth of Christian Liberty* (New York: Continuum, 2008), p. 164. Phil Donnelly's recent work also insists upon holding Milton's theology closely together with his poetry if we are properly to understand the latter. See Phillip J. Donnelly, *Milton's Scriptural Reasoning: Narrative and Protestant Toleration* (Cambridge: Cambridge University Press, 2009), esp. pp. 73-165.

4. Frank Kermode, "Adam Unparadised," in Frank Kermode, ed., *The Living Milton* (London: Routledge & Kegan Paul, 1960), p. 92.

5. Ibid., p. 91.

6. On this text and the circumstances surrounding its composition see Gordon Campbell and Thomas N. Corns, *John Milton: Life, Work and Thought* (Oxford: Oxford University Press, 2008), pp. 271ff.

7. Milton, "The Reason of Church-government Urg'd against Prelaty" (1641). For the relevant passage see the edition by Harry Morgan Ayres in Frank Allen Patterson, ed., *The Works of John Milton*, vol. 3, part 1 (New York: Columbia University Press, 1931), p. 238.

tendant upon it were at the forefront of theological conversation.[8] Among Protestant variations on Augustinianism, differing perspectives on the doctrines of grace, freedom, foreknowledge, the divine decree, and the state of human nature before and after the "fall" were bandied around as convenient markers of party allegiance, and all came to a head conveniently in contested readings of this particular biblical text. Why *did* Adam do what he did? This, of course, is an interesting religious and theological question. But in an age when religious and political visions were more difficult to disentangle than they sometimes are (in theory at least) today, the exegesis of biblical texts both informed and was in turn informed directly by the realities of public life, and a question about the conditions of Adam's fall was naturally understood to be a question about what human beings are like when push comes to shove and, consequently, how human societies might most appropriately be ordered for the common good. For Milton and his contemporaries, the true context for human action could really only be understood through an imaginative grasp on a profoundly theological vision of reality, a vision of the precise sort Milton himself offers in *Paradise Lost.*

Certain questions in particular exercised Milton throughout his life, especially those to do with human liberty and the conditions under which it may meaningfully be exercised in a moral way. Thus in *Areopagitica* (1644), attacking Parliament's efforts to curb the freedom of the press, we find the following:

> If every action which is good, or evill in man at ripe years, were to be under pittance, and prescription, and compulsion, what were vertue but a name, what praise could be then due to well-doing, what grammercy to be sober, just or continent? many there be that complain of divin Providence for suffering *Adam* to transgresse, foolish tongues! when God gave him reason, he gave him freedom to choose, for reason is but choosing; he had bin else a meer artificiall *Adam,* such an *Adam* as he is in the motions. . . . Assuredly we bring not innocence into the world, we bring impurity much rather: that which purifies us is triall, and triall is by what is contrary.[9]

Temptation, in other words, is the necessary condition not only for sin but for its opposite too, obedience and the cultivation of true virtue. Good-

---

8. See William Poole, *Milton and the Idea of the Fall* (Cambridge: Cambridge University Press, 2005), esp. chs. 3–4.

9. "Areopagitica," ed. William Haller, in Patterson, ed., *Works of John Milton,* vol. 4 (New York: Columbia University Press, 1931), pp. 319, 311.

ness that never has to grapple with evil (either because its choices are co-erced, or because the opportunities for evil are carefully airbrushed out of its world in advance) is bound only to be a shallow and morally sickly thing; and the establishment of good in place of evil impulses in human lives lies only through victories in battle rather than strategies of constant retreat. If, then, we would truly be delivered from evil, Milton is suggesting, it can only be because we have first been led into (or exposed to) temptation. And it is this, he muses, that "justifies the high providence of God, who though he command us temperance, justice, continence, yet powrs out before us ev'n to a profuseness all desirable things, and gives us minds that can wander beyond all limit and satiety."[10] Another two decades would pass before the publication of Milton's more famous attempt to "justify the ways of God to men," yet the theological and political themes explored poetically in *Paradise Lost* are here already on the table.

Milton, then, was immersed to the hilt in the political theology of his day, and we cannot glibly brush this practical, fiduciary, and intellectual context aside in the pursuit of "purely aesthetic" considerations. The beliefs, the ideas, are absolutely essential to the way the poem works *as a poem*, fusing the concerns of heart and mind and will together in an imaginative vision that challenges and reshapes not just our thinking, but in Lewis's phrase our "total response to the world."[11]

"Forewarn'd," or "Seduc'd to Foul Revolt"?

If, as I have suggested, it is important to approach *Paradise Lost* as a text that is concerned to instruct as well as to delight its readers, it is equally important to ask about the precise manner in which this instruction is duly delivered. By its very nature, the voice of poetry is generally more elusive, more indirect than that of manuals of systematic theology, demanding a far higher level of interpretation. To misidentify or mishear the "voice" of the poem is (even in cases where higher rather than lower levels of reader reception must be acknowledged as essential to the event of poetic meaning) to jeopardize the broad shape of the learning and teaching process that the poet hoped to set in motion.

How, then, in *Paradise Lost* should we think of Milton placing himself

10. Ibid., p. 320.
11. Lewis, *Preface to Paradise Lost*, p. 54.

(or rather the voice of his poem) and his readers vis-à-vis the received theological orthodoxies of his day? His poem contains many voices, and in the nature of the case they articulate many different perspectives, perspectives that often stand in stark contradiction to one another. The poem could hardly contain the drama that it does otherwise, drama being largely a matter of the careful generation and subsequent resolution of conflicts. But where amid all this complicated play of locution are we to identify the singular "word" of the poem itself speaking to us and — since Milton deliberately casts his epic within the context of prayer, transforming Homer and Virgil's appeal to the Muse into an invocation to the Spirit — for the poetically mediated Word of God?[12]

I want next briefly to identify four literary-critical answers to this question, before turning to a theological issue that lies at the very core of the poem's treatment of Genesis 3, and considering it in the light of them. On the basis of that, I shall end by proposing that a fifth alternative may need to be entertained.

According to one tradition, notoriously pioneered by Blake and Shelley, and subsequently developed by William Empson and others, Milton's poetry must finally be judged heterodox in its theological achievements, whether he intended it that way or not. So, in plate 6 of *The Marriage of Heaven and Hell* (c. 1790), William Blake suggests that "Milton wrote in fetters when he wrote of Angels & God, and at liberty when of Devils and Hell, . . . because he was a true Poet and of the Devil's party without knowing it."[13] In brief, according to this reading the character of Satan comes out of the thing on the whole rather better than God in moral terms, and the reader quickly finds himself imaginatively and sympathetically identifying with him and with the rebellion that constitutes the first "fall" in the poem. Of course, the "official" voice of the narrator and some other voices (those of God himself and of the archangel Raphael) offer a damning perspective on all this (as Milton, perhaps, realized that his poetic creation was rather running away with him, and sought to turn things around), but it is too late; the damage has been done, and we, together with our poetic recruiting agent, find ourselves too to be "of Satan's party."

A directly opposed view to this is championed by C. S. Lewis, accord-

---

12. See, e.g., 1.17-18; 3.51-52.

13. The suggestion is duly endorsed in Shelley's *Defence of Poetry* (1840). Empson insists that the main virtue of *Paradise Lost* is precisely that it unwittingly "makes God so bad." See William Empson, *Milton's God* (London: Chatto and Windus, 1961), p. 275.

ing to whom Milton's account of the fall and all that surrounds it is straightforward (for those with eyes to see), and "substantially that of St Augustine,
which is that of the Church as a whole."[14] Like most other pre-Romantic po-
ets, Lewis suggests, Milton was perfectly content to give a clear lead on matters of spiritual and moral concern, evoking "stock responses" among his
readers (in this case responses tutored by a Vincentian catholic consensus
stretching back over the centuries[15]), and thus contributing directly to the
formation and preparation of human character to meet life's various challenges and opportunities in a fitting manner. Of course there are conflicting
voices in the poem, but the discerning reader sees quickly through the boo
characters, and takes a stand with the "overwhelmingly Christian" perspective of the poetic consensus. Milton, Lewis suggests, "manipulates" his readers unashamedly rather than allowing them to make up their own minds or
wander too far off the beaten track;[16] and he does so in the unashamed interest of Christian formation.

In *Surprised by Sin*,[17] Stanley Fish builds on Lewis's identification of a
subtle manipulation of the reader by Milton, but takes it in a rather different
direction. Rather than holding the reader by the hand, as it were, what Milton
does, according to Fish, is to dump the reader down unceremoniously in the
world of his poetic creation itself, and leave him there, withdrawing the benefit of narratorial omniscience, and setting him up to be seduced by the very
same voices and alluring options that duly lead Eve and Adam themselves
into disobedience. So yes, we do find ourselves seduced by Satan's allure, at
least at first. And, when Adam falls, we are sympathetic to his choice, and
would follow him. But in the moment that we "fall" the authoritative voice of
the poem rebukes us and calls us to account. The intent of all this, Fish suggests, is not sheer sadism or harassment of the reader. *Caught up in* the poetic
action rather than simply *taught by* it, we discover the dark truth about ourselves, and emerge from the encounter (which occurs more than once in the
poem as we fail to learn the relevant lesson) chastened, and penitent. In a
sense, Fish's Milton is a supralapsarian deity who *leads his readers into temptation* precisely in order to deliver them from evil, a suggestion that echoes
ideas we have already identified in Milton's earlier musings and that is relevant to the poem's own larger theological understanding, as we shall see.

14. Lewis, *Preface to Paradise Lost*, p. 66.
15. Ibid., p. 82.
16. Ibid., p. 41.
17. Stanley Fish, *Surprised by Sin: The Reader in Paradise Lost*, 2nd ed. (Cambridge:
Harvard University Press, 1997).

In *Milton and the Idea of the Fall,* William Poole suggests that a compromising of dogmatic orthodoxy occurs in the poem, together with an unresolved conflict of perspectives, all due to the demands of the narrative genre itself. Precisely by seeking to do what Genesis 3 itself never seeks to do, namely, to offer a convincing (i.e., psychologically, emotionally, and humanly convincing) narrative account of the commission of the first sin, Milton finds himself compelled to break company with the mainstream dogmatic tradition. For this tradition Adam and Eve were, in their prelapsarian state, regal and exalted creatures unperturbed by anything and easily able to send Satan packing had they chosen to do so. Milton's poem, Poole observes, offers *just such a vision* with one hand, but then withdraws it with the other, portraying the paradisal couple at various points as frail and vulnerable, easy prey to Satan's machinations. Such inconsistency, he argues, albeit theologically problematic, is *poetically* vital, since in narrative terms there must be a struggle before a capitulation, and thus some indeterminate state leading up to and *accounting for* the "bad action" that follows. Narrative is, after all, a matter of situating events in some meaningful and persuasive order, and the sheer anomaly or surd occurrence sits ill with its aesthetic demands.

Poole's observation provokes an important question. Might the existence of conflicting and unresolved voices here in Milton's poem be driven not (as Poole suggests) by poetic and dramatic considerations alone, but by distinctly theological considerations too? Could such deliberate lack of resolution, in certain circumstances, be more a matter of theological integrity than theological compromise? Might poetry, indeed, be supposed to provide a mode of engagement better suited to the exploration of some theological questions than approaches that tend too soon and inevitably finally toward the production of a neat systematic unity? Bearing this query in mind, we turn now briefly to consider the poem's treatment of the question that echoes through it from end to end: How, in the good purposes of God, was it ever possible for sin and its progeny to enter our world?

"Sufficient to Have Stood"?

According to God's own testimony in book 3 of *Paradise Lost,* human beings were created "sufficient to have stood, though free to fall" (3.99).[18] In many

---

18. Citations from the poem are taken from Christopher Ricks, ed., *John Milton: Paradise Lost* (London: Penguin, 1968).

ways the poem constitutes a sustained reflection on the tensions inherent in this terse formulation and the ways in which it variously illuminates and complicates the dramatic action of book 9, where the fruit of the forbidden tree is actually plucked and eaten. In what sense "sufficient"? And in what sense "free"? And if both sufficient and free, whither then the fall? In grappling with the issue, Milton keeps more than one vision of prelapsarian sufficiency identifiably in play; and the question is, why?

From one angle, then, Milton's poem follows closely the mainstream Augustinian tradition, offering us a paradisal couple in full enjoyment of "unalloyed felicity," unperturbed "by any agitation of the mind, nor pained by any disorder of the body," in full control, in other words, of their passions and their will.[19] These are not the childlike, naïve foundlings of Socinian theology, but regal beings, "erect and tall,/Godlike erect, with native Honour clad/In naked Majesty" (4.288-90). The garden in which God has placed them provides everything they need and much more besides, so that the "sole commandment" is one "easily obey'd amid the choice/Of all tastes else to please their appetite" (7.48-49).[20] It is Adam who asks the relevant question: "can wee want obedience then/To him, or possibly his love desert/Who form'd us from the dust, and plac'd us here/Full to the utmost measure of what bliss/Human desires can seek or apprehend?" (5.514). It hardly seems possible, though we as readers, like God, have the relevant foreknowledge that grants the question powerful dramatic irony.

Milton also rules out any suggestion that the first sin might have been born of childlike ignorance rather than willful disobedience. In book 5 God sends the archangel Raphael on a diplomatic mission to forewarn Adam in the most explicit terms that his faithfulness will be tried, thus rendering "inexcusable" his actual capitulation when it comes. And finally, the poem disentangles the fall quite explicitly from any predestinarian scheme in which, *sub specie aeternitatis,* the fall of human beings was as much a matter of God's willing as of Eve and Adam's own, a matter of "divine overruling" or "absolute Decree," which, even in their freedom, they were in no position to resist.[21] Cleverly, Milton makes God here a more than convenient mouthpiece for his own Arminian theological sympathies.[22] At the point of sin, Eve

19. *City of God* 14.10. See Augustine, *City of God,* trans. Henry Bettenson, Penguin Classics (London: Penguin, 1984), p. 567.

20. Cf. *City of God* 14.12. See Augustine, *City of God,* p. 571.

21. See esp. 3.114-16: "As if Predestination over-rul'd/Their will, dispos'd by absolute Decree/Or high foreknowledge."

22. On Milton's Arminianism see, e.g., Campbell and Corns, *John Milton,* pp. 106,

and Adam act undetermined by anything other than their own will.[23] They are, God insists, "Authors to themselves in all/both what they judge and what they choose" (3.122-23); they decreed their own revolt (3.116), ordained their own fall (3.128). The weight placed on creaturely freedom with respect to God's purposes is quite breathtaking at points: As Eve leaves Adam for a bit of gardening on her own, the circumstance electrically charged by both their and our awareness of the impending danger, Adam contributes some dubious cheerleading: "God towards thee hath done his part," he reminds her; "do thine!" The emphasis, then, is on the capacity and the freedom to obey or to disobey (without which true obedience could not exist at all), and Milton's verdict is apparently God's own: whose fault is the fall and all that follows from it? "Whose but (man's) own" (3.96-97).

There is, though, in the poem another voice, another very different perspective on the whole matter, and it cannot, I think, be dismissed entirely as a seductive perspective that we are expected to entertain only to be duly rebuked and rescued from it, as both Lewis and Fish suggest. To be sure, it is only from Satan's lips that God's human creatures are ever described in the poem as "frail" (1.375) and "puny" (1.367). They are not that. Yet Milton's God himself is finally ambivalent about the precise state in which his human creatures meet Satan's temptation. At one moment he insists that their sin is one committed with a high hand, like that of the rebellious angels before them; yet in the same speech God admits that there is a vital difference, since the angels "by their own suggestion fell,/Self-tempted, self-deprav'd: Man falls deceiv'd/By the other first: Man therefore shall find grace,/the other none" (3.129-32). Elsewhere, Satan is likened by the authoritative voice of the narrator to the thief who climbs into God's fold to harm the flock (4.192), and to a vulture just waiting to prey on helpless newborn lambs (3.434). In book 5 Satan assaults Eve first not in waking reality but in a dream, seducing her through the organ of "Fancy" or imagination, leading her all the way to the edge of the slippery slope of disobedience, holding the forbidden fruit to her mouth; but the dream (as so often) ends and evaporates before the fatal step is taken. Adam's response, on hearing of the dream, is to reassure: Don't worry, he tells her, there is nothing culpable in having had a dream like that in and of itself; "Evil into the mind of God or Man/May come and go, so

---

274-75, 338; Neil Forsyth, *John Milton: A Biography* (Oxford: Lion, 2008), pp. 137-38; Hobson, *Milton's Vision,* pp. 41-43, 54-55; Poole, *Milton and the Idea of the Fall,* p. 159.

    23. Cf. 5.525: "good he made thee, but to persevere/He left it in thy power, ordain'd thy will/By nature free, not overrul'd by Fate/Inextricable, or strict necessity."

unapprov'd, and leave/no spot or blame behind" (5.117-19). Perhaps. Or perhaps here Satan has driven the screw of temptation in just so far, engaging the imagination in order to prepare the path in mind and heart and will for the final, decisive drive in book 9. Perhaps, in other words, there is here an initial "virtual" temptation (if not quite a virtual fall) that renders the other, when it comes, more explicable. Eve has been softened up. The moral ground has been carefully prepared. Man's fall when it occurs will, God admits in his divine foreknowledge, be "easy," all too easy in fact; and when the actual fall is narrated briefly in book 9 what we are offered is a picture of credulous seduction, all trace of "solid virtue" and sufficiency to stand now seemingly absent.

Again, Milton has Adam ask the relevant question (albeit this time from the perspective of fallen humanity): "O why did God,/Creator wise . . . create at last/This novelty on Earth, this fair defect/of Nature . . . ?" (10.888-92). The "fair defect" referred to is Eve, who falls "deceived," taken in by Satan's seductive lies. But we can translate the question; because what Milton does, moving beyond the dynamics of Genesis 3:1-6 with the permission of 1 Timothy 2:14, is to symbolize in the characters of Adam and Eve respectively the twin terms of a Kierkegaardian paradox (viz., one that we should not expect or seek to resolve). Where human freedom is concerned (even unfallen freedom),[24] in a sense we are "undeceived" and thus fully responsible moral agents (and fully "guilty" when we sin); and yet we fall precisely because we are subject to forces preying upon us from without and from within, forces that prey upon us, furthermore, with divine foreknowledge and permission. Milton's God unashamedly leaves Satan "at large to his own dark designs" and looks on as those designs bear their evil fruit; yet he does so precisely so that Satan "enrag'd might see/How all his malice serv'd but to bring forth ultimate goodness, grace, and mercy" (1.213-18). Milton's account of divine Providence here in the poem and in his earlier systematic treatise echoes that of his Arminian mentor Grotius; God is involved in the production of evil in his world inasmuch as he permits its existence, "throwing no impediment in the way of natural causes and free agents," and out of its effects God himself "eventually converts every evil deed into an instrument of good . . . and overcomes evil with good."[25]

---

24. Milton's treatment effectively softens any rigid distinction between fallen and unfallen freedom. Again, one might write this off as a necessary cost of any attempt to imagine the paradisal circumstance concretely (since we *can* only imagine an alien experience by configuring it in terms of what we know); my suggestion here, though, is that Milton does this quite deliberately in order to keep a deeper theological question in play.

25. *On Christian Doctrine* 1.8, in James Holly Hanford and Waldo Hilary Dunn, eds.,

On Milton's Refusal to Conclude

Adam's question in book 10 of *Paradise Lost* is really the one asked by Augustine in book 11 of his *Literal Commentary on Genesis:* Why did God not make his human creatures *more* "sufficient to stand" than he actually did? Milton's approach to this question through the dramatic devices of epic poetry permits him to leave the relevant tensions open and unresolved in a manner that more systematic theological treatments might not, keeping the ideas of human sufficiency and insufficiency paradoxically in play at the same time, rather than resolving them prematurely in the interests of any overarching logical unity. Lazy appeals to mystery can of course be an intellectual cop-out in theology as elsewhere; but not all appeals to mystery are lazy, and we must take care not to grant the spirit of Procrustes a dangerous foothold by tethering our notions of what counts as due intellectual rigor mistakenly to any particular mode of engagement. Arguably, Milton's open-ended poetic approach is at least faithful to the canonical pattern of biblical thought on this particular subject[26] and to the shape of our experience of evil in the world, neither of which encourages us to dignify sin and its outputs by "explaining" them and thereby justifying them, ascribing some positive meaning to them within the scheme of things. And, whether we judge a higher systematic resolution to be warranted or not, the poetry of *Paradise Lost* undeniably affords a powerful "theological" engagement with the realities of human freedom, temptation, and the commission of sin, one that admittedly raises rather than resolves the big questions, but that thereby, I would argue, charts the relevant territory more rather than less adequately. In the end, Milton points us to Augustine's own answer in the *Literal Commentary:* "Penes ipsum est" (11.10.13).[27] Why did God set things up this way? "God alone knows." But then, while it may well seem to us to be a very odd way of proceeding, God, we may reasonably trust, knows best.

De Doctrina Christiana, trans. Charles R. Sumner, in Patterson, ed., *Works of John Milton,* vol. 15 (New York: Columbia University Press, 1933), pp. 67, 79-81. Cf. Grotius's defense of Remonstrant views, e.g., in his *Ordinum Pietas* of 1613. See Edwin Rabbie, ed., *Hugo Grotius: Ordinum Hollandiae ac Westfrisiae Pietas (1613),* Studies in the History of Christian Thought 66 (Leiden: Brill, 1995).

    26. I.e., human freedom and God's sovereign responsibility for all that happens in his world.

    27. See P. Agaësse and A. Solignac, eds., *La Genèse au sens littéral en douze livres (VIII–XII),* Oeuvres de Saint Augustin 49 (Paris: Desclée de Brouwer, 1972), p. 250.

Sex or Violence?
Thinking Again with Genesis
about Fall and Original Sin

Walter J. Houston

At the Sheffield conference on Bible and Justice in 2008 I read a paper on environmental justice as conceived in the Priestly creation and flood stories in Genesis 1 and 6–9.[1] It occurred to me that the same biblical material, which speaks of the corruption of the earth by violence, might support theological rather than purely ethical conclusions. In short, is there a fall in P? And might it be possible by drawing on this material to give the doctrines of the fall and original sin in Christian theology a shot in the arm? It has to be admitted that they are not in very good shape. A survey by Richard Roberts shows that although they were given considerable emphasis by Karl Barth and Dietrich Bonhoeffer, major theologians like Jürgen Moltmann, Eberhard Jüngel, and Wolfhart Pannenberg have not made "anything more than peripheral references" to them,[2] while feminist and liberation theologies have found the original sin not in humanity as such but in particular economic and social structures.

This situation is not surprising. First, probably no one today finds in

---

1. Walter J. Houston, "Justice and Violence in the Priestly Utopia," in Matthew J. M. Coomber, ed., *Bible and Justice: Ancient Texts, Modern Challenges* (London: Equinox, 2011). I am grateful to Equinox Publishing Ltd for permission to use passages from this article (© Equinox Publishing Ltd, 2011) in the present publication.

2. Richard Roberts, "Sin, Saga and Gender: The Fall and Original Sin in Modern Theology," in Paul Morris and Deborah Sawyer, eds., *A Walk in the Garden: Biblical, Iconographical and Literary Images of Eden*, JSOTSup 136 (Sheffield: Sheffield Academic Press, 1992), pp. 244-60, here pp. 255-56.

the least plausible Augustine's hypothesis that the corruption of our human nature is transmitted from our first parents through the sex act through which each new generation comes to be. In any case, as Emil Brunner has seen, the traditional theory of original sin is "completely foreign to the thought of the Bible"; but, according to him, it nevertheless expresses two elements of the biblical (primarily Pauline) understanding of sin: that sin is "a dominant force" in human life, and that "humanity is bound together in a solidarity of guilt."[3] Brunner recognizes that Genesis 3 is a myth, though Barth refuses to use that word, but he also argues that it is a myth essential to the Christian doctrine of sin, in that it presents sin as "a turning-away from the beginning, the abandonment of the origin," and humanity, before Christ, as apostates, as turning away from God and God's grace in disobedience.[4]

Second, however, it is not easy from the exegetical point of view to interpret Genesis 3 as a story concerned essentially with either the origin of sin or the solidarity of human beings in it. It purports to account for the origin of various unhappy features of our life as human beings, but the universality of sin is not one of these. Probably death is not one either, despite Paul in Romans. James Barr has persuasively argued that the story is of a missed opportunity to gain immortality, rather than of its loss.[5] Perhaps, because it is a myth, this does not matter. Perhaps, realistically, all it has to tell is of the solidarity of human beings in turning away from God. Yet exegetically it is difficult to see this also. Theologians, including Brunner, frequently characterize the temptation offered by the serpent as that of becoming *like God,* and so the sin committed as the primal human sin of pride and self-reliance.[6] But it is more probable that כאלהים (Gen. 3:5) means "like gods," as is shown by the words of God in v. 22: "The man has become like *one of us,*"[7] not like the Creator, but merely a step higher on the scale of being. The issues in this story appear to be slighter than theologians would like to make them.

But must we concentrate the entire basis of the doctrine in a single narrative? In Genesis as we have it, it is embedded in a longer narrative of greater cosmic reach. The framework of this narrative is supplied by the "document" P, as source critics have come to call it. Later, we shall need to

---

3. Emil Brunner, *Dogmatics,* vol. 2: *The Christian Doctrine of Creation and Redemption,* trans. Olive Wyon (London: Lutterworth, 1952 [original 1949]), p. 103.

4. Brunner, *Creation,* pp. 91, 100; Karl Barth, *CD* III/1:84-90.

5. James Barr, *The Garden of Eden and the Hope of Immortality* (London: SCM, 1992).

6. Brunner, *Creation,* pp. 92-93.

7. All biblical translations are my own.

ask whether the "J" narratives embedded in it, including the garden of Eden story, may be read as complementary to it, rather than simply additional.

Three passages of divine discourse mark the turning points of the narrative. The first is that pronounced upon the creation of human beings in Genesis 1:28-30, along with the evaluation of the newly created world as "very good" in 1:31. The second is the evaluation of the earth after its corruption in 6:12, in free indirect speech, with the following speech to Noah beginning in v. 13. The third is the speech to Noah after the flood in 9:1-7, with the second speech establishing God's covenant with the earth in vv. 8-11.

Between the first and last points of the story there is a profound transformation. There is no return to the status quo after the flood. Terence Fretheim's heading, "Genesis 9:1–11:26 — A New World Order," expresses this neatly.[8] In 1:29-30 God assigns food to humans and animals respectively. Humans are to eat seeds and fruit, animals are to have the green stuff of the plants. Nothing is said about animal food for either group. It is true that it is not specifically prohibited, and some, including Calvin, have taken this as a loophole to argue that it is not excluded.[9] But human beings are specifically permitted to eat flesh in 9:3, implying, as most agree, that it was previously out of bounds.[10] The world brought into being by God's word of creation and blessing is a world without predation and without violence.[11] Humanity carries out its function of "government" of the animals by natural authority, not by coercion: this is demonstrated by Noah, who models this function to perfection, as P. J. Harland, William Brown, and Fretheim all suggest.[12] The animals simply "come" to Noah (7:9), without, it seems, needing to be driven or enticed.

At the second turning point, the determination made by God is that violence has entered this world and destroyed it. "The earth was destroyed before God; the earth was filled with violence; and God looked at the earth and saw

8. Terence E. Fretheim, *God and the World in the Old Testament* (Nashville: Abingdon, 2005), p. 83.

9. John Calvin, *Commentary on the First Book of Moses, Called Genesis,* trans. John King (1847; repr. Grand Rapids: Eerdmans, 1948), pp. 99-100; Luc Dequeker, "'Green Herbage and Trees Bearing Fruit' (Gen. 1:28-30; 9:1-3)," *Bijdragen* 38 (1977): 118-27.

10. E.g., Claus Westermann, *Genesis 1–11,* trans. John J. Scullion, CC (Philadelphia: Fortress, 1984 [original 1974]), pp. 163-64; P. J. Harland, *The Value of Human Life: A Study of the Story of the Flood (Genesis 6–9),* VTSup 64 (Leiden: Brill, 1996), p. 150.

11. Gerhard von Rad, *Genesis,* trans. John H. Marks, rev. ed., OTL (Philadelphia: Westminster, 1972), p. 61; William P. Brown, *The Ethos of the Cosmos* (Grand Rapids: Eerdmans, 1999), pp. 46-52.

12. Harland, *Value,* p. 197; Brown, *Ethos,* p. 55; Fretheim, *God and the World,* p. 52.

that it was destroyed, because every living thing [lit. 'all flesh'] had destroyed its way on the earth" (6:11-12). God uses the same verbal root as in v. 13, where the intention to destroy the earth is announced, as Anne Gardner notes.[13] I have followed Gardner in using "destroy" for שׁחת instead of the traditional "corrupt," to emphasize the verbal link with v. 13 and the sense of physical damage, and I have translated כל בשׂר (lit. "all flesh") as "every living thing," against Claus Westermann but in line with the majority of exegetes, because that is what "all flesh" means at every one of the numerous times it occurs in the flood account that follows.[14] "Violence" — חמס, the Hebrew word used in 6:11-13 — is defined by Hermann Gunkel as "criminal oppression of the unprotected by those mightier than they."[15] It is the antithesis of justice. Both human beings and animals have been practicing violence: the sequel in 9:3-6 implies that human beings have been eating animal flesh and attacking one another, and that animals have been preying on one another. Gardner interprets "have destroyed their way" by means of 1:28-30: each group has disregarded the divine commands given there.[16] In that case, the "destruction of their way" by humans could be taken to include not only disobedience to the dietary commands but also to the command to subdue the earth and rule its creatures. We shall see shortly what this might mean. Noah is exempted from God's judgment and from the consequent punishment because he stands out as an exception among his contemporaries, preserved from corruption because, like his great-grandfather Enoch (5:24), he "walked with God" (6:9). The implication may be that the animals "came" to Noah because they were able to trust him: he was not implicated in the violence of "all flesh."

It is because of this that, as God tells Noah (6:17), "I am bringing the flood on the earth to destroy everything which has the breath of life from under the sky." Yet the fresh start thus given the world is not a start over again from the original point. The charge given to humans through Noah in 9:1-7 differs in significant ways from the original one in 1:28-30: "The fear of you and the dread of you shall be upon every beast of the earth . . . : into your hands they are delivered. Every moving thing which lives may be food

---

13. Anne Gardner, "Ecojustice: A Study of Genesis 6.11-13," in Norman Habel and Shirley Wurst, eds., *The Earth Story in Genesis,* Earth Bible 2 (Sheffield: Sheffield Academic Press, 2000), pp. 117-29, here pp. 119-20.

14. Westermann, *Genesis,* p. 416, following A. R. Hulst, "*Kol Baśar* in der priesterlichen Fluterzählung," *OtSt* 12 (1958): 28-68. But see Gardner, "Ecojustice," p. 121.

15. Hermann Gunkel, *Genesis Translated and Interpreted,* trans. Mark E. Biddle (Macon, Ga.: Mercer University Press, 1997 [original 5th ed. 1922]), p. 148.

16. Gardner, "Ecojustice," p. 121.

for you; along with the green herbs, I give you everything" (9:2-3). They are to control animals by force and fear, not by their recognized authority. It seems that the relations between people and animals, and indeed between people, have been permanently altered: the flood has enabled a new start, but not a restoration of the primeval world. The irruption of violence into the original state of peace cannot be undone. Violence begets violence down through all subsequent ages of the world. This is a fact of life that we all recognize, unlike Augustine's notion of uncontrollable sexual excitement passing on the corruption of human nature to each generation.

If the blessing in Genesis 9 may be said to reflect the world as it is, that in 1:28-30 could be said to express the divine intention for the world. If Genesis places it in the ideal past, the Isaianic tradition places it in the ideal future (Isa. 11:6-9). Here the rule of the shoot from the stump of Jesse, the ideal king, who rules in justice and destroys oppressors, is figured in the peace that reigns in the animal world. The function that humanity is to discharge in Genesis 1:28 can be understood, at least in part, along the same lines. They are told to "govern" the animals. The Hebrew verb רדה in every case means "rule," "govern," "control." It is not distinctively applied to kings, but when it is it appears usually to refer to rule over foreigners and enemies (1 Kgs. 5:4 [Eng. 4:24]; Isa. 14:6; Pss. 72:8; 110:2); and as it also applies to the control of slaves and conscript labor, its connotations are far from pastoral, in the modern sense of that word. What excludes the sense of exploitation here is the context. Humanity is here being charged with responsibility, not granted license.[17] Now, a central function of government in the Hebrew conception is to check oppression, and so it is in Isaiah 11:4: "He shall vindicate the poor with justice, and decide with equity for the wretched of the land; he shall strike the tyrant with the rod of his mouth, and slay the unjust with the breath of his mouth." And "violence" — חמס — is one of the ways in which oppression is conceived in the Hebrew Bible.[18] Therefore I suggest that the authority of the human governors exists, among other things, to repress violence among the animals. But in this primordial world this does not entail coercion. As Norbert Lohfink suggests, it is to be done by peaceably taming them,[19] or rather they are tame to start with. Now this function is given to humanity in the same context as that in which

17. Cf. Brown, *Ethos*, pp. 45-46.
18. Walter J. Houston, *Contending for Justice* (London: T&T Clark, 2008), pp. 67-68, 90, 142.
19. Norbert Lohfink, "Subdue the Earth? (Genesis 1:28)," in *Theology of the Pentateuch: Themes of the Priestly Narrative and Deuteronomy,* trans. Linda M. Maloney (Minneapolis: Fortress, 1994), pp. 1-17, here p. 12.

they are said to be made "in the image of God." Whatever else this much disputed phrase may mean, it surely implies that in governing they are to act as representatives of the authority of God.

But once humans have taken to violence against one another and against the animals, they no longer validly represent God's authority, and cannot prevent violence from breaking out among the animals.[20] Thus they have lost their own authority. The "fear and dread" inspired in the animals by human beings following Genesis 9:2 maintains their government, but is a poor substitute for the charismatic authority bestowed on them by the original blessing. Interpreters in the critical period do not seem to have recognized that 9:2 implies a weakening rather than a strengthening of humanity's original authority. But earlier, Calvin, for example, speaks of "this dominion, which, although greatly diminished, is nevertheless not entirely abolished."[21] I think this is a correct perception. Even with the post-flood blessing, humanity is unable to repress violence among the animals; they can only protect themselves and use the animals for their own needs.

So the differences between 1:28-30 and 9:1-7 arise from the difference between the ideal and the real worlds. The dispensation of Genesis 1 expresses the divinely intended justice of the world order, a hierarchical order in which human beings stand between God and the rest of the earthly creation, mediating to them the blessings of God's justice.[22] The dispensation in Genesis 9 is a more ambiguous matter. It exists under the sign of God's covenant (9:8-17), which guarantees its permanence, and may be seen to express God's justice; but on the other hand justice is now entirely absent from the animal world. What we mean by "the law of the jungle" is the antithesis of justice. There is an interesting parallel in Hesiod: Zeus has decreed "that fish and beasts and winged birds should eat one another, since justice is not with them; but to human beings he has given justice."[23] However, the rules in 9:4-6 are intended to ensure that at least human beings' relationships to one another and to the animal world are governed by law, not by the unregulated greed and exploitation that constitute violence.

---

20. Gardner, "Ecojustice," p. 126; cf. Bernhard W. Anderson, "Creation and Ecology," in Anderson, ed., *Creation in the Old Testament,* Issues in Religion and Theology 6 (Philadelphia: Fortress, 1984), pp. 152-71, here pp. 163-64.

21. Calvin, *Genesis,* p. 291.

22. Cf. H. H. Schmid, "Creation, Righteousness and Salvation: 'Creation Theology' as the Broad Horizon of Biblical Theology," in Anderson, ed., *Creation,* pp. 102-17.

23. Hesiod, *Works and Days,* ll.277-79, in *Theogony, Works and Days, Testimonia,* ed. and trans. Glenn W. Most, LCL (Cambridge: Harvard University Press, 2006), pp. 208-11.

Thus P conceives of the Noachic dispensation as a dispensation of law, which exists to control the violence of people and animals, whereas the intention of creation had been a dispensation purely of blessing. There is a parallel here with Paul's idea of the function of the law, though clearly P's evaluation of this is rather more positive than Paul's, and Paul apparently only recognizes law from the time of Moses.

Is there a fall in P? At any rate there is fallenness. *That* creation has fallen from the intention of God is shown with the utmost clarity. *How* it fell cannot be answered from P alone. Either there is a lacuna in the document (if that is how P is to be characterized), or the origin of violence and corruption is deliberately veiled. There is a third alternative: that the standard critical view that J and P are independent documents is incorrect, and that one account is written in awareness of the other. Some ways of understanding Genesis diachronically are discussed in the appendix to this paper. For our main purpose it is not necessary to pursue this line of inquiry. We shall instead try to understand the narrative of Genesis 1–9 as a whole in its final form as an account of the fall of the earthly creation away from God's intention of peace and justice.

In this context, the violence of Cain and his descendant Lamech appear to typify the violence with which the earth is full.[24] But these narratives on their own do not explain the spread of violence to the animals. What of Genesis 3, to return to a starting point that we rejected above? I would argue that placing Genesis 3 in the context of the P narrative of the fallen creation, including both Genesis 1 and Genesis 9, makes it possible to understand it after all as a "fall" story. It tells that human beings have taken to themselves the authority to determine what is good and what is bad — conventionally "the knowledge of good and evil" — declining the place allotted to them, as related in 1:26-28, as mediators of divine authority. The human rebellion deplored by the theologians appears in this context not as a lust for abstract autonomy, but as the rejection of the concrete divine gift of responsibility for justice and peace in the earthly creation. It meets poetic retribution in the loss of peace and harmony in the life that human beings lead with God, with each other, with the earth, and with at least one creature of the earth; and although no precise sequence of cause and effect is traced, it is intelligible symbolically that this should be followed by the general outbreak of violence among creatures. Phyllis Trible's well-known interpretation of the Eden

---

24. Cf. Anderson, "Ecology," pp. 163-64, who also describes the events in Gen. 3 and 6:1-4 as violence; both cases are rather dubious.

story points the way here.[25] This "final-form" reading enables us to use Genesis 1–9 as a whole as part of the foundation of the doctrine of the fall. On its own, each of the strands distinguished by historical criticism is incomplete as an account of the emergence of evil in God's good creation. Taken together, they give a more rounded picture.

But the development of such a doctrine on this foundation is still far from easy. The idea of a fall in itself, taken literally, is mythical, if by "fall" is meant the loss of an *actual* initial state of obedience and blessing. Any narrative realization of it must be a myth, the P account no less so than the Eden story. Evolutionary biology suggests that the violent aspects of human nature, including our meat eating, are probably an inheritance from our primate ancestors.[26] All that humans are they have always been: there is no golden age in the past. As for the animals, there has never been a time, and could never have been a time, when no animals were predatory. The idea that, as created, animals were all herbivorous and human beings peaceful guardians of the natural world corresponds to no state of affairs actually subsisting, for however short a time, in the past. What the account in Genesis presents as the fallen state of both, on the other hand, is realistic. The Priestly author has grasped and clearly expressed two things: First, the overwhelming predominance of the human species over the natural order. This is a fact we may increasingly come to regret, but it is a fact that cannot be altered. Its consequences, however, are not predestined. Second, the solidarity of humans not only with one another but with all the natural world in the incessant competition for space and resources, often expressed in predation and parasitism, which forms the essential backdrop to Darwin's theory of natural selection. Against this the author has placed an understanding of the purpose of God in creation, the ideal justice of the created order.

We may understand this ideal in a nonnarrative, nonmythical way as the unrealized potential of creation; and in the same way we may interpret the biblical account as claiming that this potential has been deliberately rejected, rather than simply being unrealized. It is more difficult to accept this in relation to the animals than in relation to ourselves, both because the idea of a willed choice of lifestyle and behavior is only appropriate to human beings, and of course because the physiology and ecology of purely predatory

---

25. Phyllis Trible, "A Love Story Gone Awry," in *God and the Rhetoric of Sexuality,* OBT (Philadelphia: Fortress, 1978), pp. 72-143.

26. Richard Dawkins, *The Ancestor's Tale: A Pilgrimage to the Dawn of Life* (London: Weidenfeld & Nicolson, 2004), p. 89.

and parasitic animals make it impossible that they could choose to be herbivorous even if they were capable of choosing. It therefore seems impossible to integrate the idea of a swerve by all creatures from peacefulness to violence into a doctrine of the fall acceptable in an intellectual context informed by science. The recent volume *Darwin, Creation and the Fall* does not help here, since it betrays no recognition that this narrative exists, focusing on a purely human fall and attempting to integrate it as a historical event into a scientific account of human origins.[27] The attempt necessarily fails, for the reason already alluded to, that the evolutionary origin of human beings makes it impossible to offer an account of the roots of their behavior totally distinct from anything we may say of other animals.

I would suggest, nevertheless, that any future formulations of the doctrine of sin should broaden their biblical basis by taking seriously the narrative framework within which the story of Eden is set, for four reasons. First, the literary reason: the essential structural elements in Genesis 1–11 should take precedence over any single narrative within the section.

Second, the Priestly element in the account attempts, at least, to address the moral and theological problems posed by the cosmos as a whole rather than by only one species within it. It expresses a highly realistic view of the behavior of created beings. Even though it is impossible to accept its account either as literal history or as a judgment on the conduct of nonhuman animals, it should compel us to broaden the scope of the doctrine, if we retain it at all. The assumption found in so many formulations of the doctrine of the fall, that the human species is the only problem, is hardly realistic.

Third, Genesis 1–9 taken as a whole relates to the central biblical value of justice, since חמס is the antithesis of this. By integrating Genesis 3–4 into their context in the way I have suggested above, we are able to read these narratives, chapter 3 as well as chapter 4, as a rejection by human beings of the divine mandate to mediate God's justice to the whole of the earthly creation. Without this integration, it is easy for the Eden story to be read in ways that fail to relate it to central biblical values. Certainly obedience to God is one of these. But in such a text as Deuteronomy, where obedience to God is basic to the entire structure, it is clearer than it is in Genesis 3 that God's commands are intended for the good of human beings.

Finally, the central place taken in the passage by human responsibility to the earthly creation assists in theological reflection on the now desper-

---

27. R. J. Berry and T. A. Noble, eds., *Darwin, Creation and the Fall: Theological Challenges* (Nottingham: Apollos, 2009).

ately urgent issue of the human impact on the environment. I have developed the ethical aspect of this briefly in an earlier essay.[28] In the context of this theological discussion, I would now suggest that the lesson we can draw from the Priestly story is that the integrity of the whole of creation is dependent on us because we have the power to destroy it, and will do so unless we learn how to discipline our use of power. In other words, we may transfer the ideas of this narrative from a protological to an eschatological context. In contrast to the likely consequences, barring any genuine change of course, of the path on which human action and development are at present set, we may put the Isaianic vision of the peaceable kingdom — all creation at peace under the rule of the messianic king — though it can no more be read literally than the account in Genesis, as an image of the eschatological goal for the earthly creation intended by God. Just as in Genesis the human creatures who are created according to the image of God are called to exercise a kingly role, a role that they abuse, so in Isaiah the messianic king models in truth the kind of rule that was and is required of humanity as a whole. This part of the picture at least is in harmony with the nature of animals, even though it must fall within that category of events that are humanly impossible, yet possible with God.

Appendix: Diachronic Readings

A diachronic view of the text is strictly unnecessary for the purpose envisaged in this paper, since we have succeeded in reading "J" and "P" strands together in complementary fashion. But we may incidentally reflect on the possible implications of this reading for our view of the development of Genesis 1–11. That "J" and "P" appear to complement each other may cast doubt on the standard, and still possibly most widely held, critical view that the passage is composed from two originally independent documents. P might be seen in "supplementary" guise as written in awareness of the J strand. But as critical thought stands at the moment, the contrary view is more in favor, that the so-called J narrative is a late wisdom-inspired supplement to P, as suggested by Joseph Blenkinsopp and others, including Eckart Otto.[29] On its own, however, this does not account for the abrupt and un-

28. Houston, "Justice and Violence."

29. Joseph Blenkinsopp, *The Pentateuch: An Introduction to the First Five Books of the Bible* (London: SCM, 1992), pp. 64-67; Eckart Otto, "Die Paradieserzählung Genesis 2–3:

motivated appearance of violence in P, which on this showing would be the first extant Hebrew account of the origins of the world. If 6:1-4, instead of being considered part of J, were read as P's explanation for the emergence of evil, it would read more smoothly and make more sense. But this has never been considered, because the style and vocabulary of the piece, including of course the use of the divine name, mark it off clearly from P and (less strongly) link it with J.[30]

However, Philip Davies, following Blenkinsopp, has made a speculative attempt to link 6:1-4, in an earlier form, with P.[31] He suggests that the passage is a deliberate bowdlerization by J of an account of the descent of rebel "sons of God," or angels, much more like the story of the Watchers in *1 Enoch*. Here we are told: "the women became pregnant and gave birth to great giants . . . the giants turned against (the people) in order to eat them. And they began to sin against birds, wild beasts, reptiles, and fish. And their flesh was devoured the one by the other, and they drank blood. And then the earth brought an accusation against the oppressors. And Azaz'el [one of the angels] taught the people (the art of) making swords and knives, and shields and breastplates" (*1 Enoch* 7:2, 4-6).[32] According to Davies, P's original story of the irruption of violence into God's good creation was something similar to this, derived from the same source as the Enoch story, and it has been censored and reduced to unintelligibility by J in order to promote against this a view of sin as purely human in origin. Such an origin is described in Genesis 3–4, and summarized in 6:5-7, J's explanation for the flood, where the word אדם recurs four times.

In general, students of *1 Enoch* have not been inclined to agree with this view of the relationship of Genesis 6:1-4 to their text. Rather, as George Nickelsburg sets out in detail in his commentary on *1 Enoch*, it is the latter

---

Eine nachpriesterschriftliche Lehrerzählung in ihrem religionshistorischen Kontext," in Anja A. Diesel, Reinhard G. Lehmann, Eckart Otto, and Andreas Wagner, eds., *"Jedes Ding hat seine Zeit . . .": Studien zur israelitischen und altorientalischen Weisheit: Diethelm Michel zum 65. Geburtstag*, BZAW 241 (Berlin: de Gruyter, 1996), pp. 167-92.

30. John Skinner, *A Critical and Exegetical Commentary on Genesis*, ICC (Edinburgh: T&T Clark, 1910), p. 140, with note.

31. Philip J. Davies, "And Enoch Was Not, for Genesis Took Him," in C. Hempel and J. M. Lieu, eds., *Biblical Traditions in Transmission: Essays in Honour of Michael A. Knibb*, JSJSup 111 (Leiden: Brill, 2006), pp. 97-107.

32. E. Isaac, "1 (Ethiopic Apocalypse of) Enoch: A New Translation and Introduction," in James H. Charlesworth, ed., *The Old Testament Pseudepigrapha*, vol. 1: *Apocalyptic Literature and Testaments* (Garden City, N.Y.: Doubleday, 1983), pp. 5-90, here p. 16.

that has used and developed the text of Genesis.[33] This may be granted. But this does not rule out the idea that both writings may have been dependent on an earlier tradition, possibly oral; Nickelsburg elsewhere grants the possibility that in places the Enochic writings have "drawn on oral traditions related to the Scriptural narratives."[34] The authors of *1 Enoch* 6–7 will then have retold the tradition they had received using the words of the related narrative in Genesis.

33. George W. E. Nickelsburg, *1 Enoch 1: A Commentary on the Book of 1 Enoch, Chapters 1–36, 81–108*, Hermeneia (Minneapolis: Fortress, 2001), pp. 176, 183.
34. Ibid., p. 57.

Genesis and the Natural World

Interpreting the Story of Creation:
A Case Study in the Dialogue between Theology and Science

David Fergusson

In what follows, I shall explore how theologians and commentators have handled key tenets in the doctrines of creation and providence with respect to the reading of Genesis 1–3 in the encounter with modern science. On the basis of a series of historical and theological reflections, I will attempt some wider characterizations of the relationship of theology to the natural sciences. Against standard models in the field, the history of interpretation will suggest that different types of engagement can occupy the same ground.

The Doctrine of Creation in Historical Perspective

During the history of the relationship between science and theology, the book of Genesis has been the focus of contested interpretation and controversy. The reasons for this are not hard to establish. With its Septuagint title, Genesis is manifestly a book of cosmic origins, at least in its opening chapters. Its account of the origin of the world provides a putative point of contact with cosmology, whether ancient or modern. When this became a point of conflict, debates about the proper interpretation of Genesis intensified.

The encounter of exegesis with modern science is not exclusively a modern preoccupation. It does not date from the Copernican hypothesis, the geology of Hutton and Lyell, or the evolutionary theory of Darwin. Already in the early church, we find a similar preoccupation with Genesis, borne partly through a concern with its account of origins. Augustine commented at length and more than once on Genesis, while Basil's *Hexaemaron* stands as one of the classic studies of the six days of creation. The diversity of interpretive trends can already be identified in their work. Basil's tendency is to argue against allegorical readings of the text by insisting upon the literal sense of the six days as intervals of twenty-four hours determined by the revolutions of the sun.[1] Others, recognizing the oddity of such a notion prior to the creation of the sun, tend to read the Hebrew or Greek word for "day" in more symbolic ways. In *The City of God,* Augustine simply concedes that it is difficult to know exactly what a "day" can mean in the creation story. What kind of days these were it is extremely difficult or perhaps impossible for us to conceive, and how much more to say.[2]

Nevertheless, before launching into further consideration of the scientific reception of Genesis, an important feature of its theological description of the world as created needs to be registered. The doctrine of creation in the Hebrew Bible is not merely an account of how the world commenced. It gives shape to the continual relationship of dependence between the world and God, and to the manner in which a history is established. This is marked by the covenant faithfulness of its God, the rebellion of human creatures, the rootedness of human existence in society and the natural world, the companionship of other creatures, the presence of evil as a surd and menacing force, and the ongoing creative and redemptive actions of its Maker. To see God simply as a placeholder for a supernatural act of origination is to miss most of what Genesis has to say about the character of the world in relation to its Creator. The doctrine of creation is therefore as much about the status of the world as created and the ongoing narrative of its relationship to the Creator. To concentrate merely on origination is to miss many of the motifs of the creation story. These are subsequently developed by Genesis with respect to human responsibility and disobedience, land, blessing, covenant, and much else.

A similar concern should be registered with the doctrine of creation out of nothing. While modern exegesis has questioned whether the form and content of the opening verses of the Hebrew Bible require an *ex nihilo* creation, it is evident that most theologians of the church have assumed this teaching, at least from about the beginning of the third century onward. Again, however, this was not primarily on account of philosophical or cos-

1. Basil of Caesarea, *Hexaemeron,* Homily 2.8. For further discussion see Andrew Louth, "The Six Days of Creation According to the Greek Fathers," in Stephen Barton and David Wilkinson, eds., *Reading Genesis after Darwin* (Oxford: Oxford University Press, 2009), pp. 39-56.
2. Augustine, *City of God* 11.6.

mological concerns about how to provide a sufficient explanation for all that existed contingently. This emerges later as an additional consideration and even a buttress for the doctrine of creation out of nothing. Yet its initial theological appearance reflected a broader set of considerations. In particular, the *ex nihilo* doctrine was adjudged more fitting over against the leading alternatives of eternal matter and an emanation from the divine being.[3] It articulated the love, freedom, and greatness of the Creator while also describing the dependence, goodness, and reliability of the world. For Irenaeus and Tertullian, writing against their gnostic opponents, to say that creation is out of nothing is simply to say that it is not out of something. This moreover is intensified by the outcome of the Nicene controversy and the resultant need to distinguish quite sharply the relationship of God to the world from the relationships of origin among the persons of the Trinity. The eternal generation of the Son by the Father is understood to be of a different order from the freely willed creation of the world. God could be God without the world, but the Father's relationship to the Son is essential to the identity of the Trinitarian persons.[4]

While articulating the *ex nihilo* doctrine, the theologians of the early church also tended to stress the manner in which the created order was expressive of the divine being. This was never allowed to become a claim about the divinity of creation, but it did establish a relationship of correspondence between Creator and cosmos. Creation was not an occasional or random act of God lacking any relationship at all to the divine being. This is apparent in Augustine's treatment of the subject. Carol Harrison sees the doctrine of *creatio ex nihilo* as already constitutive for his theology after his conversion in 386.[5] In particular, it enables him to eschew Manichaeism, to borrow from but significantly to modify Neoplatonism, and to provide the conceptual framework for articulating important notions about the goodness of the world, evil, the human will, and grace. The world is created by divine fiat, but its being reflects the nature and purpose of God.

Augustine, moreover, insists upon the need for a constant giving of divine grace to sustain the human creature. This is not a one-off gift in terms of created capacities. Rather the fragility of the will entails its radical and on-

3. See Gerhard May, *Creatio ex Nihilo: The Doctrine of "Creation Out of Nothing" in Early Christian Thought* (Edinburgh: T&T Clark, 1994).
4. See the discussion in Thomas F. Torrance, *The Trinitarian Faith* (Edinburgh: T&T Clark, 1988), pp. 76-109.
5. Carol Harrison, *Rethinking Augustine's Early Theology* (Oxford: Oxford University Press, 2005), pp. 75-114.

going dependence upon God's grace for succor, guidance, and strength to re-sist temptation. Although this is more heavily stressed later in his career against the Pelagians, who he believed attributed too much autonomous power and moral integrity to the unaided will, it is a theme that is already present in his early embrace of creation out of nothing, as for example in the opening prayer of the *Soliloquies.* Or to take a later example, Thomas Aqui-nas, while clearly committed to some version of the cosmological argument as validating creation out of nothing, also argues quite carefully that the act of creation takes a Trinitarian form. It is not merely an impulse that pro-duces the world, as it appears to be in later strains of deism. Instead, it is an action that has a particular character. This suggests the endowment of the world with qualities that are analogically related to the divine being. All cre-ated things have three aspects that derive from their participation in God. They reflect God in their being by analogy *(analogia entis).* Every being has its origin or principle in the Father. Each thing is a particular kind of thing and reflects the Word or Wisdom that informs it. Each thing also has its place within an ordered whole, thus relating to everything else. This displays the love of the Holy Spirit, the *vinculum caritatis.*[6]

Nevertheless, cosmic origination remains a seemingly inescapable ele-ment of the doxological witness to God as Creator in Genesis, the Psalms, and elsewhere. God is the reason that the world exists. It is not self-sufficient or *causa sui.* Without God, the world would not be. Given this dependent status of the world, we cannot exclude an initial act of creation even if this cannot be conceptualized or expressed other than in poetic and mythical terms. This consideration might also be supported by the way in which re-cent readings of the Hebrew Bible have tended to depart from Gerhard von Rad's earlier thesis that cosmological themes were incidental or at least sub-ordinate to Israelite religion, its preoccupation being with the actions of God in history.[7] This is misleading insofar as God's concern for and rule over the natural world are axiomatic for the account of redemption that un-folds in the text. The book of Genesis indeed may only deal with creation in its opening chapters, the bulk of its narrative being concerned with the sub-sequent historical drama. Yet these introductory sections are not so much a prologue as the foundation to what comes later in the stories of Noah and

6. Thomas Aquinas, *Summa theologica* 1.45.7.

7. Gerhard von Rad, "The Theological Problem of the Old Testament Doctrine of Creation," in *The Problem of the Hexateuch and Other Essays,* trans. E. W. Trueman Dicken (New York: McGraw-Hill, 1966), pp. 131-43, here p. 132.

the patriarchs. As one recent commentator writes, "Set in the context of polytheistic societies, the entire message of Genesis rests on the programmatic truths established in the first two chapters, that one supreme God made everything that exists and exercises his prerogative as supreme ruler of the earth and its inhabitants."[8]

Creation and Modern Cosmology

The recent engagement with big bang cosmology, while appropriate and necessary, needs to avoid any single account of cosmic origination or evolutionary mechanisms that ties theological description too tightly to scientific theory. There are two closely related reasons for this, both of them rooted in Genesis. First, the explanation for the emergence of our world can largely be left to science without undue anxiety on the part of theology to secure particular outcomes. It is not the remit of Scripture to describe how the present state of the world was preceded by earlier cosmic events or states. Second, the doctrine of creation works largely at a different level of understanding so that it cannot be exhausted by the explanatory descriptions of natural science. A clear differentiation between the provinces of science and theology now needs to be maintained. Notwithstanding this complementarity of description types, however, the engagement with science remains a proper apologetic task. It provides a broader and inescapable context within which Scripture has to be interpreted. In this respect, attention to the prevailing worldview of contemporary science must be a condition of responsible exegesis for each generation.

Some recent writers have argued that a consilience of arguments from Scripture, philosophy, and modern cosmology supports the doctrine of creation out of nothing. According to Paul Copan and William Lane Craig, the universe has a temporal beginning about 13.7 billion years ago that can only be explained by reference to divine causal action. The argument hinges upon a series of claims about Scripture, philosophy, and cosmology. These are all rehearsed and cumulatively presented to strike a decisive blow for creation out of nothing.[9]

In relation to the opening verses of Genesis, Copan and Craig argue for creation out of nothing in terms of grammatical structure, the striking

---

8. James McKeown, *Genesis,* Two Horizons Old Testament Commentary (Grand Rapids: Eerdmans, 2008), pp. 264-65.

9. See Paul Copan and William Lane Craig, *Creation out of Nothing: A Biblical, Philosophical, and Scientific Exploration* (Grand Rapids: Baker, 2004).

differences from other ancient Near Eastern views, and the distinctive sense of ברא as a majestic bringing forth by God. Creation out of nothing, they maintain, is thus implied and taken for granted by the Hebrew writers; exegetes who maintain otherwise tend to be presented as in the grip of outmoded ideological prejudices. We might note here the slide from "asserted," "stated," or "taught," to expressions such as "implicit," "implied," and "taken for granted."

In relation to philosophy, Copan and Craig offer a version of the *kalam* cosmological argument first expounded by the Islamic philosopher Al Ghazali in twelfth-century Baghdad. This appeals to mathematical arguments against actual infinites, as opposed to potential infinites, which are really indefinites. The assumption of actual infinites leads to all sorts of absurdities, as illustrated by the paradox of Hilbert's hotel. The hotel with infinite rooms is filled with infinite guests, but one extra turns up. Yet how can there be an additional room or an additional guest if these are already infinite in number? The assumption of actual infinites renders this intelligible possibility absurd and impossible to state coherently. To allow its possibility, we must believe that there are only indefinites, not actual infinites. So, according to Copan and Craig, the universe must have had a beginning; its temporal length may be indefinite but it cannot be infinite. And since everything with a beginning must have a cause, we must assume a first cause, and only God can be an adequate candidate for this first cause.

This philosophical argument is buttressed by recent considerations in cosmology. On the basis of thermodynamics and the expansion of the cosmos, we cannot avoid the conclusion that the universe originated. To put the point negatively, we cannot say that it did not have a beginning or that it is eternal. It is argued that scientific attempts to avoid this conclusion, such as that of the Hartle-Hawking model, are expressive of a metaphysical or ideological hostility to the notion of a cosmic beginning.[10] It is significant that a similar argument is employed by Stephen Hawking to run in precisely the opposite direction. In his much-publicized comments, he claims that the initial conditions that obtained at the big bang can now be given a scientific explanation. This drives him to the conclusion that there is no room for God in explaining the origin of the world. Here again his positioning of science and theology on the same explanatory terrain is misleading.[11]

10. Ibid., pp. 219ff.

11. See the closing chapter of Stephen Hawking and Leonard Mlodinow, *The Grand Design* (London: Bantam, 2010).

Do we wish to lock a theological doctrine quite so closely into a complex philosophical argument, an interpretation of the current state of big bang cosmology, and a particular grammatical reading of Genesis 1:1? Does Genesis teach creation out of nothing, as if some version of the cosmological argument is lurking in the shadows of its opening chapter? There are at least grounds for caution here, if only because the doctrine of creation out of nothing is not explicitly taught until the church confronts the regnant philosophical commitment in the ancient world to the eternity of matter. Only as this is challenged does a declared commitment to the *ex nihilo* doctrine appear. It may be none the worse for it.

Moreover, the simple claim that the universe is uncaused is not one that is readily refuted on philosophical grounds, even if neither theologians nor scientists find it attractive. One might appeal to some hidden physical processes that are as yet unknown to us or are in principle unknowable from our vantage point. Cosmology has not reached a terminal point. Alternatively, one might invoke the hypothesis of a multiverse.

The multiverse concept has generated considerable discussion amongst cosmologists and particle physicists — it is no longer the province of speculative metaphysicians. It is the concept of many universes rather than one, although this requires careful explication. There are different ways in which the concept has been construed.[12] The most discussed in recent literature is the spatial notion of a multiverse comprising different subregions of a single, infinite space. These might be likened to bubbles of space-time that are causally disconnected from one another. Our own cosmos from the big bang onward is simply one bubble among many others. This is an option tentatively proposed by several physicists, including Martin Rees, the Astronomer Royal, who suggests ways in which an ensemble of universes might have evolved, one of which has the physical structure of our own. Since our conception of the physical universe has increased spectacularly over the last few centuries, he argues, we should not dismiss too quickly a further enlargement that accommodates the idea of a multiverse. While the principle of economy seems to militate against this, Rees claims that the multiverse hypothesis may eventually prove to be scientifically fruitful. So go easy with Ockham's razor, he advises.[13]

---

12. In what follows, I have drawn upon an earlier discussion of this issue in *Faith and Its Critics: A Conversation* (Oxford: Oxford University Press, 2009), pp. 47ff.

13. Martin Rees, *Just Six Numbers: The Deep Forces That Shape the Universe* (London: Weidenfeld & Nicolson, 1999), p. 173.

A consequence of this postulation of multiple domains, each manifesting a different physical structure, is that the strong anthropic principle is weakened. It is less surprising that this universe has exactly the right structure to accommodate conscious life forms billions of years after an initial big bang. We can no longer assume that ours is the only domain, the peculiarly biocentric bias of which requires explanation. Instead, given the multiplicity of such domains, it is less of a coincidence that one has emerged like ours and that we are here to observe it. Our universe may be an oasis within an otherwise sterile multiverse. Rees offers the illustration of a large "off the shelf" clothes shop. Given the size of the stock in store, we should not be surprised to find one suit that fits us exactly. "Likewise, if our universe is selected from a multiverse, its seemingly designed or fine-tuned features wouldn't be surprising."[14]

The theist, however, can offer a possible rejoinder. While the multiverse might one day solve the problem of why this particular universe exhibits its particular structure, one can still legitimately ask why a multiverse exists at all and why it has the right combination of laws and states to permit a universe like ours to come into being. The "why" question can always be reintroduced, no matter the impressive capacity of the natural sciences to press their "how" questions further back. A generating process that enables multiple domains, at least one of which is like ours, itself requires explanation. Why our multiverse should have a principle of generation that renders probable or inevitable at least one anthropic universe itself requires explanation since it does not appear to be obviously right or at all self-explanatory. In any case, Christian theology has sometimes explored the idea of multiple worlds as an inevitable outcome of divine creativity.[15] If this invites the charge of extravagant speculation, we might also add that the dogmatic exclusion of such possibilities may itself be the result of unwarranted conjecture, the entering upon territory that is largely remote from the concerns of Scripture and the church.

Where does this leave us? There is undoubtedly an affinity, even a convergence, of considerations surrounding Scripture, doctrine, philosophy, and science in support of an *ex nihilo* creation. But to see these in relations

14. Martin Rees, "Other Universes: A Scientific Perspective," in Neil Manson, ed., *God and Design: The Teleological Argument and Modern Science* (London: Routledge, 2003), pp. 211-20.

15. See, e.g., John Hedley Brooke, "The Search for Extra-terrestrial Life: Historical and Theological Perspectives," *Omega: Indian Journal of Science & Religion* 5, no. 1 (2006): 6-22.

of entailment or as rationally defeating all other rivals in the field represents an overdetermination of the data. What we are offered in Scripture is neither a proof of a position, nor even a set of arguments to rebut the skeptic. Instead it is the witness of a worshiping and believing community that seeks to order its life according to convictions rooted in its history and organization. These carry intellectual commitments but do not seem to entail or exclude any particular scientific story about cosmic origins, the age of the universe, or the physical processes that determine the formation of stars and planets. To this extent, Stephen Jay Gould's nonoverlapping magisterial (NOMA) is a safer, more modest model to adopt when examining the relationship of Genesis to modern science. It would be unwise to seek to eliminate scientific possibilities on theological grounds. Science can be left to take care of itself, in this respect. Let the debate about a multiverse and extraterrestrial intelligence take place without seeking a premature theological closure on any of its questions. As explanation of a different order and understanding of a different type, the doctrine of creation should be sufficiently confident of its particular domain not to be unduly anxious about developments in other fields. Nevertheless, we might have to concede that these developments have led to a keener differentiation of types of understanding and description. Our distinguishing them in this way is in itself partly attributable to the encounters with modern science that have taken place particularly since the early nineteenth century.

Evolution and Providence

As already noted, the theological significance of Genesis extends far beyond its account of cosmic origination. Creation is the first of God's works, but it is succeeded by a continual series of actions. Traditionally, these have been assigned to the categories of general and special providence — a general providence such as that attested at the end of the Noah story in the guaranteed regularity and rhythms of nature, and a special providence such as we find in the stories of Abraham, Isaac, Jacob, and Joseph. The link between general and special can bear different constructions depending on how particular and universal aspects of the divine rule are to be configured. Nevertheless, these dimensions are both present in the text and are evident in the scope of the different covenants. The life of each of the patriarchs is marked by a strong sense of divine providential oversight — indeed, the only appearance of the linguistic term *providentia* in the Vulgate is in the "Dominus providebit" announced by Abraham to Isaac in Genesis 22:8. "God himself will provide a lamb for the burnt offering, my son" (NRSV).

Of all the stories, the Joseph cycle arguably offers the strongest sense of providence, and although this is not adverted to later in the canon it provided a rich source for the Christian imagination. From out of evil, God intends good so that human sinfulness is overruled and overcome by divine redemption. Joseph's brothers sell him into slavery in Egypt but God uses this for their salvation. There are parallels here with later Christian preaching about the cross as evidencing the foresight of God and the use of Psalm 118:22 as a Christological proof text.

It is in the context of Christian claims about providence, moreover, that a further encounter with modern science has taken place. Darwinian evolution seems to strike at earlier Paleyian assumptions concerning the wise and benevolent ordering of life-forms in the cosmos. It is significant that much nineteenth-century reaction to the *Origin of Species* (1859) was not around fears about its postulation of a very old universe or its threat to the notion of God as Creator. These were quite consistent with an evolving world, and in any case theologians had been well prepared for similar conclusions by the work of geologists such as Hutton and Lyell. There was little debate about a literal six days of creation in the wake of Darwin. The more neuralgic issue surrounded that of divine providence, in particular the role seemingly assigned to "chance" by Darwinian science. Even among writers in search of an alliance with evolutionary theory, we find attempts to replace the function of chance with a more deterministic mechanism. Of course, for Darwinian theory "chance" does not refer to the inexplicable or the uncaused. Instead, it is the denial of a single deterministic trajectory followed by the evolution of life-forms. There seem to be two types of process that are characterized by the language of chance. One of these concerns the minor physiological variations that are evident through the reproduction of species, and the other is in the intersection of unrelated causal systems, for example, the impact of a sudden change in climate upon the development of species in a hitherto stable ecological niche. The mechanism governing physiological variation was not understood until the later development of genetics, and many informed critics of Darwin in the nineteenth century recognized this lacuna in his theory. As we know, it was eventually to be filled by developments in genetics, thus providing the neo-Darwinism synthesis with its twin principles of natural selection and genetic mutation that dominated explanatory theories.

Significantly, it was the random course of evolution, as described by

Darwin, that most offended Charles Hodge in Princeton. He regarded this as *practically* atheistic since there could be no governing purpose or overriding control exercised over the direction of nature. What was under threat from Darwin's account of evolution was not so much the doctrine of creation — a transcendent origination of the whole scheme could still be conceived — as the doctrine of providence. Hodge could concede that a process of evolution was consistent with a residual theism. However, the particular account offered by Darwin with its stress on natural selection led him to believe that it was metaphysically inconsistent with the teleological principle that belonged both to revealed and natural theology. If God were no longer in control of the course of life on earth, then it could not be perceived as proceeding toward an appointed end. For a Reformed theologian such as Hodge, this was tantamount to a practical atheism. Many passages from Darwin were cited to demonstrate that the appearance of design and intentionality in nature was only a veneer. The salient causal processes were basically material — these could be characterized without any reference to divine intention or interposition. Apart from his scruples about the details of Darwinian theory — and Hodge was here very well informed — he seems to have concluded that the creative role assigned to natural causes effectively rendered God otiose. "This banishing God from the world is simply intolerable and, blessed be his name, impossible. An absent God who does nothing is, to us, no God. Christ brings God constantly near to us."[16] Hodge seems to have assumed that the appearance of organs such as the eye could not be explained by a natural, incremental process. To do so was simply incredulous. In raising this possibility, Darwin himself pointed to its impossibility. It is "the most credulous men in the world (who) are unbelievers. The great Napoleon could not believe in Providence, but he believed in his star and in lucky and unlucky days."[17]

Nevertheless, within that same tradition others reached different conclusions by placing evolution within a wider context that was perceived to be providentially ordered. Asa Gray, the Harvard botanist, replied to Hodge. His difficulty with Darwin, Gray claimed, arose out of an unduly restricted account of how divine teleology works. The Creator can endow nature and organisms with the powers of evolution into states of greater complexity.

16. Charles Hodge, *What Is Darwinism? And Other Writings on Science and Religion*, ed. Mark A. Noll and David N. Livingstone (Grand Rapids: Baker, 1994), p. 88. Hodge's essay was first published in 1874.

17. Ibid.

David Fergusson

Hodge simply begs the question against this type of teleology with his commitment to an older, Paleyian type of strategy. This was also the line taken by Robert Flint in his Baird lectures, which went through numerous editions during the late nineteenth century.[18] By interacting with Darwinism, he offered a set of responses that have become standard in theological appropriations of evolutionary science. The development from lower to higher organisms is consistent with design. The tendency toward improvement and progression requires explanation. Evolutionary process can be envisioned as a vast scheme of order and beauty, rather than a grim arena of conflict and waste. This more positive vision of evolutionary complexity would be later developed by writers such as J. Arthur Thomson and Patrick Geddes.[19]

Princeton theology itself proved capable of simultaneously moving in the opposite direction to that of Hodge. James McCosh felt able to welcome key aspects of Darwinism, especially evolutionary descent, and to accommodate it within a wider teleological system. What it represented was the outworking of a vast orderly and regulated system that betokened divine design. The discernment of laws governing the evolutionary process together with the apparently inevitable rise of increasing complexity suggested for McCosh that Darwinian science and Christian theology could be reconciled. In this respect, McCosh was to be followed by B. B. Warfield, another distinguished Princeton theologian, who regarded Darwinian explanation as unavoidable within the scientific domain but as readily consistent with theological determinism. That Darwinism perceived an order, regularity, and lawfulness governing the seemingly haphazard history of life enabled theologians quite quickly to reach an accommodation and to maintain patterns of teleological explanation. This was the apologetic move argued against Huxley and Haeckel by writers such as Flint, Drummond, and George Campbell, the duke of Argyll.

The key differences between Hodge and McCosh may actually reflect a fundamental disagreement that persists among evolutionary theorists today. To what extent is the course of life a one in a million shot, a random walk, a sequence of haphazard events strung together? Stephen Jay Gould has argued that, even if replayed many times over, the tape of life would never resemble again the course of natural history on our planet. Against this, we

---

18. Robert Flint, *Theism* (Edinburgh: Blackwood, 1877).

19. J. Arthur Thomson and Patrick Geddes, *Evolution* (London: Williams & Norgate, 1912). I have discussed the nineteenth-century reception of Darwin more fully in "Providence after Darwin," in Michael Northcott and R. J. Berry, eds., *Theology after Darwin* (Milton Keynes: Paternoster, 2009), pp. 73-88.

166

find Simon Conway Morris arguing for evolutionary constraints and patterns of convergence that ensure that a species like human beings (i.e., mammals with large brains) would emerge given the setting of our planetary system.[20] This is an interesting debate to view from a distance, and theologians will doubtless incline toward the view of convergence since it has affinities with design. Nevertheless, theology can live with whatever the outcome, and it would certainly be a mistake to seek to intrude God into whatever gaps science has yet to fill.

The position adopted by Hodge again illustrates the danger of binding theology to particular scientific claims. In his case, the commitment was not to a specific account of the history of life, but more to the denial of the compossibility of Christian theology with Darwinian evolution. These two types of explanation could not be consistent, he argued; hence science had to be contested in the name of theology. What was required was a keener awareness of the different types of understanding involved, and therefore of the greater capacity of theology to accommodate sudden advances in scientific knowledge. As with modern cosmology, the lesson is that religion and science serve different purposes and function with complementary rather than competing narratives. Of course, this is a lesson that has to be learned on both sides. It is not only theologians who sometimes stray outside their field of competence. Scientists too are occasionally prone to make wider philosophical and theological claims that are unwarranted by the insights of their specialism. To this extent, Richard Dawkins's neo-Darwinism and creation science represent two sides of the same coin. Each assumes that evolution and theology cannot coexist, and that therefore one must be denied for the sake of defending the other.

To assert this claim for complementarity, however, is not to deny either the need for theological awareness of scientific claims or the importance of showing how they might fit together. Points of contact and tension will continue to exist, these generating a challenge for the theologian to suggest ways in which theology and science coexist while showing that the fit must always be sufficiently loose for the integrity of each to be respected — neither should be overly constrained by formulations in the other's domain. This can be illustrated both negatively and positively in two further ways.

In one important respect, Darwinism promoted a reexamination of fundamental claims concerning the interpretation of the fall doctrine that

20. Simon Conway Morris, *Life's Solution: Inevitable Humans in a Lonely Universe* (Cambridge: Cambridge University Press, 2003).

had for so long been embedded in Western, Augustinian Christianity. According to traditional teaching, the fall of Adam and Eve recorded in Genesis 3 fulfilled at least three functions. In the context of theodicy, it could explain the suffering and evil that afflicted human beings collectively without attributing these directly to the action of God. Second, it guaranteed the original goodness of the created order as it had been constituted in Genesis 1. Third, it provided the context for a doctrine of redemption in which both the guilt and stain of original sin were erased by the work of Christ.

In the standard expressions of the doctrine in the work of Augustine, Aquinas, and Calvin, it was assumed that the fall was a historical event involving the first human couple. After Darwin, however, scientific opinion seemed overwhelmingly to discount the possibility of a spatiotemporal fall. It could no longer be assumed that the human race had descended from a single couple created in a state of moral and physical integrity. Humans had descended from earlier hominids over a period of millions of years. Moreover, those conditions that produced suffering, conflict, and death had determined planetary life-forms long before the appearance of human beings and their deeds of transgression. The pervasiveness of evil and death could not be attributed to an initial fall from a state of perfection. In interpreting Genesis 3, therefore, commentators tended to view the ancient text as containing parabolic material that exercised an important descriptive function but not one of historical or scientific explanation. Just as Genesis 1 did not furnish us with details of scientific cosmology but with a characterization of the world as dependent upon God, so *mutatis mutandis* Genesis 3 attested the universality of sin and the alienation of human beings from God. It is description, not explanation. At the same time, some features of the text made better sense on this account, for example, the presence of the serpent (an ancient Near Eastern image of evil) in the garden prior to the fall.

Of course, as John Rogerson has pointed out, exegetes had been prepared for this already by the work of geologists stressing uniformitarian processes rather than appealing to a single catastrophic event to account for significant geological changes on the earth's surface. Strategies of interpretation were already in place, and these were evident in the handling of Genesis 3. One might also add that historical criticism was also alerting scholars to similarities between the creation stories of Israel and those of other ancient cultures. The meaning of such texts was thus to be found in their religious and anthropological significance, rather than in scientific insight.[21]

---

21. See John Rogerson, "What Difference Did Darwin Make? The Interpretation of

Two examples from the early twentieth century confirm this shift of perspective. In his Hulsean Lectures of 1901-2, the philosopher F. R. Tennant dealt at some length with the subject of the origin and propagation of sin. He is quite clear that a historical reading of the text is now excluded not only by literary and historical criticism, but also by the collective weight of the natural sciences.

> The increased light which has been thrown upon the early history of mankind, not to speak of the continuity of the human species with those lower in the scale of animal life, compels us to entertain the conviction that what was once necessarily received as a genuine tradition is rather, transfigured and spiritualised, the product of primitive speculation on a matter beyond the reach of human memory. Literary criticism and historical exegesis, Comparative Religion and Race-Psychology, Geology and Anthropology all contribute materially to the cumulative evidence on this head.[22]

Tennant, however, also claims that the doctrine of original sin (if not, the fall as its primary cause) has much to offer in terms of expressing the power of sin as habit, together with the social and physical unity of the human race. It remains a valuable corrective to more individualist notions of sin that fail to capture its corporate and universal force.

A similar position is adopted by S. R. Driver in his Genesis commentary. He argues that the most to which Genesis 2–3 commits us is the view that, when human beings became conscious of the moral law, they broke it. A state of moral and physical perfection, as in Milton's *Paradise Lost,* is not implied by the text. He then goes on to recognize that modern anthropology claims that there was no single pair but that human beings evolved in different parts of the globe. He concludes that each and every portion of the race similarly "fell," thus demonstrating the collective similarity of our moral and spiritual capacities.[23] What is significant is that Driver, notwithstanding his scholarly caution, presents these findings as if they have become standard and uncontroversial. The departure from the literal reading of the fall doc-

---

Genesis in the Nineteenth Century," in Barton and Wilkinson, eds., *Reading Genesis after Darwin,* pp. 75-92.

22. F. R. Tennant, *The Origin and Propagation of Original Sin* (Cambridge: Cambridge University Press, 1902), pp. 26-27.

23. S. R. Driver, *The Book of Genesis,* Westminster Commentary (London: Methuen, 1904), pp. 56-57.

trine is one of the more significant shifts in modern theology, and it provides a useful illustration of the way in which advances in science can impact theology, even while one maintains the different subject matter and methodology of each. To this extent, the ways in which scholarly interpretations of Genesis demarcated science and religion have tended to confirm Schleiermacher's conviction earlier in the nineteenth century that theological concerns were remote from historical and scientific accounts of human origins and, however interesting, should be detached from these.

The engagement with science, however, did not simply produce a defensive reworking of doctrinal claims. Some positive gains were proclaimed. After the publication of *Origin of Species* in 1859, theologians offered a more immanent account of divine involvement in the cosmic process. This suggested a different model of providence, one that continues to attract defenders today. In his essay in *Lux Mundi* (1889), Aubrey Moore famously wrote:

> The one absolutely impossible conception of God, in the present day, is that which represents Him as an occasional Visitor. Science had pushed the deist's God farther and farther away, and at the moment when it seemed as if He would be thrust out altogether, Darwinism appeared, and, under the disguise of a foe, did the work of a friend.[24]

Moore's claim is that Darwinism affords a positive opportunity for Christian theology to reaffirm its commitment to a perpetual involvement of the divine spirit in the natural world. Instead of the more remote and disengaged God of deism, we now have an immanent divine presence that is at work in the creative and open-ended processes of evolutionary history. Rather than posing a threat, therefore, the apparently free movement of natural forms is consonant with a God who is present and active within the creative process, in a manner analogous to God's same involvement with human history. This model of divine engagement resonated with the kenotic theologies that flourished in the late nineteenth century, and it has exercised a particularly strong hold over Anglican thinkers to the present day. The model here is of God's "letting the world become itself," not in such a way as to abandon it but in the interests of a patient accompanying that seeks to work within and alongside creative processes. A model of providence is thus

---

24. Aubrey Moore, "The Christian Doctrine of God," in Charles Gore, ed., *Lux Mundi: A Series of Studies in the Religion of the Incarnation,* 15th ed. (repr. London: Murray, 1913), pp. 41-81, here p. 73.

suggested that avoids the determinism of much of the Augustinian tradition but also the deism that had persisted from the early modern period.

More than most who sought an accommodation with Darwinism, Moore was able to see clearly some positive theological gains. The encounter with science enabled a retrieval of important scriptural and doctrinal themes that had been occluded by the dominance of Paley's apologetic theology. The occasional interventions of a remote deity could now be replaced by the constant sustaining and creative activity of the divine spirit. This has the significant benefit of correlating the Christian understanding of how God acts in nature and history. The God of the Bible is portrayed as deeply involved in the stories of Israel, Christ, and the church, an ongoing personal drama that takes a narrative shape in the successive books of Scripture. By contrast, the model of divine action suggested by deism, at least in one of its standard forms, was that of a transcendent Creator who perfectly ordered the world so that subsequent historical interaction was unnecessary, if not undesirable. After Darwin, however, theologians could see the world of nature as having a history, as being constantly in the process of making. It had a narrative shape that could increasingly be detected by advances in the natural sciences. Like history, therefore, nature was a work in progress, a construction site in which God could be seen as a sustaining, creative, guiding presence. This appearance of the natural world as undergoing significant change in the course of its existence was further confirmed by the emergence of big bang cosmology in the following century.

Much of this makes sense of what we find in the Hebrew Scriptures. God is engaged with the created world, in both its nature and its history, and each of them has a narrative. Yet this engagement is not the result of total control but involves a willingness to enter into partnership, albeit an asymmetric one as described in the language of covenant. What emerges in the writings of scholars such as Jon Levenson, Terence Fretheim, and Walter Brueggemann is an account of the God-world relationship that has affinities with theories of providence that emerge at the interface with contemporary science.

If we think of God's calling into being an interconnected world established in a continuing relationship with its Maker and Redeemer, then we can attribute a proper place to creaturely action, initiative, and power in ways that reflect the codependence of God without lapsing into synergism or Pelagianism. The divine-human relationship is asymmetric in terms of its setting, yet it is one in which God becomes reactive and in important respects dependent upon what has been made. Within this conceptual space, activities such as prayer, obedience, rebellion, forgiveness, redemption, and blessing now become possible. Fretheim writes, "God works from within a committed relationship with the world and not on the world from without in total freedom. God's faithfulness to promises made always entails the limiting of divine options. Indeed, such is the nature of this divine commitment that the relationship with Israel (and, in a somewhat different way, the world) is now constitutive of the divine identity. The life of God will forever include the life of the people of God as well as the life of the world more generally."[25]

Nevertheless, it is not sufficient merely to register the analogical relationship of an evolving natural world with a providentially ordered history. These are not identical, not least because the natural evolutionary process itself is an integral part of the world that, according to Scripture, requires redemption. Evolution cannot be assumed to deliver a divine commonwealth, as in some theological variants of social Darwinism. Creation and covenant are not identical, although the latter may require the former as its condition and setting. The survival of the fittest and the reproduction of one's genes are nowhere commended by Jesus as ordering human action in the kingdom of God. Instead, the protection of the weakest and loyalty to those who are not of one's own family, tribe, and race are commended.[26] To this extent, the work of God must in some sense counteract and overcome some of the drivers of evolution. Jürgen Moltmann speaks of the need for a *countermovement* that culminates in an eschatological transformation that is quite different from the omega point of an evolutionary process. "The raising of the dead, the gathering of victims, and the seeking of the lost bring a redemption of the world which no evolution can ever achieve."[27]

Conclusion

Theology and science are fundamentally different types of inquiry, providing diverse forms of understanding. This is confirmed by modern advances in cosmology and evolutionary theory and their theological reception. Theology does not seek to fill the gaps in science or to make good what cannot

25. Terence Fretheim, *God and World in the Old Testament: A Relational Theology of Creation* (Nashville: Abingdon, 2005), p. 20.

26. For a recent discussion of these issues see Christopher Southgate, *The Groaning of Creation: God, Evolution and the Problem of Evil* (Louisville: Westminster John Knox, 2008).

27. Jürgen Moltmann, *The Way of Jesus Christ: Christology in Messianic Dimensions*, trans. Margaret Kohl (London: SCM, 1990), p. 303.

be explained at the present stage of inquiry, a methodological error committed by both sides. One primary lesson of the modern engagement with cosmology and evolution is the need to respect complementarity. This works
both ways; it is not only theologians who have transgressed in this respect. A
commitment to the doctrines of creation and providence is not undermined
by the hyperinflated claims of natural scientists to have banished the need
for God in all human forms of understanding.

Nevertheless, there remain interesting and salutary ways in which theology must take cognizance of developments in modern science in the ongoing attempt to show how different types of understanding can be perceived
as consistent within a single worldview. In this respect, the encounter with
modern science is one in which theology itself will undergo some change,
development, and correction. To this extent, the different models often used
to describe the science-theology exchange (e.g., independence, complementarity, conflict, and integration) are all in different ways present in the modern history of the interpretation of Genesis. No single model is adequate to
the exclusion of others.

The sciences must be given their place freely to investigate and hypoth-
esize according to their methods and findings. A clearer delineation of the
differences with theology will result in recognition of peaceful coexistence
rather than a misplaced anxiety about the directions in which science might
lead us. The converse of this is that scientific description will itself need to be
challenged when it steps beyond its boundaries by seeking to "explain away"
other types of description. The explanatory descriptions of science and theology work in different ways — we might say at different levels — so that the
integrity of each can be recognized by the other. Significantly, John Brooke
and Geoffrey Cantor point out that references to natural theology tended to
disappear finally from the scientific textbooks in the latter part of the nineteenth century.[28]

A further instructive feature of the encounter with Darwinism was the
extent to which it showed the Bible and the Christian tradition capable of
providing resources for dealing with a new set of problems, in some cases resources that had been overlooked by earlier generations. The anthropocentric turn of deism might have been challenged by the place assigned to human beings in evolutionary science. However, the Bible with its more
theocentric vision could suggest a divine concern with creatures and

---

28. John Brooke and Geoffrey Cantor, *Reconstructing Nature: The Engagement of Science and Religion* (Edinburgh: T&T Clark, 1998), p. 201.

stretches of cosmic history that do not directly involve Homo sapiens. Similarly, if the Enlightenment projects of theodicy now found themselves in trouble by the end of the nineteenth century, it was open to Christian scholars to point to the lack of such theodicies in Scripture, to the rejection of easy solutions in the book of Job, and ways in which much of the response to evil was resistance, protest, and redemption through the dying and rising of Christ, rather than metaphysical explanation. If the occasional interpositions of Paley's God were now questionable, the way was opened to stress a continuous creation suffused with the divine presence and open to its agency. Amid all this, Scripture continued to offer fresh insight and vision in ways that could scarcely have been anticipated.

Humans, Animals, and the Environment in Genesis 1–3

Richard Bauckham

Creation in Seven Days (Gen. 1:1–2:4a)

The account of creation in seven days (Gen. 1:1–2:4a) is not the only creation account in the Bible. As well as Genesis 2:4b-25, generally recognized as a second creation account, there are at least four others (Job 38:4-11; Ps. 104:2b-9; Prov. 8:22-31; John 1:1-5). But the canonical placing of the seven-day account at the beginning of the Torah and the beginning of Scripture does give it an eminent role as foundational for the rest of the scriptural narrative. It is not surprising that it has had much the greatest influence on Christian understanding of the relationship between humanity and the nonhuman creation. In my view, it has had too exclusive an influence and, in the context of our age of ecological catastrophe, the perspectives of other parts of Scripture urgently need also to be appropriated,[1] but they lie outside my present task.

Structure and Meaning

The passage is carefully and intricately structured, and much of the meaning is embodied in the structure. The following diagram explicates the most important elements in the structure of the six-days narrative:

1. See Richard Bauckham, *Bible and Ecology: Rediscovering the Community of Creation* (Waco, Tex.: Baylor University Press, 2010).

Environments + Names	Inhabitants + Tasks
[precreation: earth, waters, darkness: formless and unproductive]	
(Day 1) light — separated from darkness	(Day 4) heavenly lights
God saw that it was good	Task: to separate day from night,
God names: Day and Night	to give light, to rule
	God saw that it was good
(Day 2) firmament — separates waters	(Day 5) Water produces water creatures
God names: Sky	Birds in sky
	God saw that it was good
	God blesses
	Task: to be fruitful and fill
(Day 3) dry land — by gathering waters	(Day 6) Land produces land creatures
God names: Land and Sea	*God saw that it was good*
God saw that it was good	Humans in God's image
Land produces vegetation	God blesses
God saw that it was good	Task: to be fruitful and fill and subdue
	Dominion over creatures of (5) and (6)
	All creatures of (5) and (6) to live from vegetation of (3)
	God saw all that he had made and it was very good[2]

Despite the use of a scheme of days, the allocation of material to the days follows primarily a spatial rather than a chronological arrangement. On the first three days God creates the three environments that constitute the ordered space of creation; then on the fourth, fifth, and sixth days he creates the inhabitants of each of these cosmic habitats in turn. Each of the habitats is named by God, and two of them (the waters and the land) participate in the creation of their inhabitants. Vegetation is treated as an aspect of the third environment, rather than as inhabitants of it, because it is viewed as part of the land's provision for the living creatures that inhabit it. The inhabitants are all animate creatures, including the heavenly bodies (seen as animate at least because of their regular and autonomous movement). Whereas

2. Biblical translations are based on the NRSV with some alterations.

God names the environments, he gives to each category of inhabitants (with the exception of the nonhuman land creatures)[3] a task that relates both to their specific environment and to the continuance of the created order in the future. In the cases of the creatures of sea and air and of humans the task is given along with God's blessing because it is this that enables them to procreate and multiply, sharing to that extent in God's creative work.

The scheme is primarily spatial. There is also a degree of logical sequence: the work of the third day has to follow that of the second, and the environments have to be created before their respective inhabitants. What is lacking, however, is any sense of building toward a culmination. Humans, the last creatures to be created, have a unique role within creation, but they do not come last because they are the climax of an ascending scale. The "creeping things" (reptiles and insects), created on the sixth day, are not higher, in some order of being, than the birds, created on the fifth day. So this scheme of creation has nothing in common with that progressivist reading of evolution that envisages a process of increasing complexity and increasing intelligence that culminates in human beings.

If the scheme is primarily spatial rather than chronological, we may wonder why it is set in a framework of seven days. One function of the temporal framework is to convey that, along with creating a spatially ordered creation, God created a temporal structure for that creation (the perpetuation of which is entrusted to the heavenly lights). However, that the number seven symbolizes completeness (not unconnected with the fact that a week has seven days) is also important. As well as the sequence of seven days, the microstructure of the account is replete with series of sevens, of which the most important is the sevenfold occurrence of the word ברא (to create).[4] That God completed his whole work of creation in the six days is emphasized in the account of the seventh day, on which he rested, presumably with the implication that he rested in appreciation of all that he had brought into being. The seventh day (rather than the creation of humans) is the true culmination of the work of creation, but not in the sense of ending a series that move progressively toward it. Rather the seventh day, radically different in kind from the others, relates directly to each of the six and forms the vantage point from which the work of all six days may be seen, not as a sequence but as a whole.

---

3. The reason for this omission is unclear, but that these creatures also have the task of procreating and multiplying seems to be assumed.

4. William P. Brown, *The Ethos of the Cosmos: The Genesis of Moral Imagination in the Bible* (Grand Rapids: Eerdmans, 1999), p. 52.

God's approbation and appreciation of every part of his creation are conveyed by the refrain, repeated at each stage of creation: "God saw that it was good." This indicates that each part of creation has its own value that does not depend on its value for other parts. The environments, for example, are not valued only because they serve as environments for their inhabitants. While the account stresses the importance of vegetation as food for the land animals, it does not require us to think that this is its only value. God appreciates the trees and plants also for their own sake. Nevertheless, the creation is designed to be an interconnecting and interdependent whole, and so the refrain is varied at the end of the work of the sixth day: "God saw everything that he had made, and, behold, it was very good" (1:31).[5] The value of the whole is more than the value of the sum of its parts.

The general picture of creation conveyed by the account features order, diversity, and profusion of life.

The Human Place in Creation

Humans, with their unique role in creation (to which we shall turn shortly), are essential to the design of the whole, but so are the other parts of creation. The view, which was common in much of the Christian tradition, that the rest of creation was created for the sake of humans finds no support in the text. But three features of the account, prior to the creation of humans, do show it to be written from the point of view of the human place in creation:

1. The heavenly lights are created "to separate the day from the night" and to "be for signs and for seasons and for days and years" (1:14). Though the distinguishing of light and darkness, day and night, benefits all creatures (cf. Ps. 104:20-22), the calendrical use of the movements of the heavenly bodies, implied by the second set of functions, is peculiarly human.

2. In the account of the creation of the land animals, "cattle" (בהמה) are distinguished from "wild animals of the land" (1:24, 25, 26). Usually when such a distinction is made, the "cattle" are domesticated animals, such as oxen, sheep, and goats. The account evidently sees such animals as already, at their creation, intended to share their lives with humans. Since this whole account of creation depicts humans and animals as vegetarians (1:29-30), killing domestic animals for food is not envisaged here; their roles as beasts of burden and as supplying wool and perhaps milk must be in view. Domes-

5. There are six occurrences of "God saw that it was good," and this distinctive variation is therefore the climactic seventh.

tic animals were so integral to the life of ancient Israel that humans could hardly be envisaged without such animals nor such animals apart from humans (note their inclusion in the Sabbath law [Exod. 20:10] and even in national repentance [Jonah 3:7-8]). It is not, however, implied that such animals were created solely for the sake of humans, and it could well be that the relationship between humans and domestic animals was seen as one of mutual benefit (Ps. 23 presupposes that sheep benefit from having a shepherd).[6]

3. At the creation of vegetation, it is described as "plants bearing seed, and fruit trees of every kind on earth that bear fruit with the seed in it" (1:11). Almost all of this rather cumbersome description is repeated in the following verse, and again when God grants humans their food supply: "I have given you every plant yielding seed that is upon the face of all the earth, and every tree with seed in its fruit" (1:29). By contrast, the food given to the land animals is described merely as "every green plant" (1:30). As Ellen Davis has recently argued, the full description, which insists so emphatically on seeds, alludes to agriculture, a uniquely human practice.[7] Again, this does not mean that seed-bearing plants and fruit trees were created solely so that humans could cultivate them, but it does mean that the creation of plants is viewed in the account from the perspective especially of humans dependent on agriculture for food.

Humans are one of two categories of creatures to whom God gives the special task of "ruling": the sun and the moon "rule" (מָשַׁל) the day and the night (1:16-18), while humans "rule" (רדה) all the creatures that inhabit sea, air, and land (1:26, 28). The latter are created in "the image of God" presumably, whatever more precisely the phrase may mean, because this is what makes it possible or appropriate for them to rule over other living creatures. But we need to look quite closely at the way the human dominion is introduced and described in the two divine speeches:

> Let us make humankind in our image, according to our likeness, and *let them have dominion* (רדה) *over the fish of the sea, and over the birds of the air, and over the cattle, and over all the wild animals*[8] *of the land, and over every creeping thing that creeps upon the land.* (1:26)

6. From the perspective of modern knowledge, we may note that domestication evidently took place in processes by which the animals attached themselves to human society, rather than being forcibly enslaved by humans; see Stephen Budiansky, *The Covenant of the Wild: Why Animals Chose Domestication* (London: Weidenfeld & Nicolson, 1994).

7. Ellen F. Davis, *Scripture, Culture, and Agriculture: An Agrarian Reading of the Bible* (Cambridge: Cambridge University Press, 2009), pp. 48-51.

8. "The wild animals" does not occur in MT, LXX, or Vulgate, and therefore not in

> Be fruitful and multiply, and fill the land and subdue (כבשׁ) it, and *have*
> *dominion* (רדה) *over the fish of the sea and over the birds of the air and*
> *over every living thing that moves upon the land.* (1:28)

The dominion is described in the italicized portions of the text. Despite
much confusion by exegetes,[9] the words that begin the second quotation are
not part of the mandate of dominion. They correspond rather to what God
has said to the sea creatures and the birds:

> Be fruitful and multiply and fill the waters in the seas, and let birds mul-
> tiply on the land. (1:22)

The only difference is that humans are told to "subdue" (כבשׁ) the land.
When this verb is used with humans as its object, as it mostly is in the Old
Testament, the meaning seems to be something like "to take by force" or "to
make subject" (e.g., 2 Sam. 8:11; Esth. 7:8; Jer. 34:11), but when "land" (ארץ) is
the object the meaning seems more like "to occupy" or "to take possession"
(Num. 32:22, 29; Josh. 18:1; 1 Chr. 22:18). This action, in these cases, requires
defeating the enemies who previously occupied the land, but the land itself
has only to be possessed.

In Genesis 1:28 the "land" that is to be "subdued" is the same "land"
that is to be "filled" by humans (i.e., all the land in the world), and the two
actions are closely connected. It seems likely that "subduing" the land here
refers to agriculture, since the only way humans are able to fill the land is to
cultivate it and so to make it yield more food than it would of its own accord.
If the element of force is intrinsic to the verb כבשׁ, then the reference is to
the fact that farmers must work the land to make it yield crops.[10]

English versions until recently. NRSV, JB, REB, and NIV margin supply it from the Syriac.
This correction of the MT seems very likely to be right, since "all the land/earth" in the middle of a list that is otherwise of animals is odd, and out of line with the similar lists in vv. 24,
25, and 28 (of which vv. 24 and 25 specifically mention "the wild animals"). The correction is
accepted by Claus Westermann, *Genesis 1–11*, trans. John J. Scullion, CC (Minneapolis:
Augsburg, 1984), p. 79, note on v. 26b, although his translation (p. 77) unaccountably omits
the whole of v. 26 after "image."

9. The confusion must be largely due to the text of v. 26 in MT, LXX, and Vulgate; see
n. 8 above.

10. Brown, *Ethos*, p. 46, speaks of "an ethos of order that requires effort but no weap-
onry." On the other hand, Norman Habel, "Geophany: The Earth Story in Genesis 1," in Norman C. Habel and Shirley Wurst, eds., *The Earth Story in Genesis*, Earth Bible 2 (Sheffield:
Sheffield Academic Press, 2000), pp. 34-48, here p. 46, thinks of "harsh control."

Agriculture makes the difference between fish and birds, on the one hand, and people, on the other. Without agriculture the land does not produce enough food for humans to fill it. This point must have been obvious to the biblical writers and accounts for the emphasis we have already noted on plants as seed bearing and therefore suitable for human cultivation. Since God's command to humans is not only that they should multiply, but that they should do so to the extent of filling the land, they must also "subdue" the land, that is, farm it. Other land animals, confined to habitats that supply their food without needing to be farmed, cannot fill the land. (As well as farming, it is possible that "subduing" the land alludes also to mining metals and quarrying stone; cf. Deut. 8:7-10.)

Of course, the command to "fill the land" should not be taken over-literally. The biblical writers were aware that there were some areas of wilderness in which humans could not live. But a more serious issue is that the creation account clearly assigns the land also to all the land animals. So God can hardly intend humans to "fill the land" at the expense of other animals. This is why, rather oddly, God's grant of "every green plant" to the land animals for food (1:30) is not spoken to the animals themselves, but appended, as information for humans, to his grant to them of seed-bearing plants for food (1:29). The point must be that humans should not grow food for themselves (and so fill the land) to an extent that competes with the livelihood of other living creatures. Humans and other creatures are to share the land, and humans are responsible for seeing that their own use of the land does not negate this sharing. There is a trace of this concern in Israelite land law, when the people are required to leave the land fallow every seventh year "so that the poor of your people may eat; and what they leave the wild animals may eat" (Exod. 23:11; cf. Lev. 25:7). Agriculture that is too efficient deprives not only the poor but also the wild animals. (In our contemporary context we may compare the drastic decline of wildlife as a result of industrial farming methods.)

For the mandate to fill the land and subdue it we may appropriately use the term "stewardship," since it is a right to responsible use of the land that belongs ultimately to God. But (contra most exegetes) in Genesis this is to be distinguished from the dominion over other living creatures. There is, implicitly, a connection between the two. The uniquely human practice of agriculture enables humans to multiply and spread so that they become the dominant species on earth. (Even in the OT period this must have seemed to be the case.) But the dominion granted by God presupposes more than this fact of power. It also presupposes that humans bear the divine image, so that God can authorize them to use their superior power in a way that reflects

God's own rule over his creation. Whereas they are to "subdue" the earth, they are to "rule" (רדה) the other living creatures.[11]

Unlike כבש, which is elsewhere used of land as well as people, רדה is used, outside Genesis 1, almost exclusively with human individuals or groups as its object (the only exception is the problematic Joel 4:13 [Eng. 3:13], where the word may be from a different root).[12] It is not surprising that, since it refers to rule or supremacy, it is often associated with violence or force, but this does not mean that violence or force is integral to the meaning of the word. In Ezekiel 34:4 it is used of the shepherds of the flock (representing rulers of the people) who are accused of not caring for the sheep but instead ruling (רדה) them "with force and harshness." The implication is probably that they should have ruled (רדה) with care and compassion, as God, the true shepherd of his people, does.

It is not clear whether the dominion over other living creatures includes the right to use them in any way. In the context of Genesis 1, there is no question of killing them for food: both humans and animals are vegetarian. Other uses of animals — as beasts of burden, for wool or milk — can apply only to the domestic animals, and so could constitute only a minor part of what dominion over all living creatures — in the sea, in the air, and on the land — could mean. It seems better to exclude use of animals from the meaning of dominion. The human dominion, like God's, is a matter not of use but of care. Genesis itself provides us with a paradigmatic case: Noah's preservation of the animals during the flood.[13]

It is therefore significant and intelligible that the image of God is connected not with the subduing of the earth but with the dominion over other living creatures. When humans obey the command to be fruitful and multiply, to fill the earth and subdue it, they are not imitating God in a unique way but behaving like other species. All species use their environment and, though agriculture is unique to humans, it can be seen as a peculiarly hu-

---

11. Psalm 8:7 (Eng. v. 6) does not speak of a more extensive dominion. The "all" of this verse comprises the creatures specified in the following two verses. Inanimate nature is not in view.

12. Norbert Lohfink, *Theology of the Pentateuch: Themes of the Priestly Narrative and Deuteronomy,* trans. Linda M. Maloney (Minneapolis: Fortress, 1994), pp. 11-12. But Lohfink's suggestion that the dominion refers to the domestication of animals is implausible because Gen. 1:26, as well as referring to birds and sea creatures, distinguishes "wild animals" from "cattle" (domestic animals).

13. Odil Hannes Steck, *World and Environment,* Biblical Encounters (Nashville: Abingdon, 1980), p. 106.

man extension of the right of all animals to use their environment in order to live and to flourish. If the human dominion over other creatures were merely a matter of power, it too would be only the superlative version of what other creatures have. What links it to the image of God is that it is a delegated participation in God's caring rule over his creatures.

That humans are commanded to do what other species do as well as, uniquely, to exercise dominion over other species is important to our understanding of the latter. Creation in the image of God does not make them demigods. They are unequivocally creatures. They are land animals who must live from the land as all land animals must. They participate in the ordered interdependence of the creatures as Genesis 1 portrays them. The dominion God gives them is over fellow creatures, and it reflects God's rule in a necessarily creaturely way. It is to be exercised within the created order that God has established and must serve that order.

The dominion is over living creatures, not inanimate nature. This makes the verb רדה, which elsewhere has only humans as its object, appropriate. Unlike the sun and the moon that rule only the day and the night, humans rule other sentient beings, which are to some degree subjects of their own lives just as humans are. Genesis does distinguish quite sharply between living creatures and the rest of creation. The covenant of Genesis 9 is made by God with Noah and his descendants and "with every living creature that is with you, the birds, the domestic animals, and every animal of the earth with you, as many as came out of the ark" (9:9-10). It is assumed that, unlike trees and mountains, animate creatures are suitable partners in a covenant (cf. also Hos. 2:18). (Our modern use of the term "the environment" — as a single term embracing landscape, flora, and fauna — thus fits the perspective of Genesis very badly.)

Genesis 1 as Ecotopia

As has often been observed, by contrast with other ancient creation myths, God in Genesis 1 does not battle or struggle with forces of chaos in order to wrest order from or impose order on them. God simply commands ordered form to appear out of the formless disorder of the precreation state (which in Gen. 1:2 is a kind of vividly imagined nothingness). There is no hint of a continuing threat to order from chaos. The whole process of creation proceeds in uninterrupted order, and within creation there is differentiated harmony with no hint of conflict. Crucially, neither humans nor other animals are carnivorous. So the human dominion over other living creatures involves no conflict. Its exercise ensures that there is no competition for living space or resources. All is peaceable.

This relates to the fact that everything is also finished. As we have noticed, not only the content but also the structure of the account indicates completion. The living creatures still have to multiply and to fill their environments. But this is no more than the fulfillment of the plan and potential already in place. There is no suggestion that anything could go wrong. This cosmos seems to be open neither to evil nor, in consequence, to redemption.

With a modern knowledge of the history of life on earth, we have to say: it was never like that. But the way the biblical narrative itself continues is in considerable tension with this picture of a creation already completed in the beginning. Things can go wrong and very soon do. In the light of the whole biblical narrative, the finished character of creation in Genesis 1 takes on a proleptic character, anticipating the new creation with which the narrative ends in Revelation 21–22. Only then will creation, rescued from corruption, enter into God's rest (Heb. 4:1-11).

Wolfhart Pannenberg comments:

> Only in the light of the eschatological consummation is the verdict justified that in the first creation story the Creator pronounced at the end of the sixth day when he had created the first human pair: "And God saw everything that he had made, and behold, it was very good" (Gen. 1:31). Only in the light of the eschatological consummation may this be said of our world as it is in all its confusion and pain. But those who may say it in spite of the suffering of the world honor and praise God as their Creator. The verdict "very good" does not apply simply to the world of creation in its state at any given time. It is true, rather, of the whole course of history in which God is present with his creatures in incursions of love that will finally lead it through the hazards and suffering of finitude to participation in his glory.[14]

Thus, in the light of the eschatological consummation, the human dominion, as Genesis 1 envisages it, becomes the hope for the peaceable kingdom depicted in Isaiah (Isa. 11:1-9; 65:25), in which, under the rule of the Messiah, the wild animals will live harmoniously with the domestic animals,

14. Wolfhart Pannenberg, *Systematic Theology,* trans. Geoffrey W. Bromiley, vol. 3 (Grand Rapids: Eerdmans, 1998), p. 645.

the carnivorous will become herbivorous, and the most vulnerable of humans, the small child, may play without danger from the once deadly creeping things. This is an ecotopia[15] that is both impossible to realize short of the new creation but also an invitation to practice nonviolent, caring dominion to whatever extent might be possible in the meantime. It is notable that the invitation is accepted, if only in a small way, in Israel's land law (Exod. 23:11; Lev. 25:7). As I have argued elsewhere, Mark 1:13 takes up the hope of the messianic ecotopia of Isaiah 11, seeing it as proleptically established by Jesus in his peaceable companionship with wild animals in the wilderness.[16]

Contemporary Comment

The order of the cosmos portrayed in Genesis has been unprecedentedly disrupted by modern humanity's scientific-technological project of unlimited domination of the whole world. Modern humans have overfilled the earth and grossly depleted its resources without regard to the fate of other species. Genesis 1 coheres closely with the lesson taught over and over by ecological catastrophe, already happening or unavoidably imminent: that humans must exercise their right to put the earth to use within strict ecological limits and that they exceed these limits at their own peril, as well as that of other species and the planet itself. Our modern knowledge of the interconnectedness of all life on earth can provide us with renewed appreciation of the portrayal in Genesis 1 of the ordered interrelationships of the creatures, while its emphasis on variety warrants contemporary concerns about biodiversity.

Genesis 1 does not authorize an undifferentiated human rule over the rest of creation, even when this is interpreted as stewardship. It distinguishes between human use of the earth, with its vegetation, for human life and flourishing, a right to be exercised responsibly, and human dominion over the rest of the animate creation, for which humans have a responsibility of care. Because of the interrelationships of all creatures, these two aspects of the human place in creation do tend to converge, especially in the face of ecological catastrophe, but the distinction remains important. Neglect of

15. I borrow the term from Bill Devall, *Simple in Means, Deep in Ends: Practising Deep Ecology* (London: Green Print, 1990), p. 34 ("ecotopian visions").

16. Richard Bauckham, "Jesus and the Wild Animals (Mark 1:13): A Christological Image for an Ecological Age," in Joel B. Green and Max Turner, eds., *Jesus of Nazareth: Lord and Christ: Essays on the Historical Jesus and New Testament* (Grand Rapids: Eerdmans, 1994), pp. 3-21.

this distinction and the classification of sentient creatures as simply part of the "environment" have led to all manner of cruelty to animals. Its most contemporary manifestation is the bioengineering of animals, which presupposes that humans have as much right to redesign the animal creation for their own use as they have to plant gardens and build houses.

In and out of the Garden (Gen. 2:4b–3:24)

This so-called second creation narrative doubtless originated independently of Genesis 1:1–2:4a, but in the composition of the book of Genesis it is presented not as an alternative to 1:1–2:4a but as a more detailed treatment of human origins, supplementing what 1:26-29 says on that subject.[17] I shall treat it in that way here. By comparison with 1:1–2:4a, it adopts a more exclusively anthropocentric perspective. The animals, for example, are considered only from the point of view of whether they could provide the "helper" Adam needs (2:18-20). The story itself might appear to present this as the sole reason for their creation, but were this really the case their creation would have been a mistake, since all of them fail to qualify for the role in question. But the story is a way of explicating the relationship between Adam and the animals: by naming them, he recognizes them as fellow creatures with whom he shares the world,[18] but his relationship with them is of a different order from his relationship with another human being, "flesh of his flesh."

Whereas the seven-day creation account ensures the creatureliness of humans by placing them within the order of creation, the Eden account does so, perhaps more emphatically, by stressing Adam's kinship with the earth

17. Cf., e.g., Bernard F. Batto, *Slaying the Dragon: Mythmaking in the Biblical Tradition* (Louisville: Westminster John Knox, 1992), p. 99: the Priestly editor "did not consider having two different stories of the same 'event' to be contradictory or problematic. Instead, he likely regarded them as complementary."

18. The naming is not a matter of asserting his authority over them, as many have suggested. If it were, then the same would have to be said of his naming of Eve (2:23; 3:20). Rather Adam's naming of the animals is comparable with the naming of children by parents (usually, in the OT, the mother), which does not assert authority but recognizes the independent reality of a new person. See George W. Ramsey, "Is Name-Giving an Act of Domination in Genesis 2:23 and Elsewhere?" *CBQ* 50 (1988): 24-35. According to Mark G. Brett, "Earthing the Human in Genesis 1–3," in Habel and Wurst, eds., *Earth Story in Genesis*, pp. 73-86, here p. 81, the naming is "a celebration of diversity." I see no basis for Brown's claim (*Ethos*, p. 141) that Adam determines the roles of the animals.

and the other creatures of earth. God, we are told, "formed the human being (אדם) from the dust of the soil (אדמה)"[19] (2:7) — the pun draws attention to the relationship and indicates its appropriateness. The animals are also created from the soil, all of them individually molded, like Adam, by God (2:19). God animates the clay figure of Adam by breathing into him "the breath of life" (2:7), which is the same breath that animates all living creatures (7:22). Though not specifically mentioned in the account of the creation of the animals (2:19), it must be assumed, because otherwise the animals would not be alive. The summary account probably assumes that, just as God himself formed both Adam and the animals from the soil, so God himself breathed the breath of life into both Adam and the animals. The phrase "living being" (נפש חיה), used of Adam in 2:7, elsewhere always refers to animals. Nothing in their created constitution differentiates humans from other animals.

Moreover, Adam's life remains bound up with the soil. Before we hear of him, we hear of the soil's need of him: "there was no one to till (עבד) the ground (אדמה)" (2:5). Once created, Adam is placed by God in the garden he has planted "to till (עבד) it and keep (שמר) it" (2:15). Following the description of the rivers of Eden (2:10-14), which associate it with Mesopotamia,[20] where the rivers themselves were not sufficient to make most of the land fertile, Adam's task is probably to irrigate the land in order to sustain the trees God has planted there.[21] Later he is sent to perform the same task outside Eden: "to till the ground from which he was taken" (3:23).[22] The man from the soil must work the soil in order to live from the soil's produce. The task is probably, as we have seen, much the same as that intended by the command to "subdue the land" in 1:28, but here there is a stronger sense of humanity's close relationship with the soil. It seems to be a reciprocal relationship: the soil needs Adam's work and he needs the soil's produce. There is also, in the

---

19. For אדמה as "arable land, fertile soil that can be cultivated," see Theodore Hiebert, *The Yahwist's Landscape: Nature and Religion in Early Israel* (New York: Oxford University Press, 1996), pp. 34-35.

20. I say "associate it with," rather than "locate it in," Mesopotamia, because it may be that the geography is intentionally obscure, suggesting that Eden cannot be geographically located in the ordinary sense (Batto, *Slaying*, p. 49).

21. Brown, *Ethos*, 139.

22. According to Ronald A. Simkins, *Creator and Creation: Nature in the Worldview of Ancient Israel* (Peabody, Mass.: Hendrickson, 1994), p. 180, humans are placed only temporarily in the garden, until they reach maturity and can be sent out to farm the land elsewhere.

word "keep" or "preserve," the implication that Adam takes care of the soil. He avoids exhausting it.[23]

The Old Testament often supposes a triangular relationship between God, humans, and the earth. Disruption of humanity's relationship with God affects also their relationship with the earth.[24] This is what happens in Genesis 3, when, following the primal act of disobedience to God, the ground is cursed and an element of hostility and resistance spoils the hitherto harmonious reciprocity of Adam's relationship to it (3:17-19).

Contemporary Comment

The modern project of scientific-technological domination of nature has been characterized by the desire to transcend nature, escaping from its constraints and remaking it to our own design. This is in effect a desire to be like God, with unlimited power and the freedom to create as we choose. The transfer of divine attributes from God to humans, perceived as occupying the place of God in relation to the world, not in creation but above it, is explicit in the Renaissance humanists[25] and formed much of the ethos of the modern world. It is, of course, the temptation to which Adam and Eve succumbed. In the Genesis narrative, Adam and Eve eat the fruit that the serpent tells them will make them like God, but they remain creatures, bound up with the earth, dependent on it, and destined to return to it. Similarly, the

23. Several recent studies of the passage have proposed translating עבד as "to serve," either as the sole meaning or as an additional overtone. See, e.g., Hiebert, *Yahwist's Landscape*, p. 157; Steven Bouma-Prediger, *For the Beauty of the Earth: A Christian Vision for Creation Care* (Grand Rapids: Baker Academic, 2001), p. 74; Norman Wirzba, *The Paradise of God: Renewing Religion in an Ecological Age* (New York: Oxford University Press, 2003), p. 31; Norman Habel, *An Inconvenient Text: Is a Green Reading of the Bible Possible?* (Adelaide: ATF Press, 2009), p. 69. But whereas this verb with a personal object means "to serve," there is a consistent usage of the verb to mean "to work" or "to cultivate" when the object is inanimate (Gen. 3:23; 4:12; Deut. 28:39; Isa. 19:9; cf. Prov. 12:11; 28:19; Zech. 13:5). This is the obvious meaning in Genesis 2. Davis, *Scripture*, pp. 29-30, tries to have her cake and eat it when translating both עבד and שׁמר: "to work and serve it, to preserve and observe it." But this seems to be an instance of the fallacy of attributing to a word in one occurrence the sum of the various meanings it carries in a number of other occurrences.

24. Robert Murray, *The Cosmic Covenant*, Heythrop Monographs 7 (London: Sheed & Ward, 1992), chs. 2 and 4.

25. See Richard Bauckham, *God and the Crisis of Freedom: Biblical and Contemporary Perspectives* (Louisville: Westminster John Knox, 2002), pp. 154-59.

modern project has left us once again creatures. The attempt to transcend nature, to re-create it as we would like it to be, has brought upon us the ecological disasters that are its unforeseen consequences. We are obliged now to recognize the extent to which we must respect the limits of our finite place in the ecological balance of the planet.

The modern attempt to transcend all limits was based, in the Renaissance humanists, on an interpretation of the divine image of Genesis 1:26-27. Though this neglected the limiting context within which Genesis 1 places humans, the account of humanity in Genesis 1 certainly offers more pretext for a notion of human transcendence of creation than the account in Genesis 2 does. In that sense, Genesis 2, with its stress on humanity's belonging to the earth and among the creatures of the earth, should help to bring us down to earth again.

The necessary human connection with the soil easily escapes the attention of modern urban people whose lives seem to be sustained by technology rather than by the produce of the land. The sumptuous availability of the latter in the affluent West means that we do not have to think much about their source, though uneasiness with the artificiality of modern farming methods has led to some such thinking and to the movement back to organic food. But in the face of the looming world shortage of food, likely to be disastrously intensified by climate change, a movement back to a degree of local self-sufficiency, entailing urban people's reconnection with the soil, begins to seem desirable. At the same time old-fashioned care for the soil begins to seem wiser than industrial-scale exploitation. We do not live in Eden, but even outside Eden something of Adam's symbiotic relationship with the soil, depending on it and caring for it, remains available.

Reading Genesis in Borneo:
Work, Guardianship, and Companion
Animals in Genesis 2

Michael S. Northcott

At the dawn of the modern era, in *Novum Organum,* Francis Bacon suggests that human beings recover the divinely given "empire over creation which they lost by the Fall through science and the arts."[1] At the core of the project of modernity, of which *Novum Organum* is the urtext, is the effort to dominate nature through science and technology. So intensively are modern humans now dominating and extracting value from the planet that they are using a majority of its biomass to resource their present and unprecedented levels of consumption. In the process forest cover, ocean floor, soil quality, and water sources are systematically destroyed such that biologists believe one-third of species will likely be extinct before the end of the present century. This historically unprecedented rate of species extinction is primarily because of habitat loss, whose principal causes are deforestation, destructive fishing practices, industrial agriculture, and human-induced climate change.[2]

1. Francis Bacon, *Novum Organum Scientiarum* (1620) (New York: Wiley, 1944), p. 470.

2. On the extent of marine habitat loss see Jeffrey J. Polovina, Evan A. Howell, and Melanie Abecassis, "Ocean's Least Productive Waters Are Expanding," *Geophysical Research Letters* 35 (February 2008): L03618. On bird extinctions see Cagan H. Sekercioglu, Stephen H. Schneider, John P. Fay, and Scott R. Loarie, "Climate Change, Elevational Range Shifts, and Bird Extinctions," *Conservation Biology* 22 (2008): 140-50; Wilfried Thuiller, Sandra Lavorel, Miguel B. Araújo, Martin T. Sykes, and I. Colin Prentice, "Climate Change Threats to Plant Diversity in Europe," *Proceedings of the National Academy of Sciences* 102 (2005): 8245-50.

The present wave of extinction is occurring at one hundred to one thousand times the rate at which any previous wave of extinction in geological history has taken place.[3] And the present wave is the first large extinction event provoked by the behavior of only one species. A small number of large mammals and birds in the last seventy thousand years — such as mammoths in North America and moas in New Zealand — have become extinct because of human hunting and habitat modification. But not until the modern era are large numbers of species extinguished as a direct consequence of human activities.

The root meaning of the word "extinguish" is to put out a light. In Genesis 2:18-19 species come before Adam to be named by him as potential companions, and as a mode of his *enlightenment*. In this seminal event Adam discovers his powers of language and speech, and he first engages in practical reason, discerning kinds in the world set before him, separating and naming them. As Leon Kass puts it, "the prototypical or defining human act is an act of speech, naming. Encountering the nonhuman animals actualizes the potential of human speech, thereby revealing the human difference."[4] But at the same time the narrative of Genesis 2 indicates that God brings the animals before Adam as his potential companions. Hence the work of naming also reveals Adam's creaturely companionship with other kinds.

In this essay I will explore the theological meaning of the seminal work of naming, and of Adam's given companionship with other animals, as described in Genesis 2, in the context of the extinction crisis in one particular location, Malaysian Borneo, which is part of the country in which I began my teaching career. I will suggest that when we read Genesis in the forest it has a different meaning to that which it has when read in the city. Reading it in the forest reveals anew the calling of Adam in this text to "tend and care," and to evoke and enhance in speech and action the beauty, diversity and fecundity that the Creator set within the created order. Reading it in the forest recovers the role of other animals as companions for Adam, and not just creatures to be ruled over. Reading it in the forest also resonates with the paradigmatic role of trees in salvation history. Adam and Eve fell by a tree, and the tree of death that is the cross of Christ is also revealed after the res-

---

3. Stuart Pimm, Gareth J. Russell, and John L. Gittleman, "The Future of Biodiversity," *Science* 269 (21 July 1995): 347-50.

4. Leon Kass, *The Beginning of Wisdom: Reading Genesis* (Chicago: University of Chicago Press, 2003), p. 74.

urrection as the root of the new creation. Psalmists and prophets frequently refer to trees as the standard of righteousness and truthfulness (Ps. 92:12-13). Myrtle and cypress trees "clap their hands" and flourish where once grew thorns as witnesses to redemption and "an everlasting sign that shall not be cut down" (Isa. 55:12-13).

In Borneo

Christianity is often blamed for the deteriorating condition of the earth's ecology, and in particular the opening chapters of Genesis in which dominion is granted to humankind, which is "made in the divine image." Indeed, wherever European Christians have spread over the earth their impact has been one of destruction of native biodiversity. Thus in the nineteenth century, when the eminent Victorian scientist Alfred Russel Wallace visited the Malay archipelago, which includes the tropical island of Borneo, the world's fifth largest island, he found such an abundance of wildlife that hardly a day went by in which he did not capture new species. At the end of an eight-year journey he had sent home by ship specimens that amounted to over 125,000 different species of bird, insect, mammal, plant, shell fish, and reptile.[5] But these were all dead specimens. And in the case of large mammals such as orangutans — which in Malay means "man of the forest" — they had frequently been shot by Wallace himself. The scientist, the hunter, and the colonial adventurer are all part of the identity he presents to his readers in his classic *Malay Archipelago.* There is no embarrassment, no hesitation, in recording the large number of specimens he kills, and sometimes leaves for dead in the branches of trees. Dominion for Wallace was unthinking: humans, especially wealthy Victorian ones, had the right, even the duty, to overpower the earth and its resources.

Large mammals that need significant range areas such as snow leopard, rhinoceros, pygmy elephant, and orangutan were all relatively common in Wallace's time as compared to our own. But it was not hunting in the end that reduced their numbers. The indigenous people — Dayaks, Penans, Ibans — had long hunted theses species and they were still plentiful after thousands of years of human habitation when Wallace arrived. But after 150 years of European forestry practices, timber extraction, and the spread of science-informed agriculture in the form of oil palm and rubber planta-

5. Alfred Russel Wallace, *The Malay Archipelago* (Singapore: Periplus, 2005), p. xxi.

tions, it is rare in the vicinity of the major rivers to find an intact patch of rainforest or to see a large mammal other than humans. On a flight from Kota Kinabulu to Sandakan that I took in 2008, all I could see from the plane was oil palm plantations, and the occasional small patch of secondary — that is, formerly logged — forest. Oil palm plantations have replaced more than forty percent of the great forests of Sabah and Sarawak, and much of the rest is logged over and degraded. As I write a hundred fires in Sumatra are turning an even greater percentage of that island into a large agricultural plantation for the production of palm oil for cooking, cosmetics, cleaning agents, and biofuel. And the greenhouse gas emissions from fires in this region, together with the Amazon, are so great that they exceed the weight of emissions from all the planes and cars on earth.

I visited Sabah — one of two Malaysian states in Borneo — in 2008 courtesy of the University of Malaysia Sabah where I had been speaking on religion and ecology. The university arranged for me to visit the Kinabatangan Forest Reserve, which is an area of mostly secondary forest on the upper reaches of the Kinabatangan River managed by the conservation organization HUTAN. HUTAN was founded by French primatologists Marc and Isabelle Ancrenaz in 1998. Working with the Sabah Wildlife Department and the Universiti Malaysia Sabah, HUTAN has established the Kinbatangan Orang-Utan Conservation Project (KOCP) in the upper reaches of the Kinabatangan River. KOCP has as its core objective "to restore harmonious relationships between people and the Orang-utan, which in turn will support local socio-economic development compatible with habitat and wildlife conservation."[6] The project achieves this aim by involving local residents and indigenous people who dwell in the areas still inhabited by orangutan.

The principal work of the project has focused on efforts to protect and enhance the mostly secondary forest in which orangutans live in the Kinabatangan River basin. This area was logged more than fifty years ago, and research shows that orangutans are fewer in number in logged forest.[7] However, the HUTAN project has demonstrated that orangutan numbers can be enhanced in secondary forest provided it includes a good range of tree species of sufficient size in which the animals can nest and on which

6. Red Ape Encounters and Kinabatangan Orangutan Conservation Project website at http://www.redapeencounters.com/kocp.htm.

7. Annika M. Feltona, Linda M. Engström, Adam Felton, and Cheryl D. Knott, "Orangutan Population Density, Forest Structure and Fruit Availability in Hand-logged and Unlogged Peat Swamp Forests in West Kalimantan, Indonesia," *Biological Conservation* 114 (2003): 91-101.

they can feed. KOCP employs forty local people in managing a project that includes a research station and an ecotourism project. Project scientists and guides chart the presence of nests and know most of the individuals who live in the area of the station. Besides generating scientific knowledge of these animals, the project is also intended to enhance the orangutan survival chances, and to this effect the project employs four full-time tree planters. Orangutans eat around three hundred species of tree, and they are essential to the germination of some of the tree species whose seeds expand and absorb moisture and nutrients from the feces of orangutans after being eaten. The seeds of these trees species are therefore premixed with collected orangutan feces before planting by the tree planters. The areas where the planting is done are protected with electric fences or else the elephants will come in and eat the saplings. The tree planters are all local women. Experience shows that women are better than men at tree planting. They are more careful to clear the ground, especially the *lalang* or long grass and other things growing where the sapling is planted, to dig and water it in properly, and so their plantings are more successful.

The project employs local people not only because they know the area and live nearby but also because conflicts between local people and orangutans grow as the habitat and range area of orangutan and forest and river peoples decline from the spread of palm oil plantations in which neither orangutans nor indigenous people can live. The KOCP use native guides from the river peoples who live in the forests. Such links between the project and local cultures are designed to promote indigenous resource management so that local people, instead of being excluded from deriving material benefit from protected parks and conservation projects, are actively engaged in employment and educational opportunities linked to species conservation.[8]

This approach differs from much scientific conservation management, which often assumes that conflicts between humans and other animals are intrinsic and that therefore the best strategy for conservation of endangered species is to exclude humans from the surviving habitats by declaring them wildlife reserves where humans may no longer dwell or harvest resources, even for local, customary use. The declared objective of the KOCP to foster harmony between local peoples and endemic animals is a departure from the modern practice of "wildlife" reserves. It represents an approach to con-

8. S. R. Kellert, J. N. Mehta, S. A. Ebbin, and L. L. Licthenfeld, "Community Natural Resource Management: Promise, Rhetoric, and Reality," *Society and Natural Resources* 13 (2000): 705-15.

servation grounded in human ecology, rather than human exclusion, in which there is no prior assumption of intrinsic species conflict. And it is therefore more consistent with the reading of the narrative of Eden in Genesis 2 I offer in this essay than the narrative of original conflict between humans and other animals advanced by Bacon, Descartes, Darwin, and other seminal shapers of modern scientific culture, as well as by many conservation scientists. But there is also a root of this understanding of original conflict within Christian exegesis of Genesis 1–3. And this is why it is so important rightly to discern the meaning of these three crucial chapters of the Bible. The European Christian project of colonial expansion and wealth extraction from the lawless borders of empire, a project that continues to this day, has significant roots in the Baconian reading of the Christian narrative of fall and redemption. And that reading has roots even further back in the Fathers of the Latin West.

"To till and guard" (Gen. 2:15)

Augustine reads the command to "till and guard" the garden of Eden as indicative of an original paradisiacal state where there is no physical work, and where nothing could be added by Adam to the original perfection of paradise, for "in the tranquility of the happy life, where there is no death, the only work is to guard what you possess."[9] For Augustine the war between flesh and soul, mind and body, which is the dualistic condition of sinful being, is read back into the original state of paradise: where there is no sin there is no physical work, no embodied engagement with a material world since such engagement already implies necessity, limits, death, and sin. On this hugely influential reading of the meaning of Eden there are no physical limits to human engagement with the creation other than those that arise from the condition of sin. If so, then the work of redemption is, as Bacon, Locke, and others have argued, to eschew limits in the quest to turn nature into human wealth. On this reading the work of clearing forests and draining wetlands for agriculture is a consequence of the fall and is at variance with the original and peaceable condition of life in Eden.

But there is another reading of tillage and work in Genesis 2 that we

9. Augustine, *On Genesis: Two Books on Genesis Against the Manichees; and, On the Literal Meaning of Genesis,* 2.11.15, trans. Roland J. Teske, Fathers of the Church 84 (Washington, DC: Catholic University Press of America, 1990), p. 111.

Michael S. Northcott

find in the Orthodox East. For Symeon the New Theologian the work of tending and caring is not just spiritual but physical: "In the beginning man was created with a nature inclined to work, for in paradise Adam was enjoined to till the ground and care for it, and there is in us a natural bent for work, the movement towards the good."[10] If work is part of the original calling of humankind, then this gives redemptive significance to the limits to human work already indicated in Genesis: in the original rest of God the Creator on the seventh day (2:2-3), in the story of the forbidden "tree of knowledge" that is not to be eaten (2:17), and in the story of the flood that is brought on the earth because human violence and wickedness grew beyond limit (6:5). If work in paradise is spiritual and material, then redeeming human work is a vital part of the meaning of salvation, and salvation is understood as a recovery or at least a reorientation of human embodied life on earth toward the original condition of Eden, in other words, the restoration of paradise. It is just such a reading of salvation that we find in early Christian art in the fifth century and onward, and that we find also in the development of a spirituality of manual labor in Benedictine monasticism.

Among the earliest enduring artistic depictions of salvation as incorporating all creation, and all creatures, is the mosaic apse of the basilica of San Clemente in Rome, albeit in a tenth- or eleventh-century copy of a much earlier original. The Christ depicted as redeemer in Saint Clemente is reminiscent of a Tibetan Buddhist mandala. He is connected above his head to the heavens, to God as Spirit and to the Father, and at his arms and feet to many kinds of species on earth, which are depicted encircled by swirls of green leaves emanating from the outstretched arms and feet of Christ. In the mosaic the restorative power of salvation reaches from the crucified and risen Christ throughout the cosmos, and brings wholeness to all the species of life on earth.

In the desert traditions and in Benedict there is an analogous reading of the meaning of human life after Christ, and the salvific significance of good work, that is closer to Symeon's than Augustine's reading of the meaning of work in Eden. The first monastic, Saint Antony, is said by Athanasius to have worked with his hands and to have commended this as one of the three essentials of the holy life: "He worked, however, with his hands, having heard, 'he who is idle let him not eat,' and part he spent on bread and part he gave to the needy. And he was constant in prayer, knowing that a man ought

---

10. Symeon the New Theologian, *The Discourses*, trans. C. J. DeCatanzaro (Mahwah, N.J.: Paulist Press, 1980), p. 164.

196

to pray in secret unceasingly."[11] Similarly for Cassian and Basil work is essential to the holy life because manual work makes possible almsgiving and hospitality, and because manual work is a needful occupation of the body without which it tends to be distracted by wrong desire.[12] This stance on the intrinsic relationship of manual work and holiness shapes the monastic tradition in East and West. Thus in the *Rule of Benedict* work is not punishment for sin, or a result of mortality, but a true means to the holy life: "If, however, local necessity or poverty require that they themselves are occupied in gathering the harvest, they should not be saddened; for they are then truly monks, when they live by the labour of their hands, as did our Fathers and the Apostles."[13]

Dom Rembert Sorg argues that the corruption of monasticism arises from the growing wealth of the medieval monasteries that made it possible for monks to pray and study and eat and not to work with their hands. Moreover, "the point of cleavage between healthy and decadent Benedictinism has been invariably the economic factor."[14] It was the overreaching success of the monks in cutting down forests, draining marshes, and turning the land over to sheep and cereal growing that ultimately led to their accumulated wealth and spiritual corruption. As this wealth enabled them to spend more time in church, and less in manual labor, so the fruit of manual labor was lost to them: "Its fruit in the monks is a calm, tranquil peace and silence, and his soul easily and blissfully becomes pregnant with the Wisdom of God. In contrast one may sincerely pity the flighty restlessness of meddlesome busybodies who do not know the secret and practice of manual labour."[15] In this perspective the original and first active command of God to Adam "to till and to guard" is a truly embodied and spiritual command. Good work in God's garden is an essential preservative of the goodness of human dwelling on earth because good work tends and conserves both the conscience and spirit of those who engage in it as well as the creatures among whom it is performed. Bad work, work directed by cost-benefit sums and the idle rich, deploying the power of their accumulated wealth not to protect but to destroy creaturely

---

11. Athanasius, *Life of Antony* 4, trans. Paul Halsall, *Internet Medieval Source Book* at www.fordham.edu/halsall/basis/vita-antony.html (accessed April 27, 2010).

12. For a fuller account of the status of manual labor in the Eastern Fathers see Rembert Sorg, *Holy Work: Towards a Benedictine Theology of Manual Labor* (1951; repr. Santa Ana, Calif.: Source Books, 2003), pp. 4-27.

13. *The Rule of St. Benedict,* trans. Timothy Fry (St. Paul: Liturgical Press, 1981), 48.7-9.

14. Sorg, *Holy Work,* p. xxi.

15. Ibid., p. 61.

and human habitats, is a threat to both the spiritual and ultimately the material well-being of those who command it.

So God formed from the soil every living thing of the field and every fowl of the heavens and brought each to the human, to see what he would call it. (Gen. 2:19)

The second kind of work that is given to Adam in Eden is as seminal as the command to till and to guard, for it involves the naming of the animals that are brought to him not in fear but as potential companions. This second kind of work is also seminal in a more particular way for the birth of the sciences in Christendom, and thence the flowering of the sciences and technology in the modern era. As we have seen, Francis Bacon views the scientific calling as a form of power through which humans recover the dominion over the earth that they lost at the fall. But for the editors of Genesis the calling of human beings to identify and name species — in which we see the biblical root of scientific taxonomy and all the natural sciences — is a calling given to human beings *before* the exile from Eden. Again there is division from early in the Christian era about the meaning of this passage. A number of patristic commentators on Genesis 2:18-19 reflect upon the apparent lack of animosity between Adam and the animals that come before him, and they do so in ways that indicate significant disagreement with the Augustinian tradition about the theological meaning of life in Eden before the fall. According to Ephrem the Syrian, God brings the animals to Adam

> in order that God might make known the wisdom of Adam and the harmony that existed between the animals and Adam before he transgressed the commandment. The animals came to Adam as a loving shepherd. Without fear they passed before him in orderly fashion, by kinds and species. They were neither afraid of him nor were they afraid of each other.[16]

For Isaac of Nineveh the apparent peaceableness of the animals is not because they have ceased to be predators in Eden but because there is a special quality in the holiness of this Adam before the fall that calms them:

16. Ephrem the Syrian, *Commentary on Genesis* 2.9.3, extract from Andrew Louth and Marco Conti, eds., *Genesis 1–11*, Ancient Christian Commentary on Scripture (Downers Grove, Ill.: InterVarsity Press, 2001), p. 65.

The humble man approaches ravenous beasts, and when their gaze rests upon him, their wildness is tamed. They come up to him as to their Master, wag their heads and tails and lick his hands and feet, for they smell coming from him that same scent that exhaled from Adam before the fall, when they were gathered together before him and he gave them names in paradise. This was taken away from us, but Jesus has renewed it and given it back to us through his coming. This it is that has sweetened the fragrance of the race of men.[17]

But for Augustine, who is so seminal in the development of Western Christian theology, and for Ambrose, the same action represents the great distance that there is between man and beasts, indicated by the reason that empowers Adam to name the beasts as they are paraded before him — presumably under coercion — by the angels. Thus Augustine tells us:

God first showed man how much better he was than the cattle and all irrational animals, and this is signified by the statement that all the animals were brought to him that he might see what he would call them and give them names. This shows that man is better than the animals in virtue of reason, since only reason which judges concerning them is able to distinguish and know them by name.[18]

For Ambrose also the spiritual meaning of this event is to reveal to Adam, and those who come after him, their superiority over brute beasts:

God granted to you the power of being able to discern by the application of sober logic the species of each and every object in order that you may be induced to form a judgment on all of them. God called them all to your attention so that you might realize that your mind is superior to them all.[19]

For the Fathers of the Latin West, in which tradition Bacon and Descartes stand, this story that, on a plain reading of the text, is about companionship as well as naming becomes yet another occasion for the assertion of

17. Isaac of Nineveh, *Ascetical Homilies*, 77, extract from Louth and Conti, eds., *Genesis 1–11*, p. 65.

18. Augustine, *On Genesis* 2.11.16 (p. 112).

19. Ambrose, *On Paradise*, 11.51-52, extract from Louth and Conti, eds., *Genesis 1–11*, p. 66.

human superiority over other creatures and for the claim that such creatures, in their spiritual significance, are merely expressions of misdirected human desires.

As is well known, the reading of Scripture is by no means plain. For the Fathers of the church there is a literal reading, and an allegorical or spiritual reading. As for Saint Paul, for the Fathers the spiritual reading is a reading *after* Jesus Christ, for the author of Scripture is also the God and Father of the Lord Jesus Christ. Against this traditional hermeneutics, however, the modern historical-critical method of exegesis envisages each text as a material entity locatable in space and time and whose meaning is therefore scientifically isolatable from other texts, from the canonical Scripture, and from tradition. Consequently, and paradoxically, modern exegetes, while more alive to the historical contexts of the original texts, have been less aware than the Fathers of their place in the whole narrative of salvation history, and of the location of the *reader*, as well as the text, in that narrative. This is not to deny that a fuller understanding — including scientific understanding — of the location of the text enhances the modern reading. But the knowledge acquired from this method has too often obscured the spiritual meanings of texts that arise from their location in the narrative of salvation history.[20] Analogously the historical-critical method suppresses the narrative shaping of the *reader* by Scripture and by her own life experiences.

In the light of this very brief hermeneutical excursus, a reading of Genesis 2 in a primeval forest that is ecologically closer to the primeval condition of Eden than the modern university library or a Roman city may enhance both a historical-critical and a canonical and spiritual reading of the text, and may help us to rightly deliberate on the variant spiritual readings of this text.

Companion Animals

I went into the Kinabatangan Forest Reserve on a morning in May 2008 in the hope of seeing orangutans in their natural state. I was, however, frustrated in that goal by the presence along the river of a group of pigmy elephants that were passing through the district on that day. When we got off the boat and approached the tree planting area, it became evident that orangutans were making themselves scarce because the herd of elephants —

20. For a fuller discussion see Michael S. Northcott, "Loving Scripture and Nature," *Journal for the Study of Religion, Nature and Culture* 3, no. 2 (2009): 247-53.

around twenty in all — were close by. Consequently our guide decided to call on two others from the project who were local elephant guides in order that we might have the opportunity of at least walking safely through the area. In due course our elephant guides came and led our small group of eight persons to a small tributary river. When we saw through the trees, a group of elephants were on the other side. We stood still and the group trumpeted, turned, and ran off into the woods. We held our ground. A few minutes passed in the intense midday heat. Then the elephants returned again across the stream from us. At this point they wagged their heads and trunks from side to side and our guides whispered that this meant "it's OK" and "they might be friendly." Then one of the group, a six-year-old female about five feet in height and four in width, left the herd and approached us across the stream. As she drew near she turned and began to walk backward, and finally raised a back leg in the air and wiggled it. At this point, one of our guides moved forward and patted her firmly on the rump. She ran off and undertook the same procedure again, with the same response. She then came again and this time swished her tail, which our guide then held and swished in turn. Eventually she began to approach us frontally and we found our small group being chased through the undergrowth, effectively playing "catch" with an elephant. After about twenty minutes, though it seemed a lot longer, the rest of the herd began to take an interest in joining in, and one of the large males, tusks and all, standing around seven feet tall, began to follow the younger juvenile in the game. At that point our guides suggested we back off as things could get a little too interesting.

I make no apologies in saying that for me this was a revelatory spiritual experience. During and after it I could not help but recall the passage before us now. How did the animals approach Adam? In fear and under angelic coercion, which is Augustine's suggestion? As slaves of the divine will who could do no other, which is the suggestion of another of the Fathers, Severian of Gambala?[21] Or as the elephants approached us in Borneo? Those animals were not afraid of us. They did not know us as *Homo industrialis,* who frequently kills them with a gun when the extensive incursions of the plantation industry into their terrain disturb them. They discerned in us fellow primates, communicative agents, friends, fellow wanderers in their nomadic world. They recognized us. They chose to play with us. They sought us out as companion animals. And may it not have been just so in Eden?

---

21. Augustine, *On the Literal Interpretation of Genesis* 9.14.24; Severian of Gabala, *On the Creation of the World* 6.1, extracts in Louth and Conti, eds., *Genesis 1–11,* p. 64.

Ancient and modern interpreters of Genesis 2 in Latin (Western) Europe set human agency above animal agency and suggest that the scientific enterprise whose etiology the passage evokes indicates the superiority of humans above all creation, and the human calling to order and harvest creation as the divinely intended and redemptive mode of our species' being. I suggest that on the contrary the spiritual meaning of the passage is that animals are brought to Adam to indicate to him, and to us, that they are our companions, our co-creatures here on earth, that we share the earth with them, and that they as well as we are called to fill the earth and multiply (which implies some limit on our destruction of their habitats and which few on such a reading of this passage could not now judge we have clearly exceeded).

This is not to gainsay that Genesis 2 also indicates our superiority over them. But the peculiar form of that superiority is not that we are to harvest them at will but that we are responsible, uniquely as a species, for the flourishing of Eden, and hence the earth, which we and they share. When we misconceive our creaturely relationship with God and put ourselves in the place of God, we corrupt our relationships with other beings, including trees and primates, using the ambiguous power-knowledge that our species acquired in that seminal act of eating of a forbidden fruit, of exceeding given creaturely limits, of claiming the powers of gods and not creatures. In so doing we acquired a new capacity — not given in creation — to frustrate the lives of all other beings, which both undermines our dominion and underlines how hard it is for us henceforth to till the earth in such a way as to guard the creatures in it — apart, that is, from the restorative work of Christ in vindicating and restoring the original condition of life on earth in his resurrection.

From this reading of Genesis in Borneo, the spiritual meaning of the text after the resurrection of Christ, and in the midst of ecological crisis, is that the work of science in naming and ordering the world stands as much in need of redemption as does the work of tending and guarding. Indeed, these two works are in urgent need of reconnection, for modern humans using industrial mechanical tillage have systematically degraded one-third of the available soils for agricultural production, and industrially originated climate change threatens to reduce crop output in some of the already most challenging environments for farmers.[22] Far from redeeming the earth, science and technology have conferred on *Homo industrialis* powers that have trained him to turn away from manual labor and distance himself from the

22. On soil erosion see further Michael S. Northcott, *The Environment and Christian Ethics* (Cambridge: Cambridge University Press, 1996), pp. 14-30.

soil and the forest and the garden. And while fossil-fueled wealth accumulates we also see the rotten fruit of excess wealth in the form of enforced idleness in the so-called advanced countries. In postindustrial Europe and North America good work — any work — is hard to find for many whose forebears found work, and a source of dignity and sustenance, in fields and forests and factories. There has never been a time when it was more important for Christians rightly to interpret the literal and spiritual meaning of work, guardianship, and companionship in Genesis 2.

Covenantal Ecology:
The Inseparability of Covenant
and Creation in the Book of Genesis

Brandon Frick

Introduction

As the reality of environmental degradation sets in and the threat of environmental crisis grows ever more menacing, Christian environmental orga-
nizations and environmentally conscious denominations are searching for
resources to aid them in responding to this situation. In research undertaken
at Baylor University, called the Christianity and Environmental Ethics in
North America (CEENA) project, the concept of *stewardship* was repeatedly
encountered as the motivating theological rationale for a large number of
these groups and denominations. One can see a concise example of the stewardship argument at work in Francis Schaeffer's pioneering work, *Pollution
and the Death of Man: The Christian View of Ecology*. Schaeffer argues that
the "dominion" given to humanity in Genesis 1:28 is interpreted properly
when viewed through the stewardship exhibited in the parable of the talents
(Matt. 25:14-30). Schaeffer concludes that, like the good and faithful steward,
"we are to exercise our dominion over these things not as though entitled to
exploit them, but as things borrowed or held in trust, which we are to use realizing that they are not ours intrinsically."[1]

While this approach is theologically commendable in a variety of ways,
including its attendance to Scripture and its emphasis on human action, it is

---

1. Francis Schaeffer, *Pollution and the Death of Man: The Christian View of Ecology*
(Wheaton, Ill.: Tyndale House Publishers, 1970), pp. 69-70.

also open to critique.[2] In this essay we will focus on the critique of Willis Jenkins, who points out that stewardship theologians "worry that ethical appeals to nature's status smuggle in unjustified descriptions of nature," and, in an effort to exclude philosophical and theological concepts foreign to the biblical witness, do not ascribe intrinsic integrity to creation.[3] This ultimately means that nonhuman creation often recedes into the background in many stewardship ethics, leaving the matter as fundamentally a breakdown in relationship between humanity and God, thus diminishing the significance of the rest of creation.

The attenuation of creation's significance is a highly problematic and, ultimately, unnecessary move, for the concept of covenant allows one to appreciate the intrinsic value of the created order without straying from a biblically oriented approach. Through an intertextual reading of significant portions of the book of Genesis, I argue in this essay that covenant and creation are inseparable, both because creation *provides* the means for the fulfillment of the covenant and because it is *provided for* in the covenant. Drawing heavily upon Robert Murray and Karl Barth, I first attempt to establish the inseparability of covenant and creation in the book of Genesis with an exploration of the Noachic and Abrahamic covenants. Then I take a step back to the accounts of God's interactions with the first humans in Genesis 1 and 2, arguing that while not *formally* covenantal, they might be said to be *materially* covenantal. Special attention will be paid to three important aspects of these covenants: (1) the theme of land/earth (אֶרֶץ), (2) the theme of procreation, and (3) the scope of the covenant. To conclude, the implications

---

2. Michael Northcott makes two points about stewardship. First, he notes that the fundamental problem with the metaphor of stewardship is that it does not reflect the current reality, for it implies that "humans are effectively in control of nature. . . . And yet so much of recent environmental history teaches us that we are not in fact in control of the biosphere" (*The Environment and Christian Ethics* [Cambridge: Cambridge University Press, 1996], p. 129). Second, he writes that while "stewardship" metaphors are prevalent in Western culture, "industrial humanity has a very bad record of earth-keeping" (*A Moral Climate: The Ethics of Global Warming* [Maryknoll, N.Y.: Orbis, 2007], p. 268). Finally, there is the issue of language within the Christian churches, where "stewardship" most commonly refers to the management of one's *money,* a connotation that brings with it a host of issues, not the least of which is the negative effect that current economic systems often have on the environment. Especially in our current global economic situation, we should be more than a little concerned by the idea that individuals and institutions might approach the management of the earth like the management of assets.

3. Willis Jenkins, *Ecologies of Grace: Environmental Ethics and Christian Theology* (New York: Oxford University Press, 2008), p. 83.

of the binding together of covenant and creation for stewardship ethics in particular, and environmental ethics in general, will be explored.

The Noachic Covenant

To begin, let us turn our attention to the Noachic covenant, an eternal covenant (ברית עולם) that Barth considered to be a daring proclamation of the "indissoluble relation" of creation to the "divine covenant."[4] The scope of this covenant is a matter of primary importance. In Genesis 6:18 God tells Noah that he will establish a covenant with him, a significant declaration of hope given both the enormity of the postlapsarian situation portrayed in the opening verses of this chapter and God's declaration that he will destroy everything on the earth — everything except the occupants of the ark. Here the term ברית, usually translated "covenant," is encountered for the first time in the Old Testament; yet to more fully understand the meaning of this term, the reader must continue through the narrative.

In 9:9-11 God's covenant to never again "cut off all flesh by the waters of a flood" is made not only with Noah and his descendants, but with "every living creature" housed in the ark.[5] Robert Murray notes that this covenantal inclusion of nonhuman creatures along with human beings exhibits God's concern and care for both and binds all creatures together as "the Creator's partners." Murray pushes this covenantal bond further, asking, "if both are God's covenant partners, how can they not be in some sense covenantally bound to each other?"[6]

While it might seem odd to think of any aspect of nonhuman creation as covenantally bound either to God or human beings, we must still ask if there are resources in addition to God's explicit inclusion of animals in the

---

4. *CD* IV/1:27. At the outset I must acknowledge that throughout the primeval history, and in many of the passages relating to the Abrahamic narrative that I will be drawing upon, there is a weaving together of multiple sources; while acknowledging that the imprint of at least two authorial sources can be found within these narratives, I will read and present them as single literary units. In regard to the Noachic covenant, John W. Rogerson points out that it is difficult to parse out these sources in chs. 6–9 (*Genesis 1–11* [London: T&T Clark International, 2004], pp. 70-72).

5. All biblical translations are from the NRSV.

6. Robert Murray, *The Cosmic Covenant: Biblical Themes of Justice, Peace and the Integrity of Creation* (London: Sheed & Ward, 1992), p. 102. Murray admits that while this view may *possibly* be attested to at Job 5:22-23, it is not found anywhere else in Scripture. We might also add Hos. 2:18.

covenant that might lend themselves to Murray's interpretation. There is, of course, the ark, a vessel built by human beings at the command of God, to preserve not only humanity but animal life as well. The image of the ark is compelling, as human beings and animals literally ride out the flood together, and when God remembers the ark bobbing in the floodwaters, he remembers both Noah and the animals.[7] God's concern for *all* of the creatures on the ark continues in his expressed desire that they be "fruitful and multiply" (8:17; 9:1, 7), which recalls God's commands to both human and nonhuman creatures in 1:22, 28. If humans and nonhuman creatures are to remain faithful to this particular aspect of the eternal covenant, they must respect certain boundaries that allow one another to thrive; it will entail an ark-like respect and cooperation between both humans and animals.

Yet to focus on these images is to pass over two less irenic scenarios. First, upon the postdiluvian egress from the ark, Noah offers up to the Lord a representative sacrifice of every clean bird and animal (8:20). The odor of these sacrifices pleases the Lord and prompts him to pledge the cessation of such widespread destruction. Second, animals are now filled with the "fear and dread" of human beings, and rightfully so, for animals are now given to human beings in addition to the vegetarian diet prescribed in the garden (9:1-3). Similar to their charge in the garden, human beings are again given a type of dominion over other creatures, but the environment in which this is to be exercised is no longer compliant, and therefore the relationship between humanity and the animal realm has changed (another factor that complicates the possibility of all creaturely procreation).

In addition to Walter Brueggemann,[8] there are no doubt other environmentally conscious Christians who would shy away from interpreting these relationships as covenantal; indeed, these very texts, in particular the permission and even positive assessment by God of the killing of animals, may contribute to the "growing anxiety as to whether the Flood story is a good story to think about and use at all as part of a religiously authoritative book."[9]

7. See S. van den Eynde, "The Missing Link: ברית in the Flood Narrative: Meaning and Peculiarities of a Hebrew Key Word," in André Wénin, ed., *Studies in the Book of Genesis: Literature, Redaction and History* (Leuven: Leuven University Press, 2001), p. 476.

8. While acknowledging that we are just beginning to appreciate the significance of the nonhuman in the Noachic covenant, Brueggemann states that only "human persons are covenant partners with Yahweh" (*Theology of the Old Testament: Testimony, Dispute, Advocacy* [Minneapolis: Fortress, 1997], p. 454 and n. 9).

9. R. Walter L. Moberly, *The Theology of the Book of Genesis* (New York: Cambridge University Press, 2009), pp. 106, 107.

Brandon Frick

Those unsettled by the disparity between the situation portrayed in the initial Genesis accounts and this later account have understood the flood narrative correctly, for the contrasts between the Genesis creation accounts and the flood narrative seem far from accidental. Yet this arrangement, disturbing as it may be, is nevertheless a constitutive aspect of the Noachic covenant, but one that is accompanied by God's demand that human beings and animals respect the "lifeblood" (9:4) of every living thing. The sacrifice of the animal has already been enacted and the mutual killing of one another is foreseen, but God still demands, as part of the eternal covenant he establishes with both human and nonhuman creatures, that the life that he has given each creature must be respected.

We must move to one final aspect of this covenant. God eternally covenants not only with creatures but with the earth (אֶרֶץ) as well. In v. 13 God declares, "I have set my bow in the clouds, and it shall be a sign of the covenant between me and the earth." Some may wish to understand this as a summary statement, shorthand for God's pledge to never destroy "all flesh" with another flood. Such an interpretation, however, would not be consistent with the narrative's use of אֶרֶץ. The term אֶרֶץ is repeatedly used throughout to indicate the noncreaturely aspect of God's creation in distinction from its inhabitants.[10] Therefore, it seems that the covenant between God and the earth refers to just that, a covenant between the Creator and the noncreaturely aspects of his creation, from the base of the olive tree to the "tops of the mountains" (8:5). Having been submerged for a prolonged period of time, this is a not insignificant pledge on the part of God that expresses a "solemn guarantee of the cosmic orders."[11]

To summarize: we have seen that the Noachic covenant is centered on the *entirety* of creation in its scope, and its provision of and encouragement toward procreation on the part of both human and nonhuman creatures.

The Abrahamic Covenant

God initiates the covenantal relationship with Abraham, and much like his covenant with Noah, it entails procreation. In 12:2 God informs the seventy-

10. Examples of this distinction between the earth and its inhabitants include 6:12, 13; 7:3, 21; 8:17; 9:1, 10.
11. Gerhard von Rad, *Genesis: A Commentary*, trans. John H. Marks, rev. ed., OTL (Philadelphia: Westminster, 1972), p. 134.

208

five-year-old Abraham that God will make of him "a great nation," and at 15:5, to a then one-hundred-year-old Abraham, that he will make him "exceedingly numerous." In 12:7-8 William J. Dumbrell points out that in the "extension of the covenant to succeeding generations" we find a concept similar to that of the everlasting covenant of Genesis 9.[12]

This procreative promise should lead us to appreciate how God is both Lord *over* the created order and yet not dismissive of working *through* it. As Lord of creation, the natural constraints of age that would normally prohibit offspring are removed. In the fulfilling of this covenant, we see that God is not *fettered* to the rhythms of creation, but *free* to providentially intervene in creation in order to accomplish his "covenantal will," the source of all his works.[13] Yet this is not to say that God simply dismisses a created order that he himself designed. The fulfillment of this covenant is undeniably miraculous in the sense that a one-hundred-year-old man and his ninety-year-old wife produce a son. But it still occurs through the natural process of reproduction, a process that, we might reasonably infer from the Hagar/Ishmael story, was in some way dependent upon biological and environmental factors, a reality that Abraham's descendants, who are also included in this everlasting covenant, would come to experience as they brought this covenantal promise to fruition. Given these biological circumstances, Claire Amos points out that circumcision was "an appropriate visible mark for a covenant that promised the provision of an heir supernaturally to an old man and woman well past the age of normal child-bearing."[14]

God's promise of progeny to Abraham comes with the promise of a place for them to live, making the habitation of a *specific* place essential to fulfilling the covenant. Similar to the Noachic covenant, we find in the Abrahamic covenant another, more particular, example of the significance of land (ארץ). The covenantal significance of the land of Canaan not only to Abraham but to the later generations as well cannot be overstated. Brueggemann describes the land as "the substance of the promise" God makes to Abraham.[15] God's faithfulness to the fulfillment of this covenantal promise, according to Michael Wyschogrod, establishes "an eternal link be-

12. William J. Dumbrell, *Covenant and Creation: An Old Testament Covenantal Theology* (Grand Rapids: Baker, 1984), p. 73. This covenant as an "everlasting covenant" (ברית עולם) is made explicit in 17:7.

13. Barth, *CD* IV/1:35.

14. Clare Amos, *The Book of Genesis* (Peterborough: Epworth, 2004), p. 99.

15. Walter Brueggemann, *Genesis,* Interpretation (Atlanta: John Knox, 1982), p. 150.

tween Israel and the land," in that a "people is born out of a soil which is its mother."[16] Irving Greenberg notes the profound social implications of this covenant, writing that it confirms "the significance of economic life and labor, now and forever."[17]

The scope of the Abrahamic covenant more fully expresses the cosmic dimensions briefly noted in the Noachic. In this latter covenant, and even more explicitly in numerous passages throughout the Old Testament (e.g., Exod. 7–11; Isa. 5; 33; Jer. 12:4; Hos. 4:1-4), one finds an understanding of what Murray calls the "cosmic covenant," or the "divinely willed order harmoniously [linking] heaven and earth."[18] This connection between heaven and earth carries with it two implications. First, it means that when Israel's relationship with God is distorted, the cosmic covenant is distorted as well, leading to negative effects for the created order. A succinct example of this distortion can be found in Isaiah 24:5: "The earth lies polluted under its inhabitants; for they have transgressed laws, violated the statutes, broken the everlasting covenant." Conversely, it can also have positive implications for the land, such as one later sees in the sabbatical pattern formalized in the Sinai covenant. Not only does the land receive a respite on the Sabbath, every seventh day, but also in the Sabbatical Year and the Jubilee Year, in which the land was to lie fallow and the land's inhabitants, including the wild animals, were allowed to graze upon whatever it yielded (Lev. 25:1-12).

We see this latter aspect in God's declaration in Genesis 12:2-3 that Abraham will be a "blessing," which extends the positive aspects of the covenant — "life, goodness, and well-being"[19] — out past God's explicit covenant partner Abraham, and even his descendants, for they are not only blessed, but are to be a blessing to the families of the earth.[20] Supposing that this promise to be a blessing refers to human beings only, we would do well

16. Michael Wyschogrod, "Judaism and the Land," in R. Kendall Soulen, ed., *Abraham's Promise: Judaism and Jewish-Christian Relations* (Grand Rapids: Eerdmans, 2004), pp. 91-103, here pp. 92, 103.

17. Irving Greenberg, "Judaism and Christianity: Covenants of Redemption," in Tikva Frymer-Kensky, David Novak, Peter Ochs, David Fox Sandmel, and Michael A. Signer, eds., *Christianity in Jewish Terms* (Boulder: Westview, 2000), pp. 141-58, here p. 145.

18. Murray, *Cosmic Covenant*, p. xx.

19. Terence E. Fretheim, *God and World in the Old Testament: A Relational Theology of Creation* (Nashville: Abingdon, 2005), p. 106.

20. While my reading of this text stands in a long line of Christian interpretation, Walter Moberly offers a persuasive alternative reading that asks, "May the real concern of the divine speech be not the benefit of the nations but rather the benefit of Abraham?" (*Theology of Genesis*, pp. 149-61).

to remember, as Michael Northcott states, "Human life and society are intricately bound up with the life and community of ecosystems and the biosphere."[21] To fully appreciate this observation, one need to think only of the impact of the "capitalist chariot" upon the environment or the clear-cutting of forests to meet agricultural and population demands.[22] With this ecological understanding of the interconnectedness of all life — an interconnectedness also exhibited in the Noachic covenant — it would be at the very least reasonable to understand the blessing wrought in this covenant as one that exhibits God's grace not only for Abraham or his progeny, "but for all the nations, and indeed for all creation," especially in light of our explication of the themes of procreation and land that accompany this more cosmic understanding of blessing.[23]

The Genesis Creation Narratives

If we now take a step back and view Genesis 1 and 2, we can see that land and procreation are materially significant aspects of God's covenantal interactions with the whole of creation. Murray will be the first to admit that "creation [is] not expressed in explicitly covenantal terms" in the Genesis accounts.[24] But, as we will see, the web of relationships set forth here reflects the covenantal content present in both the Noachic and Abrahamic covenants.

The earth (ארץ) in which God plants the garden of Eden plays a significant part in these covenantal interactions, especially in 2:15, which states that even *before* the garden was created, God created Adam out of the ground to "till it and keep it." As a place of rest and relationship with God, Barth considers this "sacred grove" to be a sanctuary that serves as a precursor to the tabernacle and the temple. Therefore, the gardener is a parallel to the priest, whose task was to serve and watch over the tabernacle (Num. 18:2-4) and temple, sites of extreme covenantal significance.[25] As Barth states, it is because this fruitful garden is "specially planted by God and therefore specially belongs to Him" that it "epitomises a good land desired by the husbandman or gardener . . . where it is clear that the earth which man is or-

21. Northcott, *Environment and Christian Ethics*, p. 173.
22. David K. Ma, "Destructive Creation: The Covenantal Crisis of Capitalist Society," *ThTo* 63 (2006): 150-64, here 164.
23. Barth, *CD* III/2:581.
24. Murray, *Cosmic Covenant*, p. 32. See also Hos. 6:7.
25. *CD* III/1:254.

dained to serve is also ordained to serve him."[26] The one cannot be thought of without the other: without the garden, the gardener would be without a home and a task; without the gardener, the garden would have no one to tend it and aid it in becoming fruitful. This divinely established system of mutual service is not just an ideal to which humanity must aspire, but is woven into the very fabric of reality and an integral part to creation-wide flourishing and reproduction.

The charge to procreate given in the Genesis account is also similar to the charge given in the Noachic covenant and the promise of the Abrahamic covenant. It is God's desire not only that *Adam and Eve* multiply, but that *other animals,* namely the birds of the air and the fish of the sea, multiply as well. This charge of procreation is significant, Barth writes, because for the first time "there now appears the problem of history proper as a continuation of creation, [which] appears in the form of the problem of the sequence of procreation. . . . What we have here is the beginning of its history, or at least an introductory prologue which announces the theme of this history, i.e., the establishment of a covenant between God and His creation. . . . [Even] the most remote and strange circle of the animal creation . . . must also bear witness to this covenant."[27] Implicit in the charge to procreate, then, are the charge and blessing for both human and nonhuman creatures to continuously take part in God's eternal covenant.

This leads us to our final point, the covenantal interaction between human and nonhuman creatures. Here we will follow Barth's exegesis of Genesis 1:24-31, which encompasses the well-known "dominion" passage. Barth writes: "Not as an independent partner of the covenant, but as an *attendant,* the animal will participate with man (the independent partner) in the covenant, sharing both the promise and the curse which shadows the promise."[28] The meaning of the term "attendant" is unclear in the English translation, but it does not seem to indicate what one might initially infer: that the role of the animal is only one of attending to humanity's needs. Here

26. *CD* III/1:250-51. This reciprocal service is key for Barth, for 2:15 indicates that the first humans were to tend and keep not just any garden, but one from which they themselves would be tended and kept.

27. *CD* III/1:170-71.

28. *CD* III/1:178; italics mine. Throughout his exegesis of the creation sagas, one finds a tension between Barth's understanding of humanity's exercise of dominion *over* animals on the one hand, and his insistence that if humans are to respond to God's covenant properly, they should offer praise *for* and *on behalf of* all creatures and serve them as a *primus inter pares,* a first among equals (*CD* III/1:184-85).

the German is helpful; "attendant" is a translation of German *Begleiter,*
which can mean either "companion" or "guide"; hence "attendant" should
be read, at the very least, as indicating that animals go along with humanity
as companions in the move from promise to fulfillment, and possibly indicating that they serve as guides throughout this movement.[29] God stands in
a special covenantal relationship with humanity, but covenantal participation is not excluded from animals. As creatures living alongside of, and interacting with, humanity, they experience the hope of the promise of
covenantal fulfillment and suffer the consequences of humanity's covenantal
unfaithfulness, including them in the historical movements of the covenant.
In this passage Barth does not include *all* of creation in the act of reconciliation, but this same logic of attendant participation makes creation-wide reconciliation, *at the very least,* a legitimate possibility, and covenantal participation on the part of creatures (although indirect), an actuality.

Conclusion

As we have seen in our explorations of the Noachic and Abrahamic covenants and the initial Genesis accounts, covenant and creation are inseparable in the book of Genesis, not only because the created order *provides* the
means for the fulfillment of the covenant, as in the case of procreation, but
also because creatures (both human and nonhuman) and the land are *provided for* in the covenant. To conclude, we must now turn to the ethical implications of this inseparability, specifically for stewardship theologies, and
more generally for environmental ethics.

First, this covenantal approach allows us to speak of an intrinsic integrity of creation from within the biblical witness, making it a promising tack
especially for stewardship theologies. One can now speak of the integrity of
God's creation without concern that one is *automatically* importing various
extrabiblical systems of valuation. With the covenantal approach, the
"ground and judge of what is and what exists of value is God."[30] What gives

29. Karl Barth, *Kirchliche Dogmatik,* III/1 (Zollikon/Zurich: Evangelischer Verlag,
1957), p. 199. No doubt, the proposition that this term be translated as "guide" is a provoca-
tive one. What makes the translation at the very least possible is Barth's description of animals as (only 3 sentences before our main text) *Gefährten,* which means "companion" or
"partner." Barth's use of *Begleiter* would then seem to be an intentional move that highlights
an aspect of the relationship with animals that differs from simple companionship.
30. Charles S. McCoy, "Creation and Covenant: A Comprehensive Vision for Envi-

value to every aspect of the created order is that God has created it and pledged himself to uphold and sustain it, despite the unfaithfulness of his human covenant partners.

This leads us to our second point (and here we are picking up Barth's argument), an understanding of creation's "intrinsic character" as "benefit."[31] Barth not only means that it is "benefit" in the sense that without God's choice to posit a reality other than himself nothing other than God would exist, but in addition that as the locus of covenantal fulfillment in the person and work of Jesus Christ, creation "cannot itself be hostile or indifferent, but can only be a benefit and can only be understood as such." This is not to say that creation is not, as Romans 8:22 states, "groaning." The Yes of God is undeniably accompanied by the No; but, Barth states, as a "work of God turned outwards it participates in the right, dignity and goodness of the Yes in which He is God by Himself."[32] As the work of a faithful and good Creator God, creation is eternally sustained and characterized by the divinely willed "supreme law of all benevolence and *bene esse*."[33]

Third, the covenantal approach presents us with a *covenantal ecology*. Whereas stewardship theologies focus on the divine-human relationship, a covenantal approach establishes an interconnectedness between all parties (i.e., God, humans, and nonhuman creation), for God freely enters into relationship with both human and nonhuman creation; as God's covenant is not arbitrary, neither are relationships within this covenantal ecology. God's covenant is concerned with the well-being and flourishing of all of creation; however, there is a tension here most clearly expressed in the relationship between creatures in the Noachic covenant. As we have seen, God shows an unequivocal concern for the flourishing of nonhuman creatures. Yet God also accepts the sacrifice of the animal by the human; indeed, he finds the aroma of such sacrifice "pleasing."

This tension defies any attempt to establish a simple and definitive principle for any kind of environmental ethic. However, this tension does give us a new way to think about these relationships and the significance of our faithfulness to their maintenance. This covenantally established relationship, or ecology, reminds us (1) that it is God's intention and design that

---

ronmental Ethics," in Carol S. Robb and Carl J. Casebolt, eds., *Covenant for a New Creation: Ethics, Religion, and Public Policy* (Maryknoll, N.Y.: Orbis, 1991), pp. 212-25, here p. 221.

31. *CD* III/1:330.

32. Ibid., 331.

33. Ibid.

all of life is interconnected, and (2) that creation's relationship with God places certain covenantal boundaries on the relationships between human and nonhuman creation, which must be upheld if we are to remain obedient to God's will. Therefore, I propose that we take into account this divinely initiated covenantal ecology as we evaluate how we can best live environmentally responsible lives. What does it mean that the Creator interacts covenantally with the creation? What are our responsibilities to those to whom we are covenantally bound, that is, to both God and creation? These are the questions that we must ask and answer honestly and faithfully if we truly desire the preservation, and even deepening, of the covenantal ecology that gives form and content to all of creation.

"And Without Thorn the Rose"?
Augustine's Interpretations of Genesis 3:18
and the Intellectual Tradition

Karla Pollmann

Introduction: The Fecundity of Opacity

"The enterprise of reading and interpreting Genesis will not soon cease, and the opacity of the text, its capacity for generating multiple and incompatible readings, is an important part of the reason why Genesis in general, and its third chapter in particular, serves as an excellent example of the fecundity of Scripture's opacity, and as support for the claim that it is important that Scripture not always be transparently clear and, as a result, easily exhausted."[1]

The allure, especially of the first chapters of Genesis, has endured through the ages, and goes also beyond the narrower discipline of theology. The main reason for its timeless fascination lies in that it addresses fundamental issues of the nature, position, and destiny of humankind in the world. Among the most eminent figures of intellectual history who took up the gauntlet of struggling with the interpretation of Genesis was Augustine of Hippo (354-430), arguably the most influential theological thinker of the

1. Paul J. Griffiths, *Intellectual Appetite: A Theological Grammar* (Washington, DC: Catholic University of America Press, 2009), pp. 44-45.

This essay forms part of my research in connection with the international and interdisciplinary project "After Augustine: A Survey of His Reception from 430 to 2000," which is directed by me and generously funded by the Leverhulme Trust. For further details see www.st-and.ac.uk/classics/after-augustine.

Latin West. He attempted an understanding of the creation narrative at least five times during his life.[2] Striking are his flexibility and exegetical diversity when approaching this text, where he more than once has to admit defeat (*Gn. litt.* 8.2.5; *Retr.* 1.18 and 2.24) or a change of mind (*Retr.* 1.10.3).[3] But the focus of this investigation will not be so much the plethora of interpretations offered by Augustine, but how later generations handled this legacy, by focusing on two different possible understandings of Genesis 3:18.

One Tradition of Interpreting Genesis 3:18

> Betwixt them lawns, or level downs, and flocks
> Grazing the tender herb, were interpos'd,
> Or palmy hilloc; or the flow'ry lap
> Of some irriguous valley spread her store,
> Flow'rs of all hue, and without thorn the rose. . . .

With these words John Milton (1608-1674) in *Paradise Lost* 4.252-56 describes the garden of Eden as a *locus amoenus,* one of whose characteristics is roses without thorns.[4] This implies that the rose only developed thorns as a punishment after the fall and after the expulsion of the first humans from paradise. Metaphorically this hints at the general deterioration of the human condition within a hostile environment, bringing pain, labor, danger, and eventually death. It is noteworthy that the idea that humans were immortal in paradise and their punishment for their insubordination was mortality is not supported by Genesis 2 and 3 and early Jewish literature (which assumes them to be mortal from the start), but is only the result of later interpretations.[5]

---

2. Karla Pollmann, "Augustine, Genesis and Controversy," *AugStud* 38 (2007): 203-16.

3. His general hermeneutical framework is always the same, however, as is rightly observed by Roland J. Teske, "Criteria for Figurative Interpretation in St. Augustine," in Duane W. H. Arnold and Pamela Bright, eds., *De doctrina Christiana: A Classic of Western Culture* (Notre Dame: University of Notre Dame Press, 1995), pp. 109-22.

4. I am grateful for this reference to Thomas G. Duncan, School of English, St. Andrews.

5. For this see the important article by Konrad Schmid, "Loss of Immortality? Hermeneutical Aspects of Genesis 2–3 and Its Early Receptions," in Konrad Schmid and Christoph Riedweg, eds., *Beyond Eden: The Biblical Story of Paradise (Genesis 2–3) and Its Reception History,* Forschungen zum Alten Testament 2/34 (Tübingen: Mohr Siebeck, 2008), pp. 58-78.

Karla Pollmann

In Genesis 3:18 God announces as part of his curse following Adam and Eve's transgression: "The earth shall bring forth thorns and thistles to you" *(spinas et tribulos germinabit* [sc. *terra] tibi).* Here thistles are seen as a mode of punishment. From this verse some commentators concluded already in the early Christian tradition that before the fall there were no thorns and thistles. This tradition was presumably known to Milton,[6] specifically the commentary on the six days of creation by Basil the Great and its Latin equivalent by Ambrose; both works were written in the second half of the fourth century and both were called *Hexaemeron.* Ambrose, following and enlarging Basil, said that before the fall of the first human beings the rose blossomed without thorn as an equivalent to the sinless state of the first humans.[7] After the fall the thorns were added to the rose as a mirror of the now deteriorated and more troubled state of *all* humankind *(postea spina sepsit gratiam floris, tanquam humanae speculum praeferens vitae).* Nature serves as a reminder and teacher of the postlapsarian state of human misery and harsh reality. Thus this biblical statement can also be allegorized: because of human guilt the blossoming paradisiacal state was changed through the addition of thorns of the mind and thistles of the soul *(nobis in paradisi amoenitate florentibus spinae mentis animaeque sentes iure condemnationis ascripti sunt).*[8] So we have here a theological figure of thought whose tradition spans more than thirteen hundred years, viz., at least from Basil and Ambrose to Milton.

Augustine between the Traditional and a New Interpretation

In his earliest exegetical commentary, expounding Genesis against the Manichees *(De Genesi contra Manichaeos,* written 388-390, after his conversion and before he became a priest), Augustine deals with Manichaean criticism of the account of creation as given in Genesis, which the Manichees

6. George W. Whiting, "And Without Thorn the Rose," *Review of English Studies* n.s. 10 (1959): 60-62.

7. Ambrose, *Hex.* 3.11.4; PL 14.188; Basil, *Hex.* 5.6; *Homélies sur l'Hexaéméron,* SC 26 bis, p. 300.

8. Cf. Karla Pollmann, "Wann ist der Mensch ein Mensch? Anthropologie und Kulturentstehung in spätantiken Autoren," in Barbara Feichtinger, Stephen Lake, and Helmut Seng, eds., *Körper und Seele: Aspekte spätantiker Anthropologie* (Munich: K. G. Saur, 2006), pp. 181-206, here pp. 194-95.

found difficult to harmonize with their dualist view of the world.⁹ Augustine comments on Genesis 1:11-13 (*Gn. adv. Man.* 1.13.19):¹⁰

> Here [the Manichees] are in the habit of saying: "If God gave orders for grass to spring from the earth for fodder, and also fruit trees, who gave orders for so many thorny and poisonous plants and grasses to spring up, and trees that bear no fruit?" In reply one must take care not to reveal any mysteries to the unworthy, nor to show them what things to come are being prefigured by the way things are said here.

Augustine suggests here as an answer to the Manichees:

> So then what should be said is that it was through human sin *(per peccatum hominis)* that the earth was cursed, so as to bring forth thorns, not so that the earth itself should feel the punishment, since it lacks sensation, but that it might always be setting the criminal nature of human sin before people's very eyes, and thus admonishing them to turn away at some time or other from their sins and turn back to God's commandments. As for poisonous plants, they were created for punishing mortals or putting them through their paces, and all this on account of sin, because it was after sin that we became mortal. By unfruitful trees, however, human beings are being mocked and taunted, to make them understand how they should blush for shame at lacking the fruit of good works in the field of God, that is, in the Church, and to make them afraid, because they themselves neglect unfruitful trees in their fields and do nothing by way of cultivating them, of being neglected in their turn by God and left uncultivated. So then, before human *(hominis)* sin the text does not say that the earth produced anything but grass for fodder and fruit trees, while after the first human sin we see many prickly and unfruitful things springing up from the earth, for the reason, in my opinion, that we have just given.

9. For a more detailed analysis of Augustine's exegesis of Gen. 3:18 and its implications see Karla Pollmann, "Human Sin and Natural Environment: Augustine's Two Positions on Genesis 3:18," *AugStud* 41 (2010): 69-85.

10. Translations taken from Edmund Hill, *On Genesis*, Works of Saint Augustine 1/13 (Hyde Park, N.Y.: New City Press, 2002), occasionally with modifications. See Gottfried E. Kreuz, *Pseudo-Hilarius: Metrum in Genesin. Carmen de Evangelio, Einleitung, Text und Kommentar* (Vienna: Verlag der Österreichischen Akademie der Wissenschaften, 2006), p. 106 with n. 290, who emphasizes the uniqueness of Augustine's position.

Karla Pollmann

Because the Manichees objected to allegorical interpretation if it was not applied to the myths of their founder, Mani, Augustine attempts here a relatively "literal" interpretation, which follows the quite conventional thinking patterns of nature as teacher and as a tool for God's punishment of human sinful behavior. This is reminiscent to some extent of what has already been offered by Ambrose, and follows a "traditional" interpretation of this verse.

This mode of explanation was then substantially modified when Augustine wrote his big *Literal Commentary on Genesis (De Genesi ad litteram)* in twelve books (between roughly 404 and 414).[11] He had by now become far more experienced as a biblical exegete and even more ambitious to develop a rational and consistent interpretation of Genesis that should make it acceptable even to its sternest critics, including Christians likely to be influenced or destabilized by such critics or criticism. Moreover, a close reading of the text would have revealed to him that the statement about every plant in Genesis 1:11 "bearing seed according to its kind and likeness, and whose seed is in it according to its likeness," would not allow for the claim that evil plants developed only after the fall, an explanation that moreover questioned God's comprehensive all-inclusive, once-and-for-all creation activity. Thus he comments on the creation of animals: "The question is also commonly asked about various poisonous and dangerous animals: whether they were created after the sin of the human person *(post peccatum hominis)* as a punishment, or rather had already been created as harmless, and only began after that to do sinners harm" (*Gn. litt.* 3.15.24). Augustine concedes that although "bodily trials and troubles are still necessary for training and perfecting us in virtue," Daniel survived among the lions (Dan. 6:22) and Paul was not harmed by a viper (Acts 28:3-5). So he concludes: "So it would have been quite possible for these creatures to do no harm when they were created, if no occasion had arisen for punishing vices and frightening people off them, or for testing virtue and making people perfect, when it is a matter both of giving examples of patience to help others make progress and of people growing in self-knowledge through their trials. And it is only just that the eternal salvation which has been disgracefully lost through wilfulness, should be courageously won back again through pain."

In a similar vein he writes in the context of the creation of various kinds of plants: "'Let the earth produce grass for fodder seeding seed, and fruit trees making fruit' [Gen. 1:11] — this verse is not in contradiction with the existence of thorns, thistles and those kinds of trees that bear no fruit,

---

11. For a discussion of the various datings see Michael Fiedrowicz in Hill, *On Genesis*, pp. 164-65.

because the latter will have some kind of (potentially hidden) use" (*Gn. litt.* 3.18.27-28). Regarding thorns and thistles Augustine then refers explicitly to Genesis 3:18: "Thorns and thistles shall the earth bring forth to you *(tibi),*" spoken by God to the fallen human couple. According to Augustine, this should not be understood as indicating that these things began to spring up from the earth only after the fall. Augustine is careful to avoid the demonization of nature or of living creatures, putting the focus on the inner (psychological) mechanisms in each human individual who has to consent.

There is even one later instance where the interpretation of this motif becomes vital again, namely in the final fight of the aging Augustine with his much younger, educated, and bright opponent Julian of Eclanum, in his *Incomplete Book against Julian* (*Contra Iulianum opus imperfectum,* written after 424).[12] In his vehement exchange with this formidable opponent, Augustine quotes Julian's opinion quite extensively (*c. Iul. imp.* 6.27). It is noteworthy that Julian agrees entirely with Augustine that indeed the earth had produced thorns and thistles already before the fall. There had also already been toil in paradise as can be seen from Genesis 2:15 ("And the Lord God took the man, and put him into the garden of Eden to dress it and to keep it");[13] 3:19 ("In the sweat of thy face shalt thou eat bread, till thou return unto the ground") has to be read in connection with 2:7 ("And the Lord God formed man of the dust of the ground") as information or even comfort and not as punishment. Finally, the thorns produced "to you" in 3:18 are directed at Adam personally and did not imply the entire human race. It is clear that Julian has two argumentative aims in his exegesis: he intends to lessen the difference between the pre- and the postlapsarian state of humankind,[14] which for him is more a difference in degree than in kind, and he intends to avoid a notion of original sin or a curse that was collectively extended to all of Adam's offspring. Thus the dogmatic consequences of his exegesis are markedly different from those of Augustine, although in their exegetical methods there is not much difference between the two.[15]

12. Cf. Hanneke Reuling, *After Eden: Church Fathers and Rabbis on Genesis 3:16-21* (Leiden: Brill, 2006), pp. 210-12.

13. All biblical translations are my own.

14. It is noteworthy that in a recent publication of collected essays, Schmid and Riedweg, eds., *Beyond Eden,* this seems to be an argumentative goal as well; see, e.g., pp. 194, 272-81 passim.

15. In the same direction goes, more generally, Gerald Bonner, "Augustine, the Bible and the Pelagians," in Pamela Bright, ed., *Augustine and the Bible* (Notre Dame, Ind.: University of Notre Dame Press, 1999), pp. 227-42, esp. 228.

Karla Pollmann

After Augustine

In the history of the interpretation of these verses this is a rather unusual position, which documents yet again Augustine's originality and independence
as a thinker. As I have shown elsewhere, the later exegetical tradition only
rarely follows Augustine on this innovative path.[16]

Claudius Marius Victorius, a Christian biblical poet from the first half
of the fifth century, is presumably the first, after Julian of Eclanum, to adopt
this motif of Augustine's thought, namely that pernicious plants and animals existed already before the fall. He describes in his biblical epic *Alethia*
("Truth") 1.353: *armavitque* (sc. *genitor*) *manu, cornu, pede, dente, veneno,* the
equipment of animals with harmful attributes as part of their original creation ("The Creator armed the animals with claws, horns, hoofs, teeth, and
poison").[17]

Roughly one hundred years later, Avitus (†528) enlarges this thought
in his biblical epic, *De spiritalis historiae gestis* 3.320-22: "inde truces saevire
ferae dudumque timentes / excitat ad pugnam tum primum conscia virtus /
reddit et armatas unguis, dens, ungula, cornu" ("For the same reason [sc. after the fall] savage beasts grew fierce, and for the first time an awareness of
their power stirred those once tame to attack, to use their claws and teeth,
hooves and horns as weapons").[18] Here, as in Augustine, Avitus is keen to
demonstrate that the animals had all these "wild" attributes from the beginning when they were created in paradise, but that they made harmful use of
them only after the fall. The reception of Augustine's thought in both Claudius Marius Victorius and Avitus is presumably facilitated by Lucretius, *De
Rerum Natura* 5.1036-38, where the budding horns, claws, and teeth in young
animals are highlighted although they cannot yet do any harm with them,
but they are already there from the beginning of their lives (ontogenesis instead of phylogenesis!).[19]

16. See Karla Pollmann, "Von der Aporie zum Code: Aspekte der Rezeption von
Augustins *De genesi ad litteram* bis auf Remigius von Auxerre (†908)," in Norbert Fischer,
ed., *Augustinus — Spuren und Spiegelungen seines Denkens,* vol. 1 (Stuttgart: Meiner Verlag,
2009), pp. 19-36.

17. I owe this passage and some of the following to the excellent commentary by
Manfred Hoffmann on Alcimus Ecdicius Avitus, *De spiritalis historiae gestis, Buch 3,* trans.
Manfred Hoffmann (Munich: K. G. Saur, 2005), pp. 218-22.

18. George W. Shea, trans., *The Poems of Alcimus Ecdicius Avitus* (Tempe: Arizona
State University Press, 1997), p. 97.

19. It seems appropriate to mention explicitly that, e.g., Prudentius, *Hamartigenia*

Bede (672/673-735) produced various commentaries on Genesis that borrow heavily from early Christian writers, first and foremost Augustine. These commentaries were exceedingly important as mediating Augustine's thought to medieval thinkers, some of whom, for whatever reason, did not read Augustine's commentaries directly. However, Bede feels in no way obliged to follow the text, let alone the line, of his predecessor's thought in every detail, and occasionally the editions (as far as they exist) do not make this sufficiently clear. Sometimes, unfortunately, they even give completely misguided information. I offer one striking example that is relevant in our context. When commenting on Genesis 3:17-18 the *apparatus fontium* wrongly claims that Bede quotes from Augustine, *Gn. litt.* 3.18.28, which deals with the question as to when thorns and thistles came into being.[20] But in fact Bede quotes almost verbatim from Augustine's much earlier commentary, *Gn. adv. Man.* 1.13.19 (mentioned above), which claims that harm-

---

216-49, lists fatal dangers nature developed only after the fall, thereby upsetting God's original peaceful laws through its own fault (248 *vitiis agitata suis*). It is remarkable that the "post-Augustine" biblical verse paraphrases by Pseudo-Hilary (mid-fifth century), *Metrum in Genesin*, and by Dracontius (late fifth century), *De laudibus Dei*, do not contain a reference to this particular motif; Dracontius, *Laud.* 1.454-58, stresses that there were no animals in paradise with the exception of the snake. Moreover, I was not able to trace it in Eugippius († after 530), Gregory the Great (540-604), or Isidore of Seville (570-636); cf. Pollmann, "Von der Aporie zum Code."

20. CCSL 118A:68. It seems important to quote the entire passage (lines 2178-2200), for which the *apparatus fontium* wrongly offers as a parallel *Gn. litt.* 3.11.38, which only goes from *Hos esse . . .* till *. . . teneretur;* this is then followed by an excerpt from *Gen. adv. Man.* 1.13.19, quoted practically literally from *Per peccatum* till *. . . diximus causam:* "Hos esse in terra labores humani generis quis ignorat, et quia non essent si felicitas quae in paradiso fuerat teneretur? Per peccatum enim hominis terra maledicta est, ut spinas pareret, non ut ipsa poenas sentiret quae sine sensu est, sed ut peccati humani crimen semper hominibus ante oculos poneret, quo admonerentur aliquando averti a peccatis et ad Dei precepta converti. Nam et herbae venenosae ad poenam vel ad exercitationem mortalium creatae sunt. Et hoc notandum propter peccatum, quia mortales post peccatum facti sumus. Per infructuosas quoque arbores insultatur hominibus, ut intelligant quam sit erubescendum sine fructu bonorum operum esse in agro Dei, hoc est in ecclesia, et ut timeant ne deserat illos Deus, quia et ipsi in agris suis infructuosas arbores deserunt nec aliquam culturam eis adhibent. Ante peccatum ergo hominis non est scriptum quod terra protulerit nisi herbam pabuli et ligna fructuosa; post peccatum autem videmus multa horrida et infructuosa nasci, propter eam videlicet quam diximus causam. Mystice vero terra quae in opere praevaricationis Adae maledicta esse perhibetur, non alia melius quam caro accipitur. Namque spinas iam et tribulos germinat nobis quia, per carnis concupiscentiam propagati, punctiones et incentiva vitiorum de ipsa carne patimur." The final lines appear not to be from Augustine, but to be Bede's own addition (excerpted in Hrabanus Maurus's *Commentary on Genesis* 1.19; PL 107.439).

ful plants came into being only after the fall. It is noteworthy that Augustine is here not mentioned by Bede as a source, and that Bede favors the earlier *De Genesi contra Manichaeos* over the later *De Genesi ad litteram*, which Augustine considered to be his more accomplished work.[21]

The great Carolingian thinker Erigena (810-877) does not show any interest in Augustine's approach to the issue of Genesis 3:18, but rather follows an allegorical reading as supported by Ambrose, though he allegorizes differently. In line with his general understanding of paradise as a spiritual or mental state of every human being, Erigena links Genesis 3:18 and the postlapsarian curse in general with the state of human reason *(ratio)* on its way to truth *(Periphyseon* 4, 744B): reason is ordered to reap her bread in the sweat of her face, and to go round *(lustrare)* the earth of Holy Scripture, which produces for itself *(sibi)* thorns and thistles *(spinas et tribulos)*, that is, the "thin crop of interpretations of what is divine" *(divinorum intellectuum exilem densitatem)*, till reason arrives again at truth *(ad veritatis contemplationem . . . redeundo perveniat).*[22]

Remigius of Auxerre (†908) produced perhaps the most original of all Carolingian commentaries on Genesis, and follows Augustine as one of his main authorities. However, the cento-like technique of his commentary that assembles statements from various authors with each verse allows it to juxtapose interpretations by Augustine with opinions taken from other authors that contradict what Augustine would have said. One example relevant in our context would be that Remigius explains the curse of the serpent in Genesis 3:14 as in fact directed at the devil (and not at the irrational and therefore guiltless animal), following, through the mediation of Bede and Hrabanus Maurus, the interpretation of *Gen. litt.* 11.36.49. But in the next sentence Remigius adds, following the Latin version of Flavius Josephus, *Historiae antiquitatis Iudaicae* 1.1.4, that the serpent, which had hitherto not been poisonous, became so as a consequence of God's postlapsarian curse.[23] This flatly contradicts Augustine, *Gen. litt.* 3.15.24, where Augustine emphasizes that (some) snakes were poisonous from the beginning. Of course the contradiction is not made explicit; Remigius simply uses the catena style of

21. In general, Augustine's attempt at controlling his own reception failed to a considerable degree; cf. Karla Pollmann, "Alium sub meo nomine: Augustine between His Own Self-Fashioning and His Later Reception Through Others," *ZAC* 14 (2010): 409-24.

22. Cf. John Scotus Erigena, *Periphyseon (De Divisione Naturae) Liber Quartus*, ed. and trans. Édouard A. Jeauneau and John J. O'Meara (Dublin: Institute for Advanced Studies, 1995), pp. 6-7.

23. CCCM 136:60, 1364-69.

his commentary to select and assemble statements in a way that can sometimes "correct" Augustine and represent a theology that suits Remigius
better.[24]

But Augustine's alternative thoughts on Genesis 3:18 did not get lost.
On the contrary, they were prominently included in the most influential
standard textbooks of theology in the Middle Ages, the *Four Books of Sentences,* in which Peter Lombard (c. 1100-1160) compiled biblical texts together with relevant passages taken from various Christian authors considered to be canonical, most prevalently Augustine. In book 2, which deals
with creation, in dist. 15 c. 3 (84) the question is raised as to whether animals
had been created as harmful as a punishment after the fall, or whether they
had been created as harmless and only began to be harmful to human beings
once they had become sinners after the fall. As a *solutio* Peter quotes from
Gn. litt. 3.15.25 that the latter is the case. Similarly, in *Sent.* 2 dist. 21 c. 3 (124)
and 4 (125) Peter quotes approvingly *Gn. litt.* 11.11.2.4 and 11.27.34–29.36, respectively, the latter in a strongly abbreviated way, that the serpent in paradise was not created as evil or as bad by nature but only became so through
being so used by the devil's astuteness.

Although Martin Luther still wrote glosses on Lombard's *Sentences,* we
nevertheless do not find a trace of this argument in his commentary on Genesis.[25] His *In primum Librum Mose Enarrationes* contains a preface with
methodological principles and discussions of Plato, Aristotle, and others in
connection with issues raised in Genesis and is an extremely interesting commentary engaging in a rich discussion with sources from Ovid to Nicholas of
Lyra, from Plato to Augustine (esp. *De Genesi ad litteram*). Unsurprisingly, in
this commentary many theoretical reflections are interspersed, for example,
referring to the mystical meaning of the number six in Genesis 1, de facto referring to Augustine, *Gn. litt.* 4, but without mentioning the work, only generally indicating his source with "Augustinus . . . in tractatione."[26] He holds
various opinions that can also be found in Augustine, although Luther does
not make that explicit. He takes the view that nowadays plants multiply by the
power of their seeds, whereas in the first creation they were simply made
through the power of the word *(ex virtute verbi).*[27] Philosophy does not know

24. See Pollmann, "Von der Aporie zum Code," pp. 34-35.
25. For a general evaluation of the Reformer's exegesis of the early chapters of Genesis
see Emidio Campi, "Genesis 1–3 and the Sixteenth Century Reformers," in Schmid and
Riedweg, eds., *Beyond Eden,* pp. 251-71.
26. Wittenberg 1544 (= WA 42), here WA 42, 4f.
27. Ibid., p. XIr (= WA 42, 27).

the reason why seeds always (re)generate their own kind. Several early Christian writers (including Augustine) claimed that the world was created in one moment; Luther agrees. But Luther does not seem to agree with Augustine on the rise of harmful plants: he believes that in paradise they were all good and fertile *(bonas et foecundas),* and that thorns and labor *(spinas et tribulos)* came only into being after the fall, as a punishment for the first sin *(peccati esse poenam).* Luther, like others who hold this view, does not seem to bother with how this was supposed to happen — perhaps as a kind of a second creation added by God? Luther simply claims that the expulsion from paradise meant that Adam was transferred from a happy world into thorns and fruitless labor *(Adam ex foelici mundo inter spinas positus sit).*[28]

In a similar vein, John Calvin comments on Genesis 1:11: God created plants before the sun and ordered them to multiply in order to demonstrate that everything depended on him in nature *(sed ut discamus ad eum referre omnia, nullas tunc soli et lunae partes concessit),* and that natural order and phenomena are used by God as tools.[29] Plants are not merely created as such but contain an innate power to procreate offspring to preserve their species *(inditam propagationis virtutem, ut suboles maneret).* God spoke once and so procreation goes on for all time. Calvin continues on Genesis 1:24 in like manner about the procreation of animals: *imo colligi inde potest singulis animalibus inclusam fuisse subolem.* Then on Genesis 3:18, in clear contrast to Augustine, Calvin states the marked change taking place after the fall: *non eadem erit terra quae prius, quae sinceros fructus producat: fore enim pronuntiat ut degeneret terrae fertilitas in sentes et noxia impedimenta. Quaecumque ergo vitiosa nascuntur, sciamus non nativos esse terrae fructus, sed corruptelas quae a peccato originem habent* ("The earth was not the same as before [sc. the fall] when it produced 'sincere' fruit; for God proclaimed that it should happen that the fertility of the earth should degenerate into thorns and harmful plants. Indeed, whatever harmful arises, we should know that these are not original innate fruits of the earth, but corrupt ones, which have their origin from sin").[30] Deterioration and degeneration, as consequences of (the original) sin, may eventually lead to the extinction of the whole of humankind: *ac certe periculum est, nisi resipiscat mundus, ne bona pars hominum fame et ingentibus aliis miseriis brevi tabescat* ("And there is certainly the danger, unless the world recovers, that a good part of

---

28. Ibid., p. XIIv (= W 42, 28f.; see also WA 42, 152f.).
29. *Commentarius in Genesin* (Geneva, 1554); *Calvini Opera* 23, p. 4.
30. Ibid., p. 31.

humankind should begin to waste away through famine and other huge miseries"). Although for a modern reader this reads like an ecological warning *avant la lettre,* it is in fact theological moralizing.

Conclusion: The Opacity of Fecundity

Several things emerge from this investigation. First, Augustine's large oeuvre, which has a tendency to approach certain issues from various angles, depending on the context and/or the time of writing, allows for the possibility in later reception that two opposing sides can both take statements from Augustine in support for their diverging opinions. Second, there is no linearity in this process: certain periods or thinkers may prefer one opinion of Augustine, other periods a different one. Later periods may return to an opinion that Augustine himself would have judged to be less developed. Finally, although Augustine's towering stature in the history of ideas remains uncontested at large, there exists an *unknown Augustine.*[31] In our case, Augustine's *Literal Commentary on Genesis* failed in making a lasting impression on most of his readers as far as the interpretation of Genesis 3:18 is concerned. There are, of course, other topics in this commentary concerning which this is not the case, like Augustine's concept of the *rationes seminales.* Thus this exercise will have demonstrated that not only does the opacity of Scripture generate a fecundity of interpretations, but that this also precipitates further opacity in subsequent reception. The introduction of further layers of interpreters on whose authority one's own biblical interpretation is claimed to be based obscures the fact that it is the last interpreter in this chain of receptions who makes the choice of which authorities to use to bolster his or her own point of view.

---

31. This is the title of Michael Gorman's PhD thesis (Toronto, 1974) on Augustine's *Literal Commentary on Genesis.*

Toward a Creational Perspective on Poverty: Genesis 1:26-28, Image of God, and Its Missiological Implications

Pascal Daniel Bazzell

Introduction

The creation accounts of humanity in Genesis, particularly Genesis 1:26-28, can help our churches today in their views, understandings, and engagements with poverty and the poor.[1] The reality is that neither the world that gave rise to the book of Genesis nor the world that Genesis depicts exists today. Our context of scholarship in the twenty-first-century West does not remotely resemble the context of ancient Israel. Nevertheless, aspects of the human situation portrayed in Genesis still endure. My reading of Genesis is informed by my ministry context within the margins of a city in Asia, a situation characterized by violence, murder, sex trading, generational homelessness, and extreme poverty. I believe that Genesis, especially the primeval history, speaks to the fundamental state of the human condition and the impoverishment of humanity in general. Hence my thesis: *the contextual reading of Genesis 1:26-28 in light of the creation and the first disobedience of humanity (Gen. 1–3) and in interaction with contemporary theoretical constructs of poverty provides a framework for articulating a broad*

1. David Tracy challenges us that the central theological problem of our day is the problem of those thought to be nonpersons by reigning elites. For Tracy, "this means that within Christian theology, as within the Christian churches, the option of the poor should be at the heart of every serious Christian theology today." See David Tracy, "The Christian Option for the Poor," in Daniel G. Groody, ed., *The Option for the Poor in Christian Theology* (Notre Dame, Ind.: University of Notre Dame Press, 2007), pp. 119-31, here p. 119.

understanding of poverty, which should shape our missional engagement with the poor.

Each of us has our own understanding and definition of poverty, and everyone appears to understand what it is.[2] However, if we decide to do more than speak colloquially, if we decide to act upon or to discern the tangible reality of poverty, we soon find that lines start to blur. We may view poverty from a biological aspect, where in some countries one's physical handicap, diseases, accidents, or age pushes one into a life of great dependence on others. Some economists have explained poverty as the economic restrictions of various kinds (wars, famine, the absence of livelihood possibilities, etc.). Sociologists have sometimes pointed toward the social dimension of poverty that withholds someone from satisfying social obligations and expectations. From an anthropological perspective, some point toward a (sub)culture of poverty, while others describe it as relationships that do not work. Some discussions have also been framed around a psychology of poverty that addresses the low self-image, inferiority complex, or a double consciousness in the poor. A historical perspective also provides valuable insights into the development of ideas about the poor and poverty through the different periods of history and their contexts. Within Christian circles, "spiritual poverty" has often been understood in the following ways: as alluding to a spiritual oppression; as seen across people's social economical classes in their spiritual void and emptiness; or along the lines of involuntary versus voluntary poverty. These are a few of the different aspects of poverty that evidence its multidimensional nature.

In my research on different theoretical and theological constructs of poverty, I have observed two main issues. First, there are limited dialogues occurring across different disciplines, and hence crucial discussions with great insights into poverty are kept isolated within each discipline. Thus

---

2. Poverty has traditionally been viewed as a lack of necessities (basic food, shelter, medical care, and safety) and more recently as social exclusion. Linda van Rensburg states that social exclusion "has to be understood with reference to the failure of any one or more of the following: (i) the democratic and legal system (civic integration); (ii) the labor market (economic integration); (iii) the welfare state system (social integration); and (iv) the family and community system (interpersonal integration)." See Linda Jansen van Rensburg, "A Human Rights–Based Approach to Poverty: The South African Experience," in Nanak Kakwani and Jacques Silber, eds., *The Many Dimensions of Poverty* (Basingstoke: Palgrave Macmillan, 2007), pp. 165-84, here p. 165. Furthermore, she notes that poverty is a denial of human rights and human dignity, and in that sense a lack of basic capabilities to live in dignity (p. 147).

framing a theory of poverty from the Genesis creation account in consideration of prevailing secular theories and theologies of poverty provides an interdisciplinary bridge. Second, the basic underpinnings and assumptions uttered by many theologies, and even various theoretical constructs of poverty, are often traceable to the creation and first disobedience of humanity. A creational perspective of poverty will not just augment our theoretical and theological understandings of poverty; it will also reveal missiological implications for serving the marginalized in our society.

Toward a Creational Perspective of Poverty

The account of humanity's creation in Genesis provides unique nuances that are particularly suited to addressing the question of involuntary poverty. In this study I identify four theological themes in Genesis 1:26-28 that have potential explanatory power to enhance our understanding of poverty and the poor. I will examine four elements in 1:26-28 — "in our image, according to our likeness," "Let us," "They may rule," and "male and female" — that provide the basis for articulating a creational perspective of poverty. Using that framework, I will analyze each of these four terms in light of the broader context in Genesis, and, in conversation with current theoretical constructs of poverty, I will develop four features that are often found in involuntary poverty: obscuring the royal image, reflexive oppression, repressive relationships, and oppressive structures.

Obscuring the Royal Image

The first element for discussion is the creation of humanity in the image of God. There is a proliferation of theological approaches throughout history trying to make sense of the meaning of human beings made "in our image" (בצלם), "as our likeness" (כדמות).[3] Taken together, at the very least the

3. The image of God in humans is widely debated and discussed in an utterly massive body of literature. This situation is well summarized by David Clines, who points out that "it appears that scholarship has reached something of an impasse over the problem of the image, in that different starting-points, all of which seem to be legitimate, lead to different conclusions." See David J. A. Clines, "The Image of God in Man," *TynBul* 19 (1968): 53-103, here 61. See also Karl Barth, *CD* III/1:193, 195; Sibley W. Towner, "Clones of God: Genesis 1:26-28 and the Image of God in the Hebrew Bible," *Int* 59 (2005): 341-56; and Claus

scope of these theories suggests both material and immaterial aspects present and observable in the image of God in humankind. While the image of God cannot be defined, aspects of it can still be described, or it can be described in part. In line with this, we need to keep in mind the holistic view of humanity in ancient Israel. David Clines explains that biblical scholarship has unanimously rejected the traditional view of human beings as various "parts" and has pointed out the biblical view of each person as essentially a unity. "When this insight is applied to the doctrine of the image, it is difficult to resist the conclusion that the whole man is in the image of God."[4]

If we can acknowledge that Genesis considers that the image of God is the distinctive characteristic of humanity at its creation (Gen. 1:26), that the image endures through humanity's generations (5:1-3), and that the image forms a foundation for the moral sanctity of human life (9:6), then we have in the Genesis depiction of the image of God a foundation for framing a Christian perspective on human poverty that covers theological, anthropological, and social bases. For, if *all* humans are made in the image of God, then this includes the poor by the simple virtue of their innate humanity.

Contrary to many theoretical constructs and theologies of poverty, the central premise of poverty should not be sin entering humanity and the need of development, but rather the poor being made in the image of God. There has often been a general distinction made between the poor as people versus poverty as a condition of people. However, this underestimates the complexity of poverty, as it is not just structural, situational, relational, or spiritual. What about Jesus Christ becoming flesh to live in poverty? John Calvin notes that the genealogies of Matthew and Luke were designed "to remove the stumbling-block arising from the fact, that both Joseph and Mary were unknown, and despised, and poor, and gave not the slightest indication of royalty."[5] From Luke 2:24 Calvin points out that Joseph and Mary were experiencing such deep poverty that they did not have the financial ability to offer a lamb for the purpose of redeeming their firstborn but as a substitute

---

Westermann, *Genesis 1–11*, trans. John J. Scullion, CC (Minneapolis: Augsburg, 1984), pp. 147-55, for a good overview of the different historical interpretations on the image of God in humans.

4. Clines, "Image of God in Man," p. 57. See also Gerhard von Rad, *Genesis,* trans. John H. Marks, rev. ed., OTL (Philadelphia: Westminster, 1972), pp. 58-59; and Christopher J. H. Wright, *Old Testament Ethics for the People of God* (Downers Grove, Ill.: InterVarsity Press, 2004), p. 119.

5. John Calvin, *Commentary on a Harmony of the Evangelists, Matthew, Mark, and Luke,* trans. William Pringle (Grand Rapids: Eerdmans, 1949), p. 83.

offered two young pigeons (an exception that is expressed in Lev. 5:7).[6] In contrast to current assertions about poverty, we would never say that Jesus Christ was living in spiritual poverty or that he was in bondage to poverty — powerless and entangled — and therefore needed to be empowered or to grow into true freedom. Jesus Christ is the full expression of the image of God who lived in poverty on earth, and therefore poverty in itself is not sin but has to do more with the impact of sin. Hence I would argue that it is inappropriate to negatively define poverty because it incorporates the identity of the poor, who are made in the image of God. To define poverty by what the poor do not have or use negative language for definition (such as "powerless, cycle of poverty, in need of empowerment," etc.) actually reaffirms the oppressive nature of poverty among the poor. This diminishes our ability to recognize the image of God among the poor and limits our understanding of poverty.

From a missiological perspective, the affirmation that the poor have been created in the image of God has crucial implications for our churches.[7] Any engagement we have with the poor, either to provide services, to journey with them, or to do research, should constantly be evaluated to ensure that it affirms the poor's dignity and integrity. Our terminologies, approaches, and interactions with the poor should reflect that the poor are made in God's image, and hence our missional approach should be to help them discover the image of God in themselves.

Reflexive Oppression

The next element we meet is the curious presence of the plural in Genesis 1:26. Unfortunately, the plural is notoriously obscure and therefore produces a multiplicity of interpretations. Franz Delitzsch proposes the classic view of

6. Ibid., pp. 140-41. Concerning the counterargument that the magi had just recently presented them gifts of gold, incense, and myrrh, Calvin replies: "We must not imagine that they had such abundance of gold as to raise them suddenly from poverty to wealth. We do not read, that their camels were laden with gold. It is more probable that it was some small present, which they had brought solely as a mark of respect" (p. 141).

7. Christopher J. H. Wright identifies four significant truths concerning humanity being made in the image of God, all of which are crucial to biblical mission: (1) all human beings are addressable by God; (2) all human beings are accountable to God; (3) all human beings have dignity and equality; and (4) the biblical gospel fits all. See his *Mission of God: Unlocking the Bible's Grand Narrative* (Downers Grove, Ill.: InterVarsity Press, 2006), pp. 422-24.

the "majestic plural," or "royal we."[8] Nevertheless, this solution now has been widely avoided for lack of biblical attestation. Karl Barth argues that the plural points in the direction of the Christian understanding of the Trinity, and such an interpretation is preferable to the alternatives proposed by modern biblical scholars.[9] Many other scholars argue for the presence of the "heavenly host" or "heavenly court" of divine beings.[10] However, Umberto Cassuto objects to this view of the heavenly host and notes "(1) that it conflicts with the central thought of the section that God *alone* created the entire world; (2) that the expression *Let us make* is not one of consultation; (3) that if the intention was to tell us that God took counsel, the Bible would explicitly state with whom He consulted." Cassuto concludes for a "plural of exhortation" directed reflexively from God to himself.[11] Claus Westermann calls this a reflexive "plural of deliberation." Since the text shows God self-deliberating, it is only reasonable that self-deliberation is an aspect of the image God immediately confers following the self-deliberation.[12] Jürgen Moltmann also refers to it as "a communing with his own heart." When one communes with oneself, it means that one has a relationship with oneself. With that relationship come "self-differentiation" and possibly "self-identification."[13] Hans Walter Wolff explains that "let us" is to be understood as "God's relationship to man as the

8. Franz Delitzsch and Carl Friedrich Keil, *Commentary on the Old Testament in Ten Volumes,* trans. James Martin (repr. Grand Rapids: Eerdmans, 1983), 1:62.

9. Barth, *CD* III/1:191-92.

10. Cf. von Rad, *Genesis,* pp. 58-59. He takes the fleeting presence of the plural as a device that temporarily distances God from direct relation to the creation, which is an interesting perspective when placed against Barth's and Vriezen's arguments for intimate relationship. John Sawyer acknowledges the awkwardness of reading a plural after translating the phrase "image of God." While he sees the absence of the definite article as an argument for a class of beings (divine), since the singular, ויאמר אלהים, "God said," initiates the sentence and sets the poetic style, it is difficult to read the plural into the אלהים constructions that follow. See Sawyer, "Meaning of בצלם אלהים (in the Image of God) in Genesis I–XI," *JTS* 25 (1974): 418-26, here 423. See also Barth, who notes the shift in number and attributes the heavenly host view to Delitzsch and Benno Jacob (*CD* III/1:191-92).

11. Umberto Cassuto, *A Commentary on the Book of Genesis: From Adam to Noah,* trans. Israel Abrahams (Jerusalem: Magnes Press, Hebrew University Press, 1972), p. 55.

12. Westermann, *Genesis 1–11,* p. 145.

13. Jürgen Moltmann, *God in Creation: A New Theology of Creation and the Spirit of God,* trans. Margaret Kohl (Minneapolis: Fortress, 1993), p. 217. Moltmann further explains that "the subject is then a singular in the plural, or a plural in the singular. These shifts between the singular and plural at this particular point are important: 'Let *us* make human beings — *an* image that is like *us*.' That is to say, the image of God (singular) is supposed to correspond to the 'internal' plural of God, and yet be a *single* image" (p. 217).

presupposition for man's self-understanding." Thus "man proceeds from God's address."[14] Whatever is the preferred interpretation, God addressing the other personhood in the Trinity, God addressing the heavenly host, or God addressing himself, this implies a reflexive capacity in God.

As God created humans in his own image and likeness, he created humans with this ability of reflexive capacity innate within them. This reflexive capacity, which includes aspects of *self-awareness* (identity) and *self-responsibility* (ethics), enables humans to see and to talk to themselves. As we follow the story of Genesis we then read how this reflexive capacity becomes the calamity for humankind. Westermann explains that the woman ate the fruit not to become "like God" but that in humankind there is an "urge to transcend themselves by overstepping the limits set for them."[15] The reflexive capacity gave Adam and Eve the ability to see their own state, to imagine themselves in a different state, and then to experience conflict between their perceived and actual states. Thus *das Schattenbild* was born in humanity. I have chosen to use the German term, *das Schattenbild*, literally "shadow image," to describe the conflicting, self-perceived *imago* that is created by the deceiving and oppressive voice of external influences, which operates in competition with the image of God in the psyche of humanity.

Every human being has a reflexive capacity, which means that people perceive themselves and live out their lives according to that perception. Since sin entered humankind, all of humanity is born with some sort of distorted reflexive capacity and *das Schattenbild*. However, we often see the poor develop a reflexive oppression and experience the worst oppression of *das Schattenbild* in them and from those in power. Features in the account of humanity's first disobedience (Gen. 3) show that the reflexive capacity, the self-perception, can become skewed due to external tampering and influence like the serpent's voice, resulting in oppression and destruction. Similarly, there are oppressive voices that are forced upon the poor, paralleling the voice of the serpent, skewing the self-perception of the impoverished, resulting in an ongoing cycle of reflexive oppression and destruction. This leads to a reflexive oppression pattern that reinforces on emotional and cognitive levels the shame and low self-esteem of the poor until they believe they have less worth than those who label them.[16]

---

14. Hans Walter Wolff, *Anthropology of the Old Testament*, trans. Margaret Kohl (Philadelphia: Fortress, 1974), p. 159.

15. Westermann, *Genesis 1–11*, p. 249.

16. See Ann E. Cudd, *Analyzing Oppression* (New York: Oxford University Press,

Jayakumar Christian developed the concept of the marred identity of the poor. This means that the poor are in captivity to the God complexes of the nonpoor (social, political, economic, and religious),[17] deception by principalities and powers,[18] and inadequacies in worldview,[19] which result in a tragic marring of the identity[20] of the poor.[21] Christian explains that it is these lies, a "web of lies," that keep the identity of the poor distorted.[22] It is

---

2006). For Cudd, in addition to the poor experiencing these indirect psychological forces of shame, low self-esteem, and false consciousness, they also encounter "deformed desire, which is the combined affective and cognitive process of value formation, in which the oppressed come to desire that which is oppressed in them. . . . Indirect psychological harms occur when the beliefs and values of the privileged or oppressor groups are subconsciously accepted by the subordinate and assimilated into their self-concept or value/belief scheme. Indirect forces thus work through the psychology of the oppressed to mold them and co-opt them to result in choices and decisions that harm the oppressed while benefiting the privileged. . . . They are all self-inflicted wounds, but wounds that have been inflicted with the weapon that society provides the oppressed" (p. 176).

17. Jayakumar Christian, "An Alternate Reading of Poverty," in Bryant L. Myers, ed., *Working with the Poor: New Insights and Learnings from Development Practitioners* (Monrovia, Calif.: World Vision, 1999), pp. 3-30, here p. 5. Christian explains "god complexes are clusters of power (social, economic, bureaucratic, political and religious) within the domain of poverty relationships that absolutize themselves to keep the poor powerless. These god complexes hold the poor captive."

18. Principalities and powers are considered beings that have a dominating influence over not only those involved in poverty relationships (see Dan. 10:13; Eph. 6:12), but also systems and structures within which these relationships take place.

19. Many theories of poverty from a development perspective have pointed out that the roots of poverty can be traced to a people's worldview. Christian mentions that poverty challenges cannot be adequately responded to if we do not confront the worldview inadequacies of the people involved. See Christian, "Alternate Reading," pp. 13-14.

20. Christian mentions that "poverty is about personhood and identity. By marring identity the powerful seek to inflict permanent damage to the poor." For Christian, the "powerlessness is a product of the poor's marred identity. Through oppressive social norms, stunting of the mind, retarding reflective ability and reducing the poor to mere objects, society mars the identity of the poor" (ibid., pp. 11-12).

21. Bryant L. Myers, *Walking with the Poor: Principles and Practices of Transformational Development* (Maryknoll, N.Y.: Orbis, 2002), p. 76. Myers elaborates on Christian's theory, adding that "poverty is a result of relationships that do not work, that are not just, that are not for life, that are not harmonious or enjoyable. Poverty is the absence of shalom in all its meanings" (p. 86).

22. Jayakumar Christian, "Powerless of the Poor: Toward an Alternative Kingdom of God Based Paradigm of Response" (PhD diss., Fuller Theological Seminary, Pasadena, Calif., 1994), p. 264. Christian notes that "the poor are captive in a web of flawed assumptions and interpretations. In the context of poverty relationships, this web is essentially a 'web of lies.'

the reflexive oppression, the formation and perpetuation of *das Schattenbild* in people, that believes the web of lies that eventually bereaves the poor of their identity, their dignity and integrity, their freedom, their history, their language, their rights, their hopes, their aspirations, and that even suffocates their dreams, or at least the process of attaining these dreams.[23] Therefore, reflexive oppression is a process that provokes a pattern of deception in reflection. Moreover, the reflexive oppression process among the poor does not merely accept the oppressive state of the lies of those in power; the reflexive oppression process leads the poor to incorporate those lies into their reflexive understandings of life until they start to believe its oppressive ideology.

In addition, the poor similarly experience what Adam and Eve must have experienced when they suddenly had to leave Eden to live in a new world, while surely longing for the familiarity they unwillingly left. Robert Park calls this a "cultural hybrid," which explains the cause of marginality as the internal war between two worlds, one familiar and one enticing, but neither complete.[24] Everett Stonequist builds on this concept, noting that the marginal man experiences a double consciousness as if he regards himself through two looking glasses presenting clashing images.[25] This reflexive oppression that the poor experience is a pattern of deception in reflection, which often results in a marred identity and an internal conflict of a double consciousness (rural/urban, animism/religious, superstitious/modernity, etc.). From a missiological perspective, this is essential to consider if we seek to understand poverty and the poor. Also, as we engage with the poor, we

---

Both the poor and the non-poor believe these lies and thus ensure the perpetuation of the powerlessness of the poor" (p. 264). Myers summarizes Christian's all-encompassing web of lies into five themes: the captivity to the god complexes of the nonpoor, marred identity of the poor, inadequacies in worldview, deception by the principalities and powers and weakness of mind, body, and spirit. Each disempowering theme impacts the poor's social system within which they live and their view of the social, political, economic, and religious on each theme, which reinforces an internal nature of poverty among the poor. See Myers, *Walking with the Poor*, pp. 78-79.

23. Debraj Ray notes that, because of this, "poverty and the failure of aspirations may be reciprocally linked in a self-sustaining trap." See Ray, "Aspirations, Poverty, and Economic Change," in Abhijit V. Banerjee, Roland Benabou, and Dilip Mookherjee, eds., *Understanding Poverty* (Oxford: Oxford University Press, 2006), pp. 409-22. In his chapter Ray introduces and discusses an aspiration-based view of the individual behavior and its implications for the persistence of poverty.

24. Robert Park, "Human Migration and the Marginal Man," *AJS* 33, no. 6 (1928): 881-93.

25. Everett V. Stonequist, "The Problem of the Marginal Man," *AJS* 4, no. 11 (1935): 1-3.

need to address the factors that affect reflexive oppression. In our journey with the poor, we help them realize the demeaning and abusive nature of reflexive oppression and work toward healing and reconciliation of the reflexive capacity within themselves, which is found in the image of Jesus Christ (*imago Christi*).

Repressive Relationships

This brings us to the next aspect of Genesis 1:26-28 — *male and female.* Barth sees in the two an essential interdependence of identity and the relational nature of humanity, which to him is the essence of the image.[26] Jürgen Moltmann mentions that the "likeness to God cannot be lived in isolation. It can be lived only in human community. This means that from the very outset human beings are social beings."[27] Christopher Wright notes that humanity is created in and for relationship, and "for a task that requires relational cooperation — not only at the basic biological level that only a man and a woman can produce children in order to fill the earth but also at the wider societal level."[28] Nonetheless, through Adam and Eve's acting upon their false self-perception, sin has not only disrupted the relationship with God (they hide from God) but also entered into every human's relational needs, producing unhealthy, greedy, and oppressive relationships. The poor experience these oppressive and broken relationships disproportionately more than the rest of humanity.

Peter Townsend explains poverty in the context of these oppressive social relationships. As a member of society, one has to satisfy social obligations and expectations. Not being able to access these resources and take part in society means that one is in poverty.[29] These oppressive relation-

26. See *CD* III/1:195-96. Scholars have widely interacted with Barth's position on this. For a good summary of these responses see Phyllis A. Bird, "'Male and Female He Created Them': Genesis 1:27b in the Context of the Priestly Account of Creation," repr. in Richard S. Hess and David Toshio Tsumura, eds., *"I Studied Inscriptions from before the Flood": Ancient Near Eastern, Literary, and Linguistic Approaches to Genesis 1–11* (Winona Lake, Ind.: Eisenbrauns, 1994), pp. 329-61.

27. Moltmann, *God in Creation,* pp. 222-23. See also Stanley J. Grenz, *Theology for the Community of God* (Grand Rapids: Eerdmans, 2000), p. 175.

28. Wright, *Mission of God,* p. 28.

29. Peter Townsend, "A Sociological Approach to the Measurement of Poverty — a Rejoinder to Professor Amartya Sen," *Oxford Economic Papers* 37 (1985): 659-68. See also Ray, "Aspirations," pp. 409-19, who notes that "individual aspirations are born in a social context;

ships are not just imposed from the outside, the nonpoor oppressing them, but are also seen and expressed in and among the poor. Since the poor grow up in or get acculturated into such an oppressive network of relationships, often they are not accustomed to healthy relationships and thus may also oppress one another.[30] Moreover, the competition for limited resources is part of the curse (thorns of the ground), as is disruption in the harmony of the dominion partnership (the will of the woman toward her husband and the husband's domination of the wife). *Das Schattenbild* does not just seek its own self-perceived *imago* but also seeks to abuse and diminish the image of God in the other. Hence our missional engagement should not just incorporate the poor being reconciled to God and being reconciled to the

---

they do not exist in a vacuum." Townsend also points out that poverty is deep-seated not only in the poor but in many rich countries as well. For him, it seems destined to get worse in both groups of countries unless scientific means are mobilized to fully explain current trends, and international action is taken collaboratively to counter them. According to Townsend, poverty has to be explained primarily in terms of the huge influence of international developments on social class and on style as well as conditions of life in every country. See Townsend, *The International Analysis of Poverty* (New York: Harvester Wheatsheaf, 1993), p. 3.

30. Oscar Lewis has noted that poverty involves behavior and personality traits that develop a culture of poverty (*Urban Life: Readings in Urban Anthropology* [Prospect Heights, Ill.: Waveland Press, 2002], pp. 393-404). For Lewis, once a (sub)culture of poverty comes into existence, "it tends to perpetuate itself from generation to generation because of its effect on the children" (*La Vida: A Puerto Rican Family in the Culture of Poverty — San Juan and New York* [1966; repr. New York: Random House, 1968], p. xlv). People living in a culture of poverty experience situations in which they tend to feel alienated from the goals of the larger society and at the same time these goals seem unattainable for them. Consequently, Lewis argues that they experience psychological adjustment, in that while they may express their hopelessness and despair, nevertheless, they develop traits that are coping mechanisms to meet their current needs. These traits create a lifestyle that gives birth to a common culture among the poor, or more accurately, a subculture (pp. xliv-xlv). Michèle Lamont and Mario Luis Small explain that some "think of culture as an independent variable and poverty as the outcome. Others think of culture as the outcome. Others use neither, but instead produce descriptive accounts of the operation of both variables. Still others abandon the variable-based approach all together. This heterogeneity is part of the strength of this body of work. Each approach is a lens through which to capture different dimensions of the causal process that produces inequality and poverty. As such, they can be combined, or used independently of one another. Together, they speak to how factoring in meanings can result in more comprehensive explanations of poverty" ("How Culture Matters: Enriching Our Understanding of Poverty," in Ann Chih Lin and David R. Harris, eds., *The Colors of Poverty: Why Racial and Ethnic Disparities Exist* [New York: Russell Sage Foundation, 2008], pp. 76-102, here pp. 79-80).

nonpoor but should also seek intentional reconciliation of their networks of relationships.

Oppressive Structures

Lastly, we shift our focus to the pronouncement "They may rule" (Gen. 1:26). This issue is also widely discussed in current scholastic debates;[31] hence the full scope of the argument cannot be treated here. What is relevant to our discussion is that the verb associates dominion with humankind. Barry Bandstra explains that it is ambiguous whether this statement is "indicative or directive." He renders it, "and they will rule." His analysis suggests that "this clause specifies the realm *within* which, more so than *over* which, humanity exercises authority on behalf of deity and the divine council."[32] Richard Middleton notes that Genesis 1 mentions that humans are responsible to rule over the earth and the animals, but there is no mandate in Genesis 1 for humans to rule over one another.[33]

In the creation account we see that God said to his creation that it was good and appointed human beings, male and female, to rule over creation. Adam started to name all the animals to bring order to God's creation. As the population grew, more order and structure came into place. However, following the first disobedience to God, which corrupted the hearts of humankind, many structures became oppressive and unjust in order to gain wealth and power for only a few elites.[34] Along this line, Middleton men-

31. This issue is treated by Richard J. Middleton, *The Liberating Image: The Imago Dei in Genesis 1* (Grand Rapids: Brazos Press, 2005). For a historical view see Barth, *CD* III/1:194; Westermann, *Genesis 1–11*, pp. 147-61; and Günther Wittenberg, "The Image of God: Demythologization and Democratization in the Old Testament," *JTSA* 13 (1975): 12-23.

32. Barry L. Bandstra, *Genesis 1–11: A Handbook on the Hebrew Text* (Waco, Tex.: Baylor University Press, 2008), p. 93.

33. Middleton, *Liberating Image*, pp. 204-5. Wolff comments on this: "As the *object* of rule, first of all the earth is named as a whole, and then the animals in particular. . . . Thus in principle everything is put 'under man's feet' (Ps. 8.6b). Only man himself is not to be the object of subjection (Gen. 9.6), all men having the joint task of administering and moulding creation and of having it at their disposal" (Wolff, *Anthropology of the Old Testament*, p. 163).

34. The structural theory of poverty examines how structural factors affect poverty. According to David Brady, "Structural explanations contend that macro-level labor market and demographic conditions put people at risk of poverty, and cross-sectional and over time differences in these structural factors account for variation in poverty. Groups, cities and countries disproportionately impacted by structural factors tend to have more poverty.

tions that "humans as the image of God exercise their God-given power; but not in the manner that God intended."[35] He asserts that "interhuman hierarchies of power" do not reflect God's "creational intent" as expressed in Genesis 1.[36] As sin spreads horizontally within society, Wright elucidates, "sin becomes endemic, structural. . . . So although structures may not sin in the personal sense, structures do embody myriad personal choices, many of them sinful, that we have come to accept within our cultural patterns."[37]

Any economic and/or political structure that inhibits a person from living with dignity and integrity violates our God-given right.[38] Often, *das Schattenbild* among those in power seeks their own gain and wealth, affirming their own *imago*, with the high cost of the abuse and destruction of the image of God among the poor. Therefore, the missiological implications are to address those unjust and oppressive structures by identifying factors that abuse and diminish the image of God among the poor.

Conclusion

The four themes mentioned in Genesis 1:26-28 — in our image, according to our likeness; let us; they may rule; and male and female — read in light of the early accounts of humanity (Gen. 1–3) and in interaction with other contemporary theories of poverty can provide a Christian framework to discuss poverty. Poverty takes shape differently in each context, due to its multidimensionality. For the sake of our discussion, however, I will provide a generalized definition that I have found applicable to many different contexts;

Thus, structural theory is a compositional explanation: the more people in vulnerable demographic or labor market circumstances, the more poverty exists. In this sense, structure refers to the set of labor market opportunities and/or demographic propensities that characterize the population's likelihood of being poor" ("Structural Theory and Relative Poverty in Rich Western Democracies, 1969-2000," *Research in Social Stratification and Mobility* 24, no. 2 [2006]: 153-75, here 154).

35. Middleton, *Liberating Image*, p. 220.

36. Ibid., pp. 204-5.

37. Wright, *Mission of God*, pp. 431.

38. Ronald J. Sider states, "Created in the image of God and fashioned as body-soul unities formed for community, persons possess inestimable dignity and value that transcend any economic process or system. Because our bodies are a fundamental part of our created goodness, a generous sufficiency of material things is essential to human goodness. Any economic structure that prevents persons from producing and enjoying material well-being violates our God-given dignity" (*Just Generosity: A New Vision for Overcoming Poverty in America*, 2nd ed. [Grand Rapids: Baker Books, 2007], p. 62).

Poverty is a state of distortion, abuse, and diminution of the image of God in humanity that is brought about by human beings' reflexive oppressions, repressive relationships, and oppressive structures. I feel this definition is adequate for the following reasons: First, it centers on and always relates back to the image of God in the poor; but, at the same time, it also acknowledges the reality of humanity's sinful nature. Moreover, it provides specific areas that we need to address if we desire to serve the marginalized in our society.

The missiological implication is that we must seek liberation of the image of God among the poor from reflexive oppression, repressive relationships, and oppressive structures. In light of my discussion on the church's engagement in affirming the image of God among the poor, I hope to further discussions on how to point the poor toward the fullness of the image of God, which is found in Jesus Christ. As the poor fix their eyes upon Jesus (Heb. 12:2) and build an intimate relationship with him, they will encounter a new life in the image of Jesus Christ (2 Cor. 3:18) where they may experience a restoration of the glory that was lost as a result of sin (Rom. 3:23; Heb. 2:10). The focus then becomes a restoration of the quality of life in Jesus Christ among the poor. It is a messianic calling of human beings into the *imago Christi.*[39] Therefore, our missional approach is to see the emancipation of the image of God among the poor from the abusive and destructive nature of poverty and point in the direction of the *imago Christi.*[40]

39. Moltmann, *God in Creation,* pp. 215-88.

40. I would like to express my deep appreciation to my colleagues at Fuller Theological Seminary and especially to Adam Ayers, John Goldingay, Bryant L. Myers, and Nathan MacDonald for reading this essay and making very helpful suggestions. Any defects that remain are of course my own.

Genesis and the People of God

Did God Choose the Patriarchs?
Reading for Election in the Book of Genesis

Nathan MacDonald

Introduction

Election and its related topics number among the perennial concerns of theology, though their fortunes do tend to wax and wane. Old Testament scholarship is no different in this respect. In the heyday of the biblical theology movement, strongly influenced as it was by Karl Barth and neo-orthodoxy, numerous works on election theology appeared. Most of these were animated by a belief that Old Testament conceptions were of great value for the church, but had been poorly understood because of a bias toward Aristotelian logic and ontology; biblical theologians sought to look down the telescope the right way. The preferred method of approach was often the tradition history that was in vogue at the time. Various studies plotted the development of exodus, Davidic, and Zion election theologies, especially attentive to how these traditions were reactualized for new generations.

For various reasons, which have often been retraced, the biblical theology movement collapsed and its attendant methods were overtaken by newer approaches to the biblical text. Election and its near neighbor covenant were

This research was undertaken as part of the Sofja-Kovalevskaja project on early Jewish monotheisms. I am grateful to the Alexander von Humboldt Stiftung and the German Federal Ministry of Education and Research for their support of that project. Izaak de Hulster, Joel Lohr, Joel Kaminsky, and Rob Barrett read versions of this paper and offered numerous perceptive observations and criticisms.

largely deemed to have exhausted their seams of precious metal, and fresh mines were dug in more promising places. Since 2001, however, we have seen a revival of interest in the old workings with fresh lines of inquiry being opened up. Christopher Heard traced the ambiguity of the stories in Genesis in his study *Dynamics of Diselection*. Joel Kaminsky's *Yet I Loved Jacob* has already made a noticeable impact by introducing a distinction between elect, non-elect, and anti-elect. Finally, Joel Lohr's study, *Chosen and Unchosen*, originated as a doctoral thesis under Walter Moberly and offers perceptive readings of a selection of Pentateuchal texts. To these works explicitly concerned with election we should also add Jon Levenson's profound study of child sacrifice and the chosen son, *The Death and Resurrection of the Beloved Son*.[1]

When we compare these more recent works on election to those of the previous generation, what is most striking is the new interest with election in Genesis. Each of the authors I have mentioned devotes a significant amount of their work to an exposition of election in the book of Genesis. The works of the biblical theology movement, on the other hand, focused on Deuteronomy, the books of Samuel, and Deutero-Isaiah. Part of the reason, no doubt, is the development of narrative criticism in the intervening period; an additional factor might be a concern for canonical priority. What difference does this shift make?

Election in Genesis?

The question to which we must first direct our attention is whether there is indeed a theology of election in the book of Genesis. There is the simple matter, often observed, that the book of Genesis does not employ the root בחר to speak of YHWH choosing the patriarchs. Since the tendency of recent scholarship has been to date much of this material, or at least its final redaction, after the composition of Deuteronomy and Deutero-Isaiah, the absence of בחר might appear to be less of an oversight and more of a deliberate practice. Of

---

1. R. Christopher Heard, *Dynamics of Diselection: Ambiguity in Genesis 12–36 and Ethnic Boundaries in Post-Exilic Judah*, SemeiaSt 39 (Atlanta: SBL, 2001); Joel S. Kaminsky, *Yet Jacob I Loved: Reclaiming the Biblical Concept of Election* (Nashville: Abingdon, 2007); Joel N. Lohr, *Chosen and Unchosen: Conceptions of Election in the Pentateuch and Jewish-Christian Interpretation*, Siphrut: Literature and Theology of the Hebrew Scriptures (Winona Lake, Ind.: Eisenbrauns, 2009); Jon D. Levenson, *The Death and Resurrection of the Beloved Son: The Transformation of Child Sacrifice in Judaism and Christianity* (New Haven: Yale University Press, 1993). For a perceptive survey of recent works on election see Lohr, *Chosen*, pp. 3-91.

course, arguments based on absence are particularly slippery and by no means decisive. Nevertheless, we should be mindful that Genesis is not unwilling to introduce later realities, such as blessing, covenant, or circumcision, into the lives of the fathers. Indeed, observations about the occurrence of בחר find additional support in the fact that the Old Testament speaks of the nation of Israel[2] being chosen by God and locates the moment of election in Egypt (e.g., Ezek. 20:5).[3] The book of Deuteronomy is clearest in maintaining this distinction between Israel and the patriarchs. The patriarchs are *loved* and to them a promise was given that finds its fulfillment in YHWH's *choice of Israel.* "Only YHWH set his heart in love on them, your fathers, and he chose you, their seed after them, from all the peoples" (Deut. 10:15).[4]

On one occasion, though, the Old Testament does talk about one of the patriarchs being chosen by YHWH.[5] In the recounting of Israel's history

---

2. Throughout this essay I will use "Israel" of the people rather than of the patriarch, for whom I will use the name "Jacob."

3. The election tradition of the exodus (in contrast to that of David and Zion) was a favorite theme of scholars working with a tradition-history method (e.g., Hans Wildberger, *Jahwes Eigentumsvolk: Eine Studie zur Traditionsgeschichte und Theologie des Erwählungsgedankens,* ATANT 37 (Zurich: Zwingli, 1960]; idem, "בחר *bḥr* to choose," *TLOT* 1:209-26). The attempt to derive an exodus election tradition from an earlier patriarchal election tradition is misguided. Byron E. Shafer, for example, observes the close links Deuteronomy makes between the election of Israel and the covenant and oath with the patriarchs, but then blends the two with no justification ("The Root *bḥr* and Pre-Exilic Concepts of Chosenness in the Hebrew Bible," *ZAW* 89 [1977]: 20-42).

4. All biblical translations are my own. Shafer notes: "On the basis of these dtn. passages, one concludes . . . the concept of a people chosen by Yahweh in the Exodus event and bound to him by the Sinai Covenant is specifically grounded throughout the dtn. layers in a prior oath and covenant which 'Ēl, God of the Fathers and cosmic deity, had made with the patriarchs" (Shafer, "Root *bḥr*," p. 27; cf. Josef Scharbert, "'Erwählung' im Alten Testament im Licht von Gen 12,1-3," in Katholischen Bibelwerk [ed.], *Dynamik im Wort: Lehre von der Bibel, Leben aus der Bibel* [Stuttgart: Katholisches Bibelwerk, 1983], pp. 13-33, esp. 23-24).

5. Ps. 105:6//1 Chr. 16:13 is text critically complex, but should probably be understood as referring to Israel's election and not to the patriarchs. Ps. 105:6 reads: זרע אברהם עבדו בני יעקב בחיריו. Two Hebrew manuscripts and 11QPsᵃ read the singular בחירו for בחיריו, and a number of commentators have emended MT accordingly (Hans-Joachim Kraus, *Psalms 60–150,* trans. Hilton C. Oswald, CC [Minneapolis: Augsburg, 1989], p. 307; Hermann Gunkel, *Die Psalmen,* 6th ed. [Göttingen: Vandenhoeck & Ruprecht, 1986], p. 459; Artur Weiser, *The Psalms,* trans. Herbert Hartwell, OTL [Philadelphia: Westminster, 1962], pp. 671, 673; Mitchell Dahood, *Psalms 101–150,* AB [Garden City, N.Y.: Doubleday, 1970], pp. 52-53). The reappearance of the plural as an *inclusio* in v. 43, however, tells against the emendation (rightly Leslie C. Allen, *Psalms 101–150,* WBC [Waco, Tex.: Word, 1983], p. 37). For the same reasons the Septuagint's δοῦλοι αὐτοῦ for עבדו should also be rejected (cf. v. 42).

in the great intercessory prayer of Nehemiah 9, Ezra speaks about how YHWH "chose Abram" (v. 7a).[6] Even here, the influence of the earlier tradition probably still makes its mark, for this statement is immediately followed by a figuration of the exodus election tradition in Abraham's own life: "and he brought him out of Ur of the Chaldeans" (v. 7b).[7] In addition, among the patriarchs the choice of Abraham is rather distinctive, for as we shall see when Abraham is called there is no corresponding "diselection" (to use Heard's neologism); there is no Ishmael or Esau for Abraham, as there is for Isaac and Jacob.[8] The uniqueness of Nehemiah 9 within the Old Testament is noteworthy. (The NT demonstrates a similar reticence: Acts 13:17 alone speaks clearly of the election of the patriarchs.) As such it is an important reminder that we should not assume the presence of election in the book of Genesis.[9] On the other hand, since the prayer in Nehemiah 9 appears to be working with some form of the primary history, it represents a significant, indeed canonically mandated, reception of the patriarchal material. Thus I argue that to speak about election and Genesis responsibly is to show attentiveness to exactly this problem: the Old Testament *does* and *does not* understand the patriarchal stories in Genesis to be about election.

We must recognize, then, that when we speak of the election of the patriarchs we are employing a particular strategy for reading the book of Genesis. Like all reading strategies this one may have strengths and weaknesses. Certain issues and dynamics may be highlighted, while at the same time others may be suppressed. To put it another way, Ezra's reading of the Pentateuch suggests an analogy between the election of Israel and the election of the patriarchs, as there is between Abraham's departure from Ur and Israel's from Egypt. As such there are points of similarity and points of dissimilarity. In other words, when Kaminsky responds to those who would deny that Genesis is about election by arguing that "the narratives of brotherly strug-

6. Except in quotations, for clarity I will use "Abraham," rather than the earlier name "Abram," even when discussing narratives prior to Gen. 17.

7. Scharbert, "Erwählung," p. 24. The original citation is of Gen. 15:7, but most commentators agree in finding here an intentional echo of the exodus through the use of the Hiphil of אצי (Mark J. Boda, *Praying the Tradition: The Origin and Use of Tradition in Nehemiah 9*, BZAW 277 [Berlin: de Gruyter, 1999], p. 102).

8. Lot is a rather interesting case. The element of rivalry with Abraham emerges in a muted and curtailed fashion. He is presented as a younger dependent, perhaps even a potential heir, but not really a rival.

9. Compare the hesitancy shown by Pat Miller, "Review of Joel Kaminsky, *Yet Jacob I Loved: Reclaiming the Biblical Concept of Election* (Nashville: Abingdon Press, 2007)," *RBL* http://www.bookreviews.org/pdf/6201_6898.pdf.

gle in Genesis *are* a major locus of election theology," I find myself disagreeing with both positions.[10]

The Consequences of Reading Genesis for Election

Election and the Book of Genesis

Reading Genesis in light of election provides a suggestive way of understanding the book's integrity across its different parts, for as is well known the book of Genesis includes not only the stories of Abraham, Isaac, and Jacob, but also the primeval history and the Joseph story. Nevertheless, the ways in which election is perceived to unite the book can be quite different.

Kaminsky sees the pattern of divine choice beginning in the primeval history. The story of Cain and Abel draws attention not only to a divine favoritism that is mysterious, but to the interpretive temptation to justify the divine choice. Nor is it the only story of divine choice in the primeval history. Enoch has a special relationship with God, Noah is favored in his generation, and Shem is preferred above his brothers. The election of Abraham continues this developing pattern. As Kaminsky sees it, human history is from the beginning marked with patterns of favoritism. Although this seems unfair, Kaminsky argues that God's specific love is preferable to any idea of a generic love of humankind, for it secures God's relationship to humanity. He quotes Michael Wyschogrod with approval: "The mystery of Israel's election thus turns out to be the guarantee of the fatherhood of God toward all people, elect and non-elect, Jew and gentile."[11] Pat Miller, on the other hand, sees the story differently. He highlights the centrality of the "brother" motif in the Cain and Abel story, and sees the story as primarily concerned with

---

10. Kaminsky, *Jacob*, p. 11; my emphasis. My observations suggest that we are perhaps not best served by asking what the narratives in Genesis *are* or *are not*. Kaminsky continues, "the Genesis narratives are particularly well-suited as an introduction to biblical election theology. This is so because they raise a number of central issues concerning election theology that recur in the more abstract theological reflections on election that helped shape the Pentateuch, and they had a strong influence on the Former and Latter Prophets" (Kaminsky, *Jacob*, p. 11). Even if the historical judgment were not questionable, this does appear to be working from cases where election is implied to where it is explicit, whereas it would be preferable to begin with the clear cases. Lohr is more reflective: "Does the Pentateuch address the issue of election directly? As we shall see the answer to [this] question is yes and no" (Lohr, *Chosen*, p. 94).

11. Kaminsky, *Jacob*, p. 68.

human relations rather than divine favoritism.[12] The divine election does not begin until Genesis 12. Miller seems to view the primeval history as an account of recurrent human failure. Genesis 12 marks a new beginning when YHWH focuses his attention on one family, not in order to neglect the rest of humanity, but in order to ensure its participation in the divine blessing. The choice of Abraham is ultimately centrifugal. Genesis 12, then, becomes "the pivot on which the rest of Scripture swings."[13]

Both proposals attach a central role to election in the book's structuring and its narrative dynamics, despite deeply rooted differences regarding how election and God's relationship to humanity are to be understood. The differences are deeply rooted in the biblical text itself as can be seen if we compare them to critical accounts of the shape of Genesis. Kaminsky's understanding can be naturally aligned with P's structure, which is largely agreed to have shaped the present form of the book of Genesis. The *toledot* formula, "these are the generations of . . . ," shapes Genesis according to descent with the book narrowing down to the chosen family. It is no accident that the genealogies address the excluded line before focusing on the chosen line, or that the *toledot* formula ends with the family of Jacob (37:2). National and international are related by means of two covenants, one with Noah and all humanity, and one with Abraham and all his family. Miller's account, on the other hand, might be said to prioritize the structure attributed to the Yahwist, particularly with its emphasis on Genesis 12:1-3. Already Gerhard von Rad saw these verses as the key to the primeval story and the subsequent history of Israel. "[The Yahwist] gives the aetiology of all aetiologies in the Old Testament and becomes at this point a true prophet, for he proclaims the distant goal of the sacred history effected by God in Israel to be the bridging of the cleft between God and all mankind."[14] In this account the national ultimately serves the international.

The differences, then, have often, though not always, been drawn along familiar lines between Jewish and Christian interpreters.[15] These differences reflect not least fundamental disagreements about whether, and in what way,

12. Miller, "Review," pp. 2-3.

13. Ibid., p. 3.

14. Gerhard von Rad, *Genesis,* trans. John H. Marks, rev. ed., OTL (Philadelphia: Westminster, 1972), p. 24.

15. Note, however, Jon D. Levenson's careful account of the place of the nations in late biblical eschatology, which he portrays as a restoration of the situation of primeval history: "The Universal Horizon of Biblical Particularism," in Mark G. Brett, ed., *Ethnicity and the Bible,* Biblical Interpretation 19 (Leiden: Brill, 1996), pp. 143-69, here p. 164.

the elect have a role vis-à-vis other nations and how various texts that speak about election are to be interpreted and prioritized in the construction of a theology of election. The book of Genesis does not provide a simple answer, but the decision to structure the book according to *toledot* suggests that Kaminksy's reading should be preferred, even as the present incorporation of the promise of Abraham within this structure now suggests that the nations can achieve a blessing beyond that promised to Noah.

The disagreement between Kaminsky and Miller helps to underline the fact that to find election in Genesis is to work by analogy. Although Miller believes election to begin with the story of Abraham, I think that the question of whether Cain and Abel is a story about election or family rivalry could legitimately be extended to the stories of Lot, Isaac and Ishmael, Jacob and Esau. This is clearest, though, with Joseph and his brothers, for all the sons of Jacob are within the household of Israel. Whatever is at stake in the rivalries among Jacob's sons, it is not the place of them or their descendants among the chosen people. Indeed, it is not without reason that Christopher Heard can restrict his discussion of diselection to Genesis 12–36.[16]

Although Kaminsky begins his reading of election narratives with the Cain and Abel story, I think it may be possible to reach back to Genesis 1, thus incorporating the entire book. Such a move is warranted since the *toledot* formula extends across the whole book. As I have argued elsewhere, an analogy between the *imago Dei* and election is not only theologically suggestive but can be exegetically grounded. The description of humanity being made in the image of God is notoriously underdetermined; it is, as Richard Bauckham once put it to me, a text seeking context. Since the 1950s Old Testament scholarship has found a happy coincidence between the language of dominion and ancient Near Eastern texts that speak about the king as the divine image. Unfortunately the Old Testament references to image do not make this connection.[17] In addition, the language of dominion is rarely used of kingly rule. Reading Genesis 1 within the context of the Old Testament, stronger echoes are to be heard with Israel's own experience. The command to be fruitful, multiply, and fill the earth appears to climax in the abundant Israelite tribes on the banks of the Nile (Exod. 1:7). The domination of the earth finds its closest parallels in the subjugation of Canaan during the con-

---

16. Since his concerns are the stories' ideological function in postexilic Yehud, only those stories that relate to Israel's national neighbors are of interest for Heard's thesis in *Dynamics*.

17. Phyllis A. Bird, "'Male and Female He Created Them': Gen 1:27b in the Context of Priestly Accounts of Creation," *HTR* 74 (1981): 129-59, here 140.

quest.[18] Thus humanity has a special position and role vis-à-vis creation, and most especially the animal world, which is analogous to Israel's special position and role vis-à-vis the nations. To employ the Priestly language of *toledot*, in the *toledot* of the heavens and the earth the favored descendant is the last-born of creation, the human couple.

The Non-Elect in Genesis

The universal perspective within which the Old Testament views the election of Israel draws attention to the fact that alongside the chosen appear those who have been passed over by God. In his work on election in the Old Testament, Kaminsky has made a considerable contribution to our understanding by distinguishing between the elect, the non-elect, and the anti-elect. For the moment I want to concentrate on those that Kaminsky calls the non-elect. Kaminsky's distinction is valuable and draws attention to the fact that the promise to Abraham in 12:1-3 — a key passage in the discussion of election in Genesis — is not to Israel alone. As is well known, the question of how the Niphal of ברך in the final clause is to be understood is a matter of considerable discussion. In all likelihood the final clause is best understood as the nations using the name of Abraham as a blessing, "through you will all nations of the earth bless themselves."[19] The previous clauses, however, speak of those who bless Abraham being blessed, while the exceptional individual who slights Abraham will be cursed.[20] Genesis contextualizes this

18. Nathan MacDonald, "The *Imago Dei* and Election: Reading Gen 1:26-28 and Old Testament Scholarship with Karl Barth," *International Journal of Systematic Theology* 10 (2008): 303-27; Norbert Lohfink, "'Subdue the Earth?' (Genesis 1:28)," in *Theology of the Pentateuch: Themes of the Priestly Narrative and Deuteronomy*, trans. Linda M. Maloney (Minneapolis: Fortress, 1994), pp. 1-17; A. Graeme Auld, "Creation and Land: Sources and Exegesis," in *Joshua Retold: Synoptic Perspectives*, Old Testament Studies (Edinburgh: T&T Clark, 1998), pp. 63-68.

19. The alternative translations to the reflexive are a passive, "be blessed," and a middle, "acquire blessing." For the most recent detailed discussion of the issue see Keith Nigel Grüneberg, *Abraham, Blessing and the Nations: A Philological and Exegetical Study of Genesis 12:3 in Its Narrative Context*, BZAW 332 (Berlin: de Gruyter, 2003). Note, however, the criticisms by David Carr, "Review of K. N. Grüneberg, *Abraham, Blessing and the Nations: A Philological and Exegetical Study of Genesis 12:3 in Its Narrative Context*, BZAW 332 (Berlin: W. de Gruyter, 2003)," *RBL* http://www.bookreviews.org/pdf/4079_3956.pdf.

20. See discussion in Patrick D. Miller, "Syntax and Theology in Genesis XII 3a," *VT* 34 (1984): 472-76.

promise to the patriarch with narratives that envisage those seeking Abraham's good also benefiting, while those who diminish him, even unwittingly, find themselves enduring YHWH's disfavor. However the individual elements of the promise to Abraham are to be understood, it is not the case that "non-elect" means cursed, or even that YHWH is indifferent to the non-elect. Thus reading Genesis in light of election produces an understanding of election that is more nuanced than some common construals of election theology.

The place of the unelect in Genesis underlines that election in the Old Testament is not a triumphalistic theology. Yet it is important not to evacuate Israel's special status through an instrumentalization of election.[21] Again with an eye to 12:1-3, Israel will be blessed, and this blessing results in certain specific, particularly material, benefits. As Exodus and Deuteronomy have it, Israel is a "treasured people." Thus election is not merely, as H. H. Rowley memorably expressed it, "election for service," where that service was directed toward other people and nations. To be elect is to occupy a privileged position. It is "election for service" in the sense that Israel has the unique privilege of offering cultic service to YHWH.[22]

Yet the passing over of the non-elect is not unproblematic, and the specificity of the narratives of Genesis raises particular issues that are not highlighted as directly in other biblical passages on election. The stories in Genesis tell of how Abraham and Sarah, Isaac and Rebekah, and Jacob and his family are chosen not from an amorphous and nameless mass, but in distinction from Lot, Hagar and Ishmael, and Esau. Christopher Heard puts the matter succinctly: "in Genesis, election always seems to be accompanied by a corresponding diselection."[23] (The only exception to this is Abraham. In his case there is no stress on him as the second-born; there is no preference for him over a twin or older brother. He is called out of the anonymity of Ur.)[24]

21. It is particularly modern Protestant interpreters of the OT that have sought to explain and instrumentalize election. For Horst Seebass the OT use of בחר always reflects a conscious and purposeful choice: Israel was chosen by God to exemplify right religious practice before the nations ("בָּחַר *bāchar*," *TDOT* 2:74-87). H. H. Rowley, on the other hand, held that Israel had made a particular contribution to human culture through its spiritual perceptiveness. Its election is "for service" of other nations (*The Biblical Doctrine of Election* [London: Lutterworth, 1950], p. 43 *et passim*).

22. Joel S. Kaminsky, "Loving One's Israelite Neighbor: Election and Commandment in Leviticus 19," *Int* 62 (2008): 123-32.

23. Heard, *Dynamics*, p. 3.

24. Kaminsky observes that "the pattern of having three siblings in which one is ele-

In Deuteronomy, by contrast, Israel is chosen out of the world of nations, but without any specific nation being passed over. As Deuteronomy 4 puts it, the celestial objects are allotted to the "nations" for worship, "but *you* YHWH took out of the iron-smelter, out of Egypt, to make you a people of his inheritance" (4:20).

The logic of the move from Deuteronomy to Genesis was perhaps inevitable, and it may be, as Heard's work would suggest, that this was a direction pursued in Yehud during the Persian period, perhaps in the context of Edomite territorial expansion.[25] Certainly, the issue finds clearest expression in Malachi. The opening statement of the book expresses Deuteronomic theology clearly, "'I have loved you,' says YHWH." But this seems no longer convincing in the poor, postexilic Jewish community: "How have you loved us?" Not surprisingly the divine response draws its resources from the book of Genesis: "Is not Esau Jacob's brother? I loved Jacob, but I hated Esau" (Mal. 1:2-3). In other words, it is not enough to be the recipient of God's favor — Israel also needs to know that this is at someone else's expense.

Responding as the Non-Elect

It is striking that there is a strong focus on the non-elect in recent works on election, as the titles of Heard and Lohr's books and Kaminsky's typology testify. A number of factors contribute to this shift. First, concern for the non-elect resonates strongly with the recent interest in biblical studies in the Bible's "untold stories." Although the hermeneutics of suspicion provides some conceptual resources, those who have written on election in recent times rarely deploy such methods. Second, there is concern about theologi-

---

vated, one is of medial status, and one is eliminated is also found in the story of Abram and his two siblings, Nahor and Haran, which begins in Gen 11:27. In this instance, Nahor occupies the medial position in that his family provides women to the Israelite patriarchs, and Abram is exalted while Haran's line is deselected" (Kaminsky, *Jacob,* p. 29). While this is true, my point is that the narrative makes little if anything of this. The other stories in Genesis are needed to discern any significance to the choice of Abraham rather than his siblings. I am grateful to Rob Barrett for pointing out to me the uniqueness of Abraham's election.

25. For an attempt to combine the historical relationships between Edom and Judah during and after the fall of Jerusalem together with the interpretive force of biblical traditions, see Ellie Assis, "Why Edom? On the Hostility Towards Jacob's Brother in Prophetic Sources," *VT* 56 (2006): 1-20.

cal triumphalism and the connection that violence might have to theologies of election.[26] Third, there is a growing awareness, quite different from that characteristic of previous scholarship, that Christian interpreters cannot simply claim Israel's elect status, reading the Old Testament as though what it says applies directly to us. Within this new interpretive context, it is perhaps no surprise that Genesis is seen as a particularly useful scriptural resource. In this book we find a concern with the non-elect that is strikingly different from, say, a book like Deuteronomy that, though it treats election explicitly, shows only passing interest in the non-elect.

In Genesis the non-elect are a diverse group, and are characterized by their different responses to the patriarchs. This is set out programmatically in the call of Abraham: "I will bless those who bless you, and the one who despises you I will curse" (12:3). As Pat Miller has shown, these two clauses are not balanced.[27] On the one hand, those who are blessed are plural, while the one cursed is singular. Thus the one who opposes Abraham and his seed is the exception. Or, to put it another way, God has a propensity toward blessing. On the other hand, a curse comes upon those who are merely dismissive of the patriarchal family. The Gentiles of Genesis sometimes discover this to their cost. Pharaoh and Abimelech unknowingly seize the patriarch's wife; nevertheless, temporary affliction is brought upon them.

Thus, read in the light of election, Genesis features a number of case studies of how the non-elect are to respond to the elect. Cain, Esau, and Joseph's brothers exhibit the kind of jealousy and frustration that arises from realizing that God has a special relationship and a special purpose for someone else. Their failure to come to terms with this, in the case of Cain, and their learning to submit to the divine will, in the cases of Esau and Joseph's brothers, provide alternatives for how one might respond to God's elect. The narratives of Genesis, like the narratives of 1 Samuel, are peculiarly well suited to exploring these dynamics.

The experience of the non-elect is often complex, though, as is most clearly expressed by Ishmael. Ishmael is the most ambiguous of the non-elect in Genesis, for he most approximates the elect. He is circumcised, receiving the sign of the covenant in his flesh, although God affirms that the covenant will be established with Isaac, rather than Ishmael (ch. 17). Hagar's

26. So Regina M. Schwartz, *The Curse of Cain: The Violent Legacy of Monotheism* (Chicago: University of Chicago Press, 1997).
27. Miller, "Syntax."

experience in the wilderness is portrayed in terms clearly intended to reso-
nate with Israel's own time in the wilderness (ch. 16).[28] Abraham's expulsion
of Ishmael anticipates the *Akedah,* so closely does it parallel it (ch. 21).[29] In
my view the complexity of the portrayal of Ishmael is because he embodies,
more than anyone else, the promise of 12:3. Despite George Coats's essay on
"the curse in God's blessing," it is usually overlooked that not only is Ishmael
blessed (ברך; 17:20), but he is also the cursed one. His mother, Hagar, despises Sarah, the only use of the word קלל (16:4, 5) in the patriarchal narratives outside 12:3.[30]

The response of the non-elect to the elect raises the question of
whether it is possible to move between the categories that Kaminsky proposes. Other parts of the Old Testament entertain this notion. Deuteronomy
23, for example, allows for the inclusion of some foreigners, though this is
definitely viewed as exceptional. Inclusion within the assembly of YHWH is
determined principally by descent, and the vision of Deuteronomy is of
fixed ethnic boundaries, if not absolutely so.[31] The book of Joshua can envisage Rahab moving toward inclusion within the people, just as Achan joins
the anti-elect Canaanites doomed for destruction. Some of the prophetic
books also entertain the idea that foreigners might join the worshiping community (e.g., Isa. 18, 56).

For its part the book of Genesis largely excludes such movement. As
Heard argues, the narratives of Genesis can introduce all sorts of ambiguities in its portrayal of the "diselect," but ultimately they are all excluded
from Abraham's line, the land, and the covenant. The example par excellence
is found in Genesis 34. The Shechemites seek to fuse with the family of Jacob,
becoming part of the elect, yet the opposite occurs and the Shechemites are
numbered among the anti-elect and are slaughtered. It is striking that when
the issue of joining the elect emerges, a possibility rarely envisaged by Gene-

28. Phyllis Trible, *Texts of Terror: Literary Feminist Readings of Biblical Narratives,*
SCM Classics (1984; repr. London: SCM Press, 2002), pp. 5-24.

29. Levenson, *Death,* pp. 82-110.

30. George W. Coats, "The Curse in God's Blessing: Gen 12:1-4a in the Structure and
Theology of the Yahwist," in Jörg Jeremias and Lothar Perlitt, eds., *Die Botschaft und die
Boten: Festschrift für Hans Walter Wolff* (Neukirchen-Vluyn: Neukirchener Verlag, 1981), pp.
31-41.

31. It is difficult to imagine an interpretation that reads against the grain more than
J. G. McConville's suggestion that "the permission shows that belonging to Israel depends
ultimately on faith, not on bloodline" (*Deuteronomy,* AOTC 5 [Leicester: Apollos, 2002],
p. 350; cf. Georg Braulik, *Deuteronomium II: 16,18–34,12,* NEchtB [Würzburg: Echter, 1992],
p. 171). The exception now becomes the rule.

sis, the book introduces the idea of the anti-elect, an idea otherwise not envisaged by Genesis.[32]

The Non-Elect and the Anti-Elect

The absence of the anti-elect within Genesis is striking, and now I want to examine the different foci of Genesis and Deuteronomy, a difference that raises a problematic issue when they are brought together. Together they threaten to collapse the distinction between the categories of non-elect and anti-elect. As I have already indicated, Kaminsky's distinction among the elect, the non-elect, and the anti-elect is valuable. In his typology the non-elect and the anti-elect are not to be conflated. The vast majority of the nations that are encountered in the Old Testament belong to the category of the non-elect. The anti-elect, on the other hand, are a distinct group that are ultimately destined for destruction, either because of their occupation of the land at the time of the conquest (the Canaanites) or because of their irrational opposition to Israel (the Amalekites).[33] In making this distinction Kaminsky also breaks the simple relationship between election and salvation that has been so characteristic of the Christian understanding of election.

In my view there is much to recommend Kaminsky's typology. In particular it provides a helpful way to understand election as expressed in the book of Deuteronomy, a book that contains some of the most sustained reflections on the subject.[34] Deuteronomy portrays Israel's election out of the nations, with Deuteronomy 7:6 often described as the locus classicus of the subject: "For you are a people holy to YHWH your God. YHWH chose you out of all the peoples on earth to be his people, his treasured possession." Yet this distilled statement about election occurs within the context of a command to utterly destroy the Canaanites (7:1-5). Thus Deuteronomy speaks of elect, non-elect, and anti-elect in one breath, and Kaminsky's distinction makes sense of how this is to be understood. Nevertheless, both the literary

32. An exception to Genesis's almost consistent portrayal might be found, however, in the similar story about Judah and Tamar. Through her persistence, or even her "righteous trickery," Tamar secures her place in the genealogy of Israel. This interpretation turns upon understanding Tamar as a Canaanite, a point that the text does not explicitly state, but is perhaps implied by comparison with 38:2.

33. For the Canaanites being "in the wrong place at the wrong time" see Lohr, *Chosen*, pp. 148-93, 208-25. For the irrational hatred of Amalek, see Kaminsky, *Loved*, pp. 115-16.

34. For a similar judgment see Lohr, *Chosen*, pp. 148-93.

context of the book (set on the other side of the Jordan shortly before the conquest) and the rhetorical content of the book (its frequent repudiations of the cultic practices of the Canaanites) mean that the dominant notes that are struck in this chord are Israel, the chosen people, versus the Canaanites. Israel and Canaan are portrayed as a stark contrast, elect and anti-elect, alternative realities before which the Israelites stand as they contemplate life in the land.[35]

The stories in Genesis, on the other hand, draw on quite different dynamics. Here the concentration is on one family, not all of whom will inherit all the promises delivered to Abraham. All flourish in various ways, often because of their association with the patriarchal line and sometimes because they receive their own blessing. The stories are about strife and rivalry, and not about annihilation of the other. As has often been observed, the patriarchal stories lack the strong religious contrasts that mark Israel's story from the book of Exodus on; instead there is an "ecumenical bonhomie" and patriarchs and their neighbors flourish together.[36] Most strikingly this common flourishing even includes the Canaanites. When we employ the analogy of election to Genesis, then, we find the elect and the non-elect. Although the anti-elect appear — the Canaanites and Amalek — they do not take on their anti-elect roles.

What happens then when the election language of Deuteronomy is deployed in Genesis? Is there not a danger that the rather different frameworks are merged so that the non-elect of Genesis become the anti-elect of Deuteronomy? The collapse of the anti-elect into the non-elect to create a simple dualistic contrast is an instinct that Kaminsky finds particularly prevalent in Christianity. Yet, as Kaminsky acknowledges, it is already rooted in the Old Testament; he refers especially to some late post-apocalyptic texts, such as Isaiah 65.[37] In this way Kaminsky recognizes the biblical roots of Christianity's reflections on election, while also marginalizing them. "The vast majority of texts in the Hebrew Bible" maintain Kaminsky's threefold typology.[38] My question is whether this issue might not be more deeply rooted than

35. One could certainly argue that for Israel the choice is only between acting as the elect and imitating the anti-elect. Israel does not have the possibility of repudiating its election so as to become nonelect. I am grateful to Rob Barrett for this observation.

36. Gordon J. Wenham, "The Religion of the Patriarchs," in Alan R. Millard and Donald J. Wiseman, eds., *Essays on the Patriarchal Narratives* (Leicester: IVP, 1980), pp. 157-88, here p. 184.

37. Kaminsky, *Jacob*, pp. 134-35, 175-76.

38. Ibid., p. 134.

Kaminsky suggests, finding a basis in the exegetical move to read Genesis in terms of election. Again, Malachi's interpretation of Genesis powerfully illustrates this change. It has often been observed that Malachi's "Esau I hated" moves beyond the Genesis narrative. It resonates better with the language of anti-elect than that of non-elect.[39] This is confirmed by the continuation of Malachi's prophecy: "They may build, but I will tear down. They will be called the wicked border and the people with whom YHWH is angry forever" (1:4). It is not that Esau numbers among the non-elect who have been given land beyond Israel's borders; rather Esau sounds more akin to Canaan, a link perhaps not unrelated to Esau's excursion into Judahite territory in the postexilic period.[40]

Election and Merit

Distinguishing the elect and the non-elect raises the question of whether there is a basis by which God chooses some and passes over others. The question of merit is frequently raised in relation to election, and the Old Testament itself is not inattentive to such issues. Read in light of election, the patriarchal stories can provide a narratival exposition of the unmerited nature of divine election. The recurring choice of the younger sibling emphasizes that YHWH's election does not accord with human conventions or wisdom. On the contrary, the preference for the younger would suggest that YHWH chooses those who have little or no status in the eyes of others. Their election is frequently portrayed as against the explicit wishes of the patriarchs: Abraham is content with Ishmael as heir, Isaac prefers Esau the hunter, and Joseph resists the blessings on Manasseh and Ephraim being reversed.

Read in this way the stories of Genesis are consistent with the portrayal of Israel's election elsewhere in the Old Testament, and most clearly Deuteronomy. Deuteronomy explicitly eschews any reason located in Israel's own capacities. It pursues a *via negativa* in order to base the logic of election solely upon the unmerited love of YHWH. Consequently Deuteronomy has been most attractive for modern Christian accounts of election. For example, in the opening pages of his book on election, by appeal to Deuteronomy 7

39. Cf. David L. Petersen, *Zechariah 9–14 and Malachi,* OTL (Louisville: Westminster John Knox, 1995), p. 169.

40. It is striking that the text refers to the "border" of Edom. Deut. 2:5 also betrays anxiety about the border between Judah and Edom emphasizing that Israel will not receive "so much as a foot's length of their land," and presumably the reverse is also implied.

H. H. Rowley counters J. M. Powis Smith's suggestion that election is an expression of natural racial pride: "It was not because you were the most numerous of people that YHWH set his heart upon you and chose you; for you were the least of all the people. Rather YHWH loved you" (vv. 7-8). Similarly we read in 9:5, "It is not because of your righteousness or the uprightness of your hearts that you are going in to occupy their land."[41]

Yet the parenetic style of Deuteronomy lends itself more easily to these kinds of disavowals. The narrative style of Genesis, while affirming the unmerited nature of election, also seems paradoxically unable to prevent persistent questions about the logic of election being asked. The narrative portrayal of the patriarchs raises natural questions about whether there is something about their comportment that made them particularly suitable to be a vehicle of God's elective purposes. The story of Cain and Abel in Genesis 4 provides a particularly apt example. It is possible (even preferable, I suspect) to read the narrative as a story of unexplained divine preference for the sacrifice of Abel. The text seems to studiously avoid providing any rationale for the choice of Abel's sacrifice rather than Cain's. Yet, at least as early as the Septuagint translation of the story, the instinct of many interpreters has been to seek a justification of YHWH's choice.[42] The passage's lacuna and its opaqueness have long been exploited for any hints that they may offer. Is Cain's offering less worthy than Abel's "choicest of the firstlings of his flock together with its fat"? Did Cain fail to bring the offering in the appropriate manner by not offering it "to YHWH"? Does Cain's reaction reveal some underlying moral flaw, of which YHWH was aware? The same problems confront us at every turn of the Genesis narrative. Does God prefer those who are quieter or more homey rather than those like Esau who go out on sweaty hunting expeditions? Were the character and abilities of Joseph more suited to the task of administrating Egypt and thus bringing salvation to Egypt and to his family?

The problem is embedded in the text of Genesis itself. This can be seen in two ways. First, some of the stories in Genesis are more explicit about the reasons for selection. In particular I am thinking of the story of Noah, for if there is a pattern of divine election that includes Noah, here we have a clear account of why one person might be preferred over others. Among a generation characterized by evil, Noah finds "favor in the eyes of YHWH" (6:8).

41. Rowley, *Election*, pp. 17-18.
42. See now Joel N. Lohr, "Righteous Abel, Wicked Cain: Genesis 4:1-16 in the Masoretic Text, Septuagint and New Testament," *CBQ* 71 (2009): 485-96.

This appears to be no arbitrary choice, for "Noah was a righteous man, blameless in his generation. He walked with God" (v. 9). This situation is similar to that with Noah's sons. However problematic the condemnation of Canaan may be in 9:18-29, it is somehow related to Ham's incivility; Shem and Japheth, on the other hand, are blessed because of their decency. Second, some texts raise the relationship between the actions of the patriarchs and the blessings bestowed by YHWH. This is particularly the case in some of the theological commentary that has been attributed to some of the latest redactional activity upon the stories of Genesis. The second angelic speech to Abraham after the binding of Isaac (22:15-18), for example, introduces the reaffirmation of the promise of blessing with "because (כִּי יַעַן) you have done this."[43] In some way the text envisages that "Abraham's obedience has been incorporated into the divine promise."[44] As is well known, this text has an important role in the development of the rabbinic idea of the "merit of the fathers." Similar interpretive issues arise in 26:5. With post-Deuteronomistic language Abraham is portrayed as obedient to torah. This obedience forms the basis of the promise to Abraham and his descendants. Jon Levenson sees in this verse a vindication of God's prior choice, such that Abraham's election "is no longer an act of pure grace, unrelated to the character and accomplishments of the founding father."[45] Unsurprisingly, many Protestant Christian readings of these texts look very different. Appeal is frequently made to YHWH's earlier unconditional promises, as when Westermann comments, "The promises to the fathers are, in essence, free assurances by God. To ground them, as here, on Abraham's achievement is to alter the understanding of them."[46]

The narrative of Genesis introduces, in the way that Deuteronomy does not, ambiguities that lead to significantly divergent exegetical conclusions. The main lines of argument are already laid out clearly in Paul. It is no surprise that it is to Genesis that both he and his opponents seem to appeal

43. For the redaction of Gen. 22:15-18 see Jean-Louis Ska, *Introduction to Reading the Pentateuch* (Winona Lake, Ind.: Eisenbrauns, 2006), pp. 82-83; R. W. L. Moberly, "The Earliest Commentary on the Akedah," *VT* 38 (1988): 302-23, esp. 304-11. Moberly aptly describes these verses as "the earliest commentary on the Akedah."

44. Moberly, "Earliest Commentary," pp. 320-21.

45. Jon D. Levenson, "Conversion of Abraham to Judaism, Christianity, and Islam," in Hindy Najman and Judith H. Newman, eds., *The Idea of Biblical Interpretation: Essays in Honor of James L. Kugel*, JSJSup 83 (Leiden: Brill, 2004), pp. 3-40, here p. 22.

46. Claus Westermann, *Genesis 12–36*, trans. John J. Scullion, CC (Minneapolis: Augsburg, 1985), p. 363.

for their alternative understandings of faith and obedience. Already we have arguments that the obedience of the patriarchs needs to be taken with full seriousness or that the diachronic development of the narrative needs to be respected, that is, promise precedes obedience.[47]

Suffering and Election

The existence of a profound link between election and divine testing is explored by Jon Levenson in *Death and Resurrection of the Beloved Son*. This examination of child sacrifice and the favored son in Judaism and Christianity can be read as an exposition of biblical ideas about election, especially in relation to the patriarchal narratives.[48] Levenson explores how the chosen are often subject to particularly severe testing and humiliation at YHWH's hand, the most celebrated example being Genesis 22, the *Akedah*. In Levenson's presentation of election, humiliation and exaltation are not alternatives bestowed upon the non-elect and the elect, respectively; rather they are both integral to the biblical understanding of election. "No sooner is the promise made than it is sorely tested; no sooner is exaltation conferred upon the beloved son than his humiliation begins."[49] Such observations are developed by Walter Moberly, who shows how such testing is a key ingredient of the disciplining of the chosen people.[50]

Narrative seems particularly suited for exploring the dynamics of the divine probing of the elect. The book of Job would suggest this, for it is the narrative framework of the book that expounds Job's trial by God and provides the context for the poetic exchanges between Job, his friends, and ultimately God himself. Narrative can explore human responses, while also providing a narratival perspective on divine activity. Reading Genesis in light of

---

47. For the disagreement between Paul and his opponents primarily being exegetical see Francis Watson, *Paul and the Hermeneutics of Faith* (London: T&T Clark, 2004).

48. As Levenson observes, "the first-born and the chosen are not, of course, synonymous, but their semantic fields overlap so extensively that an investigation of the one concept will inevitably illumine the other" (Levenson, *Death*, p. 60). For discussion of Levenson's understanding of election in *Death* and across other writings, see Lohr, *Chosen*, pp. 71-90.

49. Levenson, *Death*, p. 65.

50. R. Walter L. Moberly, *The Bible, Theology, and Faith: A Study of Abraham and Jesus*, Cambridge Studies in Christian Doctrine (Cambridge: Cambridge University Press, 2000).

election means that the developing relationship between God and the patriarchs, including their probing and disciplining, can be viewed as paradigmatic for later Israel. The narratives of Genesis also explore the response of the favored child to his status as well as the response of the unfavored child. Thus they provide a rich set of studies of how election should be received. The stories of Joseph and Jacob can be read as case studies of how two individuals learned to inhabit their elect status better. On the other hand, the response of Cain to YHWH's rejection is condemned, even if it is explicable.

This way of reading Genesis and thus of understanding election resonates well with other parts of the Old Testament, most obviously the exposition of election in Isaiah 40–55. In these chapters elect Israel suffers in exile, but its humiliation will lead to its exaltation and the worldwide recognition of YHWH. Similarly the servant figure — whether Israel or not — is afflicted, but will be exalted. For a Christian theology, this is an important correction to triumphalistic understandings of election and provides a suggestive way of understanding the passion of Jesus Christ.

The Elect and the Land

A final benefit and one easily overlooked, particularly by Christian interpreters, is the centrality of land to any account of election in the Old Testament. If one reads Genesis 12:1-3 as a statement of election, then land is central to the command and promise. Election entails blessing of a particular people in a specific land. Land plays an important role in the narratives of Genesis. As Heard shows, the narratives work to place the unfavored sibling not only outside the divine choice, but also outside the land. Lot goes to the Jordan plain out of his own choice, Hagar and Ishmael flee into the wilderness of Paran, while Esau settles in Seir. However much the trajectory of the patriarchs takes them outside the land, their movement is always back toward it. Abraham goes down to Egypt, but in the divine providence is thrust back out again. Jacob returns to the land as he wished to on his departure (28:21), and the Joseph narrative envisages a return to the land, even if only in death.

The importance of the land is to be found in the two most extended expositions of election in the Old Testament: Deuteronomy and Isaiah 40–55. In the case of Deuteronomy land is the fruit of election and its visible sign. When Israel fails to obey the divine covenant, its election is not jeopardized, but its possession of the land is. The non-elect and anti-elect are also defined by their relationship to the land. In Deuteronomy 20 the anti-elect status of the Canaanites seems to result from no other reason than they are in the land promised to Israel.[51] Land also has an important position in Isaiah 40–55. This is often overlooked, however, when Deutero-Isaiah is celebrated as the discoverer of monotheism and universalism. Yet central to the prophet's message is the new exodus event, which is not only salvation from Babylonian exile but leads somewhere specific: to Zion.[52]

In his challenging discussion of Israel's election, Michael Wyschogrod argues strongly for its essentially corporeal nature. The people of Israel are defined by descent. Consequently, the incorporation of a foreigner is truly a miraculous act of God. In the Old Testament election is also corporeal because of the centrality of the land.

Reading for Election across the Testaments

The dynamics that we have been examining are the consequence of Genesis having a unique role in the Old Testament. It is, as Moberly so memorably and perceptively put it, the "Old Testament of the Old Testament." Essential to the relating of the Old Testament to its older Testament is the "somewhat paradoxical combination of identity and difference, of continuity and discontinuity." As we have seen with the case of election, appropriation of Genesis to the categories of the rest of the Old Testament is "less than straightforward."[53] How much more complex, then, when for Christian theology it is necessary to take into account the New Testament. Its transformation of election is so radical that it is almost easier to avoid altogether bringing Old

---

51. Lohr develops this into a central part of his understanding of the anti-elect nature of the Canaanites, though this does play down biblical references to the injustices of the Canaanites (see Lohr, *Chosen,* pp. 148-93, 208-25). I am grateful to Joel Kaminsky for highlighting this to me.

52. See Nathan MacDonald, "Monotheism and Isaiah," in H. G. M. Williamson and David G. Firth, eds., *Interpreting Isaiah: Issues and Approaches* (Leicester: Apollos, 2009), pp. 43-61.

53. Rephrasing Moberly's observations about the relationship of Old and New Testaments: "This somewhat paradoxical combination of identity and difference, of continuity and discontinuity, characterizes a Christian approach to the Old Testament and has always made the appropriation of the Old Testament as Christian scripture less than straightforward" (R. W. L. Moberly, *The Old Testament of the Old Testament: Patriarchal Narratives and Mosaic Yahwism,* OBT [Minneapolis: Fortress, 1992], p. 127).

Testament and New into conversation on this issue. When we do, as we must, we need also to speak in terms of analogy, taking our steps carefully.

There are then three different perspectives on election to be negotiated: that of the patriarchal history, that of the Old Testament, and that of the New Testament. At this point, the theological river that should make glad the city of God arises from the boiling, seething confluence of three streams. Small wonder that the history of the church has witnessed various theological movements dragged under these waters or pushed along helplessly by surging undercurrents. For myself I can only admire the confidence of Rowley, who thought he could speak surefootedly about "*the* biblical doctrine of election."[54] In light of this I am more hesitant than usual to draw conclusions. I offer the following four observations in the hope that they will promote an ongoing discussion and prompt others to their own reflections.

First, election can be found (in a loose sense) across and throughout both the Old and New Testaments. Given that election looks somewhat different between Genesis and the rest of the Old Testament, it should not surprise us that this is true across Genesis, the Old Testament, and the New Testament. We need to be very conscious of what we are doing when we move from one part of Scripture to another.

Second, in every part of the Christian Bible, it is the family of Abraham that is the chosen people of God. This is as true of the New Testament as the Old, even if large numbers of Gentiles are now incorporated into the New Testament's vision of the Israel of the new covenant.

Third, across different parts of the Christian Bible the place of the non-elect changes. As we have seen in Genesis there is, with perhaps one exception, no move of the non-elect to become part of the elect, but in a sense there is no anti-elect. In some way this may be related to the fact that the promise of the land has not yet come to fruition. This situation changes in the rest of the Old Testament, for alongside the reality of the land, we are also introduced to the anti-elect. Is it too much to say that the appearance of the anti-elect also entails the possibility that the non-elect may join the elect? Both represent the extreme responses to Israel's election. For Kaminsky the anti-elect are those who directly oppose the elect. It is in this sense that they are *anti*-elect. They seem to represent a particular response to Israel by the non-elect, and, if that is true, then some parts of the Old Testament entertain the possibility that the opposite response might be possible.

54. So the title of Rowley's book-length study (Rowley, *Biblical Doctrine*).

That is, some might be so attracted by the worship of Israel's God to consider joining the elect community.

The New Testament might be seen as an apocalyptic exploration of this idea to its logical extreme. Jesus Christ, in some way the embodiment of all that Israel is and is called to be, is the figure to whom some response must be given in the unprecedented moment of the end times. As Jesus declares in Matthew's Gospel, "Whoever is not with me is against me, and whoever does not gather with me scatters" (12:30). In receiving authority over heaven and earth, the boundaries of his land are now extended to the extremities of the earth (Matt. 28:18-20).[55] The promise to Abraham and his descendants as Paul hears it was "that they should inherit the world" (Rom. 4:13). In this new reality there is nowhere for the non-elect to be, and the category falls away.[56]

Fourth, any theology of election deserving of the name Christian must be deeply attentive to Scripture, both Old and New Testaments. It does not have the luxury to ignore election or mold it in any way to suit its purposes. Nevertheless, a doctrine of election is also an act of theological construction. Scripture will not deliver "what the text meant" so that theologians can determine "what it means," as Krister Stendahl (in)famously put it.[57] We cannot read Genesis so as to deliver what Genesis means and so adjudicate the disagreements between Paul and his interlocutors. Instead, a theology of election will have to wrestle with different concepts of election, *and* Scripture's own wrestling with these concepts across testamental boundaries.

55. For land in the NT see William D. Davies, *The Gospel and the Land* (Berkeley: University of California Press, 1974); Walter Brueggemann, *The Land: Place as Gift, Promise, and Challenge in Biblical Faith*, 2nd ed., OBT (Minneapolis: Fortress, 2002), pp. 157-72.

56. I am grateful to Rob Barrett for drawing my attention to the possible importance of land at this point.

57. Krister Stendahl, "Biblical Theory, Contemporary," in *The Interpreter's Dictionary of the Bible*, 5 vols., ed. George A. Buttrick (New York: Abingdon, 1962), 1:418-32.

Rebekah's Twins:
Augustine on Election in Genesis

Ellen T. Charry

When asked about the place of election in Genesis, many will quickly think of the election of Abraham and his seed as a blessing for the families of the earth (Gen. 12:1-3). Further, if asked about the place of election in Western theology, many will quickly think of Augustine of Hippo, who constructed the doctrine. To close the circle, when one presses further about Augustine on election in Genesis, it becomes clear that Augustine is not reading Genesis but Romans 9 on Genesis for his thinking on election. The primary Genesis text that Paul relies on in Romans 9 is not Genesis 12:1-3 but Genesis 25:22-23, which comments on Rebekah's pregnancy: "The children struggled together within her; and she said, 'If it is to be this way, why do I live?' Therefore, she went to inquire of the Lord. And the Lord said to her, 'Two nations are in your womb, and two peoples born of you shall be divided; the one shall be stronger than the other, the elder shall serve the younger.'"[1] The elder child by perhaps a few minutes is cursed in the womb.

Indeed, ours is not a straightforward assignment. The master Western theologian read this passage not on its own terms but through Paul's filter. Thus it is more correct to speak of Augustine's Pauline doctrine of election than of his biblical doctrine of election. What was Scripture for Paul is the Older Testament for Augustine, as Paul is canonized by Augustine's day. Paul's supersessionism is unquestionable in Augustine's mind. Genesis is for

---

1. All quotations are taken from NRSV. I will follow its spelling when referring to the matriarch: Rebekah for the OT, Rebecca for the NT.

him a Christian text. This was not the case for Paul, of course, but it is for those after him.

Augustine began studying Paul in the mid-390s, and his doctrine of election elaborates and defends his reading of Romans 9 with help from Romans 11:33 and support from other biblical verses. He held very tightly to his original reading of Paul, so it is worth examining the foundational text before turning to Augustine's use of it.

Paul's Doctrine of Election in Romans 9

The Great Reversal

Paul's doctrine of election as it appears in Romans 9 is a stunning reversal of the promise to Abraham. Quite against the usual reading of the biblical text, Paul boldly says, "not all of Abraham's children are his true descendants" (Rom. 9:7).[2] He relies heavily on other verses in Genesis to testify against Genesis 12:2-3 for the sake of the Gentiles. His point is that the seed of Abraham is no longer — if it ever was — the Israel of God, but those who are in Christ (primarily Gentiles) are the children of the promise.

The crucial passage is long, but worth recalling in full, noting the scriptural texts quoted or alluded to because they become the building blocks of Augustine's doctrine.

> It is not as though the word of God had failed. For not all Israelites truly belong to Israel, and not all of Abraham's children are his true descendants; but "It is through Isaac that descendants shall be named for you" [Gen. 21:12]. This means that it is not the children of the flesh who are the children of God, but the children of the promise are counted as descendants. For this is what the promise said, "About this time I will return and Sarah shall have a son" [Gen. 18:10]. Nor is that all; something similar happened to Rebecca when she had conceived children by one husband, our ancestor Isaac [Gen. 25:21, 23]. Even before they had been born or had done anything good or bad (so that God's purpose of election might continue, not by works but by his call) she was told, "The elder shall serve the younger" [Gen. 25:23]. As it is written, "I have loved

2. Of course, he works out the great reversal in Galatians as well, but Augustine gravitates to the Romans version.

Jacob [the younger, now Gentiles], but I have hated Esau" [the older, now, the Jews; paraphrase of Mal. 1:2-3]. What then are we to say? Is there injustice then on God's part? By no means! For he says to Moses, "I will have mercy on whom I have mercy, and I will have compassion on whom I have compassion" [Exod. 33:19]. So it depends not on human will or exertion, but on God who shows mercy. (Rom. 9:6-16)

Paul makes five significant moves here. First, he turns away from Abraham and locates the promise through Isaac. Second, the promise to Abraham that his seed would be a blessing to the Gentiles is transmitted through Isaac's twin sons, who are cursed to be at odds with one another before they are born. Third, the nations appear as the younger of the twins while Israel remains the elder, but the younger, having stolen the primal blessing from his brother, is now his brother's master. That is, the Gentiles will rule over the Jews. Fourth, Paul introduces the element of hatred into the doctrine by paraphrasing Malachi 1:2-3, "I have loved Jacob but I have hated Esau." Genesis 27:41 had paved the way for this by saying that Esau hated Jacob because he had stolen his father's blessing of the firstborn and was cursed by his father instead. The import is that the Jews will hate the Gentiles who will rule over them. It is the precise opposite of the theology expressed in Psalm 2, for example. Although later the brothers almost go to war against each other, they finally make peace in Genesis 33 through Esau's good graces. Paul's fifth move is to rely on Exodus 33:19 to claim that there is no injustice here because God does what he wants to do. The great reversal of Jews and Gentiles is complete. The older brother, Esau, now the Jews, are out; the younger brother, Jacob, now the Gentiles, are in, at least according to Romans 9.

The Gentiles are now the children of the promise, and God now hates the Jews, apparently anticipatorily cursed from the womb (from eternity?). Scripture does not support the metaphor at this point, but the rhetorical effect is the goal. Of course, Paul tries to soften this blow by saying that God has by no means rejected his people (Rom. 11:1-2), but what that means precisely depends on how one interpret Romans 11:25-32 about the ultimate gift of mercy to all.

So that you may not claim to be wiser than you are, brothers and sisters, I want you to understand this mystery: a hardening has come upon part of Israel, until the full number of the Gentiles has come in. And so all Israel will be saved; as it is written, "Out of Zion will come the Deliverer; he will banish ungodliness from Jacob"; "And this is my covenant with them, when I take away their sins." As regards the gospel they are enemies of God for your sake; but as regards election they are beloved, for the sake of their ancestors; for the gifts and the calling of God are irrevocable. Just as you were once disobedient to God but have now received mercy because of their disobedience, so they have now been disobedient in order that, by the mercy shown to you, they too may now receive mercy. For God has imprisoned all in disobedience so that he may be merciful to all.

This takes us somewhat afield from Augustine on election, but not too far and we shall return to it soon. It is striking that in his doctrine of election Augustine does call upon the hope for all in Romans 11. His doctrine of Israel, and all following him, sustains Paul's great reversal in Romans 9, although he expands it considerably beyond Paul's scope. Paul's qualification of God's rejection of Israel is lost on Augustine.[3]

In the remainder of Romans 9, Paul cites numerous passages from Isaiah and Jeremiah to reinforce his argument, adding the idea that this is all fair and just in the great reversal of election because God, like a potter at his wheel, is free to take a lump of clay and do with it as he pleases. Augustine echoes Exodus 33:19: "he said, 'I will make all my goodness pass before you, and will proclaim before you the name, 'The LORD'; and I will be gracious to whom I will be gracious, and will show mercy on whom I will show mercy.'" The prophets inspire Paul's image of God as a potter, but he adds a sinister note missing from them. "Has the potter no right over the clay, to make out of the same lump one object for special use and another for ordinary use? What if God, desiring to show his wrath and to make known his power, has endured with much patience the objects of wrath that are made for destruction; and what if he has done so in order to make known the riches of his glory for the objects of mercy, which he has prepared beforehand for glory?" (9:21-23). This passage becomes central to Augustine's doctrine. Paul clinches his great reversal with Hosea's own threat of reversal. Paul concludes that its time has now come, as he said in Galatians 3:24 ("that the law was our custodian until Christ came, that we might be justified by faith"), to realize that the law was always only temporary. The election of Israel, if it ever was true, was never more than preparatory.

---

3. Unlike today's biblical scholars, Augustine is not embarrassed by God's rejection of Israel. Indeed, he will cling to it, setting the trajectory for Western Christian Israelology that was sustained by both Thomas Aquinas and Karl Barth. Pauline scholars have only pointed to Paul's "by no means" in Rom. 11:1 in the last quarter of the twentieth century.

Augustine's Tutor

Paul was Augustine's tutor on the topic of election. The key verses are Romans 9:6-13, where he brings together several testimonies from Genesis to create the great reversal in which Gentiles either replace the Jewish people as the elect of God or have been the heirs of the promise to Abraham in Genesis 12:3 all along. The bishop will add one other verse from Romans to complete his doctrine of grace/election: "O the depth of the riches and wisdom and knowledge of God! How unsearchable are his judgments and how inscrutable his ways!" (11:33). He reads it as a gloss on Paul's quotation of Exodus 33:19 at Romans 9:15.[4]

Paul's imaginative use of Scripture forebodes a sinister image of election fueled by divine hatred and wrath that Augustine will lift up and defend tirelessly, even calling it mercy. Modern scholars read Romans 9–11 as a unit dealing with Jews and Gentiles. Of course, Augustine did not read these chapters as a discrete unit. He understood the context Paul was writing in, but it was not his own. While Paul faced Jews and pagans, Augustine faced Christians and pagans and felt free to universalize Paul's message for that audience. In his hands, election was about Jewish and Christian types; Jacob and Esau typologize every human being quite apart from ethnicity or belief.

In Augustine's long fingers, Romans 9's portrayal of Jacob as Gentiles and Esau as Jews strictly applied becomes what theologians have called Augustine's terrifying or repulsive doctrine of predetermination whereby people are taken or left based on what Augustine constantly notes is God's inscrutable will.[5] Although he faced much opposition in his own day as well as in our own for his adherence to divine arbitrariness, he would not have taken himself to be constructing a doctrine of election but only drawing out the implications of Paul's teaching for his parishioners and readers. Of course, Paul did not think that the great reversal that he constructed from scriptural texts was arbitrary. For him, it was the fulfillment of Genesis 12:3. Nevertheless, it fell to Augustine to interpret Paul's teaching for the West, and he did so over the course of decades.

---

4. It is noteworthy that while he relies heavily on Rom. 11:33, he scarcely mentions 11:32: "For God has imprisoned all in disobedience so that he may be merciful to all." It could have taken his teaching of election in an entirely different direction. He does have one sermon that deals extensively with this text. I shall turn to it later on.

5. Gerald Bonner, *St. Augustine of Hippo: Life and Controversies*, 2nd ed. (Norwich: Canterbury Press, 1986), p. 392; Phillip Cary, *Inner Grace: Augustine in the Traditions of Plato and Paul* (Oxford; New York: Oxford University Press, 2008), p. xi.

Ellen T. Charry

Augustine's Doctrine of Election

Augustine's epithet is "the Doctor of Grace." Grace towers above his corpus like a rainbow after a sun shower or massive gray clouds just before a thunderstorm, depending on one's perspective on a high doctrine of divine sovereignty. Grace seems to be a work of the Holy Spirit. In some of Augustine's works, it seems to be an invisible injection of the power to be good, while in others it is the gift of the Holy Spirit given in baptism that wipes away original sin. He never directly addressed the tension between the spontaneous and ordered work of the Spirit, leaving the church to ponder how to think about the work of the Spirit. Nevertheless, although Augustine came to the doctrine of election through Paul, his teaching on grace assumes a life of its own through the story of the birth of Jacob and Esau.

Pondering Paul

Jacob and Esau appear frequently throughout Augustine's works once he becomes entranced with Paul. Both *On Christian Teaching (De doctrina Christiana)*[6] and book 1 of *To Simplician (Ad Simplicianum)*,[7] written in the same period, are examples.

On Christian Teaching (395/96-426)

On Christian Teaching is a highly influential treatise on Christian hermeneutics — how to mine Scripture for its moral and spiritual significance. Book 1 offers a signature statement that is central to Augustine's doctrine of election, indeed to all of his theology. God alone is to be enjoyed for himself. All else is to that end.[8] The purpose of life is to know, love, and enjoy God: that and that alone is happiness. Books 2 and 3 are on semiotics, with book 2 focusing on how unfamiliar or unknown signs may be interpreted for spiritual edification. Here he turns to Genesis 25:25-26 to differentiate reading signs astrologically from reading them Christianly.

Augustine regularly takes care to explain how Christianity is to be dis-

6. Augustine, *On Christian Teaching*, trans. R. P. H. Green, World's Classics (Oxford: Oxford University Press, 1997), pp. 50-51.

7. Augustine, "To Simplician — on Various Questions Book 1," in John H. S. Burleigh, ed., *Augustine: Earlier Writings*, LCC 6 (Philadelphia: Westminster, 1958), pp. 370-406.

8. Augustine, *Christian Teaching*, pp. 9-10.

tinguished from astrology, which held sway at the time. Jacob and Esau were born under the same constellation but they had quite different destinies.[9] Not by the stars but according to "some inscrutable divine plan, those who have a desire for evil things are handed over to be deluded (by corrupt angels) and deceived according to what their own wills deserve."[10] Despite this ominous judgment Augustine insists, and continues to insist, that freedom of choice is not impugned by the working of the inscrutable divine plan. It does mean, however, that after the fall human decisions are always bad because all our thinking is badly distorted. Here he departs from the Platonist view that bad decision making is from ignorance, because people are rational. Augustine gives us the idea that bad behavior is irrational. It is from distorted love that diverts attention from God even if it be only momentary. Augustine considers this to be an uncontrollable turn from God toward lesser, usually material things stemming from the sin of Eve and Adam (following Rom. 5:12-14). Augustine's defect-based psychology would carry the entire Western tradition.

On Free Will (391/95)

The foundation for Augustine's mature position appears in the early part of book 3 of *On Free Will (De libero arbitrio)* written about the same time or a bit earlier than *Christian Teaching*.[11] Although it does not cite Genesis 25, it establishes his mature position on free choice. God is good; humans, now fallen, their created nature vitiated, voluntarily turn away from God to lesser things. Any turn from God is a turn to evil, there is no neutral ground. It is a zero-sum game. Even if God anticipates this turn away from himself, it does not impugn human freedom of choice. Our bad decisions are fully our own responsibility. God is not responsible for them. Augustine will defend this position for the rest of his life when criticized for denying human freedom. His defense is warranted. He always maintained human freedom to choose ill. It is only freedom to choose well that evades us. His point remained elusive to many. If God anticipated it, did he not cause it? Augustine charges ahead at this point in *Free Will* 3 by changing the subject to the topic of happiness, but it will haunt him for decades. This led to the charge by Pelagius

---

9. One should always keep in mind that astrology was a major opponent that Augustine battled constantly.

10. Augustine, *Christian Teaching*, p. 51.

11. Augustine, "On Free Will," in *Augustine: Earlier Writings*, pp. 102-217.

that although he officially rejected Manichaean determinism it remained significant in Augustine's theology.

The abrupt turn in the dialogue is significant. In it, Augustine reveals his bottom line. His teaching on election, indeed, perhaps the point of his theology and Western theology following him, is to lead people toward happiness. The first step on the path is brutally honest self-knowledge. Knowing that one voluntarily chooses evil cultivates humility, the primary weapon against vanity *(superbia)*, the chief sin for Augustine. Lacking honest self-knowledge leads people to believe that they can choose well. He is out to disabuse them of this posturing. The pastoral point of honest self-knowledge is so that "by stages the divine mercy would bring them to wisdom. They would be neither inflated by what they discover [about themselves], nor rebellious when they fail to find the truth, by . . . recognizing their ignorance they would become more patient in seeking it."[12] The wisdom to which he refers is that taught by Genesis 25:23 and the condensation of Malachi 1:2-3, grounded in the story of the fall (Gen. 3). On one's own, no person can do anything but choose to turn away from God, yet the unexpected younger son, Jacob, is inexplicably loved and mercifully elected by the potter as a vessel for special use while all others elected for ordinary use (symbolized by Esau) are hated by God.

The truth, that is, the happiness that people seek, whether consciously or unconsciously, is enjoying God, as book 1 of *Christian Teaching* stated. Distorted self-knowledge, given over to vanity/pride/sin, that motivates spiritual, moral, and material wrong choices stands between happiness and us. The fruit of Genesis 25:23 and Paul's shorthand for Malachi 1:2-3 is that knowing ourselves to be capable of freely willing only badly is the gateway to happiness because through it we confront our limits. A question is whether that insight teaches that since we cannot choose the good we should stop playing Sisyphus and quit trying. Only divine grace can fix that problem, and that in a release from self and a turn toward God. The key to happiness is the humility not to think that we can be happy by choosing what we think best but by admitting that God must do it for us. It is counterintuitive, as Christianity generally is.

Thus when we see someone acting righteously should we conclude that she is a recipient of divine grace and perhaps become jealous that we lack the gift, or conclude that she is acting as if she had the gift all the while, exposing her sinfulness at trying to do that of which she is incapable? Alter-

---

12. Ibid., p. 173.

natively, should we conclude that those acting wickedly are the truly humble because they do not put on airs? Augustine keeps going.

To Simplician (396)

Augustine returns to Romans 9 in another treatise from that period, *To Simplician on Various Questions.*[13] In book 1 of that work, Augustine responds to two questions from Simplician, who shortly thereafter became bishop of Milan when Ambrose died (397). Simplician's first two questions are about interpreting Paul. His second question is on interpreting Romans 9:10-29, the pivotal text for Augustine's doctrine of election. Again, the theme of humility immediately appears. Augustine rises to the challenge. Paul's purpose throughout Romans "is that no man should glory in meritorious works."[14] The contrast, of course, is between Jews (Christianity's hallowed whipping boy) and Christians (inevitably morally superior to Jews).[15] Augustine applies Paul's great reversal of the identities of Jacob and Esau from being about Jews and Gentiles to being about Christians.[16] Although the divide between Jews and Christians still stands, he uses Jacob and Esau to distinguish the visible from the invisible church. The church is a mixed body of saints (the "Jacobs") and sinners (the "Esaus"). Only God can tell them apart, although followers of this doctrine have regularly tried to nose their way into God's business.

The "arrogant" Jews believe that they received "evangelical grace" to obey divine law. However, Augustine follows Paul's idea that precisely the

13. Augustine, "To Simplician," pp. 370-406.
14. Ibid., p. 386.
15. Augustine realizes that this systematic theological reversal of Jacob and Esau and the spiritualizing of Israel as the Christians are problematic. He tries to rationalize it in Sermon 4 by saying that all the true meaning of the promises in the Older Testament is spiritual, not material. Herewith the Older Testament, Jerusalem, the land of Israel, and the people of God lose their grounding in temporal existence and become spiritual constructs that fly free of material reality. Platonism has the final word. See Augustine, "Immortality of the Soul," in Gerard Watson, ed., *Soliloquies and Immortality of the Soul, Classical Texts* (Warminster: Aris & Phillips, 1990), pp. 128-63, here p. 189.
16. This is explicit in Sermon 4.12: "Now apply this. You have a Christian people. But among this Christian people it is the ones who belong to Jacob that have the birthright or right of the firstborn. Those, however, who are materialistic in life, materialistic in faith, materialistic in hope, materialistic in love, still belong to the Old Testament, not yet to the new. They still share the lot of Esau, not yet in the blessing of Jacob" (Augustine, "Immortality of the Soul," p. 192).

opposite is the case. Paul imputes Jewish obedience to the arrogance of believing that they can follow divine law, as if God would intentionally command what we cannot do. The Jews, Augustine thinks, following Paul, obey divine law, thinking that their obedience is praiseworthy. According to Paul, the ability to obey God requires a special gift of grace, a spiritual injection of sorts, and following upon faith that is a prior injection of spiritual power that cures distorted thinking and enables good behavior. Those who "know that they are sons of promise [through Jacob now representing Gentiles] . . . do not wax proud of their merits, but account themselves co-heirs with Christ by the grace of their calling."[17] At this point, Augustine adverts to the twins. The hope of the story is to "break and cast down the pride of men who are not grateful for the grace of God but dare to glory in their own merits."[18] The younger twin, Jacob (representing Gentile Christians), was elected before he was born, so his chosenness had nothing to do with his moral strength. It was solely by the mercy of God. That spiritual injection of power becomes visible as it enables him to will well, for without it he will only choose badly. It was not because of faith either, because no fetus has faith. The bishop concludes that election cannot be a reward for faith, but only the reverse. Faith is not the act of a good will but the consequence of prevenient grace, that first injection of power necessary for any righteousness. We cannot will ourselves into faith. It is an arbitrary gift. Again, the implication is that unbelievers (including all non-Christian Jews) lack prevenient grace and so are not liable for their situation.

Then Augustine turns to that sad sack elder son, Esau, now signifying the Jews according to his reading of Paul, that is, without the qualification of Romans 11 that God has by no means rejected his people. What of him/them, miserable creature(s), hated by God apparently even before birth according to Paul's logic in Romans 9?[19] Here is perhaps the most painful consequence of Augustine's pursuit of humility. God's hatred of Esau was not unkind at all, he says, because neither he nor his brother deserved anything better. Indeed, in Sermon 159B, he argues that the mercy promised by Romans 11:32 is precisely the punishment spoken of in Romans 9:21-23.[20] Rejection of Esau

---

17. Augustine, "To Simplician," p. 387.

18. Ibid.

19. To follow the analogy out, the point is that the Jews were always destined to be hated by God in order to display divine wrath. Yet, in Rom. 11, hounded by concern for his people, Paul maintains that the Jews are somehow not abandoned after all.

20. Augustine, "Sermon 159b," in *Sermons Discovered since 1990,* ed. François Dolbeau (Hyde Park, NY: New City Press, 1997), pp. 146-63.

is a merciful act of tough love on God's part, an act of mercy in disguise.[21] God justly hated Esau, but this was for his well-being so that the Esaus of this world would come to better, deeper self-knowledge because of God's rejection of them and thereby grow in wisdom, that is, toward God. Jacob was loved for no reason; he too deserved the wrath of God but escaped it. Esau got only what they both deserved. Election is not from obedience to divine law or faith, hope, love, wisdom, or any other virtue. It does not hinge on God's sensing that Jacob would be good and Esau bad. Indeed, the literal sense of the texts does not support this. Here Augustine calls in Romans 9:16 for support: "So it depends not on human will or exertion, but on God who shows mercy." It is not a good will or that God anticipates it in advance that influences his mercy. It is not that all are called but few respond, "for the effectiveness of God's mercy cannot be in the power of man to frustrate, if he will have none of it."[22] Here we have the doctrine of irresistible grace.

Election is the provenance of the unfathomable divine will, that inscrutable will of God that chooses a few from the many and loves the majority by punishing them justly for their own good. In Augustine's mouth, that lump of clay that Isaiah and Jeremiah refer to, the fate of which the potter holds in his hands to treat as he sees fit, as Paul puts it, becomes the "mass of perdition," the *massa damnata,* that characterizes humanity, including many Christians.[23] Although Augustine regularly appeals to Romans 11:33, trying to take cover in the divine mystery, in many places he does offer the divine rationale for this horrible decree of abandoning people to their worst self.

21. "See that punishment can be the work of caring or kindness, from the example of children, from that kind of thing which nobody can hate. So someone sees his son going the way of pride, setting himself up against his father, claiming more for himself than is proper, wanting to let his life trickle away in trifling pleasures, wanting to squander what he doesn't yet possess. And there he is, when he's behaving like this, cheerful, laughing, blithely enjoying himself. His father, though, brings him to heel with a rebuke, with punishment, with a whip; he wipes the grin off his face, reduces him to tears. He has apparently deprived him of what is good, and brought what is evil upon him — see what he has deprived him of: enjoyment; see what he has brought on him: groans. And yet if he had left that enjoyment unpunished, he would have been cruel; because he has reduced him to tears, he is shown to be caring and kind" (ibid., p. 149).

22. Augustine, "To Simplician," p. 395.

23. The innocent lump of clay that Isaiah and Jeremiah mention and to which Paul alludes is anthropomorphized in Augustine's homiletical mouth. The lump of clay or dough turns cancerous and is properly condemned and rejected. It becomes a pernicious contaminant in the church as Augustine plays with it in numerous texts, including Sermons 22.9 and 71.4, 169.9, and 260 D.2. We are watching a master preacher working over his audience that clamors for his erudition and delights in his flashing rhetoric.

The reason behind this terrible decree resides in Romans 9:22-23: "What if God, desiring to show his wrath and to make known his power, has endured with much patience the objects of wrath that are made for destruction; and what if he has done so in order to make known the riches of his glory for the objects of mercy, which he has prepared beforehand for glory?" God plays fast and loose with people, creating some for destruction to show his anger, power, and glory. Even his mercy is to display power and majesty. It seems that compassion and love are not ends in themselves here. If that is so, God seems to be sending an odd message. Yet Augustine pushes on; that display is not selfish on God's part but another blessing in disguise.

In *To Simplician* Augustine turns to Paul's use of Exodus 9:16, which says that God redeemed Israel from Egypt to show his power that his name may resound across the earth. In Christian perspective, the whole drama of enslavement and liberation is contrived for evangelistic purposes, and it worked. In Exodus 12:32, as Israel is running out the door, the defeated pharaoh asks Moses to ask God to bless him too. Augustine quotes Paul alluding to this incident at Romans 9:17: "For the scripture says to Pharaoh, 'I have raised you up for the very purpose of showing my power in you, so that my name may be proclaimed in all the earth.'"

The liberation from Egypt, like the predestination of Jacob and Esau, is to a common end. God's self-promotion is not a vain show, but is so that all people may realize that their true happiness and destiny lie in enjoying God as Augustine asserted at the beginning of *Christian Teaching* 1. God promotes himself so that the elect, gifted to understand readily, may draw others to God. Yet there is a catch-22 here. Advertising his anger, power, glory, and even mercy is to no avail if turning to God is not freely available but predetermined. We hang on the horns of an insoluble dilemma. One possibility is that the morally admirable are indeed blessed saints, not of their own doing, of course. They are convinced of divine favor and goodness toward them and so properly humbled. Alternatively, they only appear to be so, in which case they are deluded and the most damnable sinners because they are trying to be good when they truly cannot because they are not elected for the injection of grace. Yet again, if moral behavior is a red herring to divert people, there is no point to being righteous, for moral accomplishment itself is actually *superbia,* not *humilitas.* On this view, moral behavior is self-defeating.

Anti-Pelagian Works

Augustine's earliest opponents were monks who assumed that they could live a holy life, and they may well have assumed that grace was at the base of it. Augustine's doctrine directly challenged them to state dependence on grace louder. By 412 the Pelagian controversy was in full swing, but to appreciate its scope, a vignette from another quarter will set the stage.

A Roman priest, Sixtus, who would later become pope, had been leaning toward Pelagius but had returned to Augustine's high doctrine of grace, and the master learned of it.[24] Augustine wrote to him shortly thereafter, thanking him for rejecting the heresy (Letter 191). Some monks at Hadrumetum found a copy of the letter in the library of Evodius, bishop of Uzalis, indicating that Augustine's letters were already being collected. Armed with Augustine's doctrine, the brothers complained that on his view they should not be held responsible for misbehavior because it was not their fault but from a want of grace. In response to a return letter from Sixtus, Augustine wrote a substantial treatise (Letter 194) defending his position that free choice is not taken away and does not undermine moral responsibility, because punishment is morally motivating. He also wrote two additional works elaborating his teaching against the Pelagians, *Correction and Grace* and *Grace and Free Will*. One criticism of Augustine was and remains that his teaching undermines moral effort, although his own spiritual path had been motivated by a desire for a life of moral rigor.

This anecdote aside, Augustine's most worthy opponent, Pelagius — himself a moderate ascetic — was an excellent theologian in his own right.[25] Pelagius, a well-educated layman from western Britain, had bigger sights. His concern was with Manichaeism, a powerful religion of the day that held that the cosmos was in a great struggle between the forces of light and the forces of darkness being played out above the human realm. He took his stand in the Christian doctrine of the goodness of creation against the Manichaean belief that evil was an independent force that threatened good-

24. "Introduction to Letter 194," Augustine, *Letters 156-210*, trans. and notes by Roland Teske, ed. Boniface Ramsey, Works of Saint Augustine II/3 (Hyde Park, NY: New City Press, 2005), p. 287.

25. He was a sophisticated Antiochene biblical exegete. In his commentary on Romans (c. 405/6-410) he worked through his opposition to Augustine's already clear position on election and grace. This thus sparked the great controversy. See Theodore de Bruyn, trans. and ed., *Pelagius's Commentary on St Paul's Epistle to the Romans*, Oxford Early Christian Studies (New York: Oxford University Press, 1993).

ness. Of course, Augustine had spent nine years with the Manichees. He repudiated this religion when he became a Christian, and upon returning to Africa after his baptism (387) had to assure the populace that his Catholicism was genuine. He embarked on a written crusade against his former religion by turning to Genesis — a life-long and frustrating preoccupation for him — with a commentary on Genesis against the Manichees.[26] Several other works were in this same vein. Yet Pelagius, also an opponent of Manichaeism and a moderate ascetic, smelled a Manichaean residue in Augustine's doctrine of grace. Augustine maintained that his insistence on the enduring power of free choice — at least for ill — definitively severed his theology from Manichaean dualism, but perhaps Pelagius concluded that the master's doctrine fell short of its goal of exonerating the goodness of creation because Augustine's doctrine of grace undermines human effort.[27] Human beings remained trapped in a struggle between good and evil being played out over their heads, located in the inscrutable will of God.

Literal Meaning of Genesis (401-14)

Augustine is unperturbed by the monastic objection. He thinks that moral urging *is* forwarded by the display of divine wrath because no one is innocent. The damned receive what they deserve and the blessed receive what they do not deserve. In the *Literal Meaning of Genesis*, he again scores his pastoral point through the twins. The sanction of Esau is to capture the attention of those who "could not appreciate God's goodness . . . without observing the punishment inflicted on another . . . that is, not to be overconfidently reliant on self, but to rely on God."[28] Esau is a wake-up call, but to what end? God's display of wrath and power (Rom. 9:22-23) is to proclaim his glory that the dull may know that their well-being is from God

---

26. Augustine, "On Genesis: A Refutation of the Manichees," in *On Genesis*, ed. Michael Fiedrowicz (Hyde Park, NY: New City Press, 2001), pp. 25-102.

27. Gerald Bonner has devoted his career to deciphering this important controversy and over the course of two decades has become more appreciative of Pelagius's position. See Bonner, *Augustine of Hippo;* idem, *Freedom and Necessity: St. Augustine's Teaching on Divine Power and Human Freedom* (Washington, DC: Catholic University of America Press, 2007).

28. Augustine, "The Literal Meaning of Genesis," in Fiedrowicz, ed., *On Genesis*, p. 434. The suggestion of motivation by observing the punishment of others sounds odd. If the designation refers to punishment after death, no observation is possible that could edify us in this life. Perhaps this is a hyperbole assuming that the purportedly faithful have preachers who help them imaginatively envision the suffering of the damned.

alone. That Esau is "made for destruction" (Rom. 9:22) is to an honorable though terrifying purpose.

We now seem to be trapped in despair. The display of divine power and wrath is to frighten people into being good. Yet the nagging sense remains that being or at least trying to be good is pointless, as it indicates nothing about one's status in the face of divine wrath, or it is a show of pride at considering oneself among the elect, though Augustine says nothing about this. The theistic sanction is sinister. God makes positive use of the bad deeds or at least the anticipated bad choices of God's rejected. It is to show them that "It is from themselves of course that they have a will that is bad, from him that they have both a nature that is good and a punishment that is just, the place that is their due, providing others with an aid to training in virtue and a salutary example to fear."[29]

Answer to Two Letters of the Pelagians (419-420/21)

Inculcating fear, however, is only one pole of Augustine's pastoral interest. On yet another run at election examining Romans 9, Jacob and Esau are the "two infants[,] one is to be taken up through mercy and the other is to be left because of judgment, and in him the one who is taken up sees what would be due to him by judgment if mercy had not come to his aid."[30] The purpose here is to inspire gratitude. This is also the case in another anti-Pelagian writing, where he responds to the charge that he remains at heart a Manichee. In that analysis of Romans 9:9-23 he points out:

> Here you have God's grace as not only a help, but also as a lesson — a help in the vessels of mercy, a lesson in the vessels of anger. In the latter, he shows his anger and demonstrates his power, for his goodness is so powerful that he makes good use of even the bad and makes known in them the riches of his glory toward the vessels of mercy. For what his justice exacts as punishment from the vessels of anger, his grace forgives in the vessels of mercy as he sets them free. The benefit which is gratuitously given to some would not be clearly seen, unless to others from

---

29. Ibid., p. 435.

30. Augustine, *The Augustine Catechism: The Enchiridion on Faith, Hope, and Love,* ed. John E. Rotelle, trans. Bruce Harbert, Augustine Series 1 (Hyde Park, NY: New City Press, 1999), pp. 110-11. Thanks to Gerald Bonner for pointing me to this passage. See Bonner, *Augustine of Hippo,* pp. 380-81.

that same mass, persons equally guilty and condemned to just punishment, God showed what both of them deserved.[31]

Late Anti-Pelagian Works

Predestination of the Saints (428)

At the end of his long life, Augustine's strength to repulse his opponents remained undiminished, and he relied on Rebekah's twins to promote predestination until the very end. In *Predestination of the Saints,* he admits that very early in his episcopate he had thought that faith was our own initiative, but that by the time he wrote *To Simplician* (396/97), five years after his elevation, he came to an extreme position. Prevenient grace intends to seal any crevice into which self-assurance might sneak. Even faith is a gift of the Holy Spirit.[32] Predestination is not only to demolish pride in our ability to obey God's law; that God made vessels for perdition is also to destroy confidence that we might petition God for the good will that we need.[33] Esau's predetermined rejection by God's wrath is to wipe out any whiff of hope that we can choose anything good of our own accord. We are thoroughly bad news.

Answer to Julian

In his long and repetitious *Unfinished Work in Answer to Julian,* Augustine reiterated, "the grace of God makes us do [good works]. Let us not establish our own righteousness. Rather, let the righteousness of God be in us, that is, the righteousness which God gives us."[34] That we are miserable sinners, from whom God chooses to love a few so that by displaying his awesome power he might bring all into ever deeper humility, is the normative Western Christian self-concept.[35]

31. Augustine, *Answer to the Pelagians, II,* trans. Roland J. Teske, ed. John E. Rotelle, Works of Saint Augustine I/24 (Hyde Park, NY: New City Press, 1998), p. 152.

32. Ibid., p. 155.

33. Ibid.

34. *Answer to the Pelagians, III,* trans. Teske, ed. Rotelle, Works of Saint Augustine I/25 (Hyde Park, NY: New City Press, 1999), p. 151. This is what Luther would later call "proper righteousness." It is not what he called "imputed righteousness."

35. It is possible to read subsequent Western theology as a great debate about which

The poles of Augustine's pastoral theology are humility and gratitude motivated by fear. Yet, ironically, Augustine's moral project falls completely flat. The argument that Jews rely on their God-given ability to keep the law implies that they are arrogant, while Christians confess they cannot keep the law because they are utterly dependent on divine grace and so are morally virtuous. This argument collapses because by virtue of their "humility" Christians hold themselves to be morally superior to the Jews (whether or not they actually claim what Paul asserts them to claim) who supposedly justify themselves by appealing to law observance. Christian self-righteousness and moral superiority over the Jews have the final word. Therefore, it is Christian reliance on grace that claims the moral high ground, utterly defeating the humility claim.

Assessment

Augustine's doctrine of election is that God arbitrarily yet intentionally designates individuals for either hell or heaven, for being either saintly or dastardly. The purpose of Augustinian fatalism is to a pastoral end, as I have been arguing. In conclusion, I review the strategies employed and some implications thereof.

The Pastoral Agenda

The reason for determining people's fate is clear, though the actual selection is arbitrary. Both election and rejection are pastorally fruitful. The goal is to instill fear in people in order to humble them. Augustine believed that the "big stick" approach was the best or perhaps even only way to secure humility, to tame the black horse of Plato's famous chariot. The tension is obvious. Romans 9:22-23 is at the heart of the matter. "What if God, desiring to show his wrath and to make known his power, has endured with much patience the objects of wrath that are made for destruction; and what if he has done so in order to make known the riches of his glory for the objects of mercy, which he has prepared beforehand for glory?"

---

way of construing doctrine is likely to create the humblest people. The issue is at the core of the Protestant Reformation. One earlier great exception to this is the magisterial work of Thomas Aquinas, who was fighting against the Manichaeism of his time.

Predetermining everyone's fate is to the end of displaying divine wrath, power, and majesty. Even mercy is to this end. The arbitrariness is calculated to persuade people that they are morally helpless in order to cultivate humility and reliance on divine initiative whether one considers oneself a beneficiary of God's gracious mercy or not. On the face of it, humility appears to countenance learned helplessness. Augustine's model Christian, persuaded of his moral helplessness and sinfulness, became paradigmatic. Humility was hoisted aloft in monasticism, Calvin, Calvinism, and movements spawned by Calvinism, like Jansenism and Quietism. God is intentionally arbitrary in order that we fear him and rejoice in whatever mercy is shown — including belief in our own damnation. This defect-based psychology is the center of Augustine's Mariner's Star quilt.

Augustine never says that people can tell which camp they are in, since that is revealed only in the next life. Perhaps he hoped that everyone would consider himself or herself condemned in order to promote humility all the more. The last books of the *City of God,* on hell and heaven, promote fear and hope. The centrality of fear is clearly to urge moral responsibility. Since the saved have the grace that enables them to be morally strong, however, the implication is that morally upstanding people are the saints, and that morally weak people are those rejected through no fault of their own and about which they could do nothing. The pointlessness of moral responsibility was not lost on readers either.

Even if Augustine's use of Romans 9 is hyper-Pauline and even if Calvinism is hyper-Augustinian in its turn, Paul's use of God's curse on Rebecca's and Isaac's boys in the womb in Romans 9 bellows down the ages. Although note has been made of differences between the Bishop's construal of divine predetermination and Calvin's, there is little doubt in either mind that God has elected some for rejection to show wrath and exempted others to show mercy.[36] Paul's hope for displaced Israel at some future point, whatever that may signal, did not find its way into the Western doctrine of election. The rejected are to be satisfied with their lot, indeed embrace it because they are edified by it, as they grow into deeper self-knowledge. The elect, who cannot really identify themselves, are appropriately thrilled that they have been graciously exempted from the fate of their doomed sisters, brothers, parents, and children. Since infants have no theological birth certificates that designate their fate, parents and children alike wait expectantly for signs of good and bad behavior, hoping that it will indicate their progeny's assig-

36. Bonner, *Augustine of Hippo,* pp. 386-89.

nation. If some behave well it should be a telltale sign of the invisible spiritual injection, since without it we can only behave badly. Perhaps, since we cannot tell where we are bound when life is over, Augustine wants us all to consider ourselves among the damned, as it is the morally safer place.

Augustine cited Rebecca's twins countless times. Without examining each of them, this conclusion cannot but be provisional. To do so would require a monograph. Still, there is sufficient evidence to suggest that Genesis 25 is central to the Western doctrine of election. Even though he did not always refer to Rebecca's twins in this regard, Augustine remained close to Romans 9:10-23 all his life, with the twins as lead characters.

Pastoral Implications

Having fulfilled the assignment here, I cannot resist commenting on the import of Augustine's doctrine of election in Western Christian theology and piety. Since Augustine has pastoral ambitions, his doctrine of election should be assessed on those grounds. Put sharply, Augustine thinks that God decides to terrify people in order to get them to be the kind of people he wants — humble, grateful, dependent. It is a dour psychology. It was not until Luther laid great emphasis on hope in divine mercy through Christ that a slightly less severe view of divine pedagogy emerged, but then Calvin followed right behind reasserting Augustine's reliance on fear as both a deterrent and a motivator. Barth later sublated both Luther's and Calvin's positions in a novel and powerful address to the interminable vacillation between affection for divine anger and affection for divine mercy that characterizes Western Christian theology.

The strategy behind the austere pedagogy is first to instill fear and later to offer hope. Psalm 22:6 sums up the fundamental self-concept: "But I am a worm, and not human; scorned by others, and despised by the people" — only in Augustine's case the scorn is from God. As honored and widespread as this strategy has been, even with mitigating offers of hope that one is, or at least may be, a vessel destined for mercy, it is still open to question on pastoral grounds. One question is, is it psychologically realistic enough to be pastorally effective? Another question is, is it encouraging?

Western theology often thinks in absolute binary terms — sinner-saint, hell-heaven, us-God, evil-good, darkness-light, reprobation-salvation, and vanity-humility. Either-or, not both-and, has ruled. Perhaps this *is* a residual Manichaean fatalism. What Augustine did not say is that human psychology is not so simple. It is complex and ambiguous, not simple and clear. The problem here is not that the master Christian psychologist lived before Freud — indeed, Freud shows traces of the Platonic and Augustinian heritage — but that he could not afford to admit psychological ambiguity lest it provide a loophole for a way past utter humility. To bring that possibility to a full stop he left us with the idea that God is merciful to a few in order to display his power rather than from affection or compassion for us. One is left with the impression that God does not really like us very much and that we should follow his lead and not like ourselves too much either.

While on the one hand, having read Romans 7, Augustine gave us the divided self, recognizing the struggle of multiple loves within the human breast, with the love of God yearning to vanquish lesser loves; on the other hand, he could not allow Paul's astute psychological acumen to penetrate his doctrine of election, centering as it did on Rebecca's fated twins. The master theologian gave us the idea that the church is a mixed body of sinners and saints, but not that everybody struggles between the sinner and saint within. Rebecca's twins did not speak to him of uncertainty.

One further pastoral question is about Augustine's construal of the divine pedagogy and the strategy for implementing it. Augustine relied heavily on the motivating and deterrent power of fear and guilt, not on the encouraging power of love and approbation. Augustine bequeathed defect-based psychology to the West. Here an adversarial relationship between God and us is presupposed with each side of the binary opposition pulling in a different direction. But what if God and we are pulling in the same direction in solidarity for the sake of our well-being? What if God is not against us in order to be for us but with us in order to be for us? Strength-based theology remains untried.

We are indebted to the master of Western theology for many gifts. We will undoubtedly continue to ponder whether his doctrine of election is among them.

Abraham and Aeneas:
Genesis as Israel's Foundation Story

R. Walter L. Moberly

Introduction

One of the ways in which one can learn something about the identity, nature, and priorities of a society, at least many a premodern society, is by looking at the account it gives of its origins. Who were its founders? What sort of people were they? Where did they come from? What sort of legacy have they bequeathed? Underlying these various questions is a basic issue that I wish in a preliminary way to investigate here: What sort of society tells the particular origin stories that it tells about itself? I propose to look at the book of Genesis, as Israel's account of its origins, from this particular angle, with a view to getting some picture of Israel's self-understanding as a people and society.

In a certain way, to be sure, the role of Genesis within the Old Testament is peculiar. For Genesis is prehistory with regard to the people of Israel, the account of whose foundations is told with relation to the work of Moses in exodus and torah in the books of Exodus, Leviticus, Numbers, and Deuteronomy. Thus one could also read Exodus to Deuteronomy as Israel's origin story, with Moses as the key founding figure under God. Nonetheless, the Genesis account prefaces the account of Israel under Moses with the account

---

I am grateful to Richard Briggs, Joel Kaminsky, and my wife, Jenny Moberly, for their helpful comments on a draft of this essay.

of Abraham and Israel's other patriarchal ancestors, and deserves attention as prehistory in its own right.

Moreover, the role of Genesis as prehistory to Israel suggests a parallel with another such famous account of prehistory from antiquity. For the coming of Aeneas and the Trojans to Italy in Virgil's *Aeneid* clearly functions as an origin-story for the Rome of Augustus in his early principate. Yet all the content of the *Aeneid* is set prior to the appearance of the Romans and the founding of Rome that, according to tradition, came centuries later through Aeneas's descendant Romulus. Here it is clear that an account that must be classified as prehistory can still be of prime importance for the self-understanding of the society whose prehistory it is.

I hope that, among other things, some reflection on one significant function of Genesis, as illuminated by comparative study with the *Aeneid,* may be helpful for thinking about the genre of the text. One of the problems that regularly attends proposals for particular genre designations ("myth," "legend," "saga," "folktale," "aetiology," etc.) is that arguments about the possible wider implications of the proposed label too easily displace attention to those features of the text that give rise to the proposal; but it is attention to the latter that should in principle be most fruitful.

To be sure, some complex issues attend such a comparative exercise. For example, the *Aeneid* is epic poetry, and is hugely indebted to many earlier poems, especially the work of Homer, while Genesis is a prose narrative (with occasional poetic pronouncements) whose indebtedness to possible antecedents is largely unknown. Alternatively, it is important that a prehistory, which is to function in the way that I have outlined, be widely recognized and accepted within the society whose self-understanding it portrays. But although Genesis now prefaces Israel's Scriptures and constitutes an authoritative account within those Scriptures, it is unclear both when its content was written down and by whom, and what kind of recognition that content may originally have had and for whom in ancient Israel/Judah. Nonetheless, so as not to get bogged down in prolegomena, I will work with Genesis in its received form, as a book whose purpose within Israel's Scriptures is to constitute the normative account of Israel's prehistory, and so also self-understanding, for all those who accept those Scriptures. Such people were, in the first instance, the Jewish community in (quite likely) the province of Yehud within the Persian Empire, though numerous successor communities, Christian as well as Jewish, have also accepted these Scriptures as authoritative.

This issue is less complex with regard to Virgil, because of clear evidence of early and enthusiastic reception of the *Aeneid* as an authoritative portrayal of Rome's origins and identity. The ancient Lives of Virgil portray close links between Virgil and Augustus: Augustus writes to Virgil to inquire about the progress of his epic, and it is Augustus who overrules Virgil's deathbed request that his unfinished manuscript be burned. Whatever one's judgments about this in terms of historicity (it is entirely plausible; but who knows what imaginative and apologetic factors may have influenced the composition of the Lives?), it attests an early understanding of Virgil's work as receiving the highest possible recognition from the outset.[1] Thus, in their different ways, both Genesis and the *Aeneid* fulfill the requirement that their portrayal of origins be recognized by ongoing generations within their respective societies.

I propose therefore to approach Genesis via a heuristic comparison. I will, at least in preliminary outline, set the *Aeneid* as a picture of Roman self-understanding alongside Genesis as a picture of Israel's self-understanding. Despite possible further methodological difficulties, I will go straight to the task. The proof of the pudding will be in the eating. Although this will be, in the first instance, an exercise in ancient historical imagination, I will not remain within the bounds of ancient history, but will also say something about the possible enduring significance of the portrayal of Israel's prehistory within Genesis when we consider this material as Christian Scripture.[2]

Aeneas and Abraham as the Focus of Comparison

My chosen way to exploring the possible fruitfulness of a comparison between the *Aeneid* and Genesis is through a focus upon the resonances between Aeneas and Abraham as archetypal ancestor. Such a specific comparison is not, of course, novel. As, for example, Virgilian scholar W. A. Camps puts it:

> It is distinctive of the role of Aeneas in the *Aeneid* as "first begetter of the Roman race" [*Aen.* 12.166] that he is conceived as the instrument of a

1. "The celebrity of Virgil's works in the Roman world was immediate and lasting" (Richard J. Tarrant, "Aspects of Virgil's Reception in Antiquity" in Charles Martindale, ed., *The Cambridge Companion to Virgil* [Cambridge: Cambridge University Press, 1997], pp. 56-72, here p. 56).

2. My approach is thus rather different from that of Thomas L. Thompson, *The Origin Tradition of Ancient Israel*, JSOTSup 55 (Sheffield: JSOT Press, 1987).

providential purpose. Fate has willed that he should do and suffer what he does to begin the process in history that leads to the birth and rise of Rome. It is "by fate's will" [1.2] that he becomes an exile from his homeland. "Fate holds out the promise" [1.205] to him and his men of a new dwelling-place where they can settle in peace and Troy can rise again under the favour of heaven.[3]

In relation to this Camps points up "a strange analogy" between Aeneas and Abraham: "Like Abraham Aeneas receives a command from heaven; is told to leave his homeland for a destination still unrevealed; has the promise of a great future for his posterity; has the hope of 'an abiding city.'"[4]

Camps further notes the importance of this for the historic reception of Virgil within a Christian civilization where Rome has been of central importance: "The analogy has naturally coloured the story of Aeneas with a symbolic significance for later readers which the poet of the Aeneid could not have foreseen."[5] This — together with the way in which Camps readily depicts Abraham in terms not only of Genesis's own narrative but also of its retelling in the Epistle to the Hebrews — interestingly highlights the important point that origin-stories intrinsically acquire fuller significance, and are read with fresh nuances and perspectives, by virtue of their being received and functioning as significant in new and changed circumstances. Indeed, it is in developed and (from the perspective of tradition history) composite form that they tend to function as authoritative and imagination-forming for as long as they genuinely function as expressions of the identity of living communities. Unfortunately, the positive Christian reception of Virgil, beginning with Tertullian's depiction of Virgil as "naturally Christian" (anima naturaliter Christiana),[6] and perhaps most famously symbolized by Virgil's role as guide within Dante's Divine Comedy, lies beyond our present remit. Nonetheless, an awareness of how reception and recontextualization can affect an origin-story, especially Genesis, will be important within our discussion.

If we focus upon certain similarities between Aeneas and Abraham, this will not be to deny that there are also significant differences. For exam-

---

3. W. A. Camps, An Introduction to Virgil's Aeneid (Oxford: Oxford University Press, 1969), pp. 21-22.

4. Ibid., p. 22.

5. Ibid.

6. Apology, ch. 17.

ple, Aeneas journeys to Italy because he is thereby returning to his homeland whence came his ancestor Dardanus (*Aen.* 3.163-68; 7.205-8, 240-42), while Abraham calls not Canaan, whither he goes, but Aram, whence he comes, "my country" (Gen. 24:4). Nonetheless, the similarities are real and striking, and deserve some pondering.

Comparison 1: Providence, Blessing, Empire, and Warfare

One primary parallel in the portrayals of Aeneas and Abraham, as already highlighted by Camps, is providence, the belief displayed by the people who tell such a story that their existence, as descendants of these ancestors, is part of a divine purpose for the world.

There is, however, a further question as to the precise nature of this divine purpose. Within the *Aeneid* this is initially and most weightily portrayed in book 1, when sovereign Jupiter, "father of men and gods" (1.254), in a lengthy speech reassures Venus, Aeneas's mother, who is anxious for her son in the light of Juno's hostility and all the hardships thereby caused for Aeneas, that the promised good future is indeed assured: Aeneas will defeat his enemies; his son Ascanius/Iulus will build Alba Longa, whence his descendants will rule until Romulus founds a city and gives his name to his people, the Romans. For these Romans, Jupiter says: "On them I impose no limits of time or place. I have given them an empire that will know no end" (1.278-79: *his ego nec metas rerum nec tempora pono: imperium sine fine dedi*).[7] This empire will be ruled by a Caesar, called Julius, who will bring wars to an end and establish peace (1.257-96). Whether this Julius Caesar is the figure we know as Julius Caesar or whether he is Augustus is a moot point (though I incline to the latter), but the victorious and enduring empire under the leadership of a particular family is clear. In a nutshell, the Roman Empire is the sovereign deity's long-term gift to the world, and Romans in the Augustan principate are to envisage themselves as, by virtue of this empire, bringing the peaceful rule of law to the world. So also in a later scene, in the underworld, Aeneas's father Anchises famously says to him: "Your task, Roman, and do not forget it, will be to govern the peoples of the world in your empire. These will be your arts — and to impose a settled pattern upon peace, to pardon the defeated and war down the proud" (6.851-53:

---

7. Here and in other citations I am using the translation of David West in Virgil, *The Aeneid*, rev. ed., Penguin Classics (London: Penguin, 2003).

R. Walter L. Moberly

"tu regere imperio populos, Romane, memento/(hae tibi erunt artes), pacique imponere morem,/parcere subiectis et debellare superbos").[8]

Within Genesis one may compare YHWH's address to Abraham that frames the subsequent patriarchal narrative, and which is periodically repeated (with variations) within the continuing narrative:

> Now the LORD said to Abram, "Go from your country and your kindred and your father's house to the land that I will show you. I will make of you a great nation, and I will bless you, and make your name great, so that you will be a blessing. I will bless those who bless you, and the one who curses you I will curse; and by you all the families of the earth shall bless themselves." (Gen. 12:1-3, with margin reading of last clause).[9]

Here the keynote attaching to the nation that Abraham is to become in relation to other nations is "blessing" (ברכה), and this keynote remains in all the repetitions (18:18; 22:18; 26:4; 28:14). There are two main ways of interpreting this "blessing."[10] One is to see Abraham's descendants as channels of divine blessing to the world. This blessing is Christianly understood by Paul to mean justification for Gentiles through faith in Christ (Gal. 3:6-9); and Christopher Wright, building on the construal of this passage by Gerhard von Rad and Claus Westermann, envisages this passage as an Old Testament counterpart to the Great Commission at the conclusion of Matthew's Gospel.[11] Jews also have read the text in a not dissimilar way. For example, Abravanel in the fifteenth century says:

> All the families of the earth will be blessed, provided for and benefitted on his account, for the world will become aware of God through Abraham and his offspring. Blessing and providence will adhere to any people that adopt his discipline and his faith.[12]

---

8. Cf. also *Aen.* 1.291; 4.231.

9. OT citations in this paper, unless otherwise specified, are NRSV.

10. See more fully my *Theology of the Book of Genesis* (Cambridge: Cambridge University Press, 2009), pp. 141-61.

11. Christopher J. H. Wright, *The Mission of God* (Downers Grove, Ill.: InterVarsity Press, 2006), p. 213.

12. Cited in Moshe Greenberg, "To Whom and for What Should a Bible Commentator Be Responsible?" in *Studies in the Bible and Jewish Thought* (Philadelphia: JPS, 1995), pp. 235-43, here p. 240.

This is clearly a weighty reading, even though I am inclined to think that it is a rereading of the text in the light of a developed awareness of the dignity and responsibilities of biblically rooted faith.

The other main reading is to see Abraham's descendants as paradigms of divine blessing in such a way that others will recognize it, wish it for themselves, and invoke it upon one another — "May you be as Abraham/Israel." It is the latter that I am inclined to see as the prime sense within Genesis, and so most indicative for our concern with Israel's self-understanding as reflected in the text.

Further clarification of the sense in which Israel will be enviable is provided by two other pentateuchal passages. First, YHWH's soliloquy near Sodom sees Abraham as a fitting recipient of the divine will and purpose not only because he will become a great nation by which people shall invoke blessing but also because he is charged to teach his descendants "to keep the way of the LORD by doing righteousness and justice" (Gen. 18:19). The implication appears to be that the greatness will be at least in part constituted by the moral practice of Israel, so that, as Deuteronomy puts it, Israel's observance of torah will constitute an enviable wisdom (Deut. 4:5-8), or, as Isaiah puts it, nations will come to Zion to receive instruction in the ways of justice and peace (Isa. 2:2-4). It is a vision of a people whose way of life is so morally admirable that it attracts inquiry and invites emulation.

The other passage is when Balaam finally arrives to make pronouncements over Israel in the plains of Moab at Balak's behest. Balaam has learned the hard way en route that it is YHWH's word that he must indeed speak,[13] and so his primary depiction of Israel is:

> Here is a people living alone,
>   and not reckoning itself among the nations!
> Who can count the dust of Jacob,
>   or number the dust-cloud of Israel?
> Let me die the death of the upright,
>   and let my end be like his!

> (Num. 23:9-10)

There are three strands to this vision in Balaam's blessing. The first is Israel as a nation not competing with other nations, presumably because it

---

13. I am presupposing the reading of the story in my *Prophecy and Discernment* (Cambridge: Cambridge University Press, 2006), pp. 138-47.

has an unusual and distinctive sense of its identity and purpose. Second, Israel is numerous, in line with YHWH's promise to Abraham (Gen. 13:16; 15:5). Third, Israel is enviable, such that Balaam voices a desire (in effect, invokes a blessing upon himself) to end his days like Israel in a life of integrity.

The aspect of Israel "living alone and not reckoning itself among the nations," which in itself would seem to imply a "peaceable kingdom," needs some comment in the light of the subsequent oracles of Balaam that portray Israel's victorious military prowess. This prowess culminates — in Balaam's unsolicited oracle, after Balak has dismissed him — in the subjugation of Balak's territory, Moab, together with other nearby territories, to an unnamed but apparently specific future ruler of Israel:

> I see him, but not now;
>> I behold him, but not near —
> a star shall come out of Jacob,
>> and a scepter shall rise out of Israel;
> it shall crush the borderlands of Moab,
>> and the territory of all the Shethites.
> Edom will become a possession,
>> Seir a possession of its enemies,
>> while Israel does valiantly.

(Num. 24:17-18)

This figure who is a "star" with a "scepter" is commonly identified by interpreters as David, mainly because David, as recounted in the books of Samuel, conquered much of Transjordan in the way the text envisages. As such he perhaps invites comparison with the "Caesar" in Jupiter's words to Venus, noted above. In relation to Genesis this portrayal of victorious conquest can be read as recalling the mention in the renewed promise to Abraham after the near-sacrifice of Isaac that his descendants "shall possess the gate of their enemies" (Gen. 22:17) — an emphasis that is untypical within Genesis but that resonates to some extent with the portrayal of Abraham as leading a victorious small army in Genesis 14 (which also is untypical, as most commentators observe, but nonetheless is there in the text).

All this raises interesting questions about the interpretation of Genesis within the wider context of the Old Testament. Specifically with regard to the logic of Balaam's oracles,[14] I suggest that the best way of reading them is to

14. I am not here concerned with the interpretation of prophetic oracles elsewhere in the OT, which envisage other nations becoming subservient to Israel.

see Israel's "living alone" and "not reckoning itself among the nations" as the primary vision, the desired norm, and the depiction of the military prowess as what will happen if Israel is provoked.[15] That is, the military prowess is envisaged as defensive and reactive: Balaam's increasing visions of Israel's military prowess are in response to the progressive goading by Balak to curse Israel so that Moab may defeat them. When not provoked, Israel's priorities do not involve conquering other nations, but rather living out a vocation as the people of YHWH, a vocation that should be attractive and enviable.

So too within Genesis, the only account of warfare involving Abraham is defensive: Abraham raises an army only when Lot has been taken captive and needs rescuing. In terms of our comparison between Aeneas and Abraham, therefore, if it is basic to the portrayal of Aeneas that he is outstanding both in religious dutifulness and in military achievement (6.403: *Troius Aeneas, pietate insignis et armis* ["Trojan Aeneas, famous for his devotion and his feats of arms"]), then Abraham is outstanding primarily in the Hebrew equivalent of *pietas,* which is perhaps אמונה ("faithfulness"); he can fight on occasion, when constrained, but it is exceptional, and he is not envisaged as a soldier. The impact of Abraham's descendants on others is to be conceived in terms of the attractiveness of a vocation to a way of living in integrity that enjoys divine blessing and so is sought after by others also.

Nonetheless, within the historical books of the Old Testament, especially Judges, Samuel, and Kings, Israel takes part in warfare much like any other nation; and it is hard to read David's military undertakings in the narrative accounts as primarily defensive. There is thus a real tension, in terms of implications for identity and practice, between Genesis and other parts of Israel's Scriptures. Indeed, the lack of warfare is but one of many consistent differences of ethos between Genesis and much of the rest of the Old Testament, an issue whose handling is hermeneutically demanding.[16]

Within the Old Testament another scene that has resonance with Jupiter's divine bequest of unending empire to Aeneas's descendants, and so also bears comparison with Genesis 12:1-3, is found in the book of Daniel. Here, in a famous visionary scenario (Dan. 7), Daniel initially sees four violent and destructive beasts, who a little later are identified as kings. In addition to this he also sees a court of judgment, presided over by "an Ancient of Days"/"An-

---

15. Thus the text can be read as an implied warning, as in the famous formulation, *nemo me impune lacessit,* "nobody challenges me and gets away with it."

16. I have discussed this more fully in *The Old Testament of the Old Testament* (1992; repr. Eugene, Ore.: Wipf & Stock, 2001). Distinctives of patriarchal religion and life are discussed on pp. 79-104.

cient One," who clearly represents YHWH. Then the beasts lose their dominion, and this dominion is bestowed elsewhere:

> I saw one like a human being [son of man]
>   coming with the clouds of heaven.
> And he came to the Ancient One
>   and was presented before him.
> To him was given dominion
>   and glory and kingship,
> that all peoples, nations, and languages
>   should serve him.
> His dominion is an everlasting dominion
>   that shall not pass away,
> and his kingship is one
>   that shall never be destroyed.

At first sight this might appear simply to be a Jewish equivalent of Jupiter's gift to Aeneas's descendants of "an empire that will know no end," not least since a little later (Dan. 7:27; cf. 7:21-22) the recipient of universal and unending dominion is redescribed as "the people of the holy ones of the Most High," that is, Jewish people in some form. Nonetheless, the text has some surprising dimensions.

First, a major element in the visionary scenario is the contrast between the beasts and the human figure. As such, the vision appears to be of the supremacy of humans, who by implication live in accordance with their intrinsic dignity "in the image of God," over those whose brutalized mode of living forsakes human dignity in favor of being hardly better than animals.

Second, the narrative context of the vision is that of the people of Judah in Babylonian exile, while the likely historical context of composition of the book is that of Antiochus Epiphanes' persecution of the Jewish people in their land. Either way, the vision implies the dominion of those whose present situation seems as far removed from dominion as could be, unlike the Rome of Augustus. Moreover, even if the vision received a certain historical realization in the Maccabean struggles for Jewish independence, those military struggles were to preserve Jewish identity and hardly to dominate over others (with certain limited exceptions). The terminology "that all peoples, nations, and languages should serve him" primarily depicts *God's* sovereignty (cf. Dan. 4:3 [MT 3:33]), without necessarily envisaging a concomitant Jewish military-political reality. The scope of the vision far exceeds the political and military realities of the Maccabean period. When read in the wider canonical context of the Old Testament, it suggests that the form of the dominion is more likely to be that envisaged in Isaiah 2:2-4, that of the universal recognition of the "moral and spiritual"[17] truth within Israel's torah. When read in the light of the New Testament, where the "human figure/son of man" is identified with Jesus, and when Jesus is understood credally as the definitive realization of the true nature both of the human and of the divine, then this draws the Christian reader firmly in the direction of a "moral and spiritual" realization of the promised dominion. In other words, a Christian frame of reference can heighten the nonmilitary dimensions of the Old Testament, and direct one back with renewed attention to the enduring significance of the blessing promised to Abraham and his descendants in Genesis 12:1-3 and 18:17-19, even though its realization for the Christian takes a form not envisaged within Genesis itself.

Comparison 2: Rome and Jerusalem, Capitol and Temple

One memorable moment in the *Aeneid* occurs in book 8, when Aeneas visits the Arcadian king Evander, who takes Aeneas on a tour of his settlement, which is on the site that in the future will be Rome. Among other places, Evander takes Aeneas to the sacred center of future Rome:

> From here he led the way to the house of Tarpeia and the Capitol, now all gold, but in those distant days bristling with rough scrub. Even then a powerful sense of a divine presence in the place caused great fear among the country people, even then they went in awe of the wood and the rock. "This grove," said Evander, "this leafy-topped hill, is the home of some god, we know not which. My Arcadians believe they have often seen Jupiter himself shaking the darkening aegis in his right hand to drive along the storm clouds." (8.347-54)

The site of the Capitol is intrinsically numinous, and although the resident deity cannot be identified by Evander, the clear implication is that it may be no less than the supreme deity, Jupiter himself — as Virgil's reader knows indeed to be the case, for the temple of Jupiter Optimus Maximus, re-

---

17. I use quotation marks because of the contemporary tendency unreflectingly to narrow the sense of these terms, whereas I wish to use them with wide reference.

stored by Augustus in 26 B.C.,[18] stood there in Virgil's day. Aeneas himself, however, performs no ritual action at the site and does nothing other than let himself be guided by Evander; and after the visit Aeneas stays in Evander's modest dwelling, sleeping on leaves — in tacit contrast to the (presumed) more luxurious bedding of Aeneas's illustrious descendant. The literary impact of this scene is that of pleasurable irony, where the implied reader savors knowing fully what the heroes in the story can only anticipate and know in part. Virgil's implied reader is to enjoy the frisson of reenvisaging the grandeur of Augustan Rome as a small settlement surrounded by trees on the banks of a river, in the presence of Augustus's heroic ancestor. Insofar as there is an implication for one's imaginative picture of Aeneas, it is that he "must live for a future he will not live to see."[19]

This visit by Aeneas to the site of Rome suggests comparison with Abraham's two visits to the site of Jerusalem, a city whose Israelite significance still lies in the future for Abraham, since Jerusalem only becomes Israelite after its capture by David (2 Sam. 5:6-10), who then develops it into his capital.

The first visit is the brief meeting with Melchizedek (Gen. 14:18-20), which abruptly intervenes in the episode when Abraham, returning from his military triumph over Chedorlaomer, is met by the king of Sodom. This king of Sodom had earlier been despoiled by Chedorlaomer and now hopes to get something back; in the event he gets more than he expected as Abraham declines any personal profit from his victory. The interleaved encounter with Melchizedek is brief but richly resonant. Since the Salem of which Melchizedek is king is suggestive of Jerusalem (as specifically identified in Ps. 76:2 [MT 3]), Melchizedek here appears as a forerunner of the Davidic dynasty. Moreover, since he is also priest of El Elyon ("God Most High") and blesses Abraham, who acknowledges his authority by giving him a tithe, the figure of Melchizedek suggests not only that Judah's known worship of YHWH in the Jerusalem temple is consonant with ancient antecedents, but also that Jerusalem is a place intrinsically linked with the worship of the sovereign God — as is the Capitol with Jupiter.[20]

The second time Abraham comes to Jerusalem is in Genesis 22, when

18. See, e.g., R. Deryck Williams, *The Aeneid of Virgil, Books 7-12* (Basingstoke: Macmillan, 1973), p. 251.

19. Jasper Griffin, "Virgil," in John Boardman, Jasper Griffin, and Oswyn Murray, eds., *The Oxford History of the Classical World* (Oxford: Oxford University Press, 1986), pp. 616-35, here p. 627.

20. In this context one may usefully reflect upon the recurrent Christian tendency in former ages to build churches on existing pagan sites of worship.

commanded to offer Isaac as a sacrifice in the land of Moriah, a symbolic name like the land of Nod ("Wandering," Gen. 4:16). The name Moriah is probably to be understood as a nominal form from the verb ראה, "see"/"provide," as used elsewhere in the narrative (22:8, 14), especially in Abraham's naming the place of sacrifice "YHWH will see/provide," which is memorialized in a saying about Mount Zion current in the writer's time (22:14b). The specific place of sacrifice focuses the nature of the whole land as a place of vision and provision, and the narrative provides sufficient clues to make clear to an attentive reader that this place of Abraham's sacrifice is none other than the place where subsequently the temple stood in Jerusalem.[21] Interestingly, although the Melchizedek episode envisages a pre-Israel settlement with a priest-king, Abraham's journey and sacrifice take place in a landscape that in narrative terms feels empty apart from the characters specifically mentioned; also Abraham goes where he goes not because it is a recognized place of worship but because he is shown where to go by YHWH (22:2b, 3).

The narrative of Genesis 22 indicates that sacrificial worship in the Jerusalem temple is, as it were, established by Abraham. Although he names the place without establishing a permanent place of worship, which must await David and Solomon, Abraham's act of sacrifice not only anticipates Israel's acts of sacrifice in the place that YHWH chooses, but also interprets them. This, I suggest, is what is at stake in the substitution of a ram for Isaac — not a religio-historical development from child sacrifice to animal sacrifice or a rationale for preferring the latter to the former, but a construal of what animal sacrifice should, in principle, mean: it should represent that which is of genuine and deep value to the worshiper — given Isaac's significance for Abraham as the son he loves and the bearer of God's promise — so that the sacrifice symbolizes the worshiper's own self-giving and self-dispossession before God.

Moreover, the frisson enjoyed by the descendants of Abraham as they encounter this text is surely rather different from that enjoyed by the heirs of Aeneas when they encounter book 8 of the *Aeneid*. Although, to be sure, the implied reader/hearer will know the outcome, and so know that Isaac is preserved to fulfill his role in God's purposes, the logic of the story is that Israel's existence in this story, dependent as it is upon the survival of Isaac as the vehicle of God's promise, is, without exaggeration, on a knife-edge. It is

---

21. This is a commonplace in rabbinic understanding. For a compelling modern restatement see Jon D. Levenson, *The Death and Resurrection of the Beloved Son* (New Haven: Yale University Press, 1993), pp. 111-24; also my *Bible, Theology, and Faith* (Cambridge: Cambridge University Press, 2000), pp. 108-12.

R. Walter L. Moberly

only as Abraham shows willingness to fulfill God's requirement to reduce to ashes and smoke his love for his son and his hope for the future that he is forbidden to sacrifice Isaac and enabled to sacrifice the ram instead. Imaginatively to live through the logic of the story should invest subsequent worship in that place with freighted meaning.

Thus the Genesis portrayal of Abraham at Jerusalem is more charged than the *Aeneid*'s portrayal of Aeneas at Rome. Abraham does not just visit and have to live for a future that he will not live to see, but he foundationally enacts that which Israel will do in the temple and establishes the meaning of sacrificial worship. And the way in which Israel's future appears to be jeopardized here by God himself reminds the reader/hearer that the allegiance required by Israel's God relativizes all usual human preferences and priorities. If Israel is to be true to the heritage represented by Abraham, then their vocation under God is demanding.

Comparison 3: Italy and Israel — Storied Landscapes

Although Aeneas's visit to the future Rome and its Capitol is a high point within Virgil's anticipatory depiction of the Italy known to him and his contemporaries, many other places in Italy and Sicily, and events within Roman history, receive significance from the *Aeneid*'s story. In terms of events, most famously the historic conflicts between Rome and Carthage are rooted in the tragedy of Dido (*Aen.* 4). In terms of places, one example is the town of Acesta/Segesta in Sicily, founded by Acestes at the location of Anchises' tomb (5.700-778).

Within Genesis the site of Sodom may be comparable. In the time of all Genesis's readers/hearers, Sodom, along with Gomorrah, is known to be located in the Jordan Valley in proximity to the Dead Sea, whose high salt content makes life within the sea impossible, and whose environs are thoroughly inhospitable (with the exception of springs, such as En-gedi). How does Genesis suggest that this generally desolate area should be thought about?

Initially, in the Genesis portrayal, the Jordan Valley is the most fertile and inviting part of the promised land; for when Abraham gives Lot first choice of territory, this is the territory that Lot chooses, explicitly because of its obvious attractions:

> Lot looked about him, and saw that the plain of the Jordan was well watered everywhere like the garden of the LORD, like the land of Egypt, in

300

the direction of Zoar. . . . So Lot chose for himself all the plain of the Jordan, and Lot journeyed eastward. . . . Lot settled among the cities of the Plain and moved his tent as far as Sodom. (Gen. 13:10-12)

This is prima facie so surprising, given the known condition of the Jordan Valley in the region of Sodom, that the narrator has to include a clarifying note: "this was before the LORD had destroyed Sodom and Gomorrah" (13:10b). The narrator also includes another ominous note, after mentioning Lot's settling in Sodom: "Now the people of Sodom were wicked, great sinners against the LORD" (13:13). The narrative implication, therefore, is that Lot's choice is guided entirely by the surface attractions of the Jordan Valley, and the moral problems represented by its inhabitants apparently do not bother him.

Everything unravels, however, when YHWH decides, as it were, to check up on Sodom and see if they are as bad as their reputation (18:20-21) — which they are. Whatever the issues about justice in Abraham's famous engagement with YHWH, on the ground in Sodom the angels, when they arrive, encounter, apart from a hospitable Lot, an abusive mob — no righteous inhabitants of Sodom here. Lot is rescued, and the whole episode of his escape is memorialized in the landscape of the Jordan Valley by the pillar of salt that is all that is left of Lot's wife, who, like other renowned figures in a difficult situation (such as Eurydice being rescued by Orpheus from the underworld), could not resist the temptation to look back, despite the warning not to do so.

Thus for the people whose story Genesis is, their land invites reflections of a specific kind: surface attraction may be transient, and can be reduced to barrenness; the bleak area around the Dead Sea is eloquent of the desolate aftermath of sin; the pillar of salt intrigues the imagination with the perils of halfheartedness and delay (as in Jesus' "Remember Lot's wife," Luke 17:32). The Genesis text thus mediates between the people and their land, and gives the land a resonant and iconic quality.

Conclusion: Genesis and Models of the Church

Although both Genesis and the *Aeneid* reflect the societies for which they were written,[22] neither does so in any straightforward way. That is, each has

---

22. There are many other features of Genesis to which attention might be drawn in the course of a comparison with the *Aeneid*. My selection is illustrative and heuristic.

a complexity and depth that resist reductive rendering in terms of any simple social or political or religious ideology, and each has a literary and imaginative richness that requires and repays engagement upon its own terms.
Nonetheless, sociopolitical dimensions are clearly present in the respective
texts, and are significant for our inquiry. Each text is dialectically related to
its envisaged context of reception.

This is clearer for the *Aeneid* than for Genesis, not only because we
know more about the ancient context of the *Aeneid* than that of Genesis, but
also because Virgil is overt and explicit about the relationship between what
is depicted in the text and the envisaged context of reception in a way that the
Genesis narrator is not; indeed, so much in Genesis is left to implication and
suggestion ("let the reader understand") that many readers can overlook or
deny this dimension of the text. Whether Virgil was positive, negative, or ambivalent about Augustus and his imperial project — an issue on which the
jury is necessarily out, given the subtlety and complexity of Virgil's writing,
even if particular verdicts are returned in particular contexts — Virgil's epic
is clearly a poem for an imperial people. If the benefits of peace and civilization are to be brought to the world and sustained, it can only be on the basis
of prolonged and costly military endeavor. Although the British Empire at its
imperial zenith appears, on the whole, not to have appealed to Virgil's vision
of imperial responsibility to undergird its own self-identity,[23] much of Victorian society managed to combine piety with imperial warfare in ways that
one imagines accorded deeply, mutatis mutandis, with their combination in
early imperial Rome. For a people with imperial responsibility there may appear to be little or no intrinsic conflict between *pietas* and *arma* — as arguably remains evident in many parts of the United States today.

Genesis, by contrast, envisages largely unmilitary patriarchs, who have
minority status where they live. Deuteronomy's famous depiction of Israel's
beginnings in terms of ארמי אבד אבי — "an Aramean close to perishing
was my father" (Deut. 26:5, my trans.)[24] — can be taken as a depiction of the
patriarchs generally (and not just Jacob, as often proposed),[25] and well cap-

---

23. "Virgil is rarely deployed explicitly by Victorian translators to justify the Empire"
(Colin Burrow, "Virgil in English Translation" in *Cambridge Companion*, pp. 21-37, here p. 34).

24. Although the translation of אֹבֵד is contested, within Deuteronomy the most
common sense of the verbal root אבד is "die, perish" (e.g., 4:26; 7:20), and the participial
form אֹבֵד has this sense in Job 29:13; 31:19; Prov. 31:6. See the useful discussion of J. Gerald
Janzen, "The 'Wandering Aramean' Reconsidered," *VT* 44 (1994): 359-75.

25. Although "Aramean" is a singular form, it is common to refer to tribal/ethnic
groups in the singular, e.g., Exod. 3:8; Deut. 7:1.

tures "the humble beginnings of Israel in the patriarchal age,"[26] even if one should not interpret this depiction in isolation from its rhetorical context of contrast with plenty in the promised land, the firstfruits of which the worshiper is offering to YHWH (Deut. 26:1-11). Moreover, the likely time of initial reception of Genesis, as the authoritative prehistory to Israel's Mosaic constitution, may be the early postexilic period when Judahites were in a small province in the Persian Empire. Genesis looks to be a text more for marginal imperial subjects than for powerful imperial rulers.

What about Christian churches that read Genesis as the introit to their Scriptures? One will readily see that the prima facie difference between the implied society of the *Aeneid* and that of Genesis resonates with live contemporary debates about the status and role of the churches in contemporary Western culture, debates that often employ the typology of "Constantinian" and "post-Constantinian." According to this polarizing typology, the "Constantinian" church is the establishment church of privilege and power that (among other blind spots) sees no problem with military imposition upon others, while the "post-Constantinian" is the church in a culture that has moved away from Christian assumptions, a church that can beneficially recognize that its reduced role releases it to regain greater moral and spiritual authenticity (and be weaned off imperialistic and militaristic tendencies). If one employs the typology in this context, then Genesis could represent the non-Constantinian pattern of sociopolitical assumptions that the church should reclaim as its own, over against the Constantinian pattern either in the Davidic portions of the Old Testament or in the *Aeneid*. The Constantinian pattern was classically embodied in the medieval church "when Virgil's Rome could be used to evoke the universal authority of the Church."[27]

Yet this typology, despite a certain heuristic value, is simplistic. On the one hand, despite the privileged role given to Abraham by the New Testament, when Genesis is reread in the light of Christ, Christians need to take into account much else in the Old Testament that is suggestive of a more complex and differentiated understanding of the role of God's people within the world. On the other hand, it is naïve to denigrate the Constantinian dimensions of church history, despite all the grievous failings and betrayals,

---

26. Gerhard von Rad, "The Form-Critical Problem of the Hexateuch" (German original 1938), repr. in K. C. Hanson, ed., *From Genesis to Chronicles: Explorations in Old Testament Theology* (Minneapolis: Fortress, 2005), pp. 1-58, here p. 3.

27. Burrow, "Virgil," p. 24.

for they have contributed much of enduring value. The room in which I am writing this essay is in a building adjacent to Durham cathedral and castle; and despite all the deep ambiguities of this historic fortress site on the Durham peninsula that is, in Sir Walter Scott's memorable phrase, "half church of God, half castle 'gainst the Scot," the Norman cathedral remains a witness to a God-oriented and Christ-focused vision of reality. Moreover, that Constantinian history remains part of that continuity of Christian history and living that not only contributes for both better and worse to the identity of contemporary churches, but also constitutes a part of the plausibility structure for our still presupposing that we can and should read the Scriptures of ancient Israel and the early church as our Scripture today.

The kind of suspicion that is directed toward the Constantinian church can also regularly appear in a variety of forms in the reading of Genesis itself. David Clines, for example, has no difficulty in reading Genesis in such a way as to problematize the Abrahamic blessing:

> With blessings like this, who needs curses? . . . One does not need to be a particularly jaundiced reader of Genesis to observe that the best way to receive this famous Abrahamic blessing is to keep out of the way of the Abrahamic family as far as possible.[28]

There are, however, critical criteria both within the Genesis narrative itself and within the frames of reference provided by Jewish and Christian faiths that should make the exercise of appropriation neither wooden nor unreflective but rather a continuing process of complex, corporate, and imaginative discernment. Even if one must recognize doubtful moments on the part of Abraham, not to mention others within his family, the reader hardly need feel ethically obliged to respond in the way Clines proposes.

What then might we appropriately draw from our reading of Genesis alongside the *Aeneid* in terms of its possible implications for contemporary Christian identity? I conclude with three interrelated suggestions. First, there is Abraham's vocation to be the ancestor of a people who respond to God's call and embody God's blessing. Second, Balaam's construal of the Abrahamic vocation in terms of a vision of a people "not reckoning itself among the nations" indicates a noncompetitive nature for the people of

---

28. David J. A. Clines, "What Happens in Genesis," in *What Does Eve Do to Help? and Other Readerly Questions to the Old Testament*, JSOTSup 94 (Sheffield: JSOT Press, 1990), pp. 49-66, here p. 57.

Abraham. Third, Abraham at the holy place of Jerusalem demonstrates important qualities — on his first visit he is ungrasping and generous, on his second visit he is self-dispossessingly obedient to the divine call. These three factors together suggest an approach to construing God's blessing, both for the church and for others, that might perhaps enable the contemporary descendants of Abraham to enter more fully into their inheritance.

Genesis and Human Society:
The Learning and Teaching People of God

Mark W. Elliott

Might one assume that it is legitimate to engage the biblical text of Genesis so as to imagine that its concerns are somehow also those of Christian theology in the twenty-first century? Rusty Reno in his foreword to the Brazos Theological Commentary series is clear that this procedure is indeed just as legitimate as one that comes from a historical or linguistic angle, given that the Bible belongs at least as much to the church and the synagogue as it does to the historian of literature and culture.[1] In the Brazos series, this tends to mean very useful and insightful discussions of Genesis in the light of other parts of Scripture, or in dialogue with great interpreters from the past, rather than the imposition of the key systematic theological topic in the text (or "locus"), which have already been given their content through dialogue with contemporary theories of culture and society. Lurking in the background is the peril of theology as apologetics or, *horribile dictu,* a church theology, which issues from the church's engagement or its *Glaubensdenken* with the present world and its trends of thought. Yet if one's reflection is informed tacitly by the wisdom of the Christian tradition and other parts of the Bible, as in the Brazos way, one might want to view that inner-Christian dialogue as providing the wherewithal for encountering issues such as "human society." We could be guided by how other living theologians have done this, asking how the Bible, traditions of interpretation, and pressing systematic con-

---

1. R. R. Reno, "Series Preface," in *Genesis,* Brazos Theological Commentary on the Bible (Grand Rapids: Brazos Press, 2010), pp. 9-14.

cerns have informed one another: in the case of themes like creation and election in Genesis, names like Moltmann and Pannenberg seem like obvious choices. When it comes to "human society," however, is this at all a topic for theologians?

I would contend that there is a doctrine of "human society" and would venture that any such Christian doctrine is best located somewhere between Providence and Ecclesiology. It concerns a "seeing for" in God that does not have to do specifically with salvation and a "being in society" that, although not unrelated to salvation, is yet distinct from that concern, since God's provision is in one sense for all his human, and perhaps also nonhuman, creation. One might agree with Henry Van Til: "There is between the church and the world a grey, colorless area, a kind of no man's land, where an armistice obtains and one can hobnob with the enemy in a relaxed Christmas spirit, smoking the common weed."[2] Here we have common grace as a social or plural inflection of "image of God" theology. Yet theologians who work in that space between Ecclesiology and Providence are not so easy to come by. Is it simply better then to take what the biblical scholar comes up with, first probing it with conceptual analysis, then applying whatever remains to the world of contemporary thought? This would be the way of the "theological encyclopedia," where theology is conceived as a relay race in which each subdiscipline waits for the baton. The message of Scripture is promoted only after receiving it in a robust way of respectful interrogation. However, this tends to make biblical theology only a "moment" in dogmatics.[3] I intend to return to this problem, but first some account of "society" as reflected in Genesis needs to be given.

2. Henry R. Van Til, *The Calvinist Concept of Culture* (Grand Rapids: Baker, 1959), p. 240, quoted in Richard Mouw, *He Shines in All That's Fair* (Grand Rapids: Eerdmans, 2001), p. 92.

3. Karl Rahner, "B[iblische] Th[eologie] u[nd] Dogmatik in ihrem wechselseitigen Verhältnis," *Lexikon für Theologie und Kirche,* ed. Josef Höfer and Karl Rahner, 2nd ed., 10 vols. (Freiburg: Herder, 1957-1965), 2:449-51, here 450-51: "So haben wir doch in der Schrift u[nd] in ihr allein eine ursprünglich reine Quelle (auch quoad nos u[nd] nicht nur in se)." Scripture must be the *hēgemonikon* of dogmatics, and that refreshing stream which prevents sterility. It is not just a moment in the whole theological task. Herbert Haag glosses this to argue that the dogmatician's job is to interrogate and order church proclamation of doctrine in the light of the central themes of Scripture ("Biblische Theologie," *Mysterium Salutis* 1 [1965]: 440-59, here 459).

Society

Unlike the majority of apocalyptic-sounding modern sociologists, Aristotle was quite sanguine about human interaction: "the state is by nature clearly prior to the family and the individual, since the whole is of necessity prior to the part" (*Politics* 1.2).[4] So it is part of human nature to be supersocial, that is, political. In the case of Genesis, however, the picture is not so clear. The proto-people of God seems to do best when it is both excusing itself and excluding itself from wholehearted integration with the rest of human life, while allowing its heart to beat in time with that of the uncovenanted, not least so that blessing might flow outward. Abraham is called to leave civilization and start again with a very different style of *Lebensform,* as he and his immediate confederates and descendants live a life on the edges of society in a way that could be labeled parasitic as easily as "alternative" (i.e., as one that asks questions of that social order). That "living on the edge" only stops after the end of Genesis when, according to Exodus 1, the Israelites end up as slaves in urban Egypt, whose conditions of unhappiness will take a long time to forget. With the patriarchs' way of life one is reminded of Ferdinand Tönnies's famous distinction between (good) *Gemeinschaft* and (bad) *Gesellschaft.* The introduction to the recent Cambridge translation of this nineteenth-century classic puts it well:

> The relationship itself, and the social bond that stems from it, may be conceived either as having real organic life, and that is the essence of *Community* [*Gemeinschaft*]; or else as a purely mechanical construction, existing in the mind, and that is what we think of as *Society* [*Gesellschaft*]. . . . All kinds of social co-existence that are familiar, comfortable and exclusive are to be understood as belonging to *Gemeinschaft.* We go out into *Gesellschaft* as if into a foreign land . . . the theory of *Gemeinschaft* is based on the idea that in the original or natural state there is a complete unity of human wills.[5]

It is important to remember the late-Romantic provenance of this distinction and to be aware that, in the patriarchal narratives, "covenant" serves to

---

4. N. Luhmann, *Die Religion der Gesellschaft* (Frankfurt: Suhrkamp, 2002), p. 226: "Die Gesellschaft selbst wurde (in sehr unterschiedlichen Begriffsvarianten) als natürliche Ordnung des Zusammenlebens der Menschen oder auch als Ergebnis eines Gesellschafts-ertrages begriffen, der seinerseits durch Natur motiviert sei."

5. Ferdinand Tönnies, *Community and Civil Society,* ed. José Harris, trans. José Harris and Margaret Hollis (Cambridge: Cambridge University Press, 2001), pp. 17-18.

overcome this dichotomy. Individuals, using their free *nous (Kürwille)*, choose to enter into business partnerships, or as kinsfolk regulate their relationships, even turning "family" inside out, for the sake of a larger "cause." That the word *koinōnia* is often translated as *societas* already somewhat blurs the hard distinction drawn by Tönnies.[6] And covenanting from Isaac onward is something one is born into rather than something one chooses, as Michael Wyschogrod reminds us when he speaks of "Jewish nature."[7] In any case proto-Israel is a community stepping hesitatingly on the way to a society. Ironically, it is to be the sojourn in Egypt that will transform their identity. It is often said that the Bible starts in a garden and ends in a city. One could arguably say the same about Genesis 1–11,[8] with far from happy results, but also about Genesis 12–Exodus 12, yet with happier results, as Israel becomes a nation in political terms.

Community, therefore, is more the network of relationships than an entity with spatial coordinates. Kant's equivalent of this was to define *Gemeinschaft* as the ethical realm whereas *Gesellschaft* was the legal one.[9] For Herder *Gemeinschaft* was the spiritual depth dimension of Christianity, *Gesellschaft* the outward casing. Kant saw society as sadly becoming an end in itself rather than the means to a common end; in this context the church needed to play the role of modeling, as those who would, ethically speaking, go the extra mile. Hegel, however, valued "civil society" as that which shuttled between family and state interests and did occupy a particular "space." It is interesting that Schleiermacher used *Gemeinschaft* for communities entered into for the sake of a further common purpose, yet *Gesellschaft* as a higher good in itself, in ways that might remind one of the social philosophy of Jürgen Habermas. For Schleiermacher, the sociable *(gesellig)* impulse would create new *Gemeinschaften,* not least that of God with human nature in the life together of believers, that is, the Holy Spirit.[10]

6. It is perhaps not without significance that the Vulgate chose to translate many of the occurrences of *koinōnia* with *societas,* in the context of fellowship through the Spirit/spirit (as at 1 Cor. 1:9; 2 Cor. 6:14; and 4 times in 1 John 1; the Vulgate of Acts 2:42 is "in communicatione."

7. Michael Wyschogrod, *The Body of Faith: God and the People of Israel* (Northvale, N.J.: Jason Aaronsson, 1996).

8. We might justly label Gen. 1–11 the "Old Testament of the Old Testament of the Old Testament," to borrow and inflate Walter Moberly's coinage (R. W. L. Moberly, *The Old Testament of the Old Testament,* OBT [Minneapolis: Fortress, 1992]).

9. Here I admit my debt in this paragraph to the fine article by Hermann Ringeling, "Gemeinschaft," *TRE* 12 (1984): 346-55.

10. F. D. E. Schleiermacher, *Die Christliche Glaube* (1830/31; repr. Berlin: de Gruyter, 1999), p. 123; *The Christian Faith* (Edinburgh: T&T Clark, 1989), pp. 569-74.

Mark W. Elliott

To mention Tönnies (1855-1936) again, he wrote in an age of de-familiarization and isolation, which to his mind cried out for more "I-Thou" relationships. Similarly the earlier Romantic Richard Rothe (1799-1867) believed that the cold and abstract enlightenment civil society of equal rights of all could be transformed through "community," but added that any boundary between one and the other could be somewhat porous. The Christian community as prophetic, even messianic (in twentieth-century forms, e.g., Jürgen Moltmann), reaches out to the unconvinced through each believer's *Beruf*. Trust is that which makes business partners or fellow citizens into brothers and sisters. Opposed to the thought of legal realists like Henry S. Maine,[11] the covenant of community was the fundamental reality. For Emil Brunner community was not about likeness, but about the unlike drawing together. Resisting this were theologians like Friedrich Gogarten who saw an emphasis on "community" as sectarian, since all human society was already *Gemeinschaft* and should be included, even though it took faith to realize this. However, for Dietrich Bonhoeffer in his *Sanctorum Communio* that was just too abstract, and real communities were required as a first step. Barth's echo of this was *I am as Thou art*.[12] In short, community feels itself driven to make society more like community.

From this short account of mostly German modern theology one senses a real tussle to locate and give dimensions to the space between church and state. Any theological account of society implies an ecclesiology. Traditionally, ecclesiology has been too fixated on questions about the "location of authority," and has been inward-looking — or only outward-looking inasmuch as it serves to claim a jurisdiction that the state will recognize. But properly speaking ecclesiology should always be outward-looking and so include a space for "civil society," teaching its citizens to be good taxpayers, workers, and politicians on account of their identity as members of the invisible body of Christ. The church's concern qua institution with spokespersons will then be with other social groupings, from families to schools and working unions and other forms of civil society, the NGOs and other religious faiths, those entities that are open to the church's coworking. It will be concerned ultimately with families and individuals outside its own boundaries, as it sees itself as the instrument of divine providence toward them, as well as being on the receiving end, as it learns lessons, painfully and joyfully.

11. Henry S. Maine, *Ancient Law: Its Connection with the Early History of Society, and Its Relation to Modern Ideas* (London: J. Murray, 1874).
12. *CD* III/2:248.

Yet in all this, as the matter begins to get properly theological, any *biblical* vision of these matters seems missing. Moltmann rightly called for bringing "friendship" back into the public sphere.[13] Yet, unfortunately in his sixteen-page discussion of Israel's special calling alongside that of the church,[14] there is no sense of the Old Testament, let alone Genesis, helping us with ecclesiology. Similarly, Hans Küng's *The Church* has no references to Genesis.[15] How can we get the biblical concreteness that prevents the doctrines of society and ecclesiology from evaporating into abstraction?

The Contribution of Genesis

Let us return to my earlier positioning of a theology of society between Providence and Ecclesiology. If the foundation of a doctrine of providence is Genesis 22:14 *(Deus providebit)*, as the Puritan William Sherlock suggested, is it a feature of special election, or the kind of thing any human father might expect if he were to call upon God? To use Sherlock's terminology, there is a government of grace as well as a more general government of providence. The former consists in God's actions of sanctifying and disciplining, the latter entails how God disposes us to act toward others so that we are "instruments of Providence."[16] The Joseph story, for example, might be about both types of providence. But isn't it also about the very human means of that providence, the particular individuals and their families, who draw tribes and nations into their slipstream, such that these become blessed through those particular families? To see two distinct stories — a family one and a tribal one — running through Genesis 37–50 seems very odd.[17] Rather, Genesis seems to tell of how special and general providence at some times intersect and at other times run parallel. These stories witness to the reality of contingency with divine grace required for survival. If God is not always impartial, he is at least morally fair and generous.

---

13. Jürgen Moltmann, *The Church in the Power of the Spirit: A Contribution to Messianic Ecclesiology*, trans. Margaret Kohl (London: SCM, 1977), p. 121.

14. Ibid., pp. 133-50.

15. Hans Küng, *The Church*, trans. Rosaleen Ockenden (London: Burns & Oates, 1967).

16. Charles M. Wood, *The Question of Providence* (Louisville: Westminster John Knox, 2008), pp. 31-34.

17. See Lothar Ruppert, *Genesis: Ein kritischer und theologischer Kommentar: 11,27–25,18*, Forschung zur Bibel 98 (Würzburg: Echter Verlag, 2002), p. 95.

Second, Genesis often deals with peripheral people; Melchizedek, Lot, Abimelech, Esau, Laban, and Tamar come to mind. This makes it hard to think of a defined account of the people of God with neat parameters, for which one has to wait until Exodus. The protagonists of Genesis can be understood as receivers of revelation and not merely as spectators, yet actors only in a limited sense. Human society, according to this foundational document, exists as the context for the exercising of faith.

Third, Genesis is not just about family life; or, if it is, it is about family life faithful to God's promises on the way to larger responsibilities in faith. Thus it is pre-ecclesiological and the patriarchs are arguably "everymen," since they do not have much of an idea what it is to be elect and correspondingly precise and self-consciously distinct in their religion, even though they might be preserved from the worst of idolatry.[18] As Thomas Hieke has recently argued, the narratives of Genesis are about a select tribe on the way to an inclusive unity.[19] By keeping things intimate, the genealogies invite readers in, yet only to show them their responsibilities to a growing family of twelve tribes, a dimension that has really outgrown what it means to speak meaningfully of a tribe. So there is a focusing *(Zuspitzung)* after a broadening out *(Ausweiterung),* which demands an ethical unity that supplements, or even overrides, natural unity so as to maintain harmony as life grows more complex and mingles with "otherness." The Genesis *toledot* remind us that "we" all come from the one. If one can run the risk of crassly using terms to denote opposite meanings, then *goy* is the more territorial and outward-looking equivalent of *'am*, which is more essential to the identity of Israel.[20] As Balaam puts it, Israel is one "not reckoning itself among the nations" (Num. 23:9). The upshot is that, from its earliest formation, Israel is to be a society that is both like and unlike the nations. One can use the term "nation" for Israel only analogically, not unequivocally.

What "proto-Israel" achieves in these stories is hardly an ideal. Genesis also tells us that while it might well be natural for people to be social, nevertheless sociopathy and even violence mark their second nature. This is an

18. Compare the pushing of the boundaries of "family" where the awareness of the *bet 'ab* in the *mishpatim* shows a covenantal awareness implying a duty of care for those beyond the immediate household, not least in the "inclusive" use of "brother" as per Deuteronomy; see John Rogerson, "The Family and Structures of Grace in the Old Testament," in Stephen C. Barton, ed., *The Family in Theological Perspective* (Edinburgh: T&T Clark, 1996), pp. 25-42. This is arguably *implicit* in Genesis.

19. Thomas Hieke, *Die Genealogien der Genesis* (Freiburg: Herder, 2003).

20. See R. E. Clements and G. J. Botterweck, "גּוֹי *gôy*," *TDOT* 2:426-33.

emphasis displayed by some Jewish readings of Genesis.[21] As has been said, the outcome is frequently on a knife-edge. Crisis supplies *kairos* to *chronos*, i.e., offers the chance to change one's times, but not without a lot of messiness. Nevertheless, Genesis does give an account of society. Before going any further with that, Christian theological interpreters who have drawn on the wisdom of Genesis for a theology of society need to be heard.

Augustine and His Legacies

The message of Augustine's *City of God* is that the universal way is, contra Porphyry, not to be found by the soul's becoming aware of its divine origin, but in its very earthly need for mediation in the flesh. Augustine claims: "This is the way which purifies the whole man and prepares his mortal being for immortality, in all the elements which constitute a man."[22] It is only by following the Mediator that we are healed (the metaphor of renewal and healing quickly morphs into that of journeying through Jesus as our "way"), and by trusting the words of witnesses in Scripture that we arrive. Augustine writes in the context of iconoclasm of the claims of pagan religion; he speaks of Scripture in its promises and fulfillments being "the right road" leading to the vision of God. The two cities are intermixed but have different origins and destinations. This leads him to the second part of his great work: he outlines how the two cities start with the two classes of angels who made respective *choices*. The two communities of good and bad angels are grist to book 12's conclusion that what makes the difference is not the origin in God's good creation but the goal of their desire, in cleaving or not cleaving to the One without whom they cannot naturally be separated. So also for human society, "God's intention was that in this way the unity of human society and the bonds of human sympathy be more emphatically brought home to humanity, if people were bound together not merely by likeness in nature but also by the feeling of kinship."[23] Again, it is a matter of right desire. Cain's envy was not for political power as in the case of Romulus's slaying of Remus, but in "the diabolical envy that the wicked feel for the good, while they themselves are evil. . . . Goodness is a possession enjoyed more widely

21. E.g., Benno Jacob, *The First Book of the Bible: Genesis,* ed. and trans. Ernest I. Jacob and Walter Jacob (1974; repr. New York: Ktav, 2007).

22. *City of God* 10.32; trans. Henry Bettenson (Harmondsworth: Penguin, 1972), p. 424.

23. *City of God,* 12.22 (Bettenson, p. 502).

by the united affection of partners in that possession in proportion to the harmony that exists among them. In fact anyone who refuses to enjoy this possession in partnership will not enjoy it at all; and he will find that he possesses it in ample measure in proportion to his ability to love his partner in it."[24] This indeed is a theology of trust and friendship, and it finds its echoes in the way that, falteringly yet inexorably, Genesis 12–50 seeks to overcome Genesis 3–11. Human society is possible rather than "given." Yet as such it is precarious, and Augustine stops us from becoming too starry-eyed.

The good, Augustine continues, should not fight among themselves. However, they will fight against the wicked as well as the evil in themselves. The realism is such that the Christian communities are to be models for society as communities of *forgiveness* rather than ones of holiness. Cain's sacrifice was rightly offered but not rightly divided: "when there is not a right distinction of the places or times of sacrifice, or the material of the sacrifice or its recipient, or those to whom the victim is distributed for eating."[25] Augustine interprets "division" to mean "distinction." In the *Questiones in Heptateuchum* Augustine will interpret the same passage as evidence that Cain's problem was that he gave himself to himself. "Thus God showed that although Cain was unrighteous in not 'dividing' rightly, that is in not living rightly, and so did not deserve to have his offering approved, he was much *more* unrighteous in hating his righteous brother without a cause. The remedy is through calming ourselves for our sin to 'return' and be put in its place. . . . We should then look for a cure of those sins, as being our own, instead of condemning them as if they did not belong to us." The idea is to follow the gospel of Genesis as one of second chances.

Augustine, however, tends to glorify the image of the patriarchal "stars" in order to provide good faithful examples for believers to aspire to, rather than represent them as sinners with whose humanity we could easily identify. As had already happened in *Against Faustus,* an attempt to defend the patriarchs on all counts is undertaken.[26] In *City of God* Augustine continues:

> "Jacob . . . was a simple man, living at home." Some of our scholars have translated this as "without deceit" (instead of "simple"). But whether it is rendered "without deceit" or "simple" or (better) "without pretence" — the Greek word is *aplastos* — what deceit is there in the obtaining of a

24. *City of God,* 15.5 (Bettenson, p. 601).
25. *City of God,* 15.7 (Bettenson, p. 603).
26. Augustine, *Against Faustus* 22.48-50.

blessing by a man "without deceit"? What kind of deceit can be shown by a simple man?[27]

For Augustine, Jacob was clearly without deceit, since according to John 1:47 Nathanael was a true Israelite without deceit, by definition. He bears the sins of another and is a lesson to us. The two sons of Isaac and Rebekah are Jews and Christians, but also sinful and faithful Christians. Furthermore, Jacob had no unlawful lust for any of the four women he met in Mesopotamia. In chapters 38–41 of book 16, Augustine continues (to paraphrase): Even the angel he wrestled with was a willing loser, just as Christ was at the hands of the Jews (38). Jacob-Israel was "blessed in those who among this same people have believed in Christ, and crippled in respect of those who do not believe. For the broad part of the thigh represents the general mass of the race" (39).[28] Here I fear that Augustine is not a particularly good reader of Genesis. In any case he concludes (41) that the patriarchal narratives are all about setting aside some and keeping others when we are studying the people of Christ, in whom the city of God is on pilgrimage in this world. Not all who start the journey will finish.

When one reads the chapters dedicated to the early biblical history in *City of God,* it appears that the church appears as the instrument of instruction and judgment upon the world in the here and now. The "body of Christ" imagery is used by Augustine to emphasize the glorious state of the church, contrary to appearances. Related to this is the question of whether membership of the city of God is anything more than journeying in a direction. It might be better to interpret Augustine as talking about the group that are striving *toward* justice and serving God. Or at least that seems obvious in Genesis, a little less so in Augustine, who sounds a strong tenor of ecclesial triumphalism as *ecclesia iudicans,* for all that one admires that it is an *ecclesia in Israel* he respects.[29]

Some versions of Augustine verge on a political Augustinianism that has little hope that the state or society can get us anywhere. Most obvious is the account by Reinhold Niebuhr, who claimed that the possession and exercise of reason can make humans worse by turning instincts of animal survival into self-aggrandizement. And it is religion that makes them much worse,

27. Augustine, *City of God,* 16.37 (Bettenson, p. 700).
28. Bettenson, p. 704.
29. Cf. Joseph Ratzinger, *Volk und Haus Gottes in Augustins Lehre von der Kirche* (Munich: Zink, 1954).

Mark W. Elliott

and explains the conquistador's cruelty. "The larger the group the more certainly will it express itself selfishly in the total human community. . . . The larger the group the more difficult it is to achieve a common mind and purpose and the more inevitably will it be unified by momentary impulses and immediate and unreflective purposes . . . civilization has become a device for delegating the vices of individuals to larger and larger communities."[30] Groups foolishly think of themselves as individuals, and this increases the energy available to egoism. Niebuhr seems to work with an unhelpful view of "society" as taking up a space that, like Soviet Russia, is just too large to be conquered, let alone ruled.[31] The individuals need not bother and should stick to practicing love within small communities. In Niebuhr's opinion, the patriarchal unit was always meant to be a rolling stone gathering no moss.

John Milbank has often seen his ontology and Christian theology of society as continuous with that of Augustine. For him, "salvation is tied to the ultimacy of a particular historical practice, which is ceaselessly *constituted* as a certain 'gaze' upon history and society."[32] Maurice Blondel serves as hero, for, while Karl Rahner naturalizes the supernatural, Blondel calls us to acknowledge the supernatural as the framework for all that happens! One may affirm that each new action is a *novum,* a mystery, in life as in art — and it is human cultural creation. The exchange and process of love is eternal, it is *telos* in itself, and as praxis it is also *poiēsis* and *theōria.* Before the fall there was a constant return to God in grace by the world; post-fall, all human action requires a mediator (here, with Augustine). Blondel perhaps was not quite aware enough that one has to stand within the tradition to see that action is love.

Yet this is to eschew the discourse of justice and reconciliation (a huge theme in Genesis) for the rhetoric of love, and separate what Augustine himself would keep together. Simply accentuating the positive alone will not do if Augustine's influence thereby comes to promote an amount of modern skepticism toward political society (in inverse proportion to ecclesiological idealism), as expressed in modern theories of social contract, with the Christian individual and family rather than the church (as once was) as the interested party. In more modern times, any more positive, Thomistic account such as that of Leo XIII's *Rerum Novarum* was more about work, economy,

---

30. Reinhold Niebuhr, *Moral Man and Immoral Society* (1932; repr. Louisville: Westminster John Knox, 2002), p. 48.

31. Ibid., p. 72.

32. John Milbank, *Theology and Social Theory* (Oxford: Blackwell, 1990), p. 246.

and family and was less about "society." Rodger Charles has the promising title *Christian Social Witness and Teaching: The Catholic Tradition from Genesis to Centesimus Annus,*[33] but he does not give more than one line to Genesis in an Old Testament section that centers (very briefly) on Deuteronomy and the Prophets. The church's business is to model communities of forgiveness, not just preach love and liberty to the state.

Luther

Luther shared the Augustinian diagnosis without its attendant "ecclesiastical" remedy and notions of "mediation." Luther "devoted the last ten years in the classroom (1535-1545) to the exposition of Genesis."[34] For a start, in Luther one detects a notion also to be found in Jewish interpreters: A man finds in a wife more than just a woman, he finds a nest or home that was a stronger building when God made it in paradise.[35] In other words religion begins at home, not in the church. From this secure center much can be achieved or withstood. Curiously Mickey Mattox highlights Luther's "persistent exegetical effort to preserve the central characters of the biblical narrative from charges of serious wrongdoing."[36] That may well be the case some of the time, but in its account of characters making compromises with immoral societies, Mrs. Lot in Genesis 19 is chastened, even if she is not condemned.[37] Faith can make up for a lot of foolishness, as with Sarah and Rebekah. It might be the case that the women and other "supporting actors" in these narratives are those with whom the listener is to identify, since the heroes are just too heroic, in that they are types of Christ. For in Luther's "pastoral" approach, God indulges such things — Rachel likewise was on the way to being holy.[38] Yet to indulge is not to condone, and one of the aims of Luther's commentary was to resist antinomianism in late-1530s Wittenberg.[39] Luther is not

---

33. Rodger Charles, *Christian Social Witness and Teaching: The Catholic Tradition from Genesis to Centesimus Annus* (Leominster: Gracewing, 1998).

34. Mickey L. Mattox, *Defender of the Most Holy Matriarchs: Martin Luther's Interpretation of the Women of Genesis in the* Enarrationes in Genesim, *1535-45* (Leiden: Brill, 2003).

35. Martin Luther, *Lectures on Genesis,* LW 1:132.

36. Mattox, *Defender,* p. 21.

37. Her soul will be saved (see 1 Cor. 5:5). See Luther, *Lectures on Genesis,* p. 300.

38. Jaroslav J. Pelikan, "Die Kirche nach Luthers Genesisvorlesungen," in Vilmos Vatja, ed., *Lutherforschung Heute* (Berlin: Lutherisches Verlaghaus, 1958), pp. 102-10.

39. Cf. James A. Nestingen, "Luther in Front of the Text: The Genesis Commentary," *WW* 14, no. 2 (1994): 186-94.

Mark W. Elliott

so much interested in society as in its ordering through godly people, by which he means those whose being tempted leads them more to rely on the promise of God. As Luther saw it, even the "heroic" patriarchs provided functions in God's history, not moral examples.[40] Commenting on Genesis 41:41 he states: "We know that there are three estates in this life: the household, the state, and the church. If all men want to neglect these and pursue their own interests and self-chosen ways, who will be a shepherd of souls? Who will baptize, absolve, and console those who are burdened with sins? Who will administer the government or protect the common fabric of human society?"[41] Luther, who in his deathbed note wrote of the three holy orders as being farmers-tradesmen, civil servants, and pastors,[42] might have answered his question: "People like Joseph!"

"To be sure, the Egyptians abstained from eating with him; yet he ate in their sight and presence and had been elevated to this preeminence because of his outstanding virtue and piety. . . . For you could see many from among the courtiers who, on being elevated to some position of rank, are immediately eager to elevate and enrich their relatives and friends. But Joseph orders his brothers to be satisfied with their station. . . . Accordingly, before God we are all citizens in hope; but before the world we are sojourners in fact."[43] Luther did not believe in freedom as an ideal so abstract as to be useless, but a community-society overlap.[44] The realm of faith is not a place but oxygen that believers carry with them — out into wider society as part of a vocation that is part of God's own story. From his experience of antinomian super-spiritualism, even in Wittenberg in the 1530s, he came to appreciate the importance of "penultimate things" for the church, even as he aimed to bring the spiritual disciplines into the world: in a phrase *tentatio*,

40. A point well made by Alexander Dobbert-Dunker, "*In summa angustia animi —* Jakobs' Kampf mit Gott: Luthers Auslegung von Genesis 32 auf dem Hintergrund der patristischen Tradition," in Ulrich Heinen and Johann A. Steiger, eds., *Isaaks Opferung (Gen 22) in den Konfessionen und Medien der frühen Neuzeit* (Berlin: de Gruyter, 2006), pp. 239-57.
41. LW 7:312; WA 44:530.
42. See O. Bayer, "Von Wunderwerk: Gottes Wort recht zu Verstehen: Luthers letzter Zettel," *KD* 37 (1991): 258-79.
43. LW 8:103, 107, 115; WA 44:654, 658, 663.
44. "Wieviele Familien und Ehen geraten heute in unlösbare Konflikte, weil die Freiheit fehlt, mit Rücksicht auf den Schwächeren abstrakt berechtigte, emanzipatorische Ziele konkret zurückzustecken?" (R. Schwarz, "Die Bedeutung des Freiheitsverständnisses Luthers an der Epochenschwelle zur Neuzeit," in Karl-Heinz zur Mühlen, ed., *Martin Luther. Freiheit und Lebensgestaltung: Ausgewählte Texte* [Göttingen: Vandenhoeck & Ruprecht, 1983], pp. 228-46, here p. 243).

not *contemplatio,* followed *oratio* and *meditatio.*[45] To use the words of John Maxfield in his insightful book: "As Luther held up his and his students' experiences in the mirror of the narrative of Genesis, he taught his students to see authentic Christian existence not as a withdrawal from the world but as a living by faith in the midst of worldly life."[46]

Mann and Wénin

To stay with Joseph, Helmut Koopmann reminds us that Thomas Mann is true to the biblical account by not just presenting Joseph as the Keynesian FDR, but also as the exile-withstanding soul of the home nation.[47] In Mann's reading, it is a corrupted Egyptian society combined with a selfish individual in Egypt that creates the tragedy of Potiphar's wife. For Koopmann, the Joseph story in Mann's interpretation is about anti-fascist humanity as represented in Israel/true Christianity. Mann was about a humanizing of myth. Thus the counterworld is sketched out in all its exotic glory, color, and richness of personal interaction, and that is so different from the modern. It is not an exclusively Jewish world, but it is cosmopolitan and open. Koopmann finds something refreshing in that, whereas Claus Westermann thinks Mann suffocates the narrative, so that the last words in his great commentary are: "The period in which the narrative itself will be heard still lies before us."[48] Friedemann Golka sees Mann as providing a way of reading Genesis that values the final form (Gen. 38 and 49 belong to the rest), the scriptural intertextuality (including placing *egō eimi* on Joseph's lips), and an ancient Near Eastern mythic background.[49]

Perhaps the attention to the last of these in Mann's work has obscured

---

45. Cf. Bernd Moeller, "Die frühe Reformation in Deutschland als neues Mönchtum," in B. Moeller and S. E. Buckwalter, eds., *Die frühe Reformation in Deutschland als Umbruch* (Gütersloh: Gütersloher Verlagshaus, 1998), pp. 76-91, here p. 88, cited in John A. Maxfield, *Luther's Lectures on Genesis and the Formation of Evangelical Identity* (Kirksville, Mo.: Truman State University Press, 2008), p. 113.

46. Maxfield, *Luther's Lectures*, p. 219.

47. Helmut Koopmann, *Thomas Mann* (Göttingen: Vandenhoeck & Ruprecht, 1975). See also his *Thomas Mann–Handbuch* (Stuttgart: A. Kröner, 2001).

48. Claus Westermann, *Genesis 37–50*, trans. John J. Scullion, CC (Minneapolis: Augsburg, 1986), p. 253.

49. Friedemann W. Golka, *Joseph. Biblische Gestalt und Literarische Figur. Thomas Manns Beitrag zur Bibelexegese* (Stuttgart: Calver, 2002), pp. 206-15.

what seems the more salient point of Genesis 37–50, which is the ecclesial-social: the patriarchs take people with them, literally and metaphorically. They set themselves up for a fall, for judgment. And it comes. Genesis 34, 37, and 38 lead to Genesis 39 and dire emergency. The gloom and anguish are borne with dignity. The irony of the story serves to arouse smiling sympathy and forgiveness even while it ridicules them. Their story is not a tragedy, and just as the logic of Romans 8 (all things work together for good) leads to a discussion of a younger brother benefiting from the older brother's stumbling (Romans 9), so too with the twelve patriarchs in the Joseph story, where the Gentile world is the locus of their salvation, and not in a political way, but in the manner of *socii*.

The story is surely one of repeated interventions of God, to judge and to bless at the same time, to reverse expectations, to bring the cleverness and latent piety of a Joseph into service of the world. If Genesis 37–50 is a *Bildungsnovelle,* then the *Bildung* is one of equipping for service. André Wénin argues that the Joseph story is thus an education in learning the value of service or perhaps rather the true nature of friendship, through overcoming the violence of desire and thinking of how to think of others in close relationships.[50] Preference is indeed a problem, since a little evil arose out of Jacob's own psychological weakness and grew to have disastrous ramifications for many people. Yet by human choices, finding where a good has given force to evil, humans have a chance to amend, and good nevertheless rebounds.[51] To my ear, however, the verse to which Wénin appeals, Genesis 50:20, seems to envisage the human characters as joyful instruments, not agents.[52] Here amid all of Wénin's talk of "agency" reading Luther might be salutary.

Conclusions

While recognizing that sociology can show us the latent structures behind the appearances of things and behaviors, it is interesting that sociologists often seem gloomier than theologians. They lament that symbols of meaning and transcendence through secularization have become flexible, polyvalent, then

50. André Wénin, *Joseph ou l'invention de la fraternité* (Brussels: Lessius, 2005), p. 330: "le récit se déploie comme une sorte d'itinéraire vers la subversion du mal."

51. Ibid., p. 329.

52. See Bernhard Lang, *"Joseph in Egypt": A Cultural Icon from Grotius to Goethe* (New Haven: Yale University Press, 2009).

empty. Hans Urs von Balthasar thought sociology too depressive. In Ralf Dahrendorf's well-known saying: "society is the alienated persona of the individual, *homo sociologicus,* a shadow that has escaped the man to return as his master."[53] If tragedy is the worst that can happen, then God's redeeming presence is available: *homo sociologus* is a myth and each person has their destiny to waste or redeem in the presence of the Eternal, as each self is called to their role (as in Paul Claudel). However, that seems to leave a lonely gap between self and role, with the social offering nothing that could endure. Yet as Émile Durkheim put it: More society, less anomie: "no-one commits suicide during wars." But of course wars involve belief, being persuaded. Society then is not only to be analyzed, but to be made, not without the influencing and conquering of spiritual forces. We might welcome the "Afterword" by Gregory Baum to a reissued classic work: "Against the postmodern emphasis on otherness, I propose that, in face of the contemporary ideologies of exclusion, every sentence acknowledging the difference between people must be followed by a sentence that recognizes the similarity between them."[54]

Scripture in Genesis can inspire us: Jacob was a businessman, and Joseph was a manager. As Richard Roberts reminds us, since the mid-1990s, "Line-management structures have become almost identical with society itself. The manager has risen to become a member of the elite. Human resources management . . . is concerned far more with understanding and then linking individual human motivation with corporate goals through active *transformation* and *synthesis.*"[55]

This is more positive than the assessment by Anthony Giddens, that prophet of assessment. According to James Beckford, reflexivity is for Giddens the "constant monitoring and adjustment of ideas and practices in the light of newly acquired information. This generates uncertainty and instability. . . . He argues that it is now more difficult for individuals to cultivate a continuous thread of self-identity in the face of the needless mutability of time/space connections, the constant recombinations of social relationships out of context and the perpetual exposure of the self to fresh information about itself."[56]

53. Ralf Dahrendorf, *Essays in the Theory of Society* (Palo Alto: Stanford University Press, 1968), p. 44.

54. Gregory Baum, *Religion and Alienation: A Theological Reading of Sociology* (Maryknoll, N.Y.: Orbis, 2007), p. 234.

55. Richard H. Roberts, *Religion, Theology and the Human Sciences* (Cambridge: Cambridge University Press, 2002), p. 182.

56. James Beckford, "Postmodernity, High Modernity and New Modernity: Three

Do Joseph-like theologians have a part to play in shaping and caring for society and its anxieties? Or should they just play their own game? For the theology-church gap is almost as wide, in places arguably wider, than the theology-society gap. The Joseph of Genesis 50 is revealed as a great teacher, having been a great administrator, in a way analogous to Ambrose. He is possibly "in place of" yet also "under" (תחת) God (Gen. 50:19). God's next step, in Exodus, was to teach those who were called out to worship and listen, and that was perhaps even more of a challenge. The experience of grace in learning the hard way on the edges of society is the matrix for receiving doctrine and ethics in order to pass them on.[57] Called out so as to represent and intercede for the larger number, the church continues its mission outward as it carries on the task of the *ekklēsia*.

_____

Concepts in Search of Religion," in Kieran Flanagan and Peter C. Jupp, eds., *Postmodernity, Sociology and Religion* (London: Macmillan, 1996), p. 34.

57. Hans-Josef Klauck, "Gemeinde und Gesellschaft im frühen Christentum: Ein Leitbild für die Zukunft?" *Antonianum* 76 (2001): 225-46. Klauck argues that *ekklēsia* rather than *synagōgē* is used to name the church because the echo of "the public square" one would have heard in that term was important.

Food, Famine, and the Nations:
A Canonical Approach to Genesis

Stephen B. Chapman

For a canonical approach to Genesis, a pressing question is that of the relationship between the three major blocks of material now found within the book: the primeval history (Gen. 1–11), the ancestral narratives (Gen. 12–36), and the Joseph story (Gen. 37–50). Each of the three has maintained its own particular literary coherence within the book's received shape. But at the same time some kind of logic has presumably led to their combination and joint transmission. So how are they to be understood together?

One possibility is to search for common themes and motifs throughout the book, and in this literary fashion to develop a reading of the book as a whole.[1] But the identification of such themes can be slippery and lack sufficient critical control, especially from the perspective of historically ori-

---

1. For a few such efforts see Robert L. Cohn, "Narrative Structure and Canonical Perspective in Genesis," *JSOT* 25 (1983): 3-16; J. P. Fokkelman, "Genesis," in Robert Alter and Frank Kermode, eds., *The Literary Guide to the Bible* (Cambridge: Belknap/Harvard University Press, 1987), pp. 36-55; Everett Fox, "Can Genesis Be Read as a Book?" *Semeia* 46 (1989): 31-40; Terence E. Fretheim, "The Book of Genesis," in *NIB* 1:319-677; Sidney Greidanus, "Detecting Plot Lines: The Key to Preaching the Genesis Narratives," *CTJ* 43, no. 1 (2008): 64-77; A. K. Jenkins, "Genesis 12 and the Editing of the Pentateuch," *JSOT* 10 (1978): 41-57; Thomas W. Mann, "'All the Families of the Earth': The Theological Unity of Genesis," *Int* 45, no. 4 (1991): 341-53.

I would like to thank the organizers of the Genesis conference for their hard work and hospitality. I am particularly grateful for instructive conversations with Gary Anderson and Terence Fretheim following the delivery of my paper.

ented scholarship. Another possibility is to tie the meaning of Genesis to a historical reconstruction in which the three blocks of material (and their component sources) are sequenced and pegged to certain points within a broader reconstruction of Israelite history and religion. But hypothetical historical reconstructions have proven no less slippery in the course of the twentieth century and are now especially fragile in light of current debates about pentateuchal formation and the archaeology of preexilic Israel.

What a canonical approach attempts to do is to combine the best of both these possibilities, but to do so in a manner that defends against their methodological vulnerabilities. Rather than working exclusively on the basis of content or theme, and thereby with disregard for the problem of anachronism, a canonical approach looks for *formal* literary features indicative of larger patterns or perhaps even a conceptual framework for the entire book. But instead of using such features to isolate the earliest constitutive sources of the book and then elaborating a theory about how they may have been coordinated, a canonical approach begins and lingers at the level of a biblical book's most decisive structural features, which are concrete and not reconstructed, while at the same time probing back more cautiously into the book's likely prehistory (or "depth dimension").

Brevard Childs's analysis of Genesis therefore took as its starting point the book's ten *toledot* formulae,[2] which cross the major literary divisions of the book and thus, he argued, "structure the book of Genesis into a unified composition and . . . make clear the nature of the unity which is intended."[3] For Childs the theological point of the *toledot* structure was "to describe both creation and world history in the light of the divine will for a chosen people."[4] Yet it bears noting that Childs also perceived variation within the *toledot* formulae and was perfectly willing to entertain historical explanations for it. For example, Childs treated the formula in Genesis 2:4a as a secondary extension of an older Priestly series beginning in 5:1. Having determined on form-critical grounds that the *toledot* formulae are always introductory expressions, Childs argued that 2:4a was not originally of a piece with Genesis 1 or with Genesis 5, both Priestly passages, but repre-

2. The expression "these are the generations" is found eleven times throughout Genesis (2:4; 5:1; 6:9; 10:1; 11:10, 27; 25:12, 19; 36:1, 9; 37:2), and thus serves as a bookwide structuring device. Because the appearance of this expression in Genesis 36:9 merely recapitulates 36:1, there are ten structurally significant occurrences in the book.

3. Brevard S. Childs, *Introduction to the Old Testament as Scripture* (Philadelphia: Fortress, 1979), p. 146.

4. Ibid.

sented instead a later "linking together [of] the P and J creation accounts."[5]
Indeed, Childs also saw in this linking, with the P account (1:1–2:3) coming
first and the J account (2:4b–3:24) introduced by a *Priestly* formula, the sub-
ordination of J's creation story to P's as the text shifts to "unfolding the history of mankind as the intended offspring of the creation of the heavens and
the earth."[6] Childs also identified the importance of the often-repeated
promises to the ancestors and the prominence of genealogies for a canonical
approach to Genesis,[7] both of which in his view shape the book in a
forward-looking manner and point ahead to the book of Exodus.[8]

Using Childs's work as a model, I would like to raise the prospect of
another network of formal features and motifs in Genesis. Here I can only
chart some tentative lines. My starting point is Genesis 26:1a: "Now there
was a famine in the land, *besides the former famine that had occurred in the
days of Abraham*" (NRSV, my emphasis). This introductory statement provides a clear reference from one place in the book to another, specifically to
12:10a, "Now there was a famine in the land." Because the initial phrases are
identical in Hebrew (ויהי רעב בארץ) and because of further similarities in
both chapters, the reference to "the former famine" in 26:1a appears to be
self-conscious literary allusion rather than simply a reference to a remem-
bered event in cultural memory. In fact, in 12:10 famine is introduced as the
reason for Abram to travel to Egypt and thus provides the setting for the first
of three "wife-sister" (or "ancestress in danger") stories in Genesis, the third
of which appears in Genesis 26 (cf. 12:10-20; 20:1-18; 26:6-11). There is also a
key difference: in Genesis 26 God tells Isaac *not* to go to Egypt in spite of the
famine, and therefore Isaac settles in Gerar.[9]

This literary relationship between Genesis 12 and Genesis 26 is a commonplace of historical-critical study. However, the standard interpretation of
their common introductory statement reduces its significance to that of evidence for the priority and sequence of the three wife-sister stories. Thus 26:1a

---

5. Ibid., p. 149.
6. Ibid., p. 150.
7. Ibid., pp. 150-53.
8. Ibid., pp. 154-58.
9. However, there may well be an implication of disobedience in Gen. 12. Abram receives no divine instruction to proceed into Egypt. On the contrary, he appears to slight
God's gift of the land of Canaan, which immediately precedes his departure (12:7-8). On this
reading Abram's concern about famine and his relocation to Egypt might be indications of
his lack of trust in God. The contrast with Isaac would then be: Abram is not told to go to
Egypt but goes disobediently; Isaac is told not to go to Egypt and obediently stays put.

is typically taken to be an indication that the wife-sister story of Genesis 12 is the more original, and that the wife-sister story in Genesis 26 has been developed on analogy with it.[10] This judgment may well be accurate, but it ignores the possibility that the two cross-linked allusions to famine also exercise a broader function within the present form of the book as a whole.[11]

Such a possibility gains force from the realization that there are other structural references to famine (רעב) within Genesis, most notably in 41:53-57; 42:5; 43:1; 47:13, 20.[12] These later famine notices are particularly noteworthy because they also continue to describe the famine in relation to "land," as in 12:10 and 26:1, and because they employ heightening terms like "strong" (חזק) and "severe" (כבד). Furthermore, 41:57 features a concluding statement focused on famine, and 42:5 and 43:1 offer introductory formulae using the famine motif. Such formal markers underscore the importance of famine for the organization of the narrative. Thus in both Genesis 43 and 47 a "severe famine in the land" is said to be responsible for the presence of Joseph's family in Egypt, echoing and deepening the relationship between famine and Egypt already established in both Genesis 12 and 26.

This patterning cuts across the standard critical division between the ancestral narratives and the Joseph story, implying a larger literary framework for both.[13] In addition, as Claus Westermann also noted briefly, the

---

10. As in Claus Westermann, *Genesis 12–36*, trans. John J. Scullion, CC (Minneapolis: Augsburg, 1985), p. 161, who notes, however, that a number of eminent scholars (e.g., Ewald, Kuenen, Wellhausen, Eissfeldt, Noth) have disagreed, preferring to see Gen. 26 as the original version of the story. Westermann cites authorities such as Dillmann, Procksch, Gunkel, and von Rad for the priority of Gen. 12, with the conclusive demonstration being by Van Seters. For Gen. 12 as the story's earliest literary form, see also Josef Scharbert, *Genesis 12–50*, NEchtB (Würzburg: Echter Verlag, 1986), p. 129, although in a mediating move he argues that the tradition behind the story nevertheless has its earliest roots in the Isaac tradition. Horst Seebass, *Genesis II/2* (Neukirchen-Vluyn: Neukirchener Verlag, 1999), p. 280, resists interpreting the relationship between the two passages as primarily redactional, observing that famines happen frequently in the land of Israel. Still, he terms the Abraham literary tradition "more extensive" (*umfangreicher*).

11. Mark E. Biddle, "The 'Endangered Ancestress' and Blessing for the Nations," *JBL* 109 (1990): 599-611, similarly stresses the literary logic of the three wife-sister stories within Genesis as a book, rather than their hypothetical prehistory. He views them as all relating to the ancestral promise.

12. Other references to famine (רעב) occur in Genesis but mainly in discourse, so that although they contribute to the theme their formal significance is not as great (41:27, 30-31, 36, 50; 45:6, 11; 47:4). The same is true of רעבון in 42:19, 33. Note that these famine references cluster in the Joseph narrative.

13. For a discussion of critical issues involving the relationship between the Joseph

threat of famine is associated throughout the Old Testament with the notion of God as one who provides food,[14] a conception of God found already in the treatment of creation in Genesis 1 and 2.[15] Terence Fretheim argues that the concession to eat meat in Genesis 9 also implies famine.[16] So famine and food, as two sides of the same motivic coin, emerge as a doubled preoccupation in all three of the book's major sections. This motif is then explicitly thematized by its repetition and formal structural significance. In other words, there is an evident self-consciousness about its place and function within the overarching narrative.

An even more significant aspect to these famine references appears at the conclusion of Genesis 41, as Joseph's prophecy of seven lean years following seven years of plenty finally comes to pass. Here it is emphasized that the famine affected "*all* the lands" while "in *all* the land of Egypt there was bread (41:54, my trans., my emphasis), with the result that "*all* the world came to Egypt to receive rations, to Joseph" (41:57, my trans., my emphasis). The summative use of "all" has climactic rhetorical force. Moreover, in the years of plenty Joseph had collected grain in such quantity that it is said to have been "like the sand of the sea" (כחול הים, 41:47-49). Both the mention of "the lands" (הארצות) and this simile also recall the book's repeated ancestral promise, beginning in 12:1-3 ("I will make of you a great nation . . . and in you all the families of the earth shall be blessed," NRSV [or: "bless themselves," NRSV margin]).[17] In the reiteration of the ancestral promise found

---

material and the rest of Genesis, see Friedemann W. Golka, "Genesis 37–50: Joseph Story or Israel-Joseph Story?" *Currents in Biblical Research* 2, no. 2 (2004): 153-77. Lindsay Wilson, *Joseph, Wise and Otherwise,* Paternoster Biblical Monographs (Carlisle: Paternoster, 2004), pp. 215-36, argues persuasively for close connections between the Joseph material and the rest of Genesis, as well as Exodus.

14. For example, Ps. 65:9 (MT 10). James L. Mays, "'Maker of Heaven and Earth': Creation in the Psalms," in William P. Brown and S. Dean McBride Jr., eds., *God Who Creates: Essays in Honor of W. Sibley Towner* (Grand Rapids: Eerdmans, 2000), pp. 75-86, here p. 81, strikingly describes Ps. 65 as envisioning "the world as the farm of God."

15. Westermann, *Genesis 12–36,* 163. Cf. Ellen F. Davis, *Scripture, Culture and Agriculture* (Cambridge: Cambridge University Press, 2009), pp. 48-51.

16. Terence E. Fretheim, *God and World in the Old Testament* (Nashville: Abingdon, 2005), p. 84.

17. Both translations are syntactically possible; for further discussion of the issues involved see Keith Grüneberg, *Abraham, Blessing and the Nations: A Philological and Exegetical Study of Genesis 12:3 in Its Narrative Context,* BZAW 332 (Berlin: de Gruyter, 2003); R. W. L. Moberly, *The Theology of the Book of Genesis* (Cambridge: Cambridge University Press, 2009).

in 22:17 and 32:12 (MT 13) the same simile is employed with reference not to grain but to progeny — *and these are the only three uses of the expression "sand of the sea" in Genesis* (22:17 [slightly expanded]; 32:12; 41:49).

At the dramatic highpoint of the Joseph story in Genesis 45, this connection between ancestral promise and contemporary sustenance is made explicit. Joseph says: "for God sent me before you to preserve life. These two years the famine has been in the land; and there will be five more years without plowing and harvest. God sent me before you to preserve you as a remnant on earth, and to keep you alive by a great deliverance" (45:5-7, my trans.). From this vantage point, Joseph's provision of grain for his family, and by extension for a hungry world, is not only revealed to have a place within the divine providential scheme, it is also shown to be a specific fulfillment of God's promise to the ancestors: God uses Joseph successfully "in order to preserve a numerous people" (50:20 NRSV). Hand in hand with the recurring theme of famine in the Joseph cycle is thus the emphasis on food.[18]

This interpretive sketch provides a confirmation, and perhaps a correction, to the work of Bruce Dahlberg, who once argued for the Joseph story as "a completion and consummation to everything in the book of Genesis preceding it."[19] Dahlberg formulated his remarks as a direct rebuttal to the famous first line of Gerhard von Rad's Genesis commentary: "Genesis is not an independent book that can be interpreted by itself."[20] To the contrary, Dahlberg insisted, the Joseph material does not simply serve as a bridge from the ancestral stories to the Exodus narrative. The Joseph narrative instead functions as part of an inclusion in which the events in Eden are reversed and resolved. Where the serpent had said, "You will be like God" (3:5 NRSV), Joseph asks, "Am I in the place of God?" (50:19

18. On the pervasive use of food imagery in the Joseph cycle, see also Katie M. Heffelfinger, "From Bane to Blessing: The Significance of Food in Genesis 37–50," in Dennis Olson and Diane Sharon, eds., *Rounded Stones: Literary Readings of Genesis Narratives*, SBL Symposium Series (Atlanta: SBL, in press). For a comparison of the different terms used for food and patterns of their occurrence in this narrative, see Donald B. Redford, *A Study of the Biblical Story of Joseph (Genesis 37–50)*, VTSup 20 (Leiden: Brill, 1970), p. 173. Redford concludes that food terms are used largely synonymously throughout the narrative. However, he also observes that instances of the term "bread" cluster in Gen. 47.

19. Bruce Dahlberg, "On Recognizing the Unity of Genesis," *TD* 24, no. 4 (1976): 363.

20. Gerhard von Rad, *Genesis*, trans. John H. Marks, rev. ed., OTL (Philadelphia: Westminster, 1972), p. 13. For additional historical-critical reasons to oppose von Rad's judgment, see David L. Petersen, "The Genesis of Genesis," in André Lemaire, ed., *Congress Volume: Ljubljana 2007*, VTSup 133 (Leiden: Brill, 2010), pp. 27-40.

NRSV).[21] While death enters the world because of the events in the garden, Joseph preserves life. Dahlberg suggested that Joseph in fact accomplishes both of the main tasks given within the creation accounts: the Priestly charge for humankind to have dominion over everything (1:28) and the Yahwistic principle that the human being is to till the garden and keep it (2:15). Dahlberg commented: "Turning to the story of Joseph in Egypt, we see that he does on a grand scale what Adam was created to do but did not, back in the beginning."[22] In other words, Joseph fulfills the creation mandate that Adam had been given but betrayed.

As part of his interpretation, Dahlberg also mentioned famine, and the way in which famine functions in Genesis as a threat to Israel's survival. But then Dahlberg drew another, less satisfying, typological parallel between Joseph and Noah, with the Joseph story serving as a counterpart to the flood account.[23] What Dahlberg overlooked was the significance of the threat of famine in the ancestral narratives, and the relationship between the ancestral promise and food, as I have already described. Dahlberg did call attention to the importance of 39:5 as an explicit fulfillment of the promise in 12:3, which he took as a reflexive (= "bless themselves"). Yet it is not a reflexive sense that one gets from 39:5: "The Lord blessed the Egyptian's house for Joseph's sake; the blessing of the Lord was upon all that he had, in house and field" (NRSV). In the context of the entire book, such blessing has to be viewed as illustrating the outworking of God's promise to Abram. But if 39:5 is a fulfillment of that promise, then a nonreflexive understanding of God's promise to Abram is evident.

To supplement and slightly reframe Dahlberg's interpretation of Genesis, I would like to draw upon the work of M. Daniel Carroll R., who relates the term "families" (משפחת) in 12:3 back to the "table of nations" in Genesis 10 (vv. 5, 18, 20, 31, 32) so that, as he puts it, "whatever else the call of Abram might entail, at the very least one can see that it is designed to reach

---

21. Dahlberg, "Recognizing," p. 363. Since the same question appears in Gen. 30:2 on the lips of Jacob, the link between Joseph and Adam is not as tight in this instance as Dahlberg maintained. See further Eric I. Lowenthall, *The Joseph Narrative in Genesis* (New York: Ktav, 1973), p. 156.

22. Dahlberg, "Recognizing," p. 364. Tim Stone's contribution to this volume, "Joseph in the Likeness of Adam: Narrative Echoes of the Fall," also illustrates the prominence of the "dominion" motif within the Joseph cycle.

23. Although Dahlberg does not mention it, one stronger argument in favor of such a parallel is the way that להחיות in Gen. 45:7 echoes 6:20. On this point see Lowenthall, *Joseph Narrative*, p. 104. Lowenthall in turns credits Benno Jacob with the insight.

'all' the peoples descended from the son of Noah."[24] Carroll stresses the material and spiritual aspects of the blessing the ancestors receive, and the way in which this blessing affects the lives of others in the ancestral narratives. Thus by coming to Lot's aid in Genesis 14 Abram defeats Chedarlaomer and gains freedom for five kings.[25] Abram intercedes for Sodom, and Lot and his family are rescued (18:22-33; 19:29). Abram again intercedes on Abimelech's behalf (20:17-18). When Jacob serves Laban, Laban's flocks multiply (29:20, 27-30; 30:29-30). Carroll observes: "Potiphar's household, Joseph's fellow prisoners, the head jailer, Pharaoh, and all of Egypt are all favored because of the character and diligence of Joseph."[26] Indeed, several of these figures also learn to "recognize the presence and hand of God": for example, Abimelech in 21:22-24 (because of Abram) and 26:26-29 (because of Isaac); Laban in 24:31, 50 (because of Abraham's servant) and 30:27; 31:29, 50, 53 (because of Jacob); and climactically Pharaoh in 41:39 (because of Joseph). Carroll concludes: "Those who deal with the patriarchs not only see the benefits enjoyed by his people, [but] some of them also come to acknowledge Yahweh as the bestower of blessing."[27] According to this logic, as much as Joseph can be viewed as antitype to Adam, he is even more the culmination and fulfillment of the ancestral blessing beginning with Abram. Food in turn emerges as one crucial sign of the material aspect of that blessing — from its presence in the creation accounts all the way to Joseph's stockpiles of grain.

A recurrent threat to this blessing is represented by famine, which confronts both Abram's family and the other families of the world. When it comes to food and famine, all people are similarly dependent upon and vulnerable to the agricultural health of God's creation. Perhaps partly for this reason, food also figures centrally in the conflict between Jacob and Esau (25:29-34; 27), which is said to be about "two nations" (25:23).[28] Food is something nations must share. Yet Joseph finally feeds the *world* (41:57) at the same time that he feeds, preserves, and increases the size of his own fam-

24. M. Daniel Carroll R., "Blessing the Nations: Toward a Biblical Theology of Mission from Genesis," *BBR* 10, no. 1 (2000): 17-34, here 20.

25. See ibid., p. 28, for this and the following examples. See also Fretheim, *God and World*, p. 107.

26. Carroll, "Blessing," p. 28.

27. Ibid., p. 30.

28. There is no little irony in the later struggle against famine by Jacob and his family, given that the blessing he once stole from Esau had promised "the fatness of the earth, and plenty of grain and wine" (Gen. 27:28 NRSV).

ily. God's faithfulness to Joseph and his family is genuine faithfulness to them,[29] and simultaneously faithfulness to the whole world *through* Joseph and his family. In this manner the ancestral promise (12:3) is explicitly fulfilled: "The Lord blessed the Egyptian's house *for Joseph's sake*" (39:5 NRSV, my emphasis).[30] This thematic link is also made explicit in the scene in which Jacob blesses Pharaoh (Gen. 47:7-10).[31] In order to make sure the point is understood, Targum Pseudo-Jonathan expands the biblical account by adding the content of Jacob's blessing, which relates to fertility and famine: "May it be the will [of heaven] that the waters of the Nile be full, and that the famine may cease from the world in your days."[32]

Yet the blessing also goes in both directions. J. Gerald Janzen makes the point that inclusion of the Egyptians in mourning rites for Jacob (Gen. 50) illustrates the reciprocal blessing of the nations upon Abraham's family, also in fulfillment of 12:1-3:

> On the one hand, Joseph has been a blessing to Egypt, in saving Egypt from the famine that is ravaging the earth. In this respect he has fulfilled God's charge to Abraham to "be a blessing" (12:2). One may assume, then, that the Egyptians' mourning, and their subsequent state escort of Jacob's family for the interment at Machpelah, comes as an expression of their gratitude to Joseph for the blessing they have received through him. On the other hand, in so honoring Joseph's father, the grandson of Abraham, they are blessing him and not belittling him or holding him of no account (12:3). Thereby, according to the original promise (of which

29. It is noteworthy that the Hebrew verb for "sustain" (כול, Pilpel) is used in 45:11; 47:12; and 50:21 only in reference to Joseph's family. According to Lowenthall, *Joseph Narrative*, p. 106, it signals a special solicitude to the people of Israel.

30. Dahlberg, "Recognizing," p. 365. This conclusion thus supports the view that the ancestors are envisioned in Genesis as instruments or mediators of God's blessing rather than only examples of it; for further discussion of this debate see Biddle, "Endangered Ancestress."

31. Within the context of Genesis, Jacob is doing much more than simply offering his greetings. See Claus Westermann, *Joseph,* trans. O. Kaste (Minneapolis: Fortress, 1996), p. 102: "At the end of the history of the patriarchs in P there is the blessing of Pharaoh by Jacob as a sign that the blessing bestowed on the patriarchs and passed along from the fathers to the children . . . reaches beyond the succession of the patriarchs and is a blessing intended for humanity." Cf. Brian A. McKenzie, "Jacob's Blessing on Pharaoh: An Interpretation of Gen. 46:31–47:26," *WTJ* 45, no. 2 (1983): 386-99.

32. Michael Maher, ed., *Targum Pseudo-Jonathan: Genesis,* Aramaic Bible (Collegeville, Minn.: Liturgical Press, 1992), p. 152.

Egypt presumably was unaware), Egypt stands to receive further blessing from God.[33]

Not only does this perspective on the Joseph story confirm Dahlberg's
sense of a coherent unity within Genesis (as against von Rad), it also illuminates the narrative logic undergirding the three major portions of the book.
And it leaves us, I think, with the tantalizing possibility that the first (and
best) exegesis of 12:1-3 was perhaps Genesis 37–50.

To be sure, there is a danger of heroicizing Joseph with this line of interpretation. Joseph's expropriation of Egyptian property on Pharaoh's behalf
continues to be problematic,[34] and there are other ambiguities in Genesis 37–
50 as well. A worry about accommodation also seems to lie at the heart of the
Joseph cycle, and this anxiety complicates the picture.[35] The theocentric focus of Joseph's character, stressed so firmly early in the narrative (41:16, "It is
not in me; God will give Pharaoh a favorable answer," my trans.),[36] is undermined later on (44:15, "Do you not know that such a man as I can indeed divine?" my trans.). Janzen acidly comments: "One is tempted to suggest that,
long before there arose a new king over Egypt who knew not Joseph (Exod.
1:8), there arose a new Joseph over Egypt who had all too successfully forgotten his painful past, and in so doing had forgotten also the old Joseph."[37]
More to the point, has Joseph forgotten to give God the appropriate due?[38]

Moreover, famine is explicitly associated with Manasseh and Ephraim,
the sons Joseph bears with Asenath, the daughter of an Egyptian priest (Gen.
41:50-52).[39] The narrative refers to Joseph's marriage with Asenath three sep-

33. J. Gerald Janzen, *Genesis 12–50: Abraham and All the Families of the Earth*, ITC
(Grand Rapids: Eerdmans, 1993), p. 199.

34. For a suggestive effort to situate this action within the Mesopotamian legal tradition, see Victor Avigdor Hurowitz, "Joseph's Enslavement of the Egyptians (Gen 47:13-26) in
Light of Famine Texts from Mesopotamia," *RB* 101 (1994): 355-62.

35. See Leon Kass, *The Beginning of Wisdom* (New York: Free Press, 2003), pp. 569-72.
Cf. Aaron Wildavsky, *Assimilation versus Separation: Joseph the Administrator and the Politics
of Religion in Biblical Israel* (New Brunswick, N.J.: Transaction Publishers, 1993). Wildavsky
treats the Joseph narrative as illustrating an *antiheroic* message: how "survival must not be
gained through sin" (p. 31).

36. See also Gen. 40:8, "Do not interpretations belong to God? Tell them to me, I pray
you" (my trans.).

37. Janzen, *Genesis*, p. 182.

38. Janzen thinks that Joseph regains his earlier theocentric outlook at the conclusion
of the book (Gen. 50:19); see ibid., pp. 204-6.

39. Interestingly, another targumic expansion converts Asenath into an Israelite in a

arate times (41:45, 50; 46:20), thus emphasizing the danger.[40] The glosses given for the sons' names register the same concern about cultural-religious accommodation (e.g., "God has made me forget all my hardship and all my father's house"). In other words, another question driving the Joseph narrative is precisely how Joseph (and his family) can feed the world without becoming "captive" to its ways. (And what is the Joseph narrative finally about, if not captivity?)

The presence in Genesis of such profound reflection on the relation between food and election offers a fresh angle of vision on the practice of the Lord's Supper within Christian tradition and the historical practice of food distribution, both in the New Testament and throughout church history.[41] These practices echo Genesis by continuing to insist that divine blessing is material as well as spiritual, and that one characteristic form such blessing takes is that of food. It is no accident that Jesus uses this biblical motif of himself in saying, "I am the bread of life" (John 6:35). On analogy, and as powerfully depicted by the canonical shape of Genesis, the provision of food to the world remains a theological litmus test of the church's — and the Christian's — faithfulness to God.

---

rather blatant effort to explain away the implication of Joseph's apostasy; see Maher, *Pseudo-Jonathan*, p. 138.

40. See Janzen, *Genesis*, p. 181.

41. The literature on this point is substantial, but for further reflection see in particular: Monika Hellwig, *The Eucharist and the Hunger of the World* (Kansas City, Mo.: Sheed & Ward, 1992); John Koenig, *The Feast of the World's Redemption: Eucharistic Origins and Christian Mission* (Harrisburg: Trinity Press International, 2000); X. Leon-Dufour, *Sharing the Eucharistic Bread: The Witness of the New Testament,* trans. M. J. O'Connell (New York: Paulist Press, 1987); Robert Song, "Sharing Communion: Hunger, Food and Genetically Modified Foods," in Stanley Hauerwas and Samuel Wells, eds., *Blackwell Companion to Christian Ethics* (Oxford: Blackwell, 2004), pp. 388-400.

Index of Names

Abravanel, Judah Leon, 292
al Ghazali, Abu Hamid Muhammad ibn
    Muhammad, 160
Ambrose, 199, 218
Amos, Claire, 209
Anderson, Gary A., xv, 55, 57, 70
Anselm of Canterbury, 60-61
Aquinas, Thomas, xxii, 158, 168
Aristotle, 308
Augustine of Hippo, xviii, xix, xxi, xxii,
    117-28, 134, 136, 139, 140-41, 144, 156,
    157-58, 168, 195, 199, 201, 216-27, 267-
    68, 270-86, 313-17
Augustus, 289
Avitus of Vienne, xxi, 222

Bacon, Francis, 190, 195, 198
Bandstra, Barry Louis, 239
Barth, Karl, xx, 27, 35, 141, 206, 209, 211-
    13, 214, 233, 237, 285, 310
Basil of Caesarea, 156, 218
Bauckham, Richard, 185, 251
Baum, Gregory, 321
Beck, Edmund, 60
Beckford, James A., 321
Behr, John, 104
Berg, Werner, 65

Biddle, Mark E., 326
Bird, Phyllis A., 251
Blake, William, 133
Blenkinsopp, Joseph, 20, 22, 149
Blondel, Maurice, 316
Bloom, Harold, 26
Bonaventure of Bagnoregio, 26
Bonhoeffer, Dietrich, 310
Bonner, Gerald, 271, 284
Boyarin, Daniel, 61
Brayford, Susan A., 66
Brown, William P., 142, 177, 180, 187
Brueggemann, Walter, 171-72, 207, 209
Brunner, Emil, 141, 310

Calvin, John, 142, 145, 168, 226, 231-32,
    284, 285
Campbell, George Douglas, 166
Camps, W. A., 289-90
Carroll Rodas, M. Daniel, 329-30
Cassuto, Umberto, 233
Charles, Rodger, 316-17
Childs, Brevard S., xxiii, 62, 324
Christian, Jayakumar, 235
Clines, David J. A., 231, 304
Coakley, Sarah, 110
Coats, George W., 256

Coogan, Michael D., 28
Copan, Paul, 159-60
Craig, William Lane, 159-60

Dahlberg, Bruce T., 62, 328-29, 331
Dahrendorf, Ralf, 320-21
Darwin, Charles Robert, 164-65, 168, 171, 195
Davies, Philip J., 150
Davis, Ellen F., 179, 188
Dawkins, Clinton Richard, 147, 167
Delitzsch, Franz, 232-33
Demetracopoulos, John A., 108
De Vries, Simon J., 20
Dolidze, Tina, 109
Driver, Samuel Rolles, 169
Drummond, Henry, 166
Dumbrell, William J., 209
Durkheim, Émile, 321

Elnes, Eric E., 22
Empson, William, xviii, 133
Ephrem the Syrian, 60, 198
Eriugena, Johannes Scotus, xxi, 224
Eunomius of Cyzicus, xvii, 103, 105, 107, 108, 110, 115

Fish, Stanley Eugene, xviii, 134, 137
Flint, Robert, 166
Fretheim, Terence E., 142, 171-72, 327

Gardner, Anne, 143, 145
Gaventa, Beverly Roberts, 71
Geddes, Patrick, 166
Geerlings, Wilhelm, 118
Geller, Stephen A., 10, 12, 13, 14
Giddens, Anthony, 321
Gogarten, Friedrich, 310
Golka, Friedemann W., 319
Gould, Stephen Jay, 163, 166
Gregory of Nyssa, xvii-xviii, 103-16
Greenberg, Irving, 210
Griffiths, Paul J., 216
Grotius, Hugo, 138
Gunkel, Hermann, 95, 143

Hamilton, Victor P., 8, 12, 15, 17, 19

Hamori, Esther J., 8, 19, 22
Harland, Peter J., 142
Harrison, Carol, 157
Harrison, Verna E. F., 113
Hart, Mark D., 113
Hawking, Stephen William, 160
Heal, Kristian S., 70
Heard, R. Christopher, 253, 256, 263
Hegel, Georg Wilhelm Friedrich, 309
Hendel, Ronald S., 13, 14
Herder, Johann Gottfried, 86, 309
Hiebert, Theodore, 23
Hieke, Thomas, 312
Hobson, Theo, 129-30
Hodge, Charles, xix, 165-66, 167
Houston, Walter J., 140, 144

Irenaeus, 157
Isaac of Nineveh, 198-99

Jacobsen, Thorkild, 16, 17
Janzen, J. Gerald, 14, 331-32
Jenkins, Willis, 205
Johnson, Luke Timothy, 72, 73
Julian of Eclanum, 221

Kaminsky, Joel S., xxi, 249, 252, 253-54, 257-59, 265
Kant, Immanuel, 28, 309
Kass, Leon R., 191
Kermode, John Frank, 130
Klauck, Hans-Joseph, 322
Klein, Jacob, 17
Koopman, Helmut, 319
Kuenen, Abraham, 85-86

LaCugna, Catherine M., 128
Laird, Martin S., 113
Lec, Stanislaw Jerzy, 76
Levenson, Jon D., 22, 48, 70, 90, 171-72, 256, 261, 262
Lewis, C. S., xviii, 129, 132, 133-34, 137
Lewis, Theodore J., 18
Locke, John, 195
Lohfink, Norbert, 144, 182
Lohr, Joel N., 249, 264
Lombard, Peter, 225

Index of Names

Luther, Martin, xxii, 225-26, 317-19

Ma, David K., 211
MacDonald, Nathan, 8, 252
Mann, Paul Thomas, xxii, 319-20
Marguerat, Daniel, 73
Mattox, Mickey L., 317
Maxfield, John A., 319
McBride Jr., S. Dean, 21
McCosh, James, 166
McKane, William, 86
McKeown, James, 159
Meredith, Anthony, 114
Middleton, J. Richard, 21, 239-40
Milbank, John, 316
Miller, Patrick D., 249-50, 255
Milton, John, xviii, 66, 217
Moberly, Walter L., 6, 7, 17, 59, 207, 210,
    262, 264, 309
Moltmann, Jürgen, 172, 233, 237
Moore, Abrey Lackington, 170-71
Moore, Sebastian, xv, 25
Morris, Simon Conway, 166-67
Mosshammer, Alden A., 106
Murray, Robert, 188, 206, 210
Myers, Bryant L., 235

Nickelsburg, George W. E., 150-51
Niditch, Susan, 14
Niebuhr, Karl Paul Reinhold, 315-16
Norris, Kathleen, 25
Northcott, Michael S., 205, 210-11

Otto, Eckart, 149
Otto, Rudolf, 4

Pannenberg, Wolfhart, 184
Park, Robert E., 236
Pelagius, 279-80
Pelikan, Jaroslav J., 317
Pollmann, Karla, 217
Poole, William, 130-31, 135

Rahner, Karl, 307
Rees, Martin John, 161-62
Remigius of Auxerre, 224-25
Rendtorff, Rolf, 15

Reno, Russell R., 27, 39, 306
Roberts, Richard H., 140, 321
Rogerson, John W., 168, 206
Rothe, Richard, 310
Rowley, H. H., 253, 259-60, 265

Sailhamer, John H., 65
Sarna, Nahum M., 13, 63
Saurat, Denis, 129
Schaeffer, Francis A., 204
Scharbert, Joseph, 248
Schleiermacher, F. D. E., 27, 309
Schüle, Andreas, 3, 5, 22
Seebass, Horst, 253
Shelley, Percy Bysshe, 133
Sider, Ronald J., 240
Skinner, John, 150
Smith, J. Warren, 111
Soloveitchik, Joseph B., 40
Sommer, Benjamin D., 7, 16, 18, 23
Sorg, Dom Rembert, 197
Speiser, Ephraim Avidgor, 8, 10
Stendahl, Krister, 266
Stonequist, Everett V., 236
Sweeney, Marvin A., 5
Symeon the New Theologian, 196

Tennant, Frederick Robert, 169
Tertullian, 157, 290
Thomson, J. Arthur, 166
Tönnies, Ferdinand, 308, 310
Tracy, David, 228
Trible, Phyllis, 146-47, 256
Tuch, Friedrich, 93

van Buren, Paul Matthews, 74
van Rensburg, Linda Jansen, 229
Venerable Bede, xxi, 223-24
Victorius, Claudius Marius, 222
Virgil, 289, 290, 302
von Balthasar, Hans Urs, 110
von Rad, Gerhard, 10, 31, 62, 65, 142, 158,
    208, 250, 328-29

Wallace, Alfred Russell, xx, 192
Waltke, Bruce K., 63

Warfield, Benjamin Breckinridge, xix, 166
Weiss, Zeev, 43, 44, 51
Wellhausen, Julius, 10, 86, 92
Wenham, Gordon J., 65, 258
Wénin, André, xxii, 320
Westermann, Claus, 7, 8, 12, 62, 143, 179-180, 233, 234, 261, 319, 326-27, 331
Williams, Rowan, 114
Witte, Markus, 99-100

Wolff, Hans Walter, 233-34, 239
Wright, Christopher J. H., 237, 240, 292
Wright, Nicholas Thomas, 72
Wyschogrod, Michael, 209-10, 249, 264, 309

Yadin, Azzan, 4
Yitzhaki, Shlomo "Rashi," 35, 37

Zenger, Erich, 85

Index of Scriptures

HEBREW SCRIPTURE

Genesis   xiii, xiv, xv, xvi,
          xvii, xxi, xxii,
          xxiii, 25, 62, 75, 83-
          84, 287-88, 308,
          311-12, 314

1–12   33
1–11   xviii, 30-31, 68
1–9   xix, 146-49
1–3   xx, 325
1–2   xx, 175-86
1   21-22, 24, 26, 34,
          36, 41, 119, 124, 189,
          324, 327
1:1   35, 36-38, 42, 119-
          20
1:2   37, 39-40, 42
1:3   120
1:5   89
1:6-25   120-21
1:8   89
1:10   89
1:11   226
1:11-12   121-22
1:11-13   219-21
1:22   xx

1:24-31   212-13
1:26   xxi, 121-24
1:26-28   xxi, 230-34, 236-40
1:28   xix, xx, 204
1:28-30   144, 145
1:29-30   142
1:31   xix, 34
2–9   91
2–3   23-24, 63, 88, 186-
          89
2   xx, 24, 40, 106-7,
          191, 195-96, 202,
          211-12, 327
2:4   324
2:5   91
2:5-7   xvii
2:9   93
2:16-17   95
2:17   98
2:18-19   198-200
2:19-22   87
2:20   89
2:23   92
2:25   93
3–11   xv
3   xvii, xviii, xix, 26,
          28, 29-30, 130-31,

          133-34, 138,
          168, 234
3:1-5   94-98
3:5   141
3:6   93
3:6-7   71
3:6-7 (OG) 71-72
3:7-8   93
3:12   93
3:14   224
3:16   92
3:17   93
3:18   xx, 216-27
3:19   99
3:19-20   86-87
3:20   89
3:22   99-100, 141
4   260
4:1   24, 87
4:6   24
4:9   24
4:10   24
4:14-17   24
5–9   29, 63-64
5   324
6   xx, 67
6:9   143

6:11	63	18:17	24	32:8	11
6:11-12	xix	18:17-33	9	32:11	11
6:11-13	143	18:19	293	32:12	12
6:13	63	19:1-3	9	32:13-22	11
6:19-21	67	19:8	9	32:22-32	10-15
6:20	329	19:10	9	32:27	24
7:9	142	19:12-13	9	32:31	12
8:21	24	19:15-16	9	33:1	12
9	xx	19:17-18	8	33:3-4	13
9:1-7	xix, 143-45	19:18	7	33:10	13
9:2	145	21:12	65	33:11	13, 14
9:3	142	21:17	9, 24	33:18-20	20
9:5	68	21:22-24	330	33:26	13
9:9-10	xx, 183	21:33	6	33:28	13
9:9-11	206	22	43, 48-49, 53, 59,	35:1-4	17-18
10	90, 329-30		298-300	35:7	20
11	29-30	22:1	7	35:9-15	18
12–36	7	22:7	52	35:10	18
12–22	32	22:15-17	59, 60	35:11-13	18
12–16	64-65	22:17	294	35:14	17, 18
12	xvi, xxiii, 31, 35-36,	23:1-20	20	35:15	18
	39, 40, 42, 59	23:4	22	37–50	68, 320, 332-
12:1-3	252-53, 292-93, 331,	24:31	330		33
	332	24:50	330	37	65
12:2-3	210-11	25:25-34	272-73	39:5	329, 331
12:3	91, 255, 329, 331	25:29-34	330	39:10	xvi
12:7	20	26	xxiii, 325-26	41	327
12:7-8	209	26:5	261	41:39	330
12:10-20	325-26	26:12-33	24	41:41	318
13	301	26:24	6	41:53-57	326
13:4	6	26:26-29	330	41:54-57	67
13:14-18	7	27	330	42:5	326
14	xvi, 80, 294	27:43	65	42:22	68
14:18-20	298	28	xvi	43:1	326
15	19	28:10-22	15-18	45	xxiii, 328
15:7-21	18-19	28:17	19, 78	45:7	329
15:12	20	29:21-25	12	47:4	67
15:13-16	20	30:16	66	47:7-10	331
15:17	6, 20	30:27	330	47:13	326
16:7-14	9-10	31:29	330	47:17	67
16:8	24	31:50	330	47:20	326
17:3	6	31:53	330	50	322
18	47, 301	32–33	15		
18:1-15	7-9	32:1	11-12	**Exodus**	17, 25
18:2	11	32:3	11	3:3	5
18:9	24	32:3-13	11	3:5	5
18:16-33	8, 24	32:4	11	3:14	25

Index of Scriptures

3:14-15	5	**Judges**		**NEW TESTAMENT**		
9:16	278	8:4-9	15			
12	35			**Matthew**	75	
19:12-13	4	**1 Kings 6:29-35**	24	28:18-20	266	
19:15	4	8:27	39			
19:18-20	4	18:17-18	8	**Mark**	75	
20:1-17	4	19:8-13	5	1:13	185	
20:18a	4	19:9-18	3			
20:18 (OG)	4	19:11-12 (OG)	5	**Luke**	75	
24:9-11	5	19:15-16	5	4	71	
25–40	22, 45			9:16	72	
25:10-40	47	**2 Chronicles**		24	71-72	
28	49	3:1	48			
29	46			**John**	xiii, 75, 76-	
29:38-42	47, 50	**Nehemiah**			79, 83-84	
30:1-10	47	9:7	248	1:1	23	
32:13	59-60			1:1-3	36	
33:9	25	**Psalms**	xv, 25	1:14	23	
33:11	25	23	179	1:47	315	
33:18-23	5	110:4	xvi, 80	1:51	xvi, 23	
33:20	10			4	xvi	
33:20-23	25	**Isaiah**		8	xvi	
33:23	5	6:1-8	5			
34:5-7	5	11:1-9	184-85	**Acts**	72-73, 75	
39–40	22	11:6-9	144			
40:34-35	7	40–55	263, 264	**Romans**	75, 275	
		51:1-2	33	5:12	98	
		60	51	5:12-21	82	
Leviticus		65:25	184-85	6:4-13	33	
1:3-17	49			6:23	98	
1:11 (= Leviticus		**Hosea**		7	286	
Rabba)	49-51	12:4	13, 18	9–11	xxii, 271	
8–9	xv, 45, 46			9	271, 276-77,	
25	57	**Daniel**			284	
		4:24	57	9:6-16	268-69	
Numbers		7	295-97	9:9-23	281-82	
14:11-12	25			9:22-23	277, 280-81	
23:9-10	293-95			11	276	
24:17-18	294	**APOCRYPHA**		11:25-32	269-70	
29:3-8	50					
		Tobit		**1 Corinthians**	75	
Deuteronomy	xxi, 247,	4:9	57	15:20-28	82	
	255, 259-60,	13	51	15:42-48	82	
	263-64					
4:11-13	4	**Ben Sirach**		**Galatians**	75	
4:15	4	29:11	57			
23	256			**Ephesians**	75	
26:1-11	47					

Colossians

1:12-13	27
1:15-16	82
1:16	27
1:26	27
3:10	123

Ephesians

4:23-24	123
5	40

Hebrews   xiii, xiv, 75, 83-84

7	xvi, 80
11	xvi, 80-81

James   75

Revelation   75